EXPLORATION AND EXPLOITATION IN EARLY STAGE VENTURES AND SMEs

TECHNOLOGY, INNOVATION, ENTREPRENEURSHIP AND COMPETITIVE STRATEGY

Series Editor: Barak S. Aharonson

Recent Volumes:

TECHNOLOGY, INNOVATION, ENTREPRENEURSHIP AND
COMPETITIVE STRATEGY   VOLUME 14

EXPLORATION AND EXPLOITATION IN EARLY STAGE VENTURES AND SMEs

EDITED BY

URIEL STETTNER

Recanati Business School, Tel Aviv University,
Tel Aviv, Israel

BARAK S. AHARONSON

Recanati Business School, Tel Aviv University,
Tel Aviv, Israel

TERRY L. AMBURGEY

Rotman School of Management, University of Toronto,
Toronto, ON, Canada

United Kingdom – North America – Japan
India – Malaysia – China

Emerald Group Publishing Limited
Howard House, Wagon Lane, Bingley BD16 1WA, UK

First edition 2014

Copyright © 2014 Emerald Group Publishing Limited

Reprints and permission service
Contact: permissions@emeraldinsight.com

British Library Cataloguing in Publication Data
A catalogue record for this book is available from the British Library

ISBN: 978-1-78350-655-2
ISSN: 1479-067X (Series)

ISOQAR certified
Management System,
awarded to Emerald
for adherence to
Environmental
standard
ISO 14001:2004.

Certificate Number 1985
ISO 14001

INVESTOR IN PEOPLE

CONTENTS

LIST OF CONTRIBUTORS

Barak S. Aharonson	Faculty of Management, Recanati Business School, Tel Aviv University, Tel Aviv, Israel
Terry L. Amburgey	Faculty of Management, Rotman Business School, University of Toronto, Toronto, ON, Canada
Meriam Bezemer	QUT Business School, Queensland University of Technology, Brisbane, Australia
Peter T. Bryant	IE Business School, Madrid, Spain
Graziano Coller	Department of Economics and Management, University of Trento, Trento, Italy
Paolo Collini	Department of Economics and Management, University of Trento, Trento, Italy
Jordi Comas	School of Management, Bucknell University, Lewisburg, PA, USA
Janke Dittmer	Gilde Healthcare Partners, Utrecht, The Netherlands
Linda F. Edelman	Bentley University, Waltham, MA, USA
M. Laura Frigotto	Department of Economics and Management, University of Trento, Trento, Italy
Robert Galliers	Bentley University, Waltham, MA, USA
Moon-Goo Huh	School of Business Administration, Kyungpook National University, Daegu, South Korea

Guktae Kim   School of Business Administration,
                          Kyungpook National University,
                          Daegu, South Korea

Blake D. Mathias   College of Business Administration,
                          University of Tennessee, Knoxville,
                          TN, USA

Judy Matthews   QUT Business School, Queensland
                          University of Technology, Brisbane,
                          Australia

Joseph A. McCahery   Tilburg University, Tilburg, The
                          Netherlands

Gaëtan Mourmant   EM Strasbourg Business School,
                          Strasbourg, France

Fred Niederman   Cook School of Business, Saint Louis
                          University, St Louis, MO, USA

Craig Randall   Florida Gulf Coast University,
                          Fort Myers, FL, USA

Shengce Ren   School of Economics and Management,
                          Shanghai Maritime University,
                          Shanghai, China

Anna Sabidussi   TiasNimbas Business School,
                          Tilburg University, Tilburg,
                          The Netherlands

Sukanlaya Sawang   QUT Business School, Queensland
                          University of Technology, Brisbane,
                          Australia

Uriel Stettner   Faculty of Management, Recanati Business
                          School, Tel Aviv University, Tel Aviv,
                          Israel

Peiran Su   Business School, University of the West of
                          Scotland, Paisley, United Kingdom

Noriko Taji   Faculty of Business Administration,
                          Hosei University, Tokyo, Japan

Erik P. M. Vermeulen	Tilburg University, Tilburg, The Netherlands
Katerina Voutsina	School of Business, American College of Greece, Athens, Greece
Roxanne Zolin	QUT Business School, Queensland University of Technology, Brisbane, Australia

PART I
INDIVIDUAL LEVEL
PERSPECTIVES ON EXPLORATION
VERSUS EXPLOITATION

CHAPTER 1

THE INTERPLAY BETWEEN EXPLORATION AND EXPLOITATION IN SMEs

Uriel Stettner, Barak S. Aharonson and
Terry L. Amburgey

ABSTRACT

Despite a growing body of research on exploration and exploitation, scholars have tended to study the phenomena from a narrow perspective mostly within larger, well-established organizations. However, it is still far from obvious how top management within small-to-medium sized enterprises (SMEs) are to address the liability of newness and seek access to resources and capabilities relevant for the pursuit of exploration and exploitation. Resource sourcing and allocation decisions are particularly critical in SMEs and must be aligned with the firm's fundamental strategic intent and growth model. For example, organizations following a stage model by first developing a domestic market and then expanding globally will require different bundles of resources and capabilities than organizations that are designed to conquer the global arena. Indeed, management systems will likely need to adapt across the firm life cycle such that it can fulfill an explorative function in the earlier stages and an exploitative function in later ones. Hence, early-stage

Exploration and Exploitation in Early Stage Ventures and SMEs
Technology, Innovation, Entrepreneurship and Competitive Strategy, Volume 14, 3–13
ISSN: 1479-067X/doi:10.1108/S1479-067X20140000014020

ventures have to master the resource reallocation process which is contingent on their access to capital. Across the firm life cycle, venture capitalists can tap into the growth potential of early-stage ventures is a key factor behind their successful short-term innovative performance as well as long-term survival.

Keywords: Exploration—exploitation; SME; early-stage venture; firm life cycle; performance

Despite a growing body of research on exploration and exploitation in the management literature, scholars have tended to study these phenomena from a narrow perspective mostly within larger, well-established organizations (Gupta, Smith, & Shalley, 2006; Jansen, Simsek, & Cao, 2012; Lavie, Stettner, & Tushman, 2010). Exploration and exploitation are conflicting organizational activities that compete for firms' scarce resources and entail distinctive sets of skills and capabilities. When engaging in exploration and exploitation, organizations trade off short-term productivity for long-term innovation, as well as stability for adaptability (Lewin, Long, & Carroll, 1999; March, 1991). Although both exploration and exploitation are essential for survival and prosperity, limited resource availability compels firms to prefer one type of activity over another. Nevertheless, achieving a balance between exploration and exploitation is essential for firms' survival and economic performance (March, 1991).

Prior research has generally embraced a firm-level perspective that tends to ignore the centrality of individual and team-level behavior and decision making. In focusing on exploration and exploitation in small-to-medium sized enterprises (SMEs), it is apparent that the exploration and exploitation framework has theoretical and practical relevance for the study of entrepreneurial behavior at the individual level. At this level of analysis, two dimensions take a central role in defining exploration and exploitation activities: (a) the motivation prompting entrepreneurial activity seeking and (b) the process underlying idiosyncratic resource allocation toward exploration and exploitation. The former concerns itself with identifying behavioral aspects in response to specific types of environmental shocks that precede and drastically impact the decision to engage in entrepreneurial activities. In contrast, the latter addresses the manner by which individual entrepreneurs allocate resources for exploring new market opportunities and/or exploiting existing ones. This perspective on exploratory and exploitative thought and behavior can be assumed to interact in different ways at various stages of the entrepreneurial process (Adner & Levinthal, 2008; Jansen, Tempelaar, Van den Bosch, & Volberda, 2009; Jansen, Van Den Bosch, & Volberda, 2006). Accordingly, entrepreneurs may initiate their entrepreneurial activities as specialists rather than generalists and may acquire the capability to manage the trade-offs that arise as they shift from, for example, exploration to exploitation (Cao, Gedajlovic, & Zhang, 2009; O'Reilly & Tushman, 2008).

The two dimensions of exploration and exploitation raise a few important questions: What types of external stimuli exist that can displace the individual from the inertia of existing behavior and pave the way for the consideration of a new set of opportunities where entrepreneurship initiatives are perceived to be both feasible and desirable? How can we explain why some founder entrepreneurs demonstrate ambidextrous capabilities when others do not (Russo & Vurro, 2010; Smith & Tushman, 2005)? How important are the personal characteristics of founders in the formation of organizational capabilities? Clearly, the social psychological processes underlying the entrepreneurial process are crucial determinants.

While individual-level decision making lies at the heart of early-stage entrepreneurial activities, decision making at the upper-management team level takes center stage with the growth of the firm. The transition of the firm from an early-stage venture to an SME requires that the firm and its top management manage the trade-offs between exploration and exploitation. Among the numerous challenges, management must address central processes including resource acquisition and its alignment with an organization's exit strategies.

How do SMEs decide on sourcing strategies to explore and exploit? How does the propensity to deploy specific modes of operations arise in managerial practice? This question involving a firms' ability to develop existing competencies and create new ones, both within and across organizational boundaries, lies at the heart of the strategic management debate and of firms' sustainable competitive advantage (Benner & Tushman, 2003; Stettner & Lavie, 2013; Teece, Pisano, & Shuen, 1997). Prior research on the performance, growth, and innovation of SMEs clarify the specific conditions of SMEs compared to larger firms. However, it is still far from obvious how top management within SME's are to address the liability of newness (Stinchcombe, 1965) and seek access to resources and capabilities relevant for the pursuit of exploration and exploitation.

The decision regarding whether to develop resources internally or seek to access resources across organizational boundaries depends on the organization's perspectives on innovation and definition of performance objectives. Moreover, such resource sourcing and allocation decisions must be further aligned with the firm's fundamental strategic intent and growth model. For example, organizations following a stage model put in place to first develop a domestic market and then expand into the global market (Johanson & Vahlne, 1977) will require different bundles of resources and capabilities than organizations that are designed to conquer the global arena (Chetty & Campbell-Hunt, 2004; Knight, 1996).

When considering the firm level of analysis, one central avenue for gaining access to resources is the venture capital cycle. Venture capitalists, through their investment in early-stage high-growth companies, can jump start the exploratory efforts of an early-stage venture. Across the firm life cycle, venture capitalists can tap into the growth potential of early-stage ventures (Mason & Pierrakis, 2013). For early-stage ventures, venture capital investment across the firm life cycle is a key factor behind their successful short-term innovative performance as well as long-term survival. It is clear that a closer look at the organization and governance arrangements that are put in place by venture capitalists hold important lessons on how this balance is maintained in early-stage start-ups.

Clearly, in the short term, SME's face the liabilities of smallness; and thus, a higher risk for failure is associated in part with the lack of resources and capabilities (Aldrich, 1979; Hannan & Freeman, 1977) and the general lack of signaling capacity and reputation (Stinchcombe, 1965). Accordingly, small firms tend to face trade-offs during the R&D phase of development and, thus, may be forced to carefully and skillfully reallocate resources between exploration and exploitation activities. The degree to which early-stage ventures have to master the resource reallocation process is likely to be tied to their access to capital. Whereas access to financial slack resources is crucial for the short-term, organizational growth and long-term survival hinges also on external determinants over which the firm may have limited control.

For example, SMEs' resource allocation decisions toward exploration and exploitation in product innovation may take on different forms in a developing economy compared to stable economic systems. The different environmental conditions may require organizations to adapt their balancing mechanism to the different stages across the firm life cycle.

Evidently, organizational evolution of exploration and exploitation is inherently tied to an organization's ability to manage resources and capabilities across the firm life cycle. For example, firms' choice of management systems designed to collect information and develop knowledge (e.g., human resource management or management information systems) can assist firms with appropriate resource reallocation needs (Greve, 2007; Hess & Rothaermel, 2011; Tzabbar, Aharonson, Amburgey, & Al-Laham, 2009). Indeed, management systems will likely need to adapt across the firm life cycle such that it can fulfill an explorative function in the earlier stages and an exploitative function in later ones.

THIS VOLUME

This volume of Technology, Innovation, Entrepreneurship, and Competitive Strategy seeks to enhance our understanding of the implications of Exploration and Exploitation activities in early-stage ventures and SMEs. The various contributions explore how organizations engage the general paradox of having to balance their exploration and exploitation activities. This paradox may intensify in such firms as they generally lack an abundance of resources and capabilities (Ahuja, Lampert, & Tandon, 2008; Voss, Sirdeshmukh, & Voss, 2008) driving them away from balancing these activities and toward either exploration or exploitation.

This book is divided into two parts. Part I consists of three chapters that offer perspectives on exploration versus exploitation on the individual level of analysis. Part II contains 10 chapters that center on a firm-level analysis. Each chapter takes a distinct and autonomous perspective on the relationship between exploration and exploitation as they relate to SMEs. Together they portray the variety and complexity of the dimensions describing the ambidexterity dilemma, as well as some ways to managers and the Top Management Teams (TMTs) can address this issue. In so doing, these writings capture selected core components of contemporary network research by each offering not only a rigorous treatment of the topic but also directions for future research.

Part I of the book addresses exploration versus exploitation at the micro-individual level. In Chapter 2, "Self-Regulation and Entrepreneurial Ambidexterity," Peter T. Bryant investigates the role of social cognitive self-regulation in fostering ambidexterity as a dynamic capability among entrepreneurs. He claims (based on a multiple case study of founder managers) that complex patterns of self-regulation are associated with ambidextrous thinking and decision making among entrepreneurs, often in combination with strong values and a sense of emotional engagement. Based on his findings, Bryant proposes a model of these processes and discusses its implications.

In Chapter 3, "The Range of Shocks Prompting Entrepreneurial Employee Turnover through the Lenses of Exploration and Exploitation Framework," Katerina Voutsina, Gaëtan Mourmant, and Fred Niederman show the theoretical and practical relevance of the exploitation/exploration framework for the study of entrepreneurial behavior at individual level. The study identifies specific instances where explorative or exploitative aspects of behavior are most likely to be manifested as a response to specific types of shocks that precede and drastically impact the decision to quit and start one's own business. Voutsina et al. argue that different types of shocks or entrepreneurial events displace the individual from the inertia of existing behavior and pave the way for the consideration of a new set of opportunities where entrepreneurship initiatives are perceived to be both feasible and desirable (exploitation−exploitation). In this chapter, she analyzed 80 semistructured and longitudinal interviews with entrepreneurs who quit their "salaried job" to start their own business, examining a thorough inventory of events/shocks found to precipitate the interviewees' decision to quit and linking the various types of shocks with the prospective exploratory and/or exploratory initiatives. Voutsina et al. illustrate the dynamics of the effects of shock on entrepreneurial behavior, demonstrating what she claims to be the blurriness and interrelatedness of exploitative and exploratory aspects of entrepreneurship. She suggests that managers can use this detailed list of shocks as reference tool and be proactive in avoiding or encouraging entrepreneurial employee turnover.

Part II of the book aims at understanding the tension between exploration and exploitation at a more macro level − the firm. In Chapter 4, "The Balance between Exploration and Exploitation in the "New" Venture Capital Cycle: Opportunities and Challenges," Janke Dittmer, Joseph A. McCahery, and Erik P. M. Vermeulen look at the centrality of venture capital needed to bring innovative ideas to the market and support the further growth and development of high-growth companies. For start-up companies, venture capital is a key factor behind their successful performance, especially through the period between the initial capital contribution and the time the company starts generating a steady stream of revenue. The authors acknowledge that government funding has been associated with an imbalance between the exploration and exploitation activities within start-up companies. The authors argue that government's poor track record in selecting and nurturing winners favors exploration over exploitation, resulting in bureaucratic, cumbersome, and inefficient practices that put too much weight on exploration. However, they emphasize the benefits of a mix of government and private investors for the realization of a sustainable venture capital ecosystem in which funds are available and accessible in terms of speed, clarity, transparency, and connectivity to other stakeholders in the industry. Their research findings show that, perhaps with the exception of super-angels, crowd funding platforms and corporate venture capital as separate funding sources tend to tip the balance to exploration and exploitation, respectively. Moreover, the authors suggest that collaborative models may provide an effective and well-balanced basis for funding innovative firms that can positively contribute to the balance between exploration and exploitation. In fact, they show that the experience with public–private partnerships, such as the High-Tech Gründerfonds, confirms that the network-creating capabilities of these government-sponsored initiatives have the anticipated exploration and exploitation effects that were present in the traditional venture capital cycle.

In Chapter 5, "Losing Balance: Trade-Offs between Exploration and Exploitation Innovation," Craig Randall, Linda F. Edelman, and Robert Galliers explore the tension between shorter term exploitative development and longer term exploratory innovation activities. They argue that firms are increasingly looking to design and develop new products and services as a crucial source of competitive advantage. However, as the pressure to innovate increases, so does the tension between shorter term gains through exploitative development and longer term gains that could be achieved via exploratory innovation activities. Thus, they explore this tension using interview data from software SMEs and venture capitalist firms who invest in technology-driven companies. They show that, despite firms having established solid innovation plans, short-term exploitative demands crowd out their longer term exploration innovation during the development phase. They suggest that these findings may be driven by agency and resource dependence issues.

In Chapter 6, "Ambidexterity and Organizational Survival: Evidence from Korean SMEs," Guktae Kim and Moon-Goo Huh explore the relationship between the exploration–exploitation balance and SMEs' longevity to address two important questions from the ambidexterity perspective: (1) How does the balance between exploration and exploitation influence organizational survival? (2) How is the appropriate balance between exploration and exploitation influenced by an organization's internal and external contexts? They find, in an analysis of SMEs in the Korean IT industry during the period of 1981–2012, an inverted U-shaped relationship between the extent of exploratory innovation and organizational longevity provides support for the ambidexterity perspective. They further claim that financial slack moderates the exploration–longevity relationship.

In Chapter 7, "Exploration and Exploitation from Start-up to Sale: A Longitudinal Analysis through Strategy and MCS Practices," M. Laura Frigotto, Graziano Coller, and Paolo Collini study management system practices of exploration and exploitation through a study of an SME from the start-up stage over a 19-year period. Specifically, they analyze the different roles that management systems have played in various stages of the growth paths of the organization. They argue that the role of management systems in shaping exploration and exploitation only loosely depends on the design of these systems. They claim that the same management systems can fulfill an explorative function in one stage and an exploitative function in another, depending on how such systems are used.

In Chapter 8, "A Height–Distance View on Exploration and Exploitation," Anna Sabidussi investigates how SMEs and large firms decide the sourcing strategies to explore and exploit. Using a qualitative methodology (interviews with 35 companies and two experts), she studies the managerial practices that drive the external sourcing decision for exploration and exploitation in SMEs and large firms and suggests a series of propositions. She claims that these insights indicate that the sourcing modality depends on the height/distance positioning of the firm and the exploration/exploitation objective for which it aims. She then argues that this approach provides a framework for interpreting the explorative and exploitative endeavors of a firm. Categorizing the degree of exploration and exploitation based on the distance from the current market, technology, or product position, and the prospective target point on the horizon. The greater the distance from the core competencies is, the more explorative the endeavor is. She explains that, beyond a certain threshold, reducing the distance between a company's current status and target position requires not only increasing the company's existing resources through internal development but also making use of external resources.

In Chapter 9, "Innovation in the Australian Spatial Information Industry," Sukanlaya Sawang, Roxanne Zolin, Judy Matthews, and Meriam Bezemer conducted 20 in-depth interviews of top management team members in Spatial Information firms in Australia. They analyzed the exploitative versus exploratory perception and behavior of SMEs in Spatial Information in terms of innovations. The find that, while innovation is seen as crucial to survival and success in a competitive environment, most innovations are more exploitative than exploratory with only a few being radical innovations. They argue that, at the source, these findings are due to the high resource requirements for innovations that may not be readily available to SMEs. They further explain that the majority of the firms they studied engage in product and/or service innovations, while some also mentioned marketing, process, and organizational innovations.

In Chapter 10, "Sustaining Competitiveness in the Economic Recession: Exploration and Exploitation in Two Small- and Medium-Sized Enterprises in a Developing Economy," Peiran Su and Shengce Ren examine two SMEs in China and claim that these SMEs' approach to balancing exploration and exploitation depends on their development stages and their industrial and environmental contexts. They further propose a four-stage framework that unfolds via initiation, innovation, transformation, and expansion. According to their framework, SMEs balance exploration and exploitation by adopting temporal separation and organizational separation sequentially. Finally, they propose that SMEs may benefit from exploring a narrow scope of products and exploiting them in a wide market scope.

In Chapter 11, "Resource Acquisition in High-Tech Start-Up Global Strategies," Noriko Taji investigates the exploration–exploitation strategies of SMEs as they relate to the actions of high-tech start-ups. She examines four case studies from the region around Cambridge University in the United Kingdom. She argues that knowledge-based start-ups target global markets from the very beginning, aiming at rapid market penetration, while knowledge-intensive start-ups start in local markets and initially restrict acquisition of core technology and financial and human resources to those markets. She claims that the latter firms start exploring global markets only at a later stage, when the local business is solidly established and they have gained slack resources they can exploit.

In Chapter 12, "Exploration, Exploitation, Ambidexterity, and Firm Performance: A Meta-Analysis," Blake D. Mathias presents a meta analysis of 117 studies (which included more than 21,000 firms), examining the relationships among the activities of exploration, exploitation, ambidexterity, and firm performance. He finds strong performance effects for exploration and exploitation, yet contrary to theory, he claims that ambidexterity yields weaker effects than a focus on either exploration or exploitation.

Finally, in Chapter 13, "Juggling Exploratory and Exploitative Learning with Dynamic Networks in the Early Days of Small Companies," Jordi Comas investigates the relationship between networks and managing the exploration–exploitation dilemma. He argues that network structure can impact the ambidexterity level of the firm. He claims that exploratory learning should be positively associated with lower network density, while exploitative learning should be associated with greater network cohesion.

Together, these chapters provide novel insights into the exploration and exploitation framework in the context of early-stage ventures and SMEs. Each of the selected contributions provides a unique perspective across the various levels of analysis. In so doing, they tackle the peculiarities associated with new entrepreneurs, their ventures, and the growth of their firms. Whereas the chapters are at the forefront in this domain, they open up new avenues for future research.

REFERENCES

Adner, R., & Levinthal, D. (2008). Doing versus seeing: Acts of exploitation and perceptions of exploration. *Strategic Entrepreneurship Journal*, *2*(1), 43−52.

Ahuja, G., Lampert, C. M., & Tandon, V. (2008). Moving beyond Schumpeter: Management research on the determinants of technological innovation. *The Academy of Management Annals*, *2*(1), 1−98.

Aldrich, H. (1979). *Organizations and environments*. Englewood Cliffs, NJ: Prentice Hall.

Benner, M. J., & Tushman, M. (2003). Exploitation, exploration, and process management: The productivity dilemma revisited. *Academy of Management Review*, *28*(2), 238−256.

Cao, Q., Gedajlovic, E., & Zhang, H. (2009). Unpacking organizational ambidexterity: Dimensions, contingencies, and synergistic effects. *Organization Science*, *20*(4), 781−796.

Chetty, S., & Campbell-Hunt, C. (2004). A strategic approach to internationalization: A traditional versus a "born-global" approach. *Journal of International Marketing*, *12*(1), 57−81.

Greve, H. R. (2007). Exploration and exploitation in product innovation. *Industrial and Corporate Change*, *16*(5), 945−975.

Gupta, A. K., Smith, K., & Shalley, C. E. (2006). The interplay between exploration and exploitation. *Academy of Management Journal*, *49*(4), 693−706.

Hannan, M. T., & Freeman, J. (1977). The population ecology of organizations. *American Journal of Sociology*, *82*(5), 929−964.

Hess, A. M., & Rothaermel, F. T. (2011). When are assets complementary? Star scientists, strategic alliances, and innovation in the pharmaceutical industry. *Strategic Management Journal*, *32*, 895−909.

Jansen, J., Tempelaar, M. P., Van den Bosch, F. A. J., & Volberda, H. W. (2009). Structural differentiation and ambidexterity: The mediating role of integration mechanisms. *Organization Science*, *20*(4), 797−811.

Jansen, J., Van den Bosch, F. A. J., & Volberda, H. W. (2006). Exploratory innovation, exploitative innovation, and performance: Effects of organizational antecedents and environmental moderators. *Management Science*, *52*(11), 1661−1674.

Jansen, J. J. P., Simsek, Z., & Cao, Q. (2012). Ambidexterity and performance in multiunit contexts: Cross-level moderating effects of structural and resource attributes. *Strategic Management Journal*, *33*(11), 1286−1303.

Johanson, J., & Vahlne, J. E. (1977). The internationalization process of the firm − A model of knowledge development and increasing foreign market commitments. *Journal of International Business Studies*, *8*(1), 23−32.

Knight, G. (1996). Born Global. *Wiley International Encyclopedia of Marketing*. Retrieved from http://onlinelibrary.wiley.com/doi/10.1002/9781444316568.wiem06052/full. Accessed on February 6, 2014.

Lavie, D., Stettner, U., & Tushman, M. (2010). Exploration and exploitation within and across organizations. *The Academy of Management Annals, 4*(1), 109–155.

Lewin, A. Y., Long, C. P., & Carroll, T. N. (1999). The coevolution of new organizational forms. *Organization Science, 10*(5), 535–550.

March, J. G. (1991). Exploration and exploitation in organizational learning. *Organization Science, 2*(1), 71–87.

Mason, C., & Pierrakis, Y. (2013). Venture capital, the regions and public policy: The United Kingdom since the post-2000 technology crash. *Regional Studies, 47*(7), 1156–1171.

O'Reilly, C. A. I., & Tushman, M. L. (2008). Ambidexterity as a dynamic capability: Resolving the innovator's dilemma. *Research in Organizational Behavior, 28*, 185–206.

Russo, A., & Vurro, C. (2010). Cross-boundary ambidexterity: Balancing exploration and exploitation in the fuel cell industry. *European Management Review, 7*(1), 30–45.

Smith, W. K., & Tushman, M. L. (2005). Managing strategic contradictions: A top management model for managing innovation streams. *Organization Science, 16*(5), 522–536.

Stettner, U., & Lavie, D. (2013). Ambidexterity under scrutiny: Exploration and exploitation via internal organization, alliances, and acquisitions. *Strategic Management Journal*. doi:10.1002/smj.2195

Stinchcombe, A. L. (1965). Social structure and organizations. In J. G. March (Ed.), *Handbook of organizations* (pp. 142–193). Chicago, IL: Rand McNally.

Teece, D. J., Pisano, G., & Shuen, A. (1997). Dynamic capabilities and strategic management. *Strategic Management Journal, 18*(7), 509–533.

Tzabbar, D., Aharonson, B. S., Amburgey, T. L., & Al-Laham, A. (2009). When is the whole bigger than the sum of its parts? Bundling knowledge stocks for innovative success. *Strategic Organization, 6*(4), 375.

Voss, G. B., Sirdeshmukh, D., & Voss, Z. G. (2008). The effects of slack resources and environmental threat on products exploration exploitation. *Academy of Management Journal, 51*(1), 147–164.

CHAPTER 2

SELF-REGULATION AND ENTREPRENEURIAL AMBIDEXTERITY

Peter T. Bryant

ABSTRACT

Scholars of ambidexterity focus on the need for strategic leaders to explore and exploit opportunities synergistically. Yet it remains unclear how such dynamic capabilities develop. Addressing this question, this chapter investigates the role of social cognitive self-regulation in fostering ambidexterity as a dynamic capability among entrepreneurs. Results of a mixed method, multiple case study of founder managers suggest that complex patterns of self-regulation are associated with ambidextrous thinking and decision making among entrepreneurs, often in combination with strong values and a sense of emotional engagement. I propose a new model of these processes and discuss its implications.

Keywords: Entrepreneurship; ambidexterity; self-regulation; regulatory focus; entrepreneurial strategy

Exploration and Exploitation in Early Stage Ventures and SMEs
Technology, Innovation, Entrepreneurship and Competitive Strategy, Volume 14, 15–37
Copyright © 2014 by Emerald Group Publishing Limited
All rights of reproduction in any form reserved
ISSN: 1479-067X/doi:10.1108/S1479-067X20140000014001

INTRODUCTION

The entrepreneurial process is typically initiated by exploratory thought and behavior, as entrepreneurs seek and create new market opportunities (Bhide, 2000; Dimov, 2007). As the process evolves from exploration to active implementation, attention shifts toward more exploitative thought and behavior. Entrepreneurs then work to produce and distribute products and services that match the perceived market need or want. Exploration and exploitation are therefore fundamental aspects of the entrepreneurial process and play a central role in the recognition and exploitation of opportunities (Shane & Venkataraman, 2000). Moreover, exploratory and exploitative thought and behavior interact in different ways at various stages of the entrepreneurial process (Adner & Levinthal, 2008; Jansen, Tempelaar, Van Den Bosch, & Volberda, 2009). Opportunity recognition may involve aspects of exploitation, while opportunity exploitation may require exploratory capabilities. For all these reasons, it is important to reach a better understanding about how ambidextrous capabilities are developed and sustained, and how individuals and organizations acquire the capacity to explore and exploit simultaneously and synergistically, and the trade-offs that may follow (Cao, Gedajlovic, & Zhang, 2009; O'Reilly & Tushman, 2008).

Achieving ambidexterity is challenging, primarily because effective exploitation calls for systematic thinking and structured routines that may conflict with the imaginative thinking and creativity required for exploration (March, 1991). For similar reasons, exploration and exploitation often conflict or diverge within entrepreneurial organizations (Smith & Tushman, 2005). On the one hand, some entrepreneurs acquire strong capabilities in exploratory activities. They are dedicated to finding new opportunities, creativity, and innovation. Yet such entrepreneurs may then fail to develop strong exploitative capabilities; that is, having identified new opportunities, they are poor at exploiting those opportunities. Some entrepreneurs exhibit the opposite tendency. They may become adept at opportunity exploitation, but lose the capacity to create or discover new opportunities (see Russo & Vurro, 2010). Like many maturing organizations, entrepreneurial founders and their ventures can fall victim to the classic liabilities of incumbency, such as competency traps and learning myopia (Levitt & March, 1988). Indeed, while founders often champion a culture of innovation and risk taking, many are ill-suited to the disciplines of efficient exploitation in a maturing organization. Not surprisingly, this incapacity to adapt is a common reason for founder exit (Wasserman, 2012).

Therefore, in order to grow their firms while also embracing fresh opportunities, entrepreneurs must learn to exploit existing opportunities while continuing to explore new territory. They must become ambidextrous (O'reilly & Tushman, 2011). It is therefore important to explain why some founder entrepreneurs demonstrate ambidextrous capabilities, yet others do not (Smith & Tushman, 2005). Thus defined, ambidexterity is conceived as both an organization-level phenomenon and as an individual-level capability (Raisch & Birkinshaw, 2008). In this chapter, I focus on the individual person as the unit of analysis and investigate the foundations of ambidexterity in social cognitive self-regulation. My argument assumes that at the early stages of the entrepreneurial process, the personal characteristics of founders are critical in the formation of organizational capabilities, and especially dynamic capabilities such as ambidexterity (see Helfat & Peteraf, 2009; Zahra, Sapienza, & Davidsson, 2006). In other words, I assume that the micro-foundations of ambidexterity as a dynamic capability will be partly explained by social psychological processes (Teece, 2007).

In this chapter, I report new empirical findings and derive theoretical insights that extend understanding of the individual origins of entrepreneurial ambidexterity. Specifically, I adopt a social cognitive perspective on these questions and seek to identify the self-regulatory characteristics of ambidextrous entrepreneurs. As a fundamental feature of social cognition, self-regulation describes how people set goals and then self-direct their thought and behavior toward reaching their goals (Vancouver & Day, 2005). Thus defined, self-regulation is fundamental for the study of goal-directed decision making and behavior. Consequently, and as numerous studies already show, self-regulation plays a central role in entrepreneurial activity as goal-directed, social behavior (Hmieleski & Baron, 2008; Wu, Mcmullen, Neubert, & Yi, 2008).

Adopting this perspective, I draw especially on Regulatory Focus Theory (RFT) which describes two related self-regulatory orientations called promotion focus and prevention focus (Higgins, 1998). Promotion focus describes where growth and advancement needs motivate people to bring themselves into alignment with their ideal selves (that is, attaining high aspirational goals for the self), thereby heightening the importance of potential gains. Whereas prevention focus describes where security and safety needs motivate people to seek alignment with their ought selves (that is, being complaint with norms and doing what one ought to do), thereby increasing sensitivity to potential losses. Notably, some scholars highlight the special relevance of promotion focus for entrepreneurship, given that many entrepreneurs focus more on approaching gains than avoiding losses (Baron, 2004; Brockner, Higgins, & Low, 2004).

Building on these concepts and theories, this chapter is organized as follows. I first review the literatures on entrepreneurial ambidexterity and regulatory focus. I then report the results of a multiple case study of founder entrepreneurs in which I gathered both interview and survey data. A major finding of this study is that the interaction of both promotion focus and prevention focus appears to play a significant role in entrepreneurial ambidexterity, especially when coupled with a strong sense of values and passion. Based on these findings, I propose a new model of entrepreneurial ambidexterity and discuss its implications for future research and practice.

THEORETICAL BACKGROUND

Entrepreneurial Ambidexterity

As March (1991) argued in his seminal paper on organizational learning, firms face great challenges in synthesizing exploration and exploitation because they entail different cognitive, behavioral, and organizational capabilities. On the one hand, exploration is more creative, imaginative, open ended, and risk taking; while on the other hand, exploitation is more systematic, routine, closed, and risk avoidant. Moreover, as organizations become more adept at exploitative activities, they often lose the capacity to explore. As routines become more embedded and risk aversion develops, exploratory creativity and novelty are repressed. Learning therefore becomes myopic in its focus on the here and now and captive to existing competencies and proximal goals (Gavetti, Levinthal, & Rivkin, 2005). For all these reasons, scholars are concerned to understand how organizations can both explore and exploit simultaneously and synergistically, which is described as being ambidextrous (Raisch, Birkinshaw, Probst, & Tushman, 2009).

Ambidexterity has been extensively researched, especially by O'Reilly and Tushman (2004, 2008) who conceive of ambidexterity as a type of dynamic capability. By way of definition, dynamic capabilities are those capabilities that enable the reconfiguration of resources into new value-creating configurations, typically in response to new opportunities or dynamic shifts in the market (Eisenhardt & Martin, 2000). In this regard, ambidexterity is especially critical as a dynamic capability in entrepreneurial firms, given that entrepreneurs are consistently adapting scarce resources and capabilities to novel market conditions (Newey & Zahra, 2009). As studies demonstrate, ambidexterity positively influences innovation networks, strategic alliance formation, strategic leadership, and managing organizational change (Amrit, 2008; Gibson & Birkinshaw, 2004; He & Wong, 2004).

Perhaps the greatest challenge for entrepreneurs is to retain ambidextrous capabilities while growing the organization. During critical early growth phases, firms become more systematic and structured as they seek to improve and scale productive capacity. Formal systems evolve to ensure discipline and efficient exploitation. Roles and boundaries become more defined. Routines are entrenched and defended. For all these reasons, organizational growth and maturity can lead to a loss of exploratory capacity, even while improving exploitative capacity. That is, as entrepreneurial firms grow and mature, they often become less exploratory and therefore less ambidextrous (Smith & Tushman, 2005). Culture and values become more focused on the priorities and meanings that underpin exploitation, such as efficiency, rule following, compliance, quality control, and loss minimization (Benner & Tushman, 2003). In contrast, strongly entrepreneurial cultures encourage innovativeness, independence, positive risk taking, and tolerance of failure. Therefore, culture and values appear to play a significant foundational role in exploration and exploitation, and hence in the development of ambidexterity.

Individual and collective psychological factors, such as socio-cognitive self-regulation, also play a major role in these processes. In this regard, self-regulation is defined in terms of self-directed thought and behavior related to goal setting, goal pursuit, and outcome evaluation (Baron, 2004). Indeed, the literature on self-regulation suggests that goal-directed thought and behavior are intrinsically linked to processes of exploration and exploitation in specific task domains such as entrepreneurship (Bandura, 1997; Wood, 2005). Entrepreneurs make decisions about where to explore in search of new opportunities, and how to exploit known opportunities. In other words, socio-cognitive self-regulation plays a significant role in motivating and directing exploration and exploitation and should therefore play a key role in ambidextrous capability.

Regulatory Focus Theory

In this study, I specifically investigate entrepreneurial ambidexterity in relation to the form of socio-cognitive self-regulation known as RFT.

This theory is owing to Higgins (1998) and refers to a person's self-regulatory orientation toward future self-states. Regulatory focus is expressed as two distinct and uncorrelated orientations: promotion focus and prevention focus. Promotion focus refers to those circumstances where growth and advancement needs motivate people to try to bring themselves into alignment with their ideal selves and thus to attain desired self-states. When acting from a promotion focus, people are motivated by self-standards based on wishes and aspirations of how they would like to be, defined by Higgins as the "ideal self." Promotion focus is therefore associated with the importance of potential gains and the use of eager approach means in the pursuit of such gains. Moreover, when acting from promotion focus, people are more creative, risk seeking, adopt more distal goals and pursue them using more exploratory means (Brockner et al., 2004).

In contrast, prevention focus refers to those circumstances where security and safety needs prompt people to seek alignment with their "ought self," or the self which a person feels obliged to be. From a prevention focus, people are motivated by the need to be compliant with self-standards based on felt duties and responsibilities, and thus seek to avoid undesired self-states. Prevention focus is therefore associated with the importance of potential losses and the use of vigilant avoidance means to avoid such losses. When acting from prevention focus, people are more cautious, risk avoidant, adopt more proximal goals and fewer goal pursuit means. In summary, regulatory focus determines whether a person's primary motivation is promotional (to advance and create, aligning with the ideal self) or preventative (to protect and avoid, aligning with the ought self). As Higgins (1998, p. 2) further explains:

> A self-regulatory system with a positive reference value [promotion focus] has a desired end state as the reference point. The system is discrepancy reducing and involves attempts to move the currently perceived actual-self-state as close as possible to the desired reference point. In contrast, a self-regulatory system with a negative reference value [prevention focus] has an undesired end state as the reference point. This system is discrepancy amplifying and involves attempts to move the currently perceived actual-self-state as far away as possible from the undesired reference point.

Regulatory focus can occur as both a chronic person variable and a situationally induced variable (Shah, Higgins, & Friedman, 1998). The chronic form largely derives from a person's development and past achievement history in promotion and prevention goal attainment. At the same time, regulatory focus occurs as a situational variable. It is typically brought about by framing problems in terms of gains or nongains, triggering a promotion focus, or by framing problems in terms of losses and nonlosses, triggering a prevention focus. Moreover, both the chronic and situational forms of regulatory focus are uncorrelated and may occur in convergent or divergent combinations (Idson, Liberman, & Higgins, 2004). That is, a person acting from chronic promotion or prevention focus may be induced to adopt either a situational prevention or promotion focus. It is also possible to employ a mixture of chronic and situational orientations simultaneously. In any case, many of the effects of regulatory focus are common to both its chronic and situational manifestations.

Given that the critical decisions made by entrepreneurs are about tackling new task goals, then regulatory focus may be important for identifying the task goal orientation of entrepreneurs and what decision means they adopt in relation to those goals. In particular, entrepreneurial opportunity recognition and exploitation are almost, by definition, promotion-oriented goals and a history of success in achieving such goals may engender a strong promotion focus (Brockner et al., 2004). The potential relevance of regulatory focus is further strengthened by the fact that it relates to a person's subjective history of previous goal success, and that has also been identified as an important factor in entrepreneurship (Bruyat & Julien, 2001; Greve & Salaff, 2003). For these reasons, this study investigates the role of regulatory focus in entrepreneurial ambidexterity, as a feature of thought and behavior among a group of entrepreneurs defined as founder managers.

In fact, a number of studies investigate the role of regulatory focus in different aspects of entrepreneurship. Most findings relate features of entrepreneurial thought and behavior to either promotion focus or prevention focus. For example, studies show that entrepreneurs' promotion focus is more strongly associated with the discovery of opportunities in dynamic environments (Bryant, 2007; Hmieleski & Baron, 2008), entrepreneurial risk taking (Burmeister-Lamp, Levesque, & Schade, 2012), higher levels of moral awareness in decision making (Bryant, 2009) and with stimulating employee creativity in entrepreneurial firms (Wu et al., 2008). In contrast, the same studies show that entrepreneurs' prevention focus is more strongly associated with opportunity discovery in stable environments, less heightened moral awareness, and lower employee creativity. However, no studies investigate the combined effects of promotion focus and prevention focus among entrepreneurs, despite the fact that all persons possess both characteristics to varying degrees and despite the fact that ambidexterity calls for the integration of both promotional and preventative behaviors. To address this gap in the literature, my study investigates the combined effects of both regulatory orientations.

METHODS

Research Design

Scholars have called for more varied methods to explore the situational complexities of entrepreneurship (Ireland & Webb, 2007). At the same time, there is little theory concerning the individual-level processes that underpin ambidexterity (Lavie, Stettner, & Tushman, 2010). Therefore, the primary goal of this chapter is to develop new theoretical insights regarding the psychological antecedents of entrepreneurial ambidexterity as situated thought and behavior. And like many scholars who seek to develop and extend theory, I conduct a multiple case study (Eisenhardt & Graebner, 2007). Moreover, I adopt a mixed methods approach by gathering and integrating both interview and survey data. Mixed methods are appropriate in this case because current knowledge is itself mixed and not yet sufficiently developed to support testable detailed hypotheses, particularly at the micro-foundational or individual level of analysis (Edmondson & Mcmanus, 2007). On the one hand, the field of self-regulation is well developed and regulatory focus has been extensively researched, allowing my study to employ established survey techniques and constructs (Higgins, 2004). Yet on the other hand, there are no prior studies that focus on the psychological antecedents of ambidexterity, suggesting that in-depth case study techniques are appropriate.

Various configurations of mixed methods are possible. In this study, I transform and combine qualitative and quantitative data during analysis (Creswell, Clark, Gutmann, & Hanson, 2003). It follows that the study is philosophically pragmatic in assuming that reality is ontologically heterogeneous and can be investigated using such mixed methods (Creswell, 2003). That is, the adoption of mixed methods assumes there is no single category of reality, such as the quantifiable objective world or the interpreted subjective world (Johnson & Onwuegbuzie, 2004). Working from this perspective, the qualitative component of the study consisted of semi-structured interviews with 30 entrepreneurs regarding many aspects of deliberation and decision making. In addition, the same 30 entrepreneurs were surveyed to measure their chronic regulatory focus. These qualitative and quantitative data were then integrated during analysis for each individual entrepreneur, allowing the study to link the survey results regarding self-regulatory construct variables with the interview results (Miles & Huberman, 1994).

Sampling

Multiple case studies may explore relatively narrow research questions and may include small samples that are purposively selected to explore embedded processes (Creswell et al., 2003). In this study, the 30 entrepreneurs were purposively selected to represent a range of industries and stages of company growth. Some were long-term serial entrepreneurs, while others were novices. A few had failed and tried again. They had all been founder managers who retained a significant role in their venture. They possessed a range of ages, education levels, industry backgrounds, and seven were women. Some of their companies were start-ups less than three years old, while a few were late expansion stage over eight years old. All were based in one region of Australia. The sample of entrepreneurs is summarized in Table 1.

Measures and Data Collection

The study employed a preexisting instrument to measure participants' chronic regulatory focus and prepublished factors were applied to the results. This instrument is called the Regulatory Focus Questionnaire (Grant & Higgins, 2003; Higgins et al., 2001). Instrument items and factors are given in Appendix A. This instrument has been shown to have strong construct validity and reliability in a number of studies. It consists of 11 self-report questions relating to both parental and nonparental content. Six of the items refer to promotion-oriented characteristics and five to prevention-oriented characteristics.

To obviate potential self-report bias, interviewees were told that the study was broadly about decision making and kept unaware that it was exploring

Table 1. Summary of Entrepreneur Cases.

Company Age Years	Industry Sector	Gender	Role Tenure Years	Highest Education	Personal Age Years
(0−5) 43%	Biotech 37%	Female 23%	(<1) 17%	Certificate 3%	(20−29) 3%
(6−10) 37%	ICT 46%	Male 77%	(1−2) 17%	1st degree 27%	(30−39) 27%
(11−15) 10%	Services 7%		(3−5) 43%	2nd degree 57%	(40−49) 40%
(16−20) 7%	Retail 10%		(6−9) 13%	Other 13%	(50−59) 27%
(21+) 3%			(10+) 10%		(60+) 3%

$N = 30$.

self-regulatory processes and ambidexterity. Firstly, semi-structured interviews were conducted with all 30 entrepreneurs lasting approximately one hour each. The researcher adopted a non-participant observer role and used the same interview guide throughout. The interview questions used are given in Appendix B. They covered a range of decision-making tasks. At the end of each interview, interviewees were invited to talk openly about related topics. Each then answered the survey questionnaire that included the survey instrument described above, plus questions regarding their background, demographic profile, experience, their current role, and history of involvement in the company.

RESULTS

Interview Results

The interviews were recorded and fully transcribed, resulting in approximately 300 pages of transcript that were entered into an electronic database indexed by interviewee and question number. Using the qualitative data analysis computer application called NVivo, I then coded each interview for themes, while both reading the transcripts and listening to the audio recordings. This allowed me to analyze both the content and style of the interviews. For example, I was able to identify and note when an interviewee was pensive and paused, or when he or she became excited and spoke more assertively. The coding process was iterative over a number of months as the interviews were gathered. The number of distinct codes also evolved and grew over time, which is typical of such analytic methods (Creswell, 1998). These codes were progressively grouped into 10 major groups or trees relating to decision making, specific entrepreneurial decisions, situational stressors, self-regulation, regulatory focus, cognitive styles, personal factors (including morals and ethics), heuristics, emotion, and decision speed.

During this process, I coded each of the interviews based on the specific questions on the interview guide. Next, I coded for references to various aspects of thought and decision making, including exploratory and exploitative themes. I also coded references to relevant keywords such as "entrepreneurship," "opportunity," "exploring," and "exploiting." I also coded the interviews based on other significant emergent themes, such as references to ethical values, emotional passion, and a sense of purpose.

In addition, I coded for self-regulatory orientation. Firstly, I coded for promotion orientation based on references to seeking ideal self-states, positive goal outcomes, and the avoidance of errors of omission. Second, I coded for prevention orientation based on references to seeking ought self-states, the avoidance of potential losses and avoiding errors of commission (cf. Keller & Bless, 2006).

Evidence of ambidexterity was then identified by the logical relation, intersection, and proximal occurrence of thematic coding for exploration and exploitation. The justification for this approach is that entrepreneurs who think and speak about exploration and exploitation in an integrated fashion, and who are capable of linking exploratory and exploitative concerns, are more likely to possess ambidextrous capabilities. This approach reflects the empirical methods adopted in some other studies, in which ambidexterity is identified by the co-occurrence of exploratory and exploitative behaviors relating to innovation and firm-level strategies, although the unit of analysis is typically at the organizational level (e.g., Amrit, 2008; Gibson & Birkinshaw, 2004; He & Wong, 2004). In contrast, however, the unit of analysis in this study is the individual entrepreneur and his or her modes of thinking about exploration and exploitation.

As evidence of such capabilities, consider the following examples. One female entrepreneur linked the major aspects of innovation – research and operations – when she said that, "running a research lab, one of the things that I always did was try to capture, in concrete terms, what was being discovered. Capture the methods, get them written down, get them verified and checked, and stored appropriately." Another entrepreneur related comparable features of innovation and production in the following way: "I employ the innovative, problem solving guys to get us through the proof of concept and R&D. And then if they're keen enough to take it to the next stage, which is then the more development side if you like, and leading into production." As a final example, the following quote exemplifies the integration of systematic and adaptive approaches to product selection, research, and development: "I'll often decide to explore a particular direction, with developing a new product and so forth, and go down that path. But I think the thing that you learn when you own a smaller business is that things happen out of the blue, they're just completely unplanned." Taken together, these quotes exemplify my coding of the ambidextrous integration of thought about exploratory and exploitative activities.

This process of analysis lasted a number of months. I continually analyzed the interviews to identify patterns in the coding and/or relationships between themes as evidenced by co-occurring or proximal codes. This was done in NVivo using code matrix intersections, proximity analysis, and the analysis of keywords and cross-case comparisons. This process led to further coding and is standard practice in the analysis of qualitative data in mixed method studies (Teddlie & Tashakkori, 2003). Among other outcomes, the analysis generated a count of coding references for exploration, exploitation, and ambidexterity for each participant. These data were subsequently combined with the survey data.

Survey Results

Regarding the survey data, Kolmogorov–Smirnov tests, box plots, and histograms showed normal distribution for promotion focus and prevention focus. All items loaded correctly, and most loaded significantly onto single factors ($Rs > 0.4$), although two loaded marginally ($Rs > 0.2$) (see Ford, Maccallum, & Tait, 1986). I then tested the internal reliability of the construct variables. These results were acceptable, given the small number of items for each factor (<7) and small sample size ($N = 30$): promotion focus ($\alpha = 0.63$), and prevention pride ($\alpha = 0.79$) (Cortina, 1993). I then generated descriptive statistics for both construct variables. Owing to the relatively small sample and the retention of nonextreme outliers, nonparametric Spearman correlations were used. Table 2 shows these results. The reported scores are the factored scores divided by the number of related items for each construct. Promotion focus is uncorrelated with prevention focus, as typically reported (Brodscholl, Kober, & Higgins, 2007). Table 2 shows that subjects possessed stronger promotion focus when compared to prevention focus. This result accords with evidence from earlier studies which show that entrepreneurs tend to be more strongly inclined toward promotion-oriented behavior (Hmieleski & Baron,

Table 2. Means, Standard Deviations, and Correlations.

Variable	M	SD	1
1. Promotion focus	2.29	0.31	
2. Prevention focus	2.05	0.54	−0.14

$N = 30$; all effects are two-tailed tests.
Correlations are Spearman correlations.

2008). Although as the results of this study also demonstrate, participants possessed significant levels of prevention focus as well.

Analysis of Combined Data

I then combined the results of the survey and interview analyses (Creswell et al., 2003). Further analysis of the combined data suggested that ambidexterity is stronger when an entrepreneur possesses stronger regulatory focus, measured by his or her combined scores for promotion focus and prevention focus. In addition, based on coding frequency and proximity analysis, ambidexterity appears to be positively related to a greater awareness and concern with ethical values, a sense of purpose and a passion for entrepreneurial goals. These results are summarized in Table 3, in which coding references are reported for the 15 participants who are members of the stronger regulatory focus group, and for the 15 members of the weaker group. The table shows the frequency of ambidextrous thinking, as well as the frequencies of co-occurrence between ambidexterity and references to ethical values and a sense of passion.

The novel results concerning values and passion are exemplified by the following statements made by a very successful young entrepreneur:

> People wouldn't view a normal technology entrepreneur as someone who does a lot of research. But I do a lot of research, but not traditional, not research what people think. At night time I read a huge cross section of things, I'm highly into theoretical physics, socio-economics – like I research alternative media sites, new technologies coming out, the latest in physics, the latest in different technologies, and the latest in spiritually. I apply all this to how I run this business, because I think the only way to acquire this tool to analyze things with such a high level of abstraction is to understand how stuff works in general in a holistic sense ... . I haven't realized the vision yet, I have a mission in my life, nothing else matters as much. I've got a goal to build this enterprise, the next

Table 3. Entrepreneurial Ambidexterity and Regulatory Focus.

Coding References	Regulatory Focus Groups	
	Stronger	Weaker
Ambidexterity	36 (13)	21 (12)
Values and ambidexterity	62 (11)	39 (9)
Passion and ambidexterity	48 (10)	22 (6)

Unbracketed figures are the number of coding references.
Bracketed figures are the number of interviews coded.

Microsoft, I'm going to keep shooting at it. I could die trying. I'm trying to do that, basically bringing new technology into the market and building an enterprise from scratch.

As another example of passion and ambidexterity, one entrepreneur linked long-term vision, product development decisions, personal goals, and emotional commitment. He remarked:

What we are doing now is about a three year vision of mine that is only just now coming to market. And it has been the single most difficult thing I have ever done, to bring this one through. So it would be not surprising if there was a lot of emotion wrapped up with that ... The other thing is for me, and from an emotional perspective this is worth just saying as it is, we took a major decision only two weeks ago to make this thing we've been doing open source, and make it freely available to the sector for non-commercial use.

These results are broadly consistent with the findings of prior studies. It is already known that promotion focus is associated with more creative and exploratory behavior, the use of eagerness approach means, and stronger emotional states on the happy—sad continuum. While prevention focus is associated with more routine cautious behavior, the use of vigilant avoidance means, and stronger emotional states on the quiescence—anxious continuum (Friedman & Forster, 2001). Importantly, however, the results reported here suggest that ambidextrous thought and behavior are strongest when overall regulatory orientation is also strong, that is, when an entrepreneur has strong promotion focus as well as strong prevention focus. This particular finding sharply contrasts most prior research into regulatory focus which tends to focus on distinct patterns of thought and behavior associated with either promotion focus or prevention focus, but rarely with the interaction of the two (Keller & Bless, 2006). Finally, results also suggest that entrepreneurial ambidexterity is positively related to a feeling of passion or emotional engagement with entrepreneurial goals, and the possession of higher values, such as strong ethical norms and ideals of personal meaning and fulfillment.

DISCUSSION

This study's major finding is that a strong promotion focus combined with a strong prevention focus appears to optimize ambidextrous entrepreneurial thought and behavior. This finding compares to most prior studies of RFT and entrepreneurship, which investigate the effect of promotion versus prevention focus. In contrast, this study suggests a significant interaction effect: it suggests that overall regulatory focus antecedes the ambidextrous combination of exploration and exploitation (see Posen & Levinthal, 2012). These effects are as depicted in Fig. 1. Earlier studies suggest why this finding may be the case. Recall that promotion focus is strongly associated with the eager pursuit of gains and attainment goals. Such goals may be achieved either through exploratory means (searching for new opportunities) or exploitative means (harvesting existing opportunities), even if promotion focus is biased toward more exploratory behavior (Brodscholl et al., 2007). At the same time, prevention focus is strongly associated with the vigilant avoidance of losses and maintenance goals. Once again, however, such goals may be achieved either through exploratory means (searching for new ways to avoid losses), or exploitative means (using existing avoidance strategies), even if promotion focus is biased toward more exploitative behavior. In this fashion, promotion and prevention orientations may work together to strengthen dynamic ambidextrous capabilities.

In addition, possessing strong regulatory focus may also stimulate an associated sense of values and passion in goal pursuit — indeed, prior studies suggest that strong regulatory orientations do stimulate a heightened sense of value and stronger motivations (Camacho, Higgins, & Luger, 2003). The resulting sense of an ethical foundation or moral compass may allow entrepreneurs to adapt more readily in day-to-day decision making. Grounded in deeper values and passions, they may be more flexible and adaptable when making strategic and operational choices regarding exploration and exploitation. Having a deeper and stronger commitment to ethical values and norms (Morris, Schindehutte, Walton, & Allen, 2002) may liberate them from the potential trap of over-committing to current exploratory or exploitative activities (Joyner, Payne, & Raiborn, 2002).

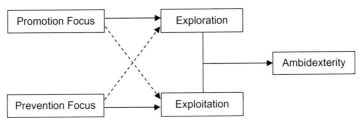

Fig. 1. Model of Entrepreneurial Ambidexterity (Dashed Lines Indicate Weaker Effects).

Thus, the study's findings suggest that by adopting strong ethical values concerning the firm's purpose and practices, founders are less captive to the immediate pressures of exploitation and execution, and at the same time less captive to the novelty drivers of exploration and innovation. In other words, the findings suggest that ethical values underpin a cognitive and behavioral framework which allows founder entrepreneurs to be more adaptive and ambidextrous. Furthermore, as Higgins and others show (Camacho et al., 2003; Higgins, 2000), people assign value to goals and outcomes based on the degree of regulatory fit between their goals, pursuit means, and dominant regulatory orientation. Hence, having a strong overall regulatory orientation will tend to be associated with a stronger sense of value.

The findings of the study also suggest that a strong moral compass or ethical climate may support desired features of both individual and organizational learning (Trevino, Weaver, & Reynolds, 2006). This suggests that strong ethical values provide a more stable, long-term framework for learning goals and objectives. Both exploration and exploitation are then framed within a fundamental ethical framework of higher purpose and principles, resulting in less vulnerability to the variable demands of either exploratory or exploitative learning behaviors (Butterfield, Trevino, & Weaver, 2000). In these respects, ethical values may serve as an antidote to myopia and rigidity in organizational learning and innovation. This further suggests that ethical values may support more expansive search and novelty in opportunity exploration and exploitation (Becker, Knudsen, & March, 2006) and nurture creative risk taking in organizational learning (March, 2006).

The chapter findings have further implications for a range of topics in entrepreneurial research and practice. Regarding research, the findings suggest that ethical values play a major role in the ambidextrous management of exploration and exploitation in entrepreneurial firms. This novel finding adds to existing research that focuses on the role of culture and cognitive frameworks in entrepreneurial strategy and ambidexterity (Smith & Tushman, 2005). This suggests a novel relationship between ethics, dynamic capabilities, and entrepreneurial strategy: that is, having a strong ethical framework may serve to guide, integrate and liberate strategic thinking and decision making in highly volatile and uncertain markets, and cement the nexus of opportunity search, recognition, and exploitation, and the dynamic reconfiguration of resources in response to new opportunities (Eisenhardt, Furr, & Bingham, 2010). In this respect, founder's self-regulatory characteristics may be a central element of the micro-foundations of dynamic capabilities, serving as a social psychological scaffold for emergent organizational values, behaviors, and capabilities (Teece, 2007).

In addition, Hmieleski and Baron (2008) show that entrepreneurs may adopt a stronger promotion orientation in more dynamic and uncertain markets, and a stronger prevention orientation in more stable and predictable markets. Noting this research, my study's findings further suggest that ambidextrous entrepreneurs may be more likely to adapt their self-regulatory approach in response to market conditions. On the one hand, in more stable markets, they may be more capable of acting from a prevention orientation, yet when confronting dynamic or unstable markets, ambidextrous entrepreneurs may be more capable of acting from a stronger promotion focus. In this sense, the complex self-regulatory characteristics of founders appear to support the emergence of both firm-level and task-level ambidexterity. Hence my study reinforces the view that it is the "dynamism of the capability itself, not the environment" that characterizes dynamic capabilities such as ambidexterity (Zahra et al., 2006, p. 925).

Regarding implications for education and practice, this chapter suggests that by enhancing the integration of promotion focus and prevention focus we may be able to strengthen ambidextrous dynamic capabilities, in areas such as strategic thinking, decision making, and other areas of executive functioning. Known techniques could be adapted for this purpose (Van-Dijk & Kluger, 2004). At the same time, ambidexterity may also be improved by encouraging greater ethical awareness and emotional engagement in decision making by entrepreneurs, and vice versa (Higgins, Shah, & Friedman, 1997). If these findings are validated in larger studies, the resulting knowledge could provide new techniques to stimulate ambidexterity, ethical behavior, and emotional commitment in rapidly growing entrepreneurial firms.

Limitations and Conclusion

As a multiple case study, this chapter seeks to extend theory, not prove it. Indeed, owing to the nonrandom, relatively small samples used in the study, the findings do not support strong claims about the general population of entrepreneurs. In addition, the data were gathered from entrepreneurs and companies based in one geographic region, and therefore the results are inherently limited in applicability to different contexts. Nevertheless, although based on a relatively small sample, the findings of this study suggest that founder entrepreneurs who possess complex self-regulatory schemes combining both strong promotion and strong prevention orientations will demonstrate more ambidextrous dynamic capabilities.

Importantly, the possession of higher order values and a sense of emotional engagement appear to support ambidexterity, possibly through providing an overarching motivational framework for goal setting and goal pursuit. That is, by having strong personal values and a sense of passionate engagement with their goals, entrepreneurs may be less constrained and conflicted by the pursuit of either exploration or exploitation. Being thus grounded in deeper motivations and values, they are more adaptive and flexible in goal pursuit. Indeed, it may also be the case that possessing strong versions of both promotion focus and prevention focus is related to the development and of higher values and emotional strength in the first instance. Future research into these topics should investigate these effects, as well as the general mechanisms of their self-regulatory development. Such research may also result in new educational and management techniques that can strengthen the self-regulatory characteristics which foster entrepreneurial ambidexterity, having practical implications for founder tenure and the management of firm growth.

REFERENCES

Adner, R., & Levinthal, D. (2008). Doing versus seeing: Acts of exploitation and perceptions of exploration. *Strategic Entrepreneurship Journal, 2*, 43−52.

Amrit, T. (2008). Do bridging ties complement strong ties? An empirical examination of alliance ambidexterity. *Strategic Management Journal, 29*, 251−272.

Bandura, A. (1997). *Self-efficacy: The exercise of control.* New York, NY: W. H. Freeman and Company.

Baron, R. A. (2004). The cognitive perspective: A valuable tool for answering entrepreneurship's basic "Why" questions. *Journal of Business Venturing, 19*, 221−239.

Becker, M. C., Knudsen, T., & March, J. G. (2006). Schumpeter, winter, and the sources of novelty. *Industrial and Corporate Change, 15*, 353−371.

Benner, M. J., & Tushman, M. L. (2003). Exploitation, exploration, and process management: The productivity dilemma revisited. *Academy of Management Review, 28*, 238−256.

Bhide, A. V. (2000). *The origin and evolution of new businesses.* Oxford: Oxford University Press.

Brockner, J., Higgins, E. T., & Low, M. B. (2004). Regulatory focus theory and the entrepreneurial process. *Journal of Business Venturing, 19*, 203−220.

Brodscholl, J. C., Kober, H., & Higgins, E. T. (2007). Strategies of self-regulation in goal attainment versus goal maintenance. *European Journal of Social Psychology, 37*, 628−648.

Bruyat, C., & Julien, P.-A. (2001). Defining the field of research in entrepreneurship. *Journal of Business Venturing, 16*, 165−180.

Bryant, P. (2007). Self-regulation and decision heuristics in entrepreneurial opportunity evaluation and exploitation. *Management Decision, 45,* 732–748.

Bryant, P. (2009). Self-regulation and moral awareness among entrepreneurs. *Journal of Business Venturing, 24,* 505–518.

Burmeister-Lamp, K., Levesque, M., & Schade, C. (2012). Are entrepreneurs influenced by risk attitude, regulatory focus or both? An experiment on entrepreneurs' time allocation. *Journal of Business Venturing, 27,* 456–476.

Butterfield, K. D., Trevino, L. K., & Weaver, G. R. (2000). Moral awareness in business organizations: Influences of issue-related and social context factors. *Human Relations, 53,* 981–1018.

Camacho, C. J., Higgins, E. T., & Luger, L. (2003). Moral value transfer from regulatory fit: What feels right is right and what feels wrong is wrong. *Journal of Personality and Social Psychology, 84,* 498–508.

Cao, Q., Gedajlovic, E., & Zhang, H. (2009). Unpacking organizational ambidexterity: Dimensions, contingencies, and synergistic effects. *Organization Science, 20,* 781–796.

Cortina, J. M. (1993). What is coefficient alpha? An examination of theory and applications. *Journal of Applied Psychology, 78,* 98–104.

Creswell, J. W. (1998). *Qualitative inquiry and research design: Choosing among five traditions.* Thousand Oaks, CA: Sage Publications.

Creswell, J. W. (2003). *Research design: Qualitative, quantitative, and mixed methods approaches.* Thousand Oaks, CA: Sage Publications.

Creswell, J. W., Clark, V. L. P., Gutmann, M. L., & Hanson, W. E. (2003). Advanced mixed methods research designs. In A. Tashakkori & C. Teddlie (Eds.), *Handbook of mixed methods in social and behavioral research.* Thousand Oaks, CA: Sage Publications.

Dimov, D. (2007). Beyond the single-person, single-insight attribution in understanding entrepreneurial opportunities. *Entrepreneurship: Theory and Practice, 31,* 713–731.

Edmondson, A. C., & Mcmanus, S. E. (2007). Methodological fit in management field research. *Academy of Management Review, 32,* 1155–1179.

Eisenhardt, K. M., Furr, N. R., & Bingham, C. B. (2010). Microfoundations of performance: Balancing efficiency and flexibility in dynamic environments. *Organization Science, 21,* 1263–1273.

Eisenhardt, K. M., & Graebner, M. E. (2007). Theory building from cases: Opportunities and challenges. *Academy of Management Journal, 50,* 25–32.

Eisenhardt, K. M., & Martin, J. A. (2000). Dynamic capabilities: What are they? *Strategic Management Journal, 21,* 1105–1121.

Ford, J. K., Maccallum, R. C., & Tait, M. (1986). The application of exploratory factor analysis in applied psychology: A critical review and analysis. *Personnel Psychology, 39,* 291–314.

Friedman, R. S., & Forster, J. (2001). The effects of promotion and prevention cues on creativity. *Journal of Personality and Social Psychology, 81,* 1001–1013.

Gavetti, G., Levinthal, D. A., & Rivkin, J. W. (2005). Strategy making in novel and complex worlds: The power of analogy. *Strategic Management Journal, 26,* 691–712.

Gibson, C. B., & Birkinshaw, J. (2004). The antecedents, consequences and mediating role of organizational ambidexterity. *Academy of Management Journal, 47,* 209–226.

Grant, H., & Higgins, E. T. (2003). Optimism, promotion pride, and prevention pride as predictors of quality of life. *Personality and Social Psychology Bulletin, 29,* 1521–1532.

Greve, A., & Salaff, J. W. (2003). Social networks and entrepreneurship. *Entrepreneurship Theory and Practice, 28,* 1–22.

He, Z.-L., & Wong, P.-K. (2004). Exploration vs. exploitation: An empirical test of the ambidexterity hypothesis. *Organization Science*, *15*, 481−494.

Helfat, C. E., & Peteraf, M. A. (2009). Understanding dynamic capabilities. Progress along a developmental path. *Strategic organization*, *7*, 91−102.

Higgins, E. T. (1998). Promotion and prevention: Regulatory focus as a motivational principle. *Advances in Experimental Social Psychology*, *30*, 1−46.

Higgins, E. T. (2000). Making a good decision: Value from fit. *American Psychologist*, *55*, 1217−1230.

Higgins, E. T. (2004). Making a theory useful: Lessons handed down. *Personality and Social Psychology Review*, *8*, 138−145.

Higgins, E. T., Friedman, R. S., Harlow, R. E., Idson, L. C., Ayduk, O. N., & Taylor, A. (2001). Achievement orientations from subjective histories of success: Promotion pride versus prevention pride. *European Journal of Social Psychology*, *31*, 3−23.

Higgins, E. T., Shah, J., & Friedman, R. (1997). Emotional responses to goal attainment: Strength of regulatory focus as moderator. *Journal of Personality and Social Psychology*, *72*, 515−525.

Hmieleski, K. M., & Baron, R. A. (2008). Regulatory focus and new venture performance: A study of entrepreneurial opportunity exploitation under conditions of risk and uncertainty. *Strategic Entrepreneurship Journal*, *2*, 285−299.

Idson, L. C., Liberman, N., & Higgins, E. T. (2004). Imagining how you'd feel: The role of motivational experiences from regulatory fit. *Personality and Social Psychology Bulletin*, *30*, 926−937.

Ireland, R. D., & Webb, J. W. (2007). A cross-disciplinary exploration of entrepreneurship research. *Journal of Management*, *33*, 891−927.

Jansen, J. J. P., Tempelaar, M. P., Van Den Bosch, F. A. J., & Volberda, H. W. (2009). Structural differentiation and ambidexterity: The mediating role of integration mechanisms. *Organization Science*, *20*, 797−811.

Johnson, R. B., & Onwuegbuzie, A. J. (2004). Mixed methods research: A research paradigm whose time has come. *Educational Researcher*, *33*, 14−26.

Joyner, B. E., Payne, D., & Raiborn, C. A. (2002). Building values, business ethics and corporate social responsibility into the developing organization. *Journal of Developmental Entrepreneurship*, *7*, 113−131.

Keller, J., & Bless, H. (2006). Regulatory fit and cognitive performance: The interactive effect of chronic and situationally induced self-regulatory mechanisms on test performance. *European Journal of Social Psychology*, *36*, 393−405.

Lavie, D., Stettner, U., & Tushman, M. L. (2010). Exploration and exploitation within and across organizations. *The Academy of Management Annals*, *4*, 109−155.

Levitt, B., & March, J. G. (1988). Organizational learning. *Annual Review of Sociology*, *14*, 319−338.

March, J. G. (1991). Exploration and exploitation in organizational learning. *Organization Science*, *2*, 71−87.

March, J. G. (2006). Rationality, foolishness, and adaptive intelligence. *Strategic Management Journal*, *27*, 201−214.

Miles, M. B., & Huberman, A. M. (1994). *Qualitative data analysis*. Thousand Oaks, CA: Sage Publications.

Morris, M. H., Schindehutte, M., Walton, J., & Allen, J. (2002). The ethical context of entrepreneurship: Proposing and testing a developmental framework. *Journal of Business Ethics*, *40*, 331−361.

Newey, L. R., & Zahra, S. A. (2009). The evolving firm: How dynamic and operating capabilities interact to enable entrepreneurship. *British Journal of Management*, *20*, S81–S100.

O'Reilly, C. A., & Tushman, M. L. (2004). The ambidextrous organization. *Harvard Business Review*, *82*, 74–81.

O'reilly, C. A., & Tushman, M. L. (2008). Ambidexterity as a dynamic capability: Resolving the innovator's dilemma. *Research in Organizational Behavior*, *28*, 185–206.

O'reilly, C. A., & Tushman, M. L. (2011). Organizational ambidexterity in action: How managers explore and exploit. *California Management Review*, *53*, 5–22.

Posen, H. E., & Levinthal, D. A. (2012). Chasing a moving target: Exploitation and exploration in dynamic environments. *Management Science*, *58*, 587–601.

Raisch, S., & Birkinshaw, J. (2008). Organizational ambidexterity: Antecedents, outcomes, and moderators. *Journal of Management*, *34*, 375–409.

Raisch, S., Birkinshaw, J., Probst, G., & Tushman, M. L. (2009). Organizational ambidexterity: Balancing exploitation and exploration for sustained performance. *Organization Science*, *20*, 685–695.

Russo, A., & Vurro, C. (2010). Cross-boundary ambidexterity: Balancing exploration and exploitation in the fuel cell industry. *European Management Review*, *7*, 30–45.

Shah, J. Y., Higgins, E. T., & Friedman, R. S. (1998). Performance incentives and means: How regulatory focus influences goal attainment. *Journal of Personality and Social Psychology*, *74*, 285–293.

Shane, S., & Venkataraman, S. (2000). The promise of entrepreneurship as a field of research. *Academy of Management Review*, *25*, 217–226.

Smith, W. K., & Tushman, M. L. (2005). Managing strategic contradictions: A top management model for managing innovation streams. *Organization Science*, *16*, 522–536.

Teddlie, C., & Tashakkori, A. (2003). Major issues and controversies in the use of mixed methods in the social and behavioral sciences. In A. Tashakkori & C. Teddlie (Eds.), *Handbook of mixed methods in social and behavioral research*. Thousand Oaks, CA: Sage Publications.

Teece, D. J. (2007). Explicating dynamic capabilities: The nature and microfoundations of (sustainable) enterprise performance. *Strategic Management Journal*, *28*, 1319–1350.

Trevino, L. K., Weaver, G. R., & Reynolds, S. J. (2006). Behavioral ethics in organizations: A review. *Journal of Management*, *32*, 951–990.

Vancouver, J. B., & Day, D. V. (2005). Industrial and organisation research on self-regulation: From constructs to applications. *Applied Psychology*, *54*, 155–185.

Van-Dijk, D. & Kluger, A. N. (2004). Feedback sign effect on motivation: Is it moderated by regulatory focus? *Applied Psychology: An International Review*, *53*, 113–135.

Wasserman, N. (2012). *The founder's dilemmas: Anticipating and avoiding the pitfalls that can sink a startup*. Princeton, NJ: Princeton University Press.

Wood, R. E. (2005). New frontiers for self-regulation research in IO psychology. *Applied Psychology: An International Review*, *54*, 192–198.

Wu, C., Mcmullen, J. S., Neubert, M. J., & Yi, X. (2008). The influence of leader regulatory focus on employee creativity. *Journal of Business Venturing*, *23*, 587–602.

Zahra, S. A., Sapienza, H. J., & Davidsson, P. (2006). Entrepreneurship and dynamic capabilities: A review, model and research agenda. *Journal of Management Studies*, *43*, 917–955.

APPENDIX A: SURVEY INSTRUMENT ITEMS

Regulatory Focus Questionnaire: Items 1, 3, 7, 9, 10, and 11 are used to derive measures for promotion focus; items 2, 4, 5, 6, and 8 are used to derive measures for prevention focus. Factor loadings are shown in brackets after each item.

1. Compared to most people, are you typically unable to get what you want out of life? (−0.65)
2. Growing up, would you ever "cross the line" by doing things that your parents would not tolerate? (−0.8)
3. How often have you accomplished things that got you "psyched" to work even harder? (0.37)
4. Did you ever get on your parents' nerves often when you were growing up? (−0.65)
5. How often did you obey the rules and regulations that were established by your parents? (0.56)
6. Growing up, did you ever act in ways that your parents thought were objectionable? (−0.84)
7. Do you often do well at different things you try? (0.54)
8. Not being careful enough has gotten me into trouble at times. (−0.55)
9. When it comes to achieving things that are important to me, I find that I don't perform as well as I ideally would like to do. (−0.51)
10. I feel like I have made progress toward being successful in my life. (0.81)
11. I have found very few hobbies or activities in my life that capture my interest or motivate me to put effort into them. (−0.53)

APPENDIX B: SEMI-STRUCTURED INTERVIEW QUESTIONS

1. What is your own approach to decision making when decisions have to be made quickly with limited information?
2. What is your own approach to decision making when the outcome is very uncertain and risky?
3. What is your own approach to decision making when you feel strongly about the issues?

4. In your own decision making, when do you rely on your intuitions or previous experience and when do you perform systematic analysis before making decisions?
5. In your decision making, how do you typically decide which opportunities you will try to exploit?
6. In your own decision making, how do you approach pursuing future gains, versus avoiding future losses?
7. Across the range of responsibilities you have — financial, strategic, HR, marketing, etc. — how confident are you in making decisions in those areas?
8. How important is decision making as part of your role in the company, relative to other aspects of the role such as leadership?
9. Why did you choose to become an entrepreneur?
10. Overall, what do you think are your main strengths and weaknesses as a decision maker?
11. Is there anything you would like to say about this topic or any other thoughts that come to mind?

CHAPTER 3

THE RANGE OF SHOCKS PROMPTING ENTREPRENEURIAL EMPLOYEE TURNOVER THROUGH THE LENSES OF EXPLORATION AND EXPLOITATION FRAMEWORK

Katerina Voutsina, Gaëtan Mourmant and Fred Niederman

ABSTRACT

This research expands the scope of the exploitation/exploration litera-ture which has generally embraced a firm-level perspective by showing the theoretical and practical relevance of this framework for the study of entrepreneurial behaviour from an individual-level perspective. The study exemplifies specific instances where explorative or exploitative aspects of behaviour are likely to be manifested as a response to specific types of shocks that precede and impact the decision to quit and start one's own business. Different types of shocks or entrepreneurial events displace the individual from the inertia of existing behaviour and pave the way for the

Exploration and Exploitation in Early Stage Ventures and SMEs
Technology, Innovation, Entrepreneurship and Competitive Strategy, Volume 14, 39–66
Copyright © 2014 by Emerald Group Publishing Limited
All rights of reproduction in any form reserved
ISSN: 1479-067X/doi:10.1108/S1479-067X20140000014010

consideration of a new set of opportunities; a new set of opportunities where entrepreneurial initiatives are perceived to be both feasible and desirable (exploitation—exploitation). Drawing upon 80 semi-structured and longitudinal interviews with entrepreneurs who quitted their 'salaried job' in order to start their own business, the study: (a) provides an inventory of events/shocks found to precipitate the interviewees' decision to quit, and (b) links the various types of shocks with the prospective explorative and/or exploitative entrepreneurial initiatives. In this respect, the dynamics that underlie the effects of shocks on entrepreneurial behaviour are illustrated, while blurriness and interrelatedness of exploitative and explorative aspects of entrepreneurial behaviour are exemplified. Such a detailed list of shocks may serve as reference tool for both prospective entrepreneurs who wish to make an entrepreneurial shift in their career, as well as managers who wish to be proactive in avoiding or encouraging entrepreneurial employee turnover.

Keywords: Shocks; exploration; exploitation; voluntary employee turnover; nascent entrepreneurship

INTRODUCTION

In management literature, the exploration and exploitation processes have been analysed in the context of large firms (Jansen, Simsek, & Cao, 2012; Lavie, Stettner, & Tushman, 2010). Exploitation activities are concerned with 'refinement, choice, production, efficiency, selection, implementation and execution' (March, 1991, p. 71), while exploration activities are concerned with 'search, variation, risk-taking, experimentation, discovery and innovation' (March, p. 71). The two types of activities are considered as conflicting, but equally important for the firm. The challenge for large firms has been to achieve a 'balance' between the two processes in order to attain survival and superior performance (e.g. Gupta, Smith, & Shalley, 2006; March, 1991; O'reilly & Tushman, 2013; Simsek, 2009; Stettner & Lavie, 2013).

Although the assumption of 'ambidexterity' has been rather employed in the analysis of large organizations, the concept seems to have theoretical and practical relevance for entrepreneurship, as well. Shane and Venkataraman (2000, p. 218) define entrepreneurship as 'the processes of discovery, evaluation and exploitation of opportunities; and the set of individuals who discover, evaluate, and exploit them'. Similarly, studies of nascent or early-stages entrepreneurship analyse the very process according to which opportunities are perceived (Krueger Jr., 2007), business ideas are conceptually generated, elaborated and adapted (Davidsson, Hunter, & Klofsten, 2004; de Koning, 1999; Hmieleski & Ensley, 2004), and entrepreneurial activities and operations are enacted (Delmar & Shane, 2004; Shane & Eckhardt, 2003; Van de Ven, 1996). Entrepreneurial behaviour seems to be manifested only when exploration and exploitation come together (Kuckertz, Kohtamäki, & Droege, 2010). Accordingly, it seemed relevant to further investigate individual's entrepreneurial behaviour along these lines.

In particular, the current study focuses on entrepreneurial behaviour of people who leave their salaried job in order to start a company. We believe that such a group is less likely to simply grow up in an entrepreneurial household, to begin entrepreneurship by inheritance or directly during their education. In some sense, those 'born to' be entrepreneurs are an important group, but are limited to a finite group; on the contrary, an alternative group of those already working who can begin new firms expands greatly the pool from which entrepreneurs can be drawn.

The aim of the chapter is twofold: (a) to present a rich repertoire of shocks that precede and drastically impact the decision to quit and start one's own business and (b) to provide some preliminary insights regarding the dynamics that underlie the effects of shocks on entrepreneurial behaviour by linking specific types of shocks with different types of entrepreneurial opportunities (i.e. explorative vs. exploitative initiatives). Different types of shock displace the individual from the inertia of existing behaviour and pave the way for the consideration of a new set of opportunities where explorative activities seem desirable, and/or exploitative activities seem feasible. The dynamics of the effects of shocks on entrepreneurial behaviour are illustrated, while blurriness and interrelatedness of exploitative and explorative aspects of entrepreneurial behaviour are exemplified.

LITERATURE REVIEW

Although the venture idea is not formed as a complete and unchangeable entity at a sudden flash of insight (Davidsson, 2004), they are moments or specific experiences which may be proved crucial in the individuals' decision to start their own business.

Shocks or entrepreneurial events are found to precede and drastically impact the individuals' decision to quit and start their own business by revealing explorative and/or exploitative opportunities which until recently remained unnoticed.

The Entrepreneurial Event

In their model of 'entrepreneurial event', Shapero and Sokol (1982) assume that inertia guides human behaviour until an event happens and this event interrupts or displaces that inertia. Any form of displacement may act as a major force pushing the individual to engage in new courses of actions. In other words, once this displacement or 'trigger event' (Shapero, 1984; Shapero & Sokol, 1982) happens, the individual may start behaving differently than before, i.e. start her own business.

The observed departure from the current state or the displacement may be negative (e.g. a job loss, non-desirable organizational changes and job dissatisfaction) or positive (e.g. salary increase, lottery, financial support and a potential business partnership) and usually precipitates a change in the behaviour. Job-related displacements are those most commonly observed (Shapero & Sokol, 1982).

As this 'trigger event' displaces the individual from the inertia of existing behaviour, it paves the way for her to reconsider a new set of opportunities where entrepreneurial initiatives are perceived to be both feasible and desirable, i.e. 'credible opportunities' (Shapero & Sokol, 1982). After the experience of such an event, the individual remains the same; yet, her perceptions have changed regarding the new circumstances and the resulting opportunities.

Elaborating on the above, Shapero and Sokol (1982) refer to the 'propensity to act' as a separate predictor of action, while Krueger Jr. and Brazeal (1994, p. 93) mention that the potential to start a business must exist prior to the displacement. 'The potential to be entrepreneurs was clearly there, but it required some sort of displacement for that potential to surface' (Krueger Jr. & Brazeal, 1994, p. 93).

In their Entrepreneurial Potential Model (EPM), Krueger and Brazeal (1994) see entrepreneurial potential as an antecedent to entrepreneurial intention – a precipitating event (displacement) intervenes in the process as the 'push' or 'pull' factor that causes entrepreneurial intention. It is worth mentioning that empirical studies on displacement have been rather limited and unable to demonstrate a strong predictive ability of this concept (Krueger, Reilly, & Carsrud, 2000).

One possible explanation for the inconsistent results is the mixture in the targeted population of both those who are led to entrepreneurship by inheritance or family ownership with those who voluntarily leave a job to start a company. We argue that it is worth looking at those leaving jobs to start companies because they are an 'actionable' group and potentially larger than the group of the entrepreneurs by inheritance or family ownership; we argue that mixing the two groups may dull what is a sharp distinction for the selected group. On this basis, this study focuses exclusively on those who voluntarily leave salaried job positions to start new firms.

Shock and Voluntary Employee Turnover

In the 21st century, turnover behaviour remains one of the most persistent challenges facing organizations (Barrick & Zimmerman, 2005; Griffeth, Hom, & Gaertner, 2000; Maertz & Griffeth, 2004; Mitchell & Lee, 2001). The unanticipated loss of well-trained or talented employees has a substantial impact on firms in terms of their financial state and competitive power in the market (Cascio, 1991; Glebbeek & Bax, 2004; Lumpkin & Dess, 2001; Mohr, Young, & Burgess Jr., 2011; Pfeffer & Fong, 2005). Mitchell and Lee (2001), quoting Horn and Griffeth (1995), estimate more than 1,000 recent studies on employee turnover.

The notion of shock as an important factor in employee turnover was initially introduced over a decade ago through the unfolding model of voluntary turnover (Lee & Mitchell, 1994). This process model identifies stages that individuals follow sequentially moving toward leaving their jobs. A shock is the first stage in the turnover process. Lee, Mitchell, Holtom, McDaniel, and Hill (1999, p. 451) describe it as 'a particular jarring event that initiates the psychological analyses involved in quitting a job'. This definition provided by Lee et al. (1999) has been extended by Holtom, Mitchell, Lee, and Inderrieden (2005, p. 341), who view shock as '... an event that generates information or provides meaning about a person's job, and then is interpreted and integrated into the person's system of beliefs and images'.

In particular, after the shock is experienced, individuals reassess their current position regarding their values, goals and plans for goal attainment (Beach, 1998; Lee et al., 1999) and they adjust their behaviour accordingly: they decide to leave or to stay. A shock may trigger the enactment of a pre-existing plan of action, based on past experience or cultivated expecta-tions and thus directly enforces the individual's decision to leave; it may prompt the employee to re-evaluate her 'fit' with the organizational values; or it may create a misalignment between the individual's values, goals and strate-gies for goal attainment and those of the employing organization (Lee et al., 1999, pp. 451–452). Holtom et al. (2005) and Morrell, Loan-Clarke, and Wilkinson (2004) examine the notion of shocks by testing specific hypotheses regarding the nature, content and role of shocks in turnover decisions.

In Morrell et al. (2004) study the relationship between the nature (perso-nal vs. job-related), the anticipated (or not) character (expected vs. unex-pected) and the valence of the shock (positive, neutral or negative) is tested. For instance, shocks that are expected are more likely to be positive and personal, while negative shocks are more likely to be work-related and associated with dissatisfaction. Holtom et al. (2005) classify shocks accord-ing to the following criteria: (a) they *may* or *may not be expected*, (b) they may be *personal/external to the job itself* or they may be *organizational/ job-related* and (c) they may be *positive, neutral* or *negative*. It is important to note that while Lee et al. (1999) understand the notion of shock as 'a single particular event' (Lee et al., 1999, p. 461), others have considered the possibility of multiple shocks (Kammeyer-Mueller, Wanberg, Glomb, & Ahlburg, 2005; Maertz & Griffeth, 2004; Mourmant, Gallivan, & Kalika, 2009). Although the shock precipitates the decision to quit, it may not always lead to actual quitting. For an individual, it may take more than one shocks to leave her company.

To emphasize the need to further investigate this concept, Morrell et al. (2004, p. 337) point out that 'contemporary research has incorporated shock into as yet untested models (Allen & Griffeth, 2001; Griffeth, Gaertner, Robinson, & Sager, 1999) or as an explanatory/heuristic device (Hom & Kinicki, 2001)'. Although there is some evidence that job leaving behaviour can be sparked by a shock, it is not clear that all shocks will trig-ger the same results. The literature identifies indeed various types of shocks; it is worth considering whether there are systemic variations in the results observed due to the different types of shocks.

Taking into account the above and the fact that the linkage between entrepreneurial pathways and shocks has not been thoroughly analysed so far (Holtom et al., 2005; Morrell et al., 2004), the present study aspires to shed light to the role of shocks in the individual's decision to quit her job and start a business.

It is worth mentioning that both in the entrepreneurship literature and in the employee turnover literature, entrepreneurial events or shocks are implicitly or explicitly intertwined with the creation of new opportunities where new courses of activities are conceived as desirable and feasible; yet, there is no much discussion about how shocks may be linked to various explorative or/and exploitative entrepreneurial initiatives.

Exploration and/or Exploitation

The urgency for large firms to both exploit existing resources and explore new opportunities has been a longstanding theme in management literature. Exploitation activities are concerned with 'refinement, choice, production, efficiency, selection, implementation and execution' (March, 1991, p. 71), while exploration activities are concerned with 'search, variation, risk-taking, experimentation, discovery and innovation' (March, p. 71). The two types of activities are approached as conflicting but equally important for the survival and growth of the firm. The challenge for managers has always been how to balance 'operating efficiency' (through better exploitation of existing resources) with 'innovation' (through exploration of uncharted waters), while at the same time acknowledging that these two imperatives require very different structures and skills (Gupta et al., 2006; March, 1991; O'reilly & Tushman, 2013; Simsek, 2009; Stettner & Lavie, 2013). Literature on 'ambidexterity' inspired a continuous stream of research which has been analysed in the context of large firms (Jansen et al., 2012; Lavie et al., 2010).

Although the assumption of ambidexterity has been mostly employed in the analysis of large organizations, the concept seems to have theoretical and practical relevance for entrepreneurship, as well. Shane and Venkataraman (2000, p. 218) define entrepreneurship as 'the processes of discovery, evaluation and exploitation of opportunities; and the set of individuals who discover, evaluate, and exploit them'. Similarly, studies of nascent or early-stages entrepreneurship analyse the process according to which opportunities are perceived (Krueger Jr., 2007), business ideas are conceptually generated, elaborated and adapted (Davidsson, Hunter, & Klofsten, 2004; de Koning, 1999; Hmieleski & Ensley, 2004), and entrepreneurial activities and operations are enacted (Delmar & Shane, 2004; Shane & Eckhardt, 2003; Van de Ven, 1996). Entrepreneurial behaviour seems to be manifested only when exploration and exploitation come together (Kuckertz et al., 2010).

Taking into account the above, it seemed relevant to further investigate individual's entrepreneurial behaviour along exploitation−exploration lines. To this end, we studied the role of shocks in the individual's decision to quit her job and start a business: we identified which are the various types of shocks implicated in this decision and how they are linked to different types of explorative or/and exploitative entrepreneurial opportunities.

We note that the initial definitions of exploitation and exploration provided by March (1991) were quite broad and allowed many interpretations and refinements which in their turn blurred the line between the two processes. Assuming that exploration refers to 'a pursuit of new knowledge', whereas exploitation refers to 'the use and development of things already known' (Levinthal & March, 1993, p. 105), in which category should we classify the refinement of existing knowledge (Gupta et al., 2006)?

In this study, although we acknowledge that exploration and exploitation are intricately entwined and difficult at times to distinguish, we embrace the definitions provided by Müller, Volery, and Von Siemens (2012) commenting on what entrepreneurs actually do: exploration refers mostly to 'actions related to searching, recognizing and exploring opportunities', while exploitation refers mostly to 'actions related to implementation and execution of existing opportunities' (Müller et al., 2012, p. 1005).

METHOD

This study is based on the analysis of 80 interviews with entrepreneurs, focusing on how they decided to quit their job and start their business. The selection of interviewees followed the snowball sampling technique (Charmaz, 2006). In the absence of a well-defined population of nascent entrepreneurs, this technique was considered as a viable solution for the exploration of the problem under investigation. Entrepreneurs were citizens of and/or created their new companies in one of the following countries: France, US, Canada, Greece and China. These companies operated in a range of industries including Information Technology, Real Estate and Marketing. These companies have reached different sizes ranging from single, self-employed individuals to firms with staff numbering several hundred employees. The pursuit of this variety in the pool of our respondents was intended to maximize the richness of shocks potentially stimulating a transition from salaried employment to entrepreneurship.

In this chapter, we use standard coding techniques (Corbin & Strauss, 2008) and content analysis methods (Miles & Huberman, 1994). This approach begins with the identification of individual statements from the interview transcript. We focused on statements which referred to shocks[1] or to vividly memorable events. We removed duplicate statements regarding the same shock/event since our purpose was not to draw inferences regarding frequency nor statistical generalization. Our purpose was to analyse the range of shocks and pursue the rationale of analytic generalization (Yin, 2003) through the detailed investigation of multiple discrete shocks.

Based on the dimensions found in the literature (positive/negative/neutral, work-related/personal) (Lee et al., 1999) and on some dimensions that emerged from the analysis of our data (internal to the individual/external to the individual), each researcher independently coded each shock. On the first round of coding, 62% of the shocks were registered under the same label dimension by the three researchers. Thereafter, the remaining shocks were discussed by the researchers until a consensus was reached. All disagreements were resolved by additional consideration of the context of the shock, as the latter was described in the interview transcript (e.g. the shock 'reading an article' could be interpreted/experienced differently across various contexts. An article on the glamorous lifestyle of an entrepreneur could be seen as a positive, external to the individual and non-work-related shock).

FINDINGS AND ANALYSIS

The Range of Observed Shocks

In contrast to Mitchell and Lee's (2001) summarization of 'entrepreneurial' shock as a single type of shock, this study suggests that the wide array of observed shocks may trigger the beginning of job leaving to start a new company (Table 1).

Each shock is categorized in terms of the following three dimensions:

(1) external to the individual/internal to the individual;
(2) work-related/home-related; and
(3) positive, neutral, negative.

The first dimension, *external/internal*, pertains to whether the shock originates from an external source (a change in the individual's micro or macro world) or from an internal source/process (a shift in the individual's internal attitude about something). For example, an internal shock may be

Table 1.   List of Entrepreneurial Events and Their Categories.

Entrepreneurial Events

Internal to the individual, positive, work

Idea of a product the entrepreneurs always wanted to develop.

Internal to the individual, negative, work

Having to execute non-challenging tasks which devaluate their dexterities and skills. For the entrepreneurs, this is a move backwards to their professional career.

Not being proud for what they are doing. This is a personal issue to them.

Not having a meaningful work and not meeting high-quality standards – this is directly related to their self-image/self-esteem.

Encountering long-hours at work and exhaustion – this leads to a desire for more flexibility and control of your work time.

External to the individual, positive, home

Having a talk with a friend, an entrepreneur, a family member, spouse, etc. It could be an inspirational talk, a reality check talk, a family-supportive talk, etc.

Someone tells you 'you can do this!!'

External to the individual, positive, work

Participating in an entrepreneurial contest and winning the first prize.

Receiving a job offer (from a friend or a stranger or from the wider network of peers or virtual network) and as a consequence, having a boost of self-confidence.

Having prior clients expressing the will to contract the services of the future entrepreneur on an individual basis – this could lead to the first contract and first opportunity recognition for the entrepreneur.

Having a partnership offer through loosely coupled networks (e.g. a friend).

Receiving European funding for young entrepreneurs who want to build their own company.

Seizing learning opportunities.

Experiencing a sudden awareness of the funding possibilities and administrative details for new venture creation. It could be accidentally from a friend, from an advertisement on the radio, from seminars, etc.

Detecting a company need and realizing that there is no company having my vision

Random acquaintances with people which serve as role models of entrepreneurs (during the attendance of a seminar or conference or alumni events).

A key member leaves the company.

A friend or relative opens her own company.

Unexpected or expected promotion, leading to a boost of self-confidence.

Being involve in various projects of the company, interaction with various work teams and travels abroad leading to a sudden increase of the entrepreneurs' confidence in his skills.

Realizing that they have an installed base of prospective customers (networks) even before the taking up of the new endeavour; leading to the sudden epiphany that the market is ready.

Table 1. (*Continued*)

Entrepreneurial Events

External to the individual, negative, home

Encountering health issues of the closer or the wider family—friends context

External to the individual, neutral, work

A book, a film, advertisement in the tube/Internet/magazines on entrepreneurship seminars

External to the individual, negative, work

Experiencing the deterioration of work conditions due to the economic crisis, leading to an increased feeling of great insecurity.

Experiencing a massive drop in the value of the stock options

Discussing with peers – sharing of work-related experiences – about the limited future of corporations and realizing the insecurity of the current situation.

Sudden realization of the deteriorating conditions in the future entrepreneur's department; the rest of the company conceive this department as a black hole which absorbs their money with no ROI (e.g. IT department).

Bankruptcy of the company.

Merger or acquisition leading to culture clash, bad work atmosphere and/or lack of fit between the future entrepreneur and the organization.

Receiving a negative annual evaluation report. For example, lack of (expected) bonus, lack of recognition or negative report resulting from internal political intrigues.

Unfair treatment of the future entrepreneur – the expected promotion were not given (lack of meritocracy)

Unfair treatment of peers leading to the future entrepreneur challenging his trust in the organizations ethics.

During the contract renewal, realization that there is no prospect of career advancement in this company.

Major changes in the internal policies: chain of command (too much of bureaucracy), more control and measurements, less autonomy.

Fight with the boss, e.g. triggered by a lack of understanding or narrow-minded approach (from the future entrepreneur's perspective).

Fight with colleagues in the same project team.

Experiencing a strong rejection for internal politics.

Not classified, as too complex or belonging to several categories

Major change in the working style, e.g. working remotely – the perception of the shock may depend if the boss or the employee wants to work remotely (*work*). It could also have *negative* or *positive* effect related to *family*.

Realization of the employee's boredom – it may vary if this is a general attitude (*internal*) or the result of a change in the working conditions (*external*).

Strong desire for a new lifestyle – depending on the lifestyle desired, it could be either *work* or *home* or both.

Table 1.   (*Continued*)

Entrepreneurial Events
Doing the math: How I can finance my company?
Having or taking some time to think (e.g. holidays, long weekend) – it could be related to both *home* or *work*, it also depends on what to think about.
Fight with the spouse over a *work–family* conflict.
Ending a cycle; e.g. at the end of a project. The individual feels that she needs to do something new (*home/work, internal/external; positive/negative*).
Perceived easiness/difficulty to start your own business.
Major influence of the media (e.g. advertisement and radio) related to the life style of an entrepreneur and how it is socially portrayed in the society (*negative/positive, home/work*).
The spouse got a new employment – it could be a new source of income (*positive*), or it could be the necessity to move (*positive/negative*).

the newly formed desire expressed by the individual for a more meaningful career. While an external shock may be the positive influence of an inspiring training seminar or the negative feelings associated with a peer's dismissal. We found that a great variety of shocks seem to originate in the external environment.

The second dimension, *work-related/home-related* pertained to the domain from which the shock originated. Examples of home-related shocks are family members' health issues and work–family conflicts. We found no cases of shocks from a change in family status such as marriage, the movement of a spouse or birth of a child in our sample; yet, we would expect these shocks to impact the individual's entrepreneurial turnover decision. We notice that the variety of shocks (36 different shocks) which came from the arena of work is richer than the variety of home-related shocks.

The third dimension pertains to the general emotion associated with the shock. For example, a *positive* event, e.g. winning a contest or getting a promotion, may boost the individual's self-efficacy and increase the perceived feasibility of the prospective entrepreneurial endeavour. In contrast, a *negative* event, e.g. an unfavourable or unjust performance evaluation or long hours of exhaustion, may increase the individual's discomfort with the organization and reinforce the perceived desirability of an entrepreneurial pathway. The only *neutral* shocks were related to 'a book', 'a film' or 'an advertisement'.

It is worth mentioning that the emotive content of the shock could not always be anticipated upfront and could only be assessed after its contextualization within the overall experience of the individual. The use of this dimension should be treated with caution as the very same event may trigger multiple reactions. For example, the offer of a new job to a spouse that requires moving from the home town may have a positive aspect (e.g. increased revenue), but also a negative aspect (e.g. disruption of daily routine and future uncertainties).

We observed that the shocks which originate in the sphere of work and are triggered by external events display a great variety indeed (see Table 1). We note that while we tend to believe that the proportion of shocks by category is likely to be correlated with the number of experienced shocks among actual job leavers, in this study we have analysed only the proportion of shocks by category. Therefore, the possibility of high frequencies among some of the smaller clusters of shock types remains possible. In other words, although there are many different types of shocks coming from the arena of work, we cannot argue that these types of shocks are more 'dominant', 'frequent' or 'influential' by comparison to others.

Types of Shocks and Types of Entrepreneurial Behaviour: Exploration and Exploitation

We found that particular types of shocks tend to be linked to certain types of entrepreneurial behaviour. Although we don't have a representative sample so that we can claim statistical generalization of findings and even if it may need more than one shocks for an individual to display a particular entrepreneurial behaviour, we notice that some types of shocks tend to be linked to exploration, others to exploitation, while others can lead to any of the two processes. Let us be more specific.

Our findings suggest that the decision to quit salaried employment and start one's business is very much related to the perception of 'credible' opportunities or immediate/forthcoming threats which come to the fore after the individual experiences the shock. In line with the literature (Shapero & Sokol, 1982), once the shock is experienced, the inertia which is governing existing behaviour is interrupted and *a new set of opportunities* which makes the potentiality of the new venture both feasible and desirable is revealed.

The newly perceived feasibility of the new venture is related to exploitation opportunities and refers to operational practicalities, e.g. financing and availability of resources while the newly perceived desirability of the new venture is related to exploration opportunities and refers to the individual's drive to experiment and explore alternative solutions that will allow her to start a new business.

Negative Shocks

All negative shocks, regardless of whether they were internal to the individual/external to the individual or work-related/home-related, tend to go hand-in-hand with the potentiality of explorative behaviour. After the experience of the shock, the individual realizes that she cannot afford to be a salaried employee anymore. Therefore, escape into entrepreneurship seems to her as the only viable solution. The desirability of the entrepreneurial pathway has been clearly perceived. In this sense, after the experience of a negative shock, the individual is likely to start exploring new or available opportunities which will allow her to escape from salaried employment and start her own business.

Negative-External to the Individual-Work-Related Shocks. Negative-external-work shocks refer to events which occur either in the corporate environment or in the wider socio-economic context. These shocks are accompanied by negative feelings in respect to (a) the way the individual currently experiences organizational life, (b) how she anticipates her future in the current organization and (c) how she anticipates the future longevity of her current organization within the economic context. These shocks include events such as downsizing, financial crisis, large or small layoffs, lack of organizational transparency and meritocracy, and are perceived as immediate threats against which the individual needs to take action.

Lack of fit between the individual's values, goals and aspirations and the organizational culture, vision or rationality lead to discomfort, dissatisfaction, feelings of unfairness and injustice (Joseph, Ng, Koh, & Ang, 2007; Lee et al., 1999) and thus turnover behaviour. This is something widely studied in the general turnover literature. Yet, the difference between general turnover behaviour and entrepreneurial turnover behaviour lies in the fact that the respondents' negative feelings were not only triggered by firm-specific events, but also − and most importantly − by the inherent characteristics of corporate life.

Although some of the negative feelings experienced by the respondents were due to politics ('informal' organization), many of their work-related negative experiences were due to the rigidities and inefficiencies inherent in the formal structuring of an organization (formal organization). The individual's disagreement with the formal rules of the organization reflected a disapproval of the generic rationality governing corporate affairs. In other words, even if these negative work-related shocks were triggered by events which occurred at the premises of a specific organization, they rather signalled the individual's denial to adapt to the idiosyncrasies of corporate life.

Individuals motivated by this sort of shock seem to experience significant job dissatisfaction or discomfort in their work or perceive some sort of threat in their work. They feel that the pathway to entrepreneurship is the only solution for them. Setting up a business is their opportunity to escape from the irrationalities of the corporate world. In this sense, the experience of such a shock is accompanied by the propensity to explore all possible alternatives which will bring them closer to entrepreneurship. To them, the road towards entrepreneurship is now perceived as a clearly desirable choice, as a first priority in their agenda.

Negative-Internal to the Individual-Work-Related. Negative-internal-work shocks refer to events which occur once the individual experiences some sort of internal shift in one or some of her attitude(s) towards her fit in corporate world. Boredom, loss of pride, loss of meaning in work are some realizations related to this type of shocks. These internal shocks are accompanied by negative feelings, as the individual shifts from a state of comfort to a state of discomfort. In reaction to that, the latter feels the need to explore opportunities which will allow her to stop her discomfort: this is the moment when the individual decides to take a chance on entrepreneurship. Rather than being coincidental, entrepreneurship is often associated with positive feeling regarding the individual's freedom to choose challenging and meaningful tasks.

Negative-External to the Individual-Home-Related Shocks. Similarly to the above shocks, negative-external-home-related shocks are accompanied by the individual's vivid desire to quit her job and start her own business, no matter what it takes. Explorative initiatives in the form of search of entrepreneurial opportunities emerge as the 'number one' priority.

Positive Shocks
Positive shocks are related to the potentiality of either explorative or exploitative behaviour or both. For instance, when the experienced positive shock is much relevant to the implementation and execution of existing opportunities, i.e. acquisition of specific resources and competencies critical to the setup of the new firm, the individual is more likely to display the propensity to engage in exploitative initiatives and specific courses of action

which will make the new company to run. The newly perceived feasibility of the new venture reinforces the individual's commitment in the new venture creation. When the experienced positive shock is relevant to some sort of general desirability towards entrepreneurship – as an alternative to her current work status – the individual is more likely to start exploring new or available opportunities which will allow her to set up the new business.

Positive-External-Work-Related Shocks. Positive-external-work shocks refer to events found in the immediate organizational environment or wider socio-economic context within which the individual operates; they are accompanied by positive feelings in respect to the taking up of an entrepreneurial endeavour.

Individuals motivated by this sort of shock do not seem to experience any job dissatisfaction or discomfort in their work (Lee et al., 1999). They rather decide to leave their company and start their own business, once they realize that they are indeed capable of doing so (perceived self-efficacy) or because the necessary resources are suddenly available to them. Their perception about the new venture creation which now seems attainable in their eyes is rooted in a new sort of awareness brought about the experience of the shock.

Shocks related to the realization that some of the practical, procedural or skills-related key issues in starting a business can now be sorted or managed, are accompanied by the individual's propensity to engage in exploitative initiatives. For instance, shocks which raise the awareness of (a) funding opportunities from a friend, a stranger or an advertisement, (b) the prospect of a job offer(s) from a friend, i.e. loose partnership or a prior – client or (c) simplification of legal and financing processes related to the take up a business endeavour after the attendance of a seminar (Baucus & Human 1994; Kolvereid, 1996), are most likely to bring to the fore the consideration of actionable strategies which will make the new business to happen (exploration).

Similarly, increased self-efficacy seems to go hand-in-hand with the eventuality of exploration. Reaching such entrepreneurial self-efficacy is usually related to events occurring within the organizational premises of the organization (e.g. after job rotation, the individual perceives that she possesses the right mix of skills and capabilities (Lazear, 2002, 2004; Wagner, 2006) to start her own business), or in the wider social–professional context (e.g. the individual wins the prize in a professional context. This event gives a boost in her self-efficacy (Davidsson, 2006), and increases her visibility in the market). The next step for the individual is to decide how to leverage these resources, how to act upon what it is already available to her so that her company starts running.

Individuals who are motivated by this sort of shock tend to choose between two entrepreneurial pathways: they exploit the newly discovered opportunity by starting either a brand new business which is completely independent, or a new business which is in some sort of partnership with the former employer.

In both scenarios, the nascent entrepreneur decides to invest into an entrepreneurial activity in which she has previous work experience. And often, because of the fact that the entrepreneurial pathway has emerged as a positive alternative worth pursuing (not as the only alternative which the individual is forced to follow) the entrepreneur feels more confident, optimistic and less the need to plan everything in advance (Sarasvathy, 2001).

If the new awareness does not refer to the availability of key resources and skills, but it rather refers to a generalized perceived desirability towards entrepreneurship, e.g. random acquaintance who serve as role model (Carter, Gartner, Shaver, & Gatewood, 2003), then the individual is prone to engage in explorative search (exploration) regarding the very way she would tailor the lessons learnt from the role model to her reality.

Positive-Internal to Individual-Work-Related Shock. The idea of a product that the entrepreneur always wanted to develop is a shock which may be accompanied either by explorative or exploitative initiatives according to the perceived feasibility of the idea and self-efficacy of the individual.

Positive-External to the Individual-Home-Related Shock. Subjective norms which are positive to entrepreneurship (e.g. family members as role models of entrepreneurs) tend to enhance the household members' perceived desirability towards entrepreneurship and nurture exploration activities.

Neutral Shocks

Finally, neutral shocks refer to random events that the individual faces in her daily life. These may originate from the attendance of an entrepreneurial seminar, the reading of a book or the notice of an advertisement. These shocks are accompanied by exploitation initiatives, if reference to implementation strategies and skills activation is made; they are accompanied by exploration initiatives, if general desirability towards entrepreneurship is raised, without reference to neither necessary courses of actions or availability of resources being made.

CONTRIBUTION TO THE LITERATURE

This study is particularly relevant to the research stream of exploration/ exploitation. It exemplifies specific instances where explorative or exploitative aspects of behaviour are likely to be manifested as a response to specific types of shocks that precede and impact the decision to quit and start one's own business. Once the shock is experienced by the individual, the inertia which usually guides human behaviour is interrupted and the individual's propensity to act and eventually start a new business is favoured (Hornsby & Naffziger, 1993; Krueger & Brazeal, 1994). In this sense, the shock is related to a cognitive shift experienced by the individual and her propensity to act upon this shift (exploration and/or exploitation). In other words, the shock operates as the 'trigger' which paves the way for the individual to consider a new set of opportunities (exploration–exploitation) where entrepreneurship initiatives are perceived to be both desirable and feasible.

The contribution of the study is fourfold:

First, the exploitation/exploration stream of literature is enriched, because this framework is applied to the study of enterprising individuals, instead of large firms. Second, the effects of shocks/events are found to be related to the potentiality of a mixture of exploration and exploitation behaviours. The study of shocks exemplifies the blurriness and interrelatedness of exploitative and explorative initiatives. Third, more detail is provided about the dynamics that explain why there is an effect of shock on entrepreneurial behaviour. And fourth, there is a cataloguing of types of shocks based on three dimensions and discussion on how these shocks affect entrepreneurial behaviour. Let us be more specific.

This research expands the scope of the exploitation/exploration literature which has generally embraced a firm-level perspective (Jansen et al., 2012; Lavie et al., 2010). It indicates that the exploitation/exploration framework have indeed theoretical and practical relevance for the study of entrepreneurial behaviour from an individual-level perspective (Müller et al., 2012; Shane & Venkataraman, 2000).

This study provides a fine-grained description of multiple types of shocks which are found to precede and impact the individual's decision to quit her job and start a new business. Particular types of shocks are linked to certain types of entrepreneurial behaviour. Shocks pave the way for the consideration of a new set of opportunities where explorative activities seem desirable, and/or exploitative activities seem feasible. The newly perceived feasibility of the new venture is related to exploitation opportunities and refers to specific aspects of operational practicalities, e.g. financing, while the newly perceived desirability of the new venture is related to exploration opportunities and refers to the individual's drive to experiment and explore alternative solutions that will allow her to start a new business.

The importance of the above observation lies in the following point: interventions which stimulate explorative initiatives or support exploitative initiatives might be differentiated by shock type in order to achieve more targeted positive results. We note that Shapero and Sokol (1982) report that job-related displacements are the most commonly observed type of a trigger event. In our study, although there is no evidence that these shocks are more 'frequent' by comparison to others; their rich variety suggests that individuals may now perceive multiple windows of explorative or exploitative opportunities in their attempt to initiate change in their prospective entrepreneurial behaviour.

We note that the majority of strategic management scholars have attempted to find ways to reconcile the competing imperatives of exploration and exploitation − the ambidexterity premise (O'reilly & Tushman, 2013; Stettner & Lavie, 2013). Yet, this study exemplified the blurriness and interrelatedness of exploitative and explorative initiatives, by shedding light to the conditions under which the explorative and exploitative aspects of entrepreneurial behaviour emerge. The study of the interrelatedness of the two sub-processes is not something new in the literature (Davidsson, 2004; Gupta et al., 2006; Lavie et al., 2010; Li, Vanhaverbeke, & Schoenmakers, 2008; March, 1991). Yet, the present study offers a fine-grained analysis of a real-life contingency where the exploitation and exploration aspects of the observed behaviour is about to be manifested. In other words, it attempts to cut through the actual lived experience of the people who have been in the process of quitting their job and start their own business, and according to the type of shock they have experienced, they are faced either with the option to explore, or with the option to exploit or both. The potentiality of an explorative or exploitative activity is found to go hand-in-hand with the experience of particular types of shocks.

It is worth noticing that although specific types of shocks are linked to the eventuality of exploration and/or exploitation, it is often difficult to draw the line between the two aspects of entrepreneurial behaviour. In the study, we linked the negative shocks to the potentiality of explorative initiatives. In the case of negative shocks, we observed that after the experience of a negative shock, the individual is likely to start exploring new or available entrepreneurial opportunities. One could argue though that 'finding ways to explore existing opportunities' or 'leveraging existing knowledge' could be classified under the concept of exploitation. Yet, we note that the reason we linked negative shocks to the potentiality of explorative initiatives has been the individual's articulated desire primarily to escape into the entrepreneurship and secondarily to consider the 'how to do what'; this would imply, at least to a certain degree, that exploration of various alternatives is the individual's priority. This has been the rationale underlying the matching of shocks to explorative or exploitative aspects of entrepreneurial behaviour.

In addition, providing a rich list of shocks has been a first attempt to gain a primitive yet comprehensive image of the prospective role of shocks in entrepreneurial behaviour of the employee who decides to leave her job in order to start her own company through the exploration/exploitation framework. Few empirical studies (Holtom et al., 2005; Lee & Mitchell, 1994; Morrell et al., 2004; Shapero & Sokol, 1982) have examined the role of shocks/events in the individuals' decision to leave their company or make an entrepreneurial shift in their career. Both the notion of shock and the notion of entrepreneurial event − although they have been found to precipitate one's decision to leave a job or to start a company respectively − have been rather under-investigated and repeated calls have been made for their study (Krueger et al., 2000; Morrell et al., 2004). In their model, Shapero and Sokol (1982) refer to negative entrepreneurial events, without distinguishing the voluntary ones from the involuntary ones, i.e. job loss or job dissatisfaction. Yet, the dynamics of the condition underlying the voluntary decision to quit one's job to start a new business are quite special and are often accompanied by a strong engagement to entrepreneurial take-ups. Being forced to leave one's job is believed to bear upon different implications than deliberately/voluntary leaving one's job. Rather than being accidental, our decision to study people who quit their job to start a business was made on the basis of the belief that the group of people who voluntary leave their salaried job to become entrepreneurs constitute a dynamic and expanding pool from nascent entrepreneurs can be drawn.

Furthermore, there is a cataloguing of types of shocks based on three dimensions and discussion of how these differentially affect entrepreneurial behaviour. The dimensions provide a 'condensed', readable and fine-grained image of the range of shocks which are observed when an employee decides to leave salaried employment in order to start his own business and are related to the potentiality of specific explorative and/or exploitative activities. Some of the dimensions used were already known in the literature (positive/negative/neutral, work relatedness or not), while others emerged from the analysis of our data (internal to the individual/external to the individual). It's worth noticing that when previous studies refer to the distinction between internal versus external shocks, they usually refer to shocks related to personal life or work life. In our study, the internal shocks experienced by people were the result of a changing internal attitude and were not necessarily related to the individual's personal life. Similarly, external shocks were the result of a change of an external state which was not necessarily related to the individual's work life.

Finally we conclude this section with two remarks: First, although not all leaving decisions experienced by the respondents in these studies can be traced back to a particular shock (Lee & Mitchell, 1994), the role of shock in the actual entrepreneurial employee turnover behaviour emerged from the data as critical in the majority of the individuals' decisions. This corresponds largely to the Lee and Mitchell (1994) unfolding model of turnover which holds that a major pathway for employee turnover commences with a shock.

Second our study is in line with the assumption made by Shapero and Sokol (1982). After the displacement in one's life path, not everyone will take the initiative to start a new business. The perceived desirability and feasibility may favour the taking up of new entrepreneurial endeavours, but if the propensity to act (Shapero & Sokol, 1982) is not there, or it is there but it is not converted into a materializable course of action, then we cannot claim that new venture will be created. The intention or the decision to act is triggered as the result of the interaction between the situational factors or precipitating events with individual variables, i.e. personality traits (Hornsby & Naffziger, 1993; Krueger Jr. & Brazeal, 1994). Differences in the above factors and in the specific form of interaction among them may be useful in explaining why someone will eventually start a business while someone else will not. 'Each entrepreneurial event occurs as a result of a dynamic process providing situational momentum that has an impact upon individuals whose perceptions and values are determined by their social and cultural inheritance and their previous experience' (Elfving, Brännback, & Carsrud, 2009, p. 24).

The inherent complexity in studying the above may probably explain why there is a limited number of studies on entrepreneurial events (Krueger et al., 2000). Nevertheless, we strongly believe that although we cannot claim whether and when a particular type of shock will eventually lead to the decision to quit and start one's own business, the awareness of a rich repertoire of these events/shocks enriches our understanding of the conditions that underlie the actual process of entrepreneurial employee turnover.

IMPLICATIONS FOR PRACTICE: SHOCKS AS THE TRIGGER FOR OPPORTUNITY RECOGNITION AND EXPLOITATION

Being aware of the various types of actual shocks which are found to be accompanied by the potentiality of exploitative and explorative initiatives relevant to entrepreneurial employee turnover behaviour is of critical importance for both managers and nascent entrepreneurs.

For entrepreneurs, recognition of the various types of shocks which are strongly implicated in the decision to quit their job and become entrepreneurs and are related to exploitation and/or exploration aspects of their behaviour, allows them to be more conscious of both the inner and outer stimuli, as well as some of the mechanics of the process that might prompt their switch from salaried employee to entrepreneur. Although literature suggests that the intention or the decision to act is not solely triggered by the precedence of entrepreneurial events (Hornsby & Naffziger, 1993; Krueger Jr. & Brazeal, 1994), awareness of entrepreneurial events do change the individual's perceptions about the new circumstances (Krueger Jr. & Brazeal, 1994). This opens a window of opportunity for exploitative and explorative initiatives which was not visible to her before. Upon recognition of such an intention to transition, the individual might more consciously pursue clarification of her priorities (desirability of entrepreneurial pathway and exploration opportunities), additional skill building, resource seeking (feasibility of entrepreneurial pathway and exploitation opportunities) in preparation of her 'readiness' to start a new business. In this way, the individual learns practical ways about how to expose herself in circumstances where the new entrepreneurial opportunity either in terms of exploration or exploitation, may emerge. Due to the detailed description of the full range of shocks, i.e. their types and the context within which they emerge, the individual gets concrete ideas of exploitation/exploration opportunities and subsequent initiatives. For instance, the professional may seek to participate in professional associations and networks of practice to increase opportunities of new idea generation or to increase opportunities of a future partnerships or expansion of an installed base of prospective customers.

In the same token, by being able to identify commonalities in the conditions underlying shocks and her current condition, as well linkages between the types of shocks and explorative/exploitative initiatives, the individual may possibly form a more concrete image of where she stands and where she heads towards.

Managers face the dual challenges of retaining good professionals, as a key to competitive advantage (Pfeffer & Fong, 2005), but also confront the prospect of former employees launching businesses possibly in direct competition with them. By understanding the various types of entrepreneurial shocks, it may be possible for them to defer or even decrease the likelihood that their good business professional will quit their job in order to become entrepreneurs. Managers may be able to pre-emptively reduce or ameliorate formal and informal constraints within their own organizations, thus decreasing the probability of individuals experiencing these types of shocks. They may also recognize other shocks, internal, family and home, or opportunities and respond quickly and positively to develop a retention plan for key employees.

For example, the manager recognizes that a shock linked to the realization of a lack of challenge or prospect of career advancement may be one of the reasons the business professional no longer wishes to remain in the corporate world and wishes to start her own company. In order to reduce this possibility, the manager can give the professional extra responsibilities and autonomy, encourage her to participate to multi-divisional teams and introduce personal schemes of career advancement in accordance to the employees' skills and will. In general, CEOs who want to retain their good business professional can decrease the possibility of generation of shocks by altering their human resources strategies directly related to organizational and job-related attributes. Shifts at the level of rewards, enhancement of perceived job security, introduction of flexibility programs, etc. can possibly inhibit or delay the generation of shocks leading to turnover decisions.

On the other hand, such a strategy of retaining highly skilled personnel could be proved to be a double-edged sword. For instance involvement in various teams and work projects (e.g. interacting with customers) may increase the employee's self-confidence, and cultivate her potential to achieve a balance of soft skills (e.g. communication, marketing, business planning) and technical skills. Such activities may lead to work-related positive external shocks that make the employee realize that she is ready to quit and become an entrepreneur.[2] In this example, the manager needs to think twice about how to introduce Human Resource Management (HRM) strategies to retain her employees as she encounters the likelihood of contradictory shocks which may equally trigger the turnover and new venture creation decision. Strangely enough, in cases when the cost of retaining professional employees is too high or there are indications that the professional employee will quit anyway, it may be at the interest of the manager to examine to what extent she can outsource part of the work to a future business partner, so as to decrease the possibility of direct competition and increase the savings of the company. For instance, in the extreme case where the business professional has obvious talent, but does not fit well into the organizational culture, the firm might gain value from helping the individual to set up a firm that provides complementary products. Future research should consider under which conditions companies may benefit either by retaining good professionals or helping them to become entrepreneurs — their prospective business partners.

LIMITATIONS AND FUTURE RESEARCH

The limitation of this study lies in the fact that although we provide a rich repertoire of shocks, a detailed range of shocks, we are not able to assess the frequency or relative importance of each shock to decision to quit and start one's own business. The lack of a well-defined population of entrepreneurs and the subsequent choice of snowball sampling techniques do not allow statistical generalization of our findings. Further research aiming at statistically validating the frequencies, relevance and intensity of the various types of shocks is required. Another potential limitation derives from the retrospective nature of interview data collection. We embrace Holtom et al. (2005, p. 342) remark that '… empirical evidence suggests that critical events such as organizational departure create strong images that are less likely to decay than other memories (Symons & Johnson, 1997; Wheeler, Stuss, & Tulving, 1997)'.

This line of research adds to our understanding of the dynamics that lead individuals to entrepreneurship. We recognize that many communities seek to enhance their workforce by encouraging new businesses. Nowadays, we see the number of people becoming entrepreneurs through family inheritance as representing an important but limited in size group from whom to draw new enterprise. While adding entrepreneurs from exciting educational programs is important, journeymen in the business field represent a body of people with rich experiences, insights into business processes and needs, and the potential to effectively fill an important role in economic growth.

NOTES

1. We note that the notion of shocks bears important conceptual similarities with the notion of Entrepreneurial Event. In this study we will use the two notions

interchangeably. The word 'shock' is more frequently used in the following sections of the chapter for the sake of abbreviation and immediacy.

2. An investigation of the correlation between the development policies of employees and turnover behaviour can be found in the study by Benson (2006).

REFERENCES

Allen, D. G., & Griffeth, R. W. (2001). Test of a mediated performance's turnover relationship highlighting the moderating roles of visibility and reward contingency. *Journal of Applied Psychology*, *86*(5), 1014−1021.

Barrick, M. R., & Zimmerman, R. D. (2005). Reducing voluntary, avoidable turnover through selection. *Journal of Applied Psychology*, *90*(1), 159−166.

Baucus, D. A., & Human, S. E. (1994). Second-career entrepreneurs: A multiple case study analysis of entrepreneurial processes and antecedent variables. *Entrepreneurship Theory and Practice*, *19*(4), 41−71.

Beach, L. R. (1998). *Image theory: Theoretical and Empirical Foundations*. Mahwah, NJ: Lawrence Erlbaum Associates.

Benson, G. S. (2006). Employee development, commitment and intention to turnover: A test of 'employability' policies in action. *Human Resource Management Journal*, *16*(2), 173−192.

Carter, N. M., Gartner, W. B., Shaver, K. G., & Gatewood, E. J. (2003). The career reasons of nascent entrepreneurs. *Journal of Business Venturing*, *18*(1), 13−39.

Cascio, W. F. (1991). *Costing human resources: The financial impact of behaviour in organizations* (3rd ed.). Boston: PWS-Kent .

Charmaz, K. (2006). *Constructing grounded theory: A practical guide through qualitative analysis*. London: Sage.

Corbin, J., & Strauss, A. L. (2008). *Basics of qualitative research: Techniques and procedures for developing grounded theory* (3rd ed.). Thousand Oaks, CA: Sage.

Davidsson, P. (2004). *Researching entrepreneurship*. New York, NY: Springer.

Davidsson, P. (2006). *Nascent entrepreneurship: Empirical studies and developments*. Hanover, MA: Now publishers Inc.

Davidsson, P., Hunter, E., & Klofsten, M. (2004). The discovery process: External influences on refinement of the venture idea. In S. Zahra et al. (Ed.), *Frontiers of entrepreneurship research*. (pp. 327−337). Wellesley, MA: Babson College.

de Koning, A. (1999). *Conceptualising opportunity formation as a socio-cognitive process*. Doctoral dissertation, INSEAD, Fontainbleau, France.

Delmar, F., & Shane, S. (2004). Legitimating first: Organizing activities and the survival of new ventures. *Journal of Business Venturing*, *19*(3), 385−410.

Elfving, J., Brännback, M., & Carsrud, A. (2009). Toward a contextual model of entrepreneurial intentions. In A. L. Carsrud & M. Brännback (Eds.), *Understanding the Entrepreneurial Mind: Opening the black box*, (pp. 23−33) Dordrecht: Springer.

Glebbeek, A. C., & Bax, E. H. (2004). Is high employee turnover really harmful? An empirical test using company records. *Academy of Management Journal*, *47*(2), 277−286.

Griffeth, R. W., Gaertner, S., Robinson, J. M., & Sager, J. K. (1999). Taxonomic model of withdrawal behaviors: The adaptive response model. *Human Resource Management Review*, *9*(4), 577−590.

Griffeth, R. W., Hom, P. W., & Gaertner, S. (2000). A meta-analysis of antecedents and corre-
lates of employee turnover: Update, moderator tests, and research implications for the
next millennium. *Journal of Management, 26*(3), 463–488.

Gupta, A. K., Smith, K., & Shalley, C. E. (2006). The interplay between exploration and
exploitation. *Academy of Management Journal, 49*(4), 693–706.

Hmieleski, K. M., & Ensley, M. D. (2004). An investigation of improvisation as a strategy
for exploiting dynamic opportunities. In W. D. Bygrave et al. (Eds.), *Frontiers of entrepreneurship*. (pp. 596–604). Babson Park, MA: Babson College.

Holtom, B. C., Mitchell, T. R., Lee, T. W., & Inderrieden, E. J. (2005). Shocks as causes of
turnover: What they are and how organizations can manage them. *Human Resource
Management, 44*(3), 337–352.

Horn, P. W., & Griffeth, R. W. (1995). *Employee turnover*. Cincinnati, OH: South-Western
College Publishing.

Hom, P. W., & Kinicki, A. J. (2001). Toward a greater understanding of how dissatisfaction
drives employee turnover. *Academy of Management Journal, 44*(5), 975–987.

Hornsby, J. S., & Naffziger, D. W. (1993). An interactive model of corporate entrepreneurship
process. *Entrepreneurship, Theory & Practice, 17*(2), 29–37.

Jansen, J. J. P., Simsek, Z., & Cao, Q. (2012). Ambidexterity and performance in multiunit
contexts: Cross-level moderating effects of structural and resource attributes. *Strategic
Management Journal, 33*(11), 1286–1303.

Joseph, D., Ng, K.-Y., Koh, C., & Ang, S. (2007). Turnover of information technology professionals: A narrative review, meta-analytic structural equation modeling, and model
development. *MIS Quarterly, 31*(3), 547–577.

Kammeyer-Mueller, J. D., Wanberg, C. R., Glomb, T. M., & Ahlburg, D. (2005). The role of
temporal shifts in turnover processes: It's about time. *Journal of Applied Psychology,
90*(4), 644–658.

Kolvereid, L. (1996). Organizational employment versus self-employment: Reasons for career
choice intentions. *Entrepreneurship Theory and Practice, 20*(3), 23–32.

Krueger, N. F., Jr. (2007). The cognitive infrastructure of opportunity emergence. In
Entrepreneurship (pp. 185–206). Berlin Heidelberg: Springer.

Krueger, N. F., Jr., & Brazeal, D. V. (1994). Entrepreneurial potential and potential entrepreneurs. *Entrepreneurship: Theory & Practice, 18*(3), 91–104.

Krueger, N. F., Reilly, M. D., & Carsrud, A. L. (2000). Competing models of entrepreneurial
intentions. *Journal of Business Venturing, 15*(5–6), 411–432.

Kuckertz, A., Kohtamäki, M., & Droege, C. (2010). The fast eat the slow – the impact of
strategy and innovation timing on the success of technology-oriented ventures.
International Journal of Technology Management, 52(1–2), 175–188.

Lavie, D., Stettner, U., & Tushman, M. L. (2010). Exploration and exploitation within and
across organizations. *The Academy of Management Annals, 4*(1), 109–155.

Lazear, E. P. (2002). *Entrepreneurship*. Working Paper No. 9109. National Bureau of
Economic Research.

Lazear, E. P. (2004). Balanced skills and entrepreneurship. *American Economic Review, 94*(2),
208–211.

Lee, T. W., & Mitchell, T. R. (1994). An alternative approach: The unfolding model of voluntary employee turnover. *The Academy of Management Review, 19*(1), 51–89.

Lee, T. W., Mitchell, T. R., Holtom, B. C., McDaniel, L. S., & Hill, J. W. (1999). The unfolding model of voluntary turnover: A replication and extension. *Academy of Management
Journal, 42*(4), 450–462.

Levinthal, D. A., & March, J. G. (1993). The myopia of learning [Special issue]. *Strategic Management Journal, 14*(S2), 95–112.

Li, Y., Vanhaverbeke, W., & Schoenmakers, W. (2008). Exploration and exploitation in innovation: Reframing the interpretation. *Creativity and Innovation Management, 17*(2), 107–126.

Lumpkin, G. T., & Dess, G. G. (2001). Linking two dimensions of entrepreneurial orientation to firm performance: The moderating role of environment and industry life cycle. *Journal of Business Venturing, 16*(5), 429–451.

Maertz, C. P., & Griffeth, R. W. (2004). Eight motivational forces and voluntary turnover: A theoretical synthesis with implications for research. *Journal of Management, 30*(5), 667–683.

March, J. G. (1991). Exploration and exploitation in organizational learning. *Organization science, 2*(1), 71–87.

Miles, M. B., & Huberman, A. M. (1994). *Qualitative data analysis* (2nd ed.). Thousand Oak, CA: Sage.

Mitchell, T. R., & Lee, T. W. (2001). The unfolding model of voluntary turnover and job embeddedness: Foundations for a comprehensive theory of attachment. In B. M. Staw & R. I. Sutton (Eds.). *Research in Organizational Behavior 23*, 189–246, Greenwich, CT: JAI Press.

Mohr, D. C., Young, G. J., & Burgess, J. F. Jr. (2011). Employee turnover and operational performance: The moderating effect of group-oriented organisational culture. *Human Resource Management Journal., 22*(2), 216–233.

Morrell, K., Loan-Clarke, J., & Wilkinson, A. (2004). The role of shocks in employee turnover. *British Journal of Management, 15*(4), 335–349.

Mourmant, G., Gallivan, M. J., & Kalika, M. (2009). Another road to IT turnover: The entrepreneurial path. *Special Issue of the European Journal of Information Systems on "Meeting the Renewed Demand for IT Workers", 18*(5), 498–521.

Müller, S., Volery, T., & Von Siemens, B. (2012). What do entrepreneurs actually do? An observational study of entrepreneurs' everyday behavior in the start-up and growth stages. *Entrepreneurship Theory and Practice, 36*(5), 995–1017.

O'reilly, C. A., & Tushman, M. L. (2013). Organizational ambidexterity: Past, present, and future. *The Academy of Management Perspectives, 27*(4), 324–338.

Pfeffer, J., & Fong, C. T. (2005). Building organization theory from first principles: The self-enhancement motive and understanding power and influence. *Organization Science, 16*(4), 372–388.

Shapero, A., & Sokol, L. (1982). The social dimensions of entrepreneurship. In C. Kent, D. Sexton, & K. H. Vesper (Eds.), *The Encyclopedia of entrepreneurship* (pp. 72–90). Englewood Cliffs, NJ: Prentice Hall.

Sarasvathy, S. (2001). Causation and effectuation: Toward a theoretical shift from economic inevitability to entrepreneurial contingency. *Academy of Management Review, 26*(2), 243–263.

Shane, S., & Eckhardt, J. (2003). The individual-opportunity nexus. In Z. J. Acs & D. B. Audretsch (Eds.), *Handbook of entrepreneurship research* (pp. 161–194). Dordrecht, NL: Kluwer.

Shane, S., & Venkataraman, S. (2000). The promise of entrepreneurship as a field of research. *The Academy of Management review, 25*(1), 217–226.

Shapero, A. (1984). The entrepreneurial event. In C. A. Kent (Ed.), *The environment for entrepreneurship* (pp. 21–40). Lexington, MA: Lexington Books.

Simsek, Z. (2009). Organizational ambidexterity: Towards a multilevel understanding. *Journal of Management Studies, 46*(4), 597–624.

Stettner, U., & Lavie, D. (2013). Ambidexterity under scrutiny: Exploration and exploitation via internal organization, alliances, and acquisitions. *Strategic Management Journal.* doi:10.1002/smj.2195

Symons, C. S., & Johnson, B. T. (1997). The self-reference effect in memory: A meta-analysis. *Psychological Bulletin, 121*(3), 371–394.

Van de Ven, A. H. (1996). The business creation journey in different organizational settings. Symposium paper presented at the Academy of Management meeting, Cincinnati, August 1996.

Wagner, J. (2006). Are nascent entrepreneurs 'Jacks-of-all-trades'? A test of Lazear's theory of entrepreneurship with German data. *Applied Economics, 38*(20), 2415–2419.

Wheeler, M. A., Stuss, D. T., & Tulving, E. (1997). Toward a theory of episodic memory: The frontal lobes and autonoetic consciousness. *Psychological Bulletin, 121*(3), 331–354.

Yin, R. K. (2003). *Case study research: Design and methods* (3rd ed.). Thousand Oak, CA: Sage.

PART II
EXPLORATION AND EXPLOITATION IN EARLY-STAGE VENTURES AND SME

CHAPTER 4

THE BALANCE BETWEEN EXPLORATION AND EXPLOITATION IN THE "NEW" VENTURE CAPITAL CYCLE: OPPORTUNITIES AND CHALLENGES

Janke Dittmer, Joseph A. McCahery and
Erik P. M. Vermeulen

ABSTRACT

There is arguably a balance between exploration and exploitation within a commercial organization which leads to sustainable growth and value creation. Exploratory activities are associated with search, innovation, risk-taking and experimentation. Activities, such as selection, implementation and execution are considered exploitative in nature. We show that the governance structures and mechanisms that are typically employed in venture capital-backed companies ensure an optimum balance between the exploratory behavior of entrepreneurs and the exploratory focus of venture capitalists. New players in the venture capital cycle, such as

Exploration and Exploitation in Early Stage Ventures and SMEs
Technology, Innovation, Entrepreneurship and Competitive Strategy, Volume 14, 69–95
ISSN: 1479-067X/doi:10.1108/S1479-067X20140000014000

crowdfunding platforms and corporate venture capital units, often fail to understand the importance of the interaction and interrelation between the apparently opposing exploratory and exploitative activities. However, collaborative venture capital models that are currently emerging appear to restore the necessary equilibrium in the "new" venture capital cycle.

Keywords: AngelList; corporate venture capital; crowdfunding; micro-venture capital funds; public—private partnerships; venture capital

INTRODUCTION

Venture capital arguably plays a dual role in the innovation process. Careful screening and financial analysis of business prospects have enabled venture capitalists to not only make reasonable projections about how to unleash a start-up company's long-term, exploratory potential, but also make adequate predictions about its short-term, exploitative opportunities. Unsurprisingly, venture capital is considered to be the main driver behind "disruptive" innovations. The reason for this is simple: venture capitalists have traditionally made investments in early-stage high growth companies that are characterized by their exploratory behavior. This behavior can be recognized by the companies' focus on search, variation, risk-taking, experimentation, play, flexibility, discovery and innovation (March, 1991).

While venture capitalists are often associated with the creation of high growth start-ups and investments in disruptive innovation and technologies, the real challenge is tapping the growth potential of the most promising start-ups companies (Pierrakis & Westlake, 2009). Indeed, there is consensus that venture capital is needed to bring innovative ideas to the market and support the further growth and development of high growth companies (Gompers & Lerner, 2001). For start-up companies, venture capital is a key factor behind their successful performance through the "valley of death" (which can be defined as the period between the initial capital contribution and the time the company starts generating a steady stream of revenue). The focus throughout is on exploitation, which is defined in the literature with terms like "refinement, choice, production, efficiency, selection, implementation and execution" (March, 1991).

The examples of entrepreneurs that started their businesses — and developed their innovative ideas — in garages and basements and built them with the help of venture capitalists into global market leaders show the importance of balancing exploration and exploitation in start-up organizations (Lavie, Stettner, & Tushman, 2010). It is clear that a closer look at the organization and governance arrangements that are put in place by venture capitalists hold important lessons on how this balance is maintained in early-stage start-ups. For instance, it has long been acknowledged that involving other venture capital funds in the screening and monitoring process (through forming syndicates with other renowned funds) can help companies meet their exploratory and exploitative goals (McCahery & Renneboog, 2003). Other techniques, such as the issuance of convertible preferred securities to venture capitalists, staged financing, actively monitoring of management teams, and the advice, expertise and networks offered to entrepreneurial firms are also essential in striking the necessary balance between the company's exploratory and exploitative activities (Ellis, Sagic, & Drori, 2005). The dominant use of convertible preferred equity contracts by venture capitalists is not surprising. The right of investors to interfere in a company's affairs when expectations are not met appears to be an effective mechanism to deal with the trade-off between the entrepreneurs' focus on exploration and the venture capitalists' exploitative orientation (Lerner, 2009).

Over the last two decades an array of legal and regulatory measures has been introduced in an effort to replicate the success of the world's most successful venture capital ecosystem: Silicon Valley. This model, however, is not easily replicated (Hwang & Horowitt, 2012). While governments around the world try to stimulate innovation, they do usually not take into account how the specific characteristics of Silicon Valley — the interactions among venture capitalists, other public and private capital providers and their advisors — help maintain an appropriate balance between exploration and exploitation (Hwang, 2013). To be sure, policymakers, particularly European, are concerned in the aftermath of the financial crisis and the subsequent economic downturn with establishing a sustainable venture capital ecosystem. However, largely because private venture capital has become a less accessible funding source in the earlier stages of a company's life cycle, governments have become the main source of post-financial crisis investment. Data from the European Venture Capital Association show that 39.1% of the €4.1 billion that was raised by European venture capitalists in 2011 originated from government agencies. In 2007, this figure was 9.9% (of €8.2 billion). In addition, investments by the European Investment Bank, the European Investment Fund and other European Commission resources account for approximately 23% of the total capital raised in 2011.

Certainly, from an exploration point of view, disruptive innovations and technologies require financial government support, particularly in the areas of biotechnology and clean technology. Indeed, governments are generally more inclined than private venture capital providers to make highly risky and long-term investments in "proof of concept"/"seed capital" projects, which are simply too early to be relevant to the more "exploitation-oriented" venture capitalists (Mazzucato, 2013). However, even governments that favor long-term investments cannot bridge the gaps that have emerged in the financing of high growth companies. Several reasons have been proposed to explain why governments are prevented from funding a greater share of the private sector's investments. First, government-backed venture capital funds are still relatively small in number and often have a regional focus. The regional bias does not seem to change if a fund's capital is committed by European government agencies. In this respect, it is interesting to see that in 2011 more than 50% of the 42 funds that attracted investments from EU resources, such as the European Investment Fund, had a domestic focus. Second, and more important in light of the discussion in this chapter, government funds tend to underperform, particularly if non-financial objectives, such as contributing to structural/regional/sectorial development policies, prevail (Kelly, 2011).

This chapter supports the prior literature by showing that too much government funding can create an imbalance between the exploration and exploitation activities within start-up companies. Researchers in venture capital suggest that governments can only play a very limited role in the emergence and development of high growth and innovative companies (Lerner, 2009). In general, government initiatives are characterized by a lack of understanding of the "exploitation dimension" (Hwang & Horowitt, 2012), resulting in bureaucratic, cumbersome and inefficient practices that put too much weight on exploration. Empirically it is well known that governments have a poor track record in selecting and nurturing winners. Furthermore, a second strand of the literature shows that a mix of government and private investors is crucial to the realization of a sustainable venture capital ecosystem in which funds are available and accessible in terms of speed, clarity, transparency and connectivity to other stakeholders in the industry (Brander, Du, & Hellmann, 2010).

In principle, the entry of new types of investors may be an efficient way to stimulate private sector investment and restore the balance between exploration and exploitation in the venture capital industry after the financial crisis. In effect, the funding gaps in the venture capital cycle are likely to be filled partially by "new" investors, such as super-angels (or micro-venture capital funds) and crowdfunding platforms. We also find evidence that corporate venture capital increasingly has the potential to significantly contribute to the growth of small and medium-sized companies.

This chapter's contribution is fourfold. First, the chapter contributes to the emerging literature on new venture capital investors. We find that, perhaps with the exception of super-angels, crowdfunding platforms and corporate venture capital as separate funding sources tend to tip the balance to exploration and exploitation respectively. Second, the chapter contributes to the literature by proposing that collaborative models may provide an effective and well-balanced basis for funding innovative firms. The structure and organization of super-angel funds seems to confirm that incentive design and connectivity to other stakeholders in the venture capital ecosystem appear to be the key to their success. Our findings shed light on the new collaborative arrangements in corporate venture capital and how corporations have become anchor investors in early-stage venture capital funds that invest in related and unrelated industries. Third, we show that the experience with public–private partnerships, such as the High-Tech Gründerfonds, confirms that the network creating capabilities of these government-sponsored initiatives have the anticipated exploration and exploitation effects that were present in the traditional venture capital cycle. Finally, our results reveal that collaborative funding models supported by online platforms positively contribute to the balance between exploration and exploitation.

This chapter proceeds as follows. The second section presents the framework of the traditional venture capital model. More importantly, it gives an overview of the funding gaps in this cycle that slowly but surely emerged after the Internet bubble burst in 2000. The third section examines the recent trends and developments in the venture capital industry, which have arguably created a "new" venture capital cycle. As we will show, some of the developments (that were recently introduced in practice) have proven to be an effective first step in bridging the gaps in this cycle. However, in order to maintain an appropriate balance between both exploration and exploitation, collaborative models have emerged. It is only to be expected that these models will develop further and become more effective in the future. The fourth section concludes.

THE VENTURE CAPITAL CYCLE AND ITS CHALLENGES

The Traditional Venture Capital Cycle

Before presenting how new investors can assist in the revival of venture capital, we begin with an account of the development of certain characteristics of the "venture capital cycle" model over the last two decades and show how the cycle has maintained a balance between the exploratory and exploitative needs of start-up companies. The venture capital cycle traditionally starts with the creation of funds that raise capital from institutional investors — which are generally viewed as reliable investors that are able to commit capital for the entire life of the fund — in order to back high potential start-up companies (Smith & Smith, 2004). This is captured in Fig. 1, which also shows that the balance between exploration and exploitation in a venture capital-backed start-up company is generally achieved through a combination of what is referred to in the literature as a "contextual ambidexterity" (Gibson & Birkinshaw, 2004) and a gradual "temporal separation" (Lavie & Rosenkopf, 2006). Indeed, a fund's duration is usually 10 years with a five-year investment period, making it possible for entrepreneurs/start-up companies to estimate with reasonable accuracy when the exploitative attitude of the venture capitalists (by increasingly focusing on a possible exit strategy) will start to prevail over the entrepreneurs' initial exploratory behavior (Ellis, Sagie, & Drori, 2005).

As depicted in Fig. 1, a newly established venture capital fund will first select a manageable number of portfolio companies, which they nurture and support by contributing capital that these companies need to reach the next stage in their development. In addition, they offer advice on operations management and governance. Initially, the focus will be on exploration (without losing sight of the exploitative aspects of the start-up

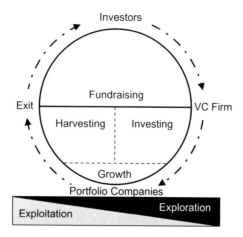

Fig. 1. Exploration and Exploitation in the Venture Capital Cycle.

company). Ideally, this continues until the moment that the fund managers decide to exit the portfolio companies and reap the fruits of the investments. Ultimately, an exploitative strategy will prevail in the endgame since a significant part of the returns will be distributed back to the funds' investors, enabling the restart of a new venture capital cycle (Gompers & Lerner, 2001).

In the end, the evidence appears to point that a rapid and smooth process of raising, structuring, operating and exiting funds is not only crucial to start and restart venture capital cycles, but also to develop a sustainable and robust venture capital industry in which exploration and exploitation constantly interact and interrelate with each other (He & Wong, 2004). It is here where the traditional venture capital cycle reveals significant flaws. To be sure, the venture capital cycle served as a good description of the venture capital ecosystem as it existed in Silicon Valley in the late 1980s and 1990s. For example, during this period there was an almost perfect balance between the supply and demand of venture capital. Venture capital fund investments were typically made across a wide range of investment stages, from seed/start-up to early-stage, expansion and finally later stage investments. However, it became immediately apparent post-crisis that the venture capital cycle could not stand up to the test of time and location (McCahery & Vermeulen, 2013).

It has even been argued that concerns about the viability of venture capital cycle came to fore in early 2000 as the Internet bubble was about to burst (Vermeulen & Nunes, 2012). The next section, however, shows that the cycle is not broken, but it is evolving in response to important imperfections in the model. To illustrate, consider some recent developments such as the revival of corporate venture capital, the move of venture capital investments to later stage start-up companies and the emergence and development of micro-venture capital funds/super-angels, the increasing role of family offices and the introduction of crowdfunding platforms. Clearly, this analysis sheds light on the evolution of the venture capital cycle (which should be taken into account by entrepreneurs), but also should provide important lessons for governments on the optimal strategies for their venture capital policies.

Crowdfunding and the Venture Capital Cycle

We have assumed so far that an analysis of venture capital over the last decade highlights how the industry has generally failed to live up to the expectations of entrepreneurs, investors and policymakers, given its risk profile. For instance, most traditionally structured venture capital firms have, with a few notable exceptions, delivered uninspiring returns (Mulcahy, 2013). These results have not only led to a significant decrease in the number of venture capital funds, but also led many funds toward the less risky financing of later and growth stage companies. As expectations declined, it stimulated remaining funds to focus on companies founded by "serial entrepreneurs" with considerable exploratory and exploitative track records. It is encouraging to see how this trend has not only resulted in a significant increase in the returns to investors in venture capital funds since 2012, but also find that it created "funding gaps" in the development of early to mid-stage companies. European policymakers refer to these gaps as the first and second "valley of death" (Fig. 2).

On the one hand, the crisis in venture capital returns has exposed tensions in the investment model. It is easy to see why venture capital funds have moved toward more conservative investments in the form of expansion and later stage venture capital rounds. On the other hand, we observe new categories of investors, such as crowdfunding platforms, super-angels and multinational corporations, that have stepped up to fill the "funding"

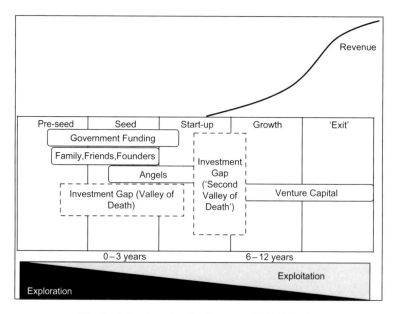

Fig. 2.   The Gaps in the Venture Capital Cycle.

gaps in the earlier stages of the corporate life cycle. The reasons for these new investors to provide financing are similar to those who provided funds earlier: access to investment in small and medium businesses in the expectations of a financial return if the business does well. Consider the example of crowdfunding. Accessibility and speed are the key drivers behind the emergence and development of crowdfunding platforms. Moreover, crowdfunding has evolved from a way to finance creative projects, such as books, films and games, into a new type of entrepreneurial finance that has the potential to dramatically change the venture capital ecosystem. In terms of the underlying economics of crowdfunding, it makes it possible for early-stage start-up companies to raise "venture capital" from a large group of individuals, sidestepping the traditional fundraising process that includes lengthy due diligence periods and tough negotiations over the pre-money valuation and contractual terms. The implication also is that "crowd" investors, who invest relatively small amounts through internet-based platforms – the crowdfunding websites – and/or through social networks – such as Facebook, Twitter and LinkedIn, need less contractual protection (the small investment amounts do not justify close involvement in the exploratory and exploitative growth process of the start-up companies).

We can roughly distinguish between four categories of crowdfunding platforms: (1) donation-based crowdfunding, (2) reward-based crowdfunding, (3) lending-based crowdfunding and (4) equity-based crowdfunding. If investors follow the donation-based crowdfunding model, they generally contribute to a charitable, creative or social project without the expectation of being compensated. This stands in contrast to the reward-based model where the "crowd" that decides to donate receives a reward, such as a finished product, perks or recognition in the credits of a movie, in return. Given the apparent benefits, start-up companies and entrepreneurs typically use lending-based crowdfunding and equity-based crowdfunding to attract investments from the general public. Lending-based crowdfunding and equity-based crowdfunding are jointly called "investment crowdfunding." If the companies grow and prosper, the investors usually receive a financial return. For example, in the lending-based model, they will receive their investment back including interest (the rate of which is dependent on the risk level). Investors that contribute cash through equity-based crowdfunding platforms indirectly or directly become beneficial owners or shareholders of the start-up company. Equity-based crowdfunding increasingly attracts attention from start-up companies, investors and the media. Evidence from data collected by crowdsourcing.org show that approximately 26% of the crowdfunding platforms have adopted the equity-based model (Fig. 3).

It is now well documented that equity crowdfunding, despite its popularity and growth, poses several challenges. First, it requires some experience in making a pitch to smaller investors (Lewis, 2013). And, moreover, there are usually no one-to-one conversations with interested investors. One specific rule is that all the relevant information should be made available upfront, which in turn could easily lead to confidentiality and transparency issues. Second, unlike business angels and venture capitalists, crowdfunding investors typically do not actively pursue an exploitative strategy (through intensive monitoring and supporting the business in the post-investment era). Some literature suggests that, in order for the start-up to succeed, risk investors must be willing to provide the entrepreneur with "value-added" services, thereby striving towards a balance between exploration and exploitation (McCahery & Vermeulen, 2008). These services include identifying and evaluating business opportunities, including management, entry or growth strategies, negotiating further investments, tracking the portfolio

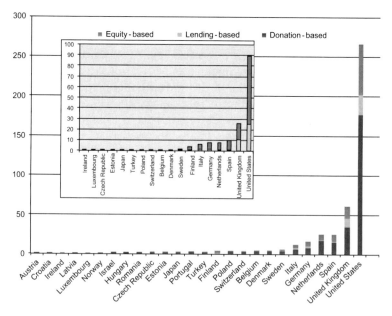

Fig. 3. The Evolution of Crowdfunding Platforms. *Source*: Derived from http:\\www.crowdsourcing.org.

firm and coaching the firm participants, providing technical and management assistance, and attracting additional capital. When assessing the potential of crowdfunding, it is clear that the absence of real value-added services could become significant and may have the potential to retard growth.

Third crowdfunding may lack connectivity to follow-on investors, key stakeholders and other advisors. High potential growth companies, particularly in highly capital-intensive sectors (such as biotechnology and medical), must prove the ability to attract follow-on funding from later stage investors. Because of the connectedness between early-stage investors and the venture capital community, companies tend to have improved access to external financing. As a consequence, crowdfunding investors that typically follow a "spray and pray" strategy when it comes to making investment decisions (and therefore) have less resources and/or incentives to assist portfolio companies in securing the next stage of finance. Moreover, the disincentive is likely exacerbated by the fact the companies that pitch for crowdfunding investors may end up with a multitude of investors. As such, these circumstances not only enhance the free-rider problem amongst investors, but also add an additional "negotiation challenge" to potential follow-on investor, as it is easier to negotiate the funding with only a few "earlier round" investors (Kolodny, 2013). To summarize, if one adds these challenges to the legislative and regulatory issues that surround crowdfunding, it is clear that this potentially attractive source of finance will only be able to play a limited role in the new venture capital industry in the near future.[1]

Corporate Venture Capital and the Venture Capital Cycle

In terms of bridging the funding gaps in the venture capital cycle, corporate venture capital is a useful starting point. It is noteworthy that the average deal size with corporate venture capital involvement is currently significantly larger than deals without corporate funding (Fig. 4). Many mature corporations have established dedicated corporate venture capital arms or structures, seeking competitively advantageous innovations, whilst capitalizing on their own ability to provide a broad range of strategic benefits from industry partnerships, distribution opportunities and product development insights. Interestingly, the recent financial crisis has moved corporate venture capital initiatives from a mainly exploitative investment to a more exploratory relationship with start-up companies (Hill & Birkinshaw, 2008).

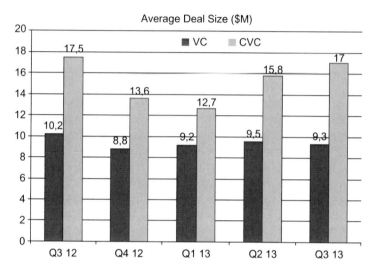

Fig. 4. Average Deal Size with and without Corporate Investors. *Source*: Data derived from CB Insights.

Arguably, this change in behavior is due to the new early-bird approach to corporate venture capitalist strategies (finding-the-next-big-thing attitude) (McCahery & Vermeulen, 2010). The consequences of this changed approach have led to an interesting interplay amongst corporations, venture capitalists and entrepreneurs with respect to innovative projects. So what are the implications of this development for venture financing? First, corporations could decide to spin-out a technology by establishing a new entity that acquires the technology and issues new shares to another corporation that pursues an outside–in strategy. Second, venture capitalists could select spin-out/spin-off companies of a corporation of its portfolio companies. Finally, corporations could decide to actively approach venture capital funds or young innovative companies to help act as a catalyst or offer managerial support.

It is also important to recognize that corporate venture capital strategies also experience challenges, particularly with tenure (and can exist at the whim of prevailing executive sentiment), access to appropriate deal flow and a perception that their focus on "strategic" (exploitative) benefits is not completely in line with the entrepreneur's own exploratory aspirations. In theory, corporations are an attractive and sustainable source of venture capital. One key question is the extent of the financial constraints on the exploratory and exploitive behaviors and strategies of corporate venture capital. Fig. 5 seems to provide part of the answer. To be sure, conflicting aims shape corporate venture capital. However, corporate venturing units are reliant on the ongoing sponsorship of their corporate owners, and can be abandoned without due cause for reasons entirely disconnected with the operations of the units themselves. This arguably makes corporate venture capital volatile.

In this environment, it should come as no surprise that the corporate venture capital share of the total venture capital investments in the United States declined from 24.6% to 14.4% after the Internet Bubble burst in 2000 and again from 21.4% to 12.7% after the recent financial crisis in 2007–2008. Clearly, the volatility raises doubts as to whether corporate venture capital schemes can effectively deal with the imbalance between exploration and exploitation in the "new" venture capital cycle. These doubts are shared by venture capitalists who generally believe that only the most active corporate venture capital units that are affiliated to relatively

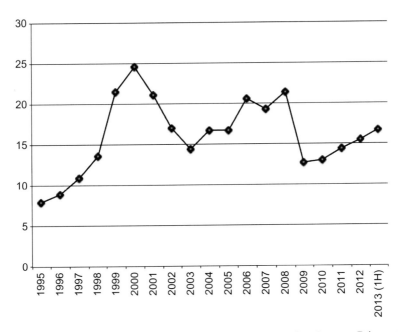

Fig. 5. Corporate Involvement in Venture Capital Deals. *Source*: Pricewater-houseCoopers/National Venture Capital Association MoneyTree™ Report, Data: Thomson Reuters.

young listed (venture capital-backed) companies, such as Google, Intel, Cisco, Comcast, SAP and Qualcomm, are able to restore the "exploration–exploitation" balance. The next section shows that the potential of corporations to "fix" the venture capital cycle increases if they pursue a collaborative strategy by partnering with existing venture capital funds.

THE NEW "COLLABORATIVE" VENTURE CAPITAL CYCLE

In the previous section we described the funding challenges associated with the venture capital cycle. One solution to bridge the gaps in funding is the entry of new types of investors. While there is broad agreement on the need for new pools of financing, it is not clear that crowdfunding and corporate venture capital alone will provide the magnitude of funding across the venture capital cycle. We consider the recent trends that arguably lead towards a new equilibrium between exploratory and exploitative strategies in the venture capital industry. To see this, we focus on the emergence of collaborative venture capital arrangements. In this respect, consider super-angel funds or micro/boutique venture capital funds. These funds appeared in the mid-2000s and we foresee an increase in the number of collaborative venture capital funds in which strategic investors often act as an anchor investor. Particularly, multinational corporations (in their search for the "next big thing") are altering their investment strategies from mere financial participations in promising start-ups to more explorative and strategic investment modes, thereby entering into partnership-type relationships with venture capital firms. In the following sections, we will provide examples of venture capital funds that are characterized by their collaborative nature and focus again on both exploratory and exploitative value creation. We will first discuss micro-venture capital funds/super-angels and then turn to "collaborative" venture capital models.

The Emergence of Super-Angels/Micro-Venture Capital Funds

According to a recent report by the European Venture Capital Association (EVCA) (2013), micro-venture capital funds (or super-angel funds), which first emerged in the United States, are increasingly established in the venture capital industry. Generally, these funds are managed by former entrepreneurs. In contrast to traditional angel investors operating alone or in concert with other angels, micro-venture capital funds also attract other investing interests from wealthy individuals, family offices, foundations and corporate investors that are often looking for innovative investment opportunities. There is a tendency for managers of micro-venture capital funds to contribute a significant amount of capital to the fund, making the organization of the fund more of a collaborative nature than a typical "venture capitalist—institutional investor" relationship. Table 1 gives an overview of some of the most notable micro-venture capital funds in the United States and Europe. Interestingly, but not surprisingly, these funds are currently able to secure capital commitments in the amount of $20 million to $100 million, an amount that is rapidly growing.

The fact is investing with proven entrepreneurs is very appealing. The basic idea is that since fund managers are extremely well connected in their former line of business, micro funds are often better positioned than traditional venture capitalists to pick out winners at a seed or early stage. Also, they are able to mentor them through the very early-stage start-up phases, increasing the possibility of follow-on investments from "traditional" venture capital funds and corporate venture funds. In fact, data provider CB Insights seems to indicate that micro-venture capital funds have a higher

Table 1. Mirco-Venture Capital Funds in the United States and Europe (2008−2012).

Micro-Venture Capital Firm	Country	No. of Investments	Aggregate Deal Value (US$ million)
Founder Collective	US	111	285.64
Floodgate Fund	US	105	488.28
SoftTech VC	US	99	330.72
Baseline Ventures	US	72	363.05
Felicis Ventures	US	68	354.44
Launch Capital	US	56	94.54
Atomico	UK	53	505.01
Harrison Metal	US	49	289.28
Freestyle Capital	US	36	76.22
Lowercase Capital	US	32	156.24
Seedcamp	UK	14	13.88
Notion Capital	UK	13	56.57
Passion Capital	UK	12	8.4
ISAI	France	9	25.42
Jaina Capital	France	2	4

Source: Data derived from Preqin − Venture Deals Analyst.

post-financial crisis rate of follow-on investments than traditional angel investors. That said, their position between the traditional angel investors and venture capital funds arguable make these micro-venture capital funds a perfect collaborator in terms of pursuing both exploratory and exploitative strategies.

Collaborative Corporate Venture Capital Models

The EVCA (2013) also identified a new breed of corporate venture capital players that have an interest in investing across all start-up stages and sectors. This is an important development since, as we have seen above, corporate involvement in the venture capital industry significantly declined after the Internet bubble in 2000. That fact that a number of corporate venture capital funds persisted and even weathered the 2007–2008 financial crisis much better than their traditional venture capital counterparts should not be surprising (Lerner, 2013). As we can see in Fig. 5, corporations have, in the wake of the financial crisis, stepped up their involvement and investments in innovative technology companies, thereby attempting to regain market share.

Nevertheless, despite the prospect of real gains, there are reasons to be skeptical about the merits of corporate venture capital. Indeed, there are a number of challenges on the path to success. First, the mission and scope of corporate venture capital divisions (exploration vs. exploitation) are often unclear making it difficult to assess results objectively. Second, corporations often lack the experience and expertise that is needed to succeed in the venture capital industry. Third, it is difficult to establish effective governance and compensation systems within a corporate environment. Fourth, the venture capital industry is highly networked based on deep interpersonal relationships and it is difficult for corporate venture capital staff to penetrate these networks to identify the right investment opportunities. Fifth, managing minority interests in portfolio companies is often daunting from an accounting point of view and sometimes even from an antitrust perspective. Sixth, many start-ups fear that accepting investments from a corporate venture fund will restrict their exit opportunities and bring about the risk of "negative signaling" should the corporate venture capital fund decide not to support the investment in the future.

At the same time, new venture models are beginning to emerge. We can distinguish among four collaborative models: (1) the outsourced venture model, (2) the minority corporate venture model, (3) the multi-corporate venture model and (4) the corporate collaboration venture model.[2] In particular, venture capitalists are increasingly establishing partnerships with mature corporations. Empirical research shows that 62% of the 135 reported announcements of corporate venture capital initiatives in 2012 and the first quarter of 2013 can be characterized as a "collaborative venture capital model" (data derived from www.globalcorporateventuring) (Fig. 6).

Unilever is an interesting example of a European corporation that has well-documented history with the "collaborative venture capital model." Note that this multinational divested in 2007 one of its "independent" corporate venture capital arms, Unilever Technology Ventures, which was at that time structured as a separate venture capital unit with Unilever as its sole investor. It replaced this structure by a collaborative model in which Unilever became an anchor investor in Physic Ventures, an early-stage venture capital fund based in San Francisco. The fund was established by Unilever to invest in consumer-driven health, wellness and sustainable living. Even though Unilever remains the largest investor, Physic has gone on to attract a number of financial as well as strategic investors including PepsiCo and health insurance company Humana.

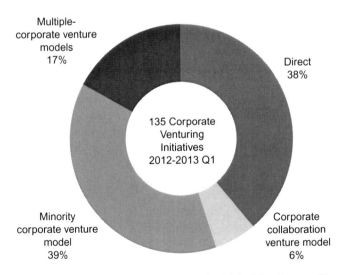

Fig. 6. Collaborative Corporate Venture Capital Models. *Source*: Data derives from http:\\www.globalcorporateventuring.com.

Collaborative venture capital models between corporations and venture capitalists have the potential to lead to "win-win" situations. On the one hand, the corporation can benefit from the "exploitative" experience and expertise of the fund managers, whereas on the other hand the venture capital firm can profit from an active corporate investor that may not only prove helpful in selecting the right portfolio companies, but may also provide the necessary support to the "exploratory" development of these start-up businesses. The collaborative model would most likely lead to an appropriate level of balance between exploration and exploitation. For instance, the collaborations are targeted to opening "exploratory" doors to innovative technology companies in emerging markets with strong growth potential. But from the venture capitalists' point of view, the collaborative models should also offer numerous benefits. For instance, consider how corporations can provide possible "exploitative" exit opportunities (in the event of it being interested in acquiring the venture capital-backed technology), but at the same time create real "explorative" investment options to spin-out or spin-off companies.

The Unilever-Physic model is a notable example of an "outsourced venture model." Presently, there is a tendency for this model to evolve toward a "minority corporate venture model" in which the corporation makes a minority investment in a venture capital fund in return for a strategic collaboration. The fact is that, under certain circumstances, this allows corporates to leverage investments from other strategic or financial investors without having to consolidate their own investment in their profit and loss statements. Depending on the cash situation of the corporation, this can make a minority investment more attractive than in-house research and development.

We observe an array of collaborative models that to a greater or lesser extent may establish an equilibrium between exploratory and exploitative strategies (Fig. 7). For instance, the partnership between Index Ventures and two competing pharmaceutical companies, GlaxoSmithKline and Johnson & Johnson, could be categorized as a "multi-corporate venture model." The €150 million fund mainly invests in single assets that have the potential to become leading products in the future, the so-called asset-centric investment model. The corporate investors provide advice to Index Ventures by appointing in-house experts on a scientific advisory committee. In order to avoid potential conflicts of interest, however, the two multinationals have not obtained any preferential rights (of first refusal) to promising drugs that could emerge from this partnership. If either party wishes to acquire an "asset," they will need to engage in an open competitive

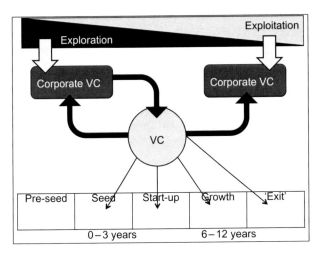

Fig. 7. The Exploration and Exploitation Balance in Collaborative Models.

bidding process. In summary, Index Ventures hopes through a supportive, but at the same time independent attitude of its corporate investors, to establish a partnership that can lead to a joint development of new drugs and medicines.

Finally, one interesting idea is the Glass Collective, a program established by venture capitalists Kleiner Perkins Caufield & Byers, and Andreessen Horowitz in conjunction with Google Ventures in 2013. The structure involves a new twist on the collaborative venture capital model. While the venture capitalists (and Google Ventures) make independent investments (without setting up a new fund), they leverage their relationships to identify and accelerate the emerging glass technologies. This constitutes a form of the "corporate collaboration venture model."

Collaborative Government Venture Capital Models

As described above, government interventions do not always have their intended effect. One reason advanced is that government venture capital schemes often ignore the exploitative aspects in the venture capital cycle. To be sure, there are always exceptions. For instance, recent academic research shows that Australian initiatives were successful in spurring innovation (exploration) and entrepreneurship (exploitation) (Cumming & Johan, 2012;

Humphery-Jenner, 2012). What is probably most suggestive here is that the funds operate as "public–private partnerships" in which public funds are pooled with capital from private investors. The funds are managed by private sector fund managers who are, as we have seen, not only in a better position to pick "winners," but also ensure that the funds are connected to the existing venture capital industry. Venture capital fund managers and private investors are thus essential for the success of the government programs. In essence, the government acts as a strategic investor. Its main aim is the focus on innovation and the development of a robust venture capital ecosystem.

Thus, in order to continue to make investments in the future, the government initiatives are organized as "revolving programs," which means that the government needs to participate in the distributions of returns and interests from initial investments in order to be able to reinvest the proceeds and ensure the long-term sustainability of the government program. Indeed, profit distribution arrangements require the fund managers to first return the invested capital to the government and private investors before venture capital fund managers participate in the upside. Often there is even an additional hurdle rate in place to ensure that the investors first receive their paid in capital and their cost of capital. However, unlike most government support programs, the Australian program is designed to attract and incentivize private investors and venture capitalists. The remaining profits (if and when realized) are split disproportionally with the government receiving 10% and 90% going to the private investors.

Arguably, the idea that a capped upside for the government is attractive to the private sector investors is not new. The Yozma program – viewed by many as one of the prime examples of how government initiatives should be organized – introduced this incentive mechanism to attract experienced international venture capitalists and investors to Israel. By doing so, the Yozma program fostered the relationship between Israeli start-up companies and experienced American venture capitalists, leading to an impressive and low-cost development of Israel's venture capital ecosystem in the late 1990s. Evidence from Israel's IT sector, for instance, suggests that the connection to the US venture capital industry with its exit opportunities, such as the stock exchange NASDAQ, introduced the necessary balance between exploration and exploitation in the "venture capital equation."

During recent years, European policymakers also have begun to mount an interest in public–private partnerships. Consider the High-Tech Gründerfonds in Germany. Interestingly, the fund is designed to meet two key components: access to venture capital and connectivity to other advisors and investors. First, the German public—private partnership currently manages in excess of €550 million of committed capital over two fund generations (€272 million in Fund I and €301.5 million in Fund II) and invests mainly in emerging start-up companies in Germany. The German Federal Ministry of Economics and Technology as well as KfW Banking Group are the "strategic" anchor investors in the two funds. As for the connectivity, the High-Tech Gründerfonds gives access to an impressive network of coaches, such as university professors, angel investors and venture capital funds. These coaches do not only offer value-added services to existing portfolio companies, but are also responsible for providing investment opportunities (Brandkamp, 2011).

But there is more. Both funds have been able to attract a significant number of corporate investors. Corporate investors in Fund I (which started to make investments in 2005) include BASF, Robert Bosch, Daimler, Siemens, Deutsche Telekom, and Carl Zeiss. Fund II, which commenced investing on 27 October 2011 and had a second close of EUR 301.5 million in December 2012, was able to attract even more corporate interest with commitments from ALTANA, BASF, B. Braun, Robert Bosch, CEWE Color, Daimler, Deutsche Post DHL, Deutsche Telekom, Evonik, LANXESS, m + mv, Metrogroup, Qiagen, RWE Innogy, SAP, Tengelmann and Carl Zeiss. Together, the involvement of these companies is important to supply key technical and market support to the entrepreneurial businesses. The High-Tech Gründerfonds is one of Europe's most active venture capital funds with 215 investments from 2008 to 2012 (with an aggregate deal value of US$ 298.06 million). Overall, the necessary interactions and interrelations between exploratory and exploitative activities appear to have been the starting point in the design of the High-Tech Gründerfonds (with the fund managers as the coordinators of both the exploratory and exploitative activities) (Fig. 8). Indeed, we view properly structured public—private partnerships as a strong tool in restoring the balance between exploration and exploitation in the venture capital cycle. The next section will show that the same can be said about online platforms.

Collaborative Online Platforms

Online platforms that offer equity-based crowdfunding are becoming increasingly popular as a source of funding. However, as we have seen, crowdfunding in itself — with a mere focus on supporting exploratory initiatives — will be unable to deal with the gaps in the venture capital

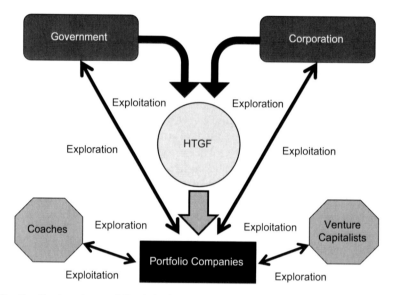

Fig. 8.   Exploration and Exploitation in the High-Tech Gründerfonds (HTGF).

cycle. It is a development that could change if angel investors and venture capitalists begin to work through the crowdfunding platforms (Colao, 2012). Of course, there is some evidence of such activity emerging in the United States. Consider AngelList, an online platform that streamlines the fundraising process by matching start-ups with investors. This platform, which commenced in January 2010, is clearly meeting the pent-up demand of start-up companies to obtain easy and speedy access to a "social network" of qualifying and sophisticated angel investors (with over 1 million in personal wealth). Perhaps because AngelList offers a platform for start-up companies to quickly connect and negotiate seed and early-stage financing, it can effectively provide transparency to the ecosystem by making it possible for investors to "follow" companies and track their explorative and exploitative potential.

For their part, the growing popularity of AngelList among start-up companies has gradually drawn venture capital firms, corporate venture capital units and other institutional investors (that are eager to find early-stage winners) to its network (Hindman, 2011). According to data collected by AngelList, 3,325 start-up companies were able to raise seed financing — ranging from US$ 50,000 to US$ 1 million — in the period 2010–2012 (in reality these numbers are probably much higher since not all deals are reported) (Fig. 9). Moreover, companies that are "listed" on AngelList have also been successful in attracting follow-on rounds of finance: They have raised 230 series A rounds of financing, 49 series B, 5 series C and 60 companies were acquired. It is only to be expected that this number will rise significantly as AngelList has recently introduced several "crowdfunding-type" services.

For instance, it became possible for accredited investors to pour small amounts of at least US$ 1,000 alongside other (angel) investors. In this context, AngelList would notify the start-up company as soon as a minimum of US$ 200,000 had been "committed." The start-up company was then offered two options: (1) it closes the deal or (2) continues fundraising. The key benefit of AngelList is to prevent companies having to deal with a large number of small investors which complicates follow-on investment rounds and, in turn, causes an imbalance between exploration and exploitation. Perhaps most importantly, AngelList's crowdfunding service was established as a partnership with SecondMarket (a company that provides liquidity to start-up companies and their investors) that acts as the broker-dealer. The idea was that SecondMarket created and managed a separate

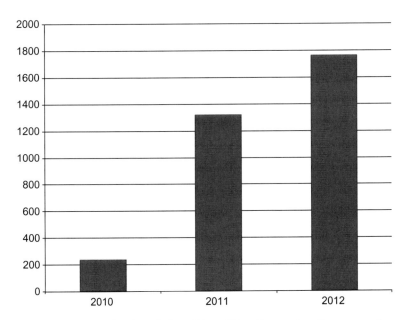

Fig. 9. The Increasing Popularity of AngelList. *Source*: http:\\www.angel.co.

fund that pools the contributed "crowdfunding" investments which, in turn, becomes a shareholder in the start-up company. The service was only available, given the investor protection problems, to accredited investors who were expected to appreciate the risks involved in early-stage finance transactions. Another, more recent, initiative is the "syndicates" service, which offers investors (backers) the opportunity to invest alongside notable angels or venture capital funds (syndicate leads) in promising portfolio companies. This service has several benefits that stimulate collaborations. First, there are no management fees (backers pay a carry — percentage of the syndicate's profits — of 5–10%).[3] Second, AngelList's syndicates provide flexibility to the backers in that they can exit the syndicate at any time or they can opt-out of specific deals. Thus, offering "crowd" investors the possibility to passively invest alongside professional "venture capital" investors has the advantage of increasing the amount of available "early-stage" resources without running the risk of disturbing the balance between exploration and exploitation (which was one of the downsides of crowdfunding platforms).

CONCLUSION

The chapter started with a discussion of the venture capital cycle in the context of the "exploration and exploitation" literature. The cycle begins with the creation of venture capital funds (fundraising), which subsequently select and invest in start-up companies (investing). These funds nurture and support their portfolio companies by contributing money and services that these companies need to reach the next stage in their development (growing). Ideally, this process continues until the moment that the venture capital funds decide to exit (harvesting), thereby distributing part of the returns back to the initial investors and restarting a new venture cycle.

The interplay between entrepreneurs and venture capital funds in the venture capital cycle is crucial as it maintains a necessary balance between the entrepreneurs' focus on exploration and the venture capitalist "increasing" attention to exploitation. Even so, this balance may not hold in the aftermath of the financial crisis. Indeed, this chapter examines the emergence of funding gaps in the early to mid-stages of a start-up company's development. We noted however, that these gaps are largely due to traditional venture capital providers moving towards less risky financing of later and growth stage companies. Two important points arise from the analysis.

First, new types of investors have emerged to begin filling the gaps, such as government venture capital, super-angels and crowdfunding platforms. Second, corporate venture capital is increasingly viewed as smart capital that has the potential to significantly influence the growth of small and medium-sized companies.

The question arises of whether these new types of "venture capital" have the potential of restore the balance between exploration and exploitation. An analysis of the new investors found that they suffer from certain structural limitations. For instance, the design of crowdfunding platforms and government funding makes it difficult to measure and develop the exploitative opportunities of the start-up company. Corporate venture capital, on the other hand, is better placed to opportunistically exploit the start-ups business to its own advantage.

Finally, we found that new collaborative venture capital models, which are gaining traction in the venture capital industry, appear to offer an adequate solution. They may provide an effective basis for funding innovative projects. For instance, one of the features of these models is that corporations have become anchor investors in early-stage venture capital funds. Our results also point to the emergence of an outsourced venture model or minority corporate venture model. In these models, venture capital funds, which are managed by independent venture capitalists with outstanding track records, make investments in start-up firms on behalf of large corporations. The experience with public–private partnerships, such as the German High-Tech Gründerfonds, confirms that the network creating capabilities of these initiatives has the anticipated productivity effects on the venture capital cycle. The results suggest, moreover, the support of online platforms which also appear to have a positive effect on the emergence of collaborative funding models. These collaborative models are highly beneficial under the circumstances in being able to restore the necessary balance between exploration and exploitation.

NOTES

1. We can already observe several regulatory initiatives that should give a boost to equity crowdfunding. An example of a self-regulatory initiative can be found in the United Kingdom where a self-regulatory body has been established under the UK Crowdfunding Association (UKCFA). These initiatives have also appeared at the European level. Consider the European Crowdfunding Network (ECN). The goal of the self-regulatory bodies is clear: To provide transparency and ensure that

members operate to minimum standards without sacrificing the accessibility and speed that made crowdfunding a success. The question, however, remains whether the venture capital ecosystem can fully rely on self-regulation? Presumptively, the payoff for ensuring the compliance with and wide diffusion of self-regulatory standards is significant. It should therefore come as no surprise that the Italian market regulator has recently taken the first regulatory steps regarding online fundraising platforms. The main purpose of the "regulation-light" approach is to provide a measure of legal certainty for market participants. In Italy, this is accomplished through a simple registration procedure for crowdfunding venues, designed to distinguish them from other market participants such as Regulated Markets or Multilateral Trading Facilities, both of which are subject to more stringent rules. In addition, the new Italian rules set out a code of conduct. In view of the examples discussed above, the challenge is to find the right mix of self-regulatory and government measures that encourage transparency and investor protection.

2. The categorization of the models is derived from Claudia Iannazzo, Pereg Ventures CEO and partner.

3. AngelList receives a 5% carry from the syndicate lead.

REFERENCES

Brander, J., Du, Q., & Hellmann, T. (2010). *Governments as venture capitalists: Striking the right balance, in globalization of alternative investments.* Globalization of Alternative Investments, Working Papers Volume 3: The Global Economic Impact of Private Equity Report 2010, World Economic Forum.

Brandkamp, M. (2011). Seed capital for good ideas, FYB 2011.

Colao, J. J. (2012). Fred Wilson and the death of venture capital. *Forbes*, May 8, 2012.

Cumming, D., & Johan, S. (2012). *Venture's economic impact in Australia.* Working Paper.

Ellis, S., Sagic, T., & Drori, I. (2005). Exploration–exploitation dilemmas of venture capital companies: The role of organizational slack and time horizon. *Israel Venture Capital & Private Equity Journal, 5*(3), 16–17 and 44.

EVCA (European Venture Capital Association). (2013). Smart choice: The case for investing in European venture capital. Retrieved from http://www.evca.eu/publications/VC_report_interactive.pdf

Gibson, C. B., & Birkinshaw, J. (2004). The antecedents, consequences, and mediating role of organizational ambidexterity. *Academy of Management Journal, 47*(2), 209–226.

Gompers, P. A., & Lerner, J. (2001). *The money of invention: How venture capital creates new wealth.* Cambridge, Massachusetts: Harvard Business School Press.

He, Z. L., & Wong, P. K. (2004). Exploration vs. exploitation: An empirical test of the ambidexterity hypothesis. *Organization Science, 15*(4), 481–494.

Hill, S. A., & Birkinshaw, J. (2008). Strategy-organization configurations in corporate venture units: Impact on performance and survival. *Journal of Business Venturing, 23*, 423–444.

Hindman, N. C. (2011). Naval Ravikant, AngelList: A social network that connects startups with investors. *The Huffington Post*, September 20, 2011.

Humphery-Jenner, M. (2012). Stimulating venture activity through government investment in venture funds. *European Business Organizations Law Review, 13*, 103–124.

Hwang, V. W. (2013). How to grow a venture capital ecosystem. *Forbes*, August 27, 2013.

Hwang, V. W., & Horowitt, G. (2012). The rainforest. California: Regenwald.

Kelly, R. (2011). *The performance and prospects of European venture capital*. Working Paper No. 2011/09. EIF Research & Market Analysis.

Kolodny, L. (2013). AngelList and beyond: What VCs really think of crowdfunding. *The Wall Street Journal* (Venture Capital Dispatch), October 8, 2013.

Lavie, D., & Rosenkopf, L. (2006). Balancing exploration and exploitation in alliance formation. *Academy of Management Journal, 49*(4), 797–818.

Lavie, D., Stettner, U., & Tushman, M. L. (2010). Exploration and exploitation within and across organizations. *The Academy of Management Annals, 4*(1), 109–155.

Lerner, J. (2009). *Boulevard of broken dreams: Why public effort to boost entrepreneurship and venture capital have failed – and what to do about it*. Princeton, NJ: Princeton University Press.

Lerner, J. (2013). Corporate venturing: More and more smart companies are going VC to find their next breakthroughs. *Harvard Business Review, 5*(October), 86–94.

Lewis, N. (2013). Business angels vs equity crowdfunding – 7 key differences. iBusinessAngel.

March, J. G. (1991). Exploration and exploitation in organizational learning. *Organization Science, 2*(1), 71–87.

Mazzucato, M. (2013). *The entrepreneurial state: Debunking public vs. private sector myths*. London: Anthem Press.

McCahery, J. A., & Renneboog, L. (2003). *Venture capital contracting and the valuation of high technology firms*. Oxford: Oxford University Press.

McCahery, J. A., & Vermeulen, E. P. M. (2008). *Corporate governance of non-listed companies*. Oxford: Oxford University Press.

McCahery, J. A., & Vermeulen, E. P. M. (2010). Venture capital beyond the financial crisis: How corporate venturing boosts new entrepreneurial clusters (and assists governments in their innovation efforts). *Capital Markets Law Journal, 5*(4), 471–500.

McCahery, J. A., & Vermeulen, E. P. M. (2013). *Conservatism and innovation in venture capital contracting*. Lex Research Topics in Corporate Law & Economics Working Paper No. 2013-2; ECGI - Law Working Paper No. 213.

Mulcahy, D. (2013). Myths about venture capitalists. *Harvard Business Review, 5*(May), 80–83.

Pierrakis, Y., & Westlake, S. (2009, June). Reshaping the UK economy: The role of public investment in financing growth. NESTA.

Smith, R. L., & Smith, J. K. (2004). *Entrepreneurial Finance*. Hoboken, NJ: Wiley.

Vermeulen, E. P. M., & Nunes, D. (2012). The evolution and regulation of venture capital funds in Europe. *EUIJ-Kyushu Review, 2012*(2), 1–68.

CHAPTER 5

LOSING BALANCE: TRADE-OFFS BETWEEN EXPLORATION AND EXPLOITATION INNOVATION

Craig Randall, Linda F. Edelman and
Robert Galliers

ABSTRACT

Low labor costs and market access are no longer competitive differentia-tors; increasingly companies are looking to design and develop new products and services as a crucial source of competitive advantage. As the pressure to innovate increases, so does the tension between shorter-term exploitative development and longer-term exploratory innovation activities. We explore this tension using interview data from software SMEs and venture capitalist firms who invest in technology-driven companies. Findings indicate that, despite firm's having established solid innovation plans, short-term exploitative demands crowd out their longer-term exploration innovation during the development phase. Agency and resource dependence theories are used to start to explore some of the reasons for this shift. Implications and suggestions for future research are discussed.

Keywords: Innovation; agency theory; exploitation; exploration; small and medium-sized enterprises; resource-dependence theory

Exploration and Exploitation in Early Stage Ventures and SMEs
Technology, Innovation, Entrepreneurship and Competitive Strategy, Volume 14, 97–121
Copyright © 2014 by Emerald Group Publishing Limited
All rights of reproduction in any form reserved
ISSN: 1479-067X/doi:10.1108/S1479-067X20140000014002

INTRODUCTION

New product and service innovation remains challenging for many companies. A recent study of 519 firms in the USA, UK, and France by Accenture found that while 51% of respondents reported they had recently increased their innovation funding, just 18% of CEOs say that they are seeing their investments in innovation pay off (http://www.accenture. com/us-en/Pages/insight-low-risk-innovation-costly.aspx). Indeed, 45% of executives said that their company had become more risk adverse when considering breakthrough ideas, and hence see their company pursuing a portfolio of smaller, safer opportunities rather than seeking the next big breakthrough. This suggests that innovation dollars are increasingly being spent on incremental or exploitative innovation, shifting the priority away from exploratory projects.

The distinction between the exploration of new possibilities and the exploitation of old certainties, introduced by March in 1991, has become widely used to examine technological innovation (see Medcof, 2010, for a review). Exploration, defined as "things captured by terms such as search, variation, risk taking, experimentation, flexibility discovery, and innovation," and exploitation, defined as "things such as refinement, choice, production, efficiency, selection, implementation, and execution," are two critical activities in the product development process (March, 1991, p. 71). Since the article's publication, exploration and exploitation have become powerful themes in the innovation literature (see, for example, Hoang & Rothaermel, 2010; Li, Lin, & Chu, 2008; Voss, Sirdeshmukh, & Voss, 2008). Empirical research has primarily focused on two dimensions of exploration and exploitation: technology development and market development (Danneels, 2007; Lavie & Rosenkopf, 2006; Smith & Tushman, 2005). Firms can develop new products for their existing market or to enter a new market and gain new customers, and they can employ technology that is either familiar to them or novel. When both the technology and the market are known, firms engage in exploitation activities that refine and extend their competencies to serve current customers. However, when both the technology and the market are novel, firms engage in exploration activities as they experiment with new technologies for unknown markets (March, 1991, p. 71).

Researchers recommend that firms pursue a balance of exploration and exploitative innovation activities (Gupta, Smith, & Shalley, 2006; He & Wong, 2004). However, the way in which that balance is achieved is less clear. Questions around ambidexterity (Benner & Tushman, 2003; Burgelman, 1991;

Levinthal, 1997) versus punctuated equilibrium (Burgelman, 2002; Levinthal & March, 1993; Siggelkow & Levinthal, 2003; Tushman & Romanelli, 1985; Vermeulen & Barkema, 2001) remain central to the overall debate. Indeed, some literature suggests that firms cannot successful pursue a strategy of both explorative and exploitative innovation and instead must focus on only one innovation type (Benner & Tushman, 2003).

Despite work that argues for a balance between these two types of innovation (Gupta et al., 2006; He & Wong, 2004), research suggests that firms continue to undertake an insufficient amount of exploration innovation (Benner & Tushman, 2003; Rosenkopf & Almeida, 2003). Reasons why exploitation activities take precedence over exploration can be found in the firm's structure, reward system, culture, competences, identity, and the level of experience of the senior management team (O'Reilly & Tushman, 2008). The implication is that firms tend to focus on existing customers and are subject to organizational inertia, causing their existing practices and processes to obstruct more novel product or market development plans.

While the arguments above clearly reflect ongoing controversy in the literature, for the most part they take a large firm perspective and hence assume some level of resource munificence. In contrast, the context for this inquiry is small and medium-sized enterprises (SMEs). Liabilities of small-ness suggest that SMEs face higher risks for survival as small firms are assumed to have fewer resources to weather bad times (Aldrich & Auster, 1986). Potential customers, suppliers, collaborators, and investors tend to be less knowledgeable about the reliability and ability of smaller enterprises, either because they have not previously transacted with them or because of their less verifiable reputations (Hannan & Freeman, 1984; Stinchcombe, 1965). This suggests that while the need for novel, exploratory innovation is necessary for future growth, resource scarcity and legitimacy concerns force small firms to make strategic trade-offs with respect to where to focus their limited innovation dollars.

This study has two objectives. Initially it examines the broad question of resource trade-offs that small firms make during the R&D phase of development as they try to not only develop new exploratory products, but also meet new and existing customer demands for modifications to existing products. Hence the initial research question is "Are small firms forced to make trade-offs between exploration and exploitation innovation projects during the R&D process of development"? We examined that research question by looking at the movement of manpower across projects, noting that small firms regularly moved engineers from exploration projects to exploitation projects.

As the interviews progressed, it seemed quite clear that these trade-offs in resources, and in particular manpower, not only existed, but that they presented some unique challenges for small and medium-sized firms. Therefore, the research shifted focus away from the baseline question about the existence of resource trade-offs and instead moved toward trying to gain an understanding of the factors which motivated those resource trade-offs. Reflecting this shift in focus, the second research question is "What are the forces that motivate firms to make resource trade-offs during the R&D process of development?" Our finding indicate that, unlike much of the exploration/exploitation literature which grounds itself in the resource-based view of the firm, resource dependence and agency theory provide a better explanation of the external and internal factors that pressure firms to choose between exploration and exploitation research during development.

Our chapter begins with a discussion of the exploration and exploitation innovation literature. We then discuss our methods and provide details about the specific sites where the data was collected. We go on to discuss our findings, suggesting propositions which while drawn from our research, could also serve as avenues for future inquires. Specifically, we find that tenets drawn from both agency theory and from resource dependence theory help to further our understanding of the exploration/exploitation trade-off. We conclude with the limitations of our present inquiry.

EXPLORATION, EXPLOITATION, AND THE PROCESS OF INNOVATION

Innovation is either a tangible output or a process (Larson & Brahmakulam, 2002). It is defined as a "new technology," a "management practice that is being used for the first time," or as a "significant improvement in a process or product" (O'Neill, Pouder, & Buchholtz, 1998). When viewed as a process, innovation is logically partitioned into different temporal phases through which innovations proceed. The phases include idea search; selection; design; development; production, and market launch (Cooper & Kleinschmidt, 1986; Dooley & O'Sullivan, 2001; Knox, 2002; Rogers, 1995).

Exploration and exploitation research has primarily focused on the search, selection, and design phases of the innovation process (Lavie & Rosenkopf, 2006; Li et al., 2008; Medcof, 2010). Innovation research, using exploration/exploitation perspectives, has viewed the engineering/ development phase as a "black box" where development proceeds unhindered or unchanged (Garcia, Calantone, & Levine, 2003). This is because successful product development, regardless of its exploratory or exploitative nature has been found to require similar skills (Cooper, Edgett, & Kleinschmidt, 2004; Kahn, Barczka, & Moss, 2006). For instance, Goktan and Miles (2011) conducted a survey of 500 technology firms and found that, contrary to expectations; radical product innovation development was not negatively related to the amount of time spent on a particular project. Projects under development had similar development productivity. Their study considered new products for new customers and newness to the firm as the most radical and exploratory. Similar results were found by Parry, Song, and Weerd-Nederhof (2009) in a study of technology oriented product firms. Their study also found that, when projects involving breakthroughs were underway, they did not exceed planned development more than incremental projects.

To date, however, researchers have not studied the exploration and exploitation trade-off phenomenon as projects proceed through the development phase of the product development process. In other words, research has not investigated the extent to which resources are removed or added to projects, or whether projects are delayed or eliminated after planning ends and development begins. Comparing the progress of exploration projects with the progress of exploitation projects under conditions where everyday forces, such as the need to acquire revenue, has been overlooked in scholarship. Yet, these issues may significantly alter the firms' priorities and hence the balance of these types of projects that are completed.

Therefore, to understand innovation rates and also at outcomes in the market after development is over, exploration research has looked predominantly at strategy-planning phases prior to engineering in larger firms (Li et al., 2008; Sidhu, Commandeur, & Volberda, 2007). In contrast, we consider whether exploration outcomes are dependent on all of the phases of product development including the R&D phase which commences after plans are set, and whether the amount of exploration innovation that progresses changes. In addition, we look at this in resource constrained SMEs.

METHODS

This investigation was an exploratory qualitative study of the innovation practices of twelve firms; nine in the software industry and three venture capital (VC) firms that invest in early stage software firms. The unit of analysis is the planned portfolio of development projects as it proceeds through R&D. What the detailed analysis of nine software firms provides us with, that other research design cannot, is an intensive investigation of processes, which reveals the common patterns among projects. The limits of qualitative research are well documented: we do not know the extent that findings from this inquiry can be generalized to larger populations. The value of the research instead lies in its ability to provide insights through rich detail, and to provide directions for future inquiries.

Sample Criteria and Selection

The research was undertaken to specifically explore the balance between exploration and exploitation projects in software SMEs. Software was chosen as the focal industry because the industry is both highly innovation intensive, and most of the innovation is generated by the firms in the industry and not by external suppliers (Medcof, 1999). The inquiry focused on SMEs because they were likely to be more resource constrained and so if there was a tension between exploration and exploration innovation, that tension would be evident in smaller organizations.

The nine software firms investigated had a number of things in common. All of them had frequent product development projects and demonstrated product development competence. In addition, all of them engaged in both exploratory and exploitative research and development projects. While still relatively young firms, all of the firms have been in business for at least three years, and so were past the initial start-up challenges that many new ventures encounter. The firms differed in size from small ($N = 10$ employees) to medium sized ($N = 500$ employees); however, all of the firms that were studied were large enough to have individuals who performed distinct functions, and therefore chains of command and reporting relationships were well established. Finally, the overall competitive environment for software was relatively similar across the nine firms, thereby controlling to at least some extent, differences arising for disparate external environments.

In addition to interviewing principals from the software industry, in this inquiry we also included data from interviews with three VC firms. These VC firms all invest in software development (although not specifically in the nine software firms that we interviewed) and so are familiar with the tensions inherent in small firms. In our study, each VC firm has historically made many investments in small software development firms and currently has multiple software firms in their investment portfolio. As is typical in VC, the venture capitalist interviewed held a board seat and has regular interaction with the software firms in its portfolio. As such, their close work with managers of many software firms provide them with insight gained from many experiences – versus the narrower insight an employee of a single software firm might bring. Given that our objective in this qualitative inquiry was to uncover possible explanations for the shift in innovation practices, adding evidence from investment firms helps to add robustness to our findings.

Data Collection and Analysis

Interviewing was adopted as the main method of investigation because of its ability to capture rich detail and also because there is a strong indication in the literature that understanding the context in which development occurs is extremely important (Eisenhardt, 1989; Eisenhardt & Grabner, 2007). Interviews were conducted with 16 individuals across the nine software organizations over a 12-month period (Table 1). The interviewees were mostly with the CEO and the head of development (R&D). Complexity of organization varied at firms; interviews were extended to other key personnel when available. The average length of interview was 1.25 hours, although interviews varied in length from 0.75 hour to over 2 hours. In addition, we interviewed three VC partners, each of whom had extensive experience working with and investing in, software development firms. Each of the partners interviewed currently sat on multiple boards of directors; however over the course of their careers, all of the venture capitalists interviewed had been integral members of many software development firms' boards. In their role as a member of the governing board, the VCs were privy to all of the debates, challenges, and trade-offs made by software development firms as they struggled to balance new and existing product development demands. Table 1 provides a breakdown of the number of individuals interviewed per organization and the length of each contact.

All of the interviews were conducted by the lead author and followed a predesigned interview protocol, which included preliminary questions about firm history and organization. Questions in the interview protocol were developed based on extensive review of the innovation literature as well as the wealth of experience that one of the members of the research

Table 1. Interview Data.

Organizational Type	Number of Organizations	Location	Business Focus	Number of Interviews Conducted	Interviewees
Venture capital	Three	MA	Technology Early- and mid-stage investments	Three plus follow-up	Board members Firm partners
Midsize software firm	Four	MA	Business-to-business Hardware and software	Six plus follow-up	CEO, VP engineering, product manager, VP sales
Small software firm	Five	MA	Business-to-business Software	Seven plus follow-up	CEO, VP engineering, VP sales

team had in the software development field. Appendix A presents the interview protocol. Only after the interviews were completed and the was data analyzed did findings emerge which not only highlighted the exploration/ exploitation trade-off challenges in the development phase of the software development innovation process, but also pointed to possible theoretical lenses through which to understand those challenges.

As is typical in inductive studies, analyzing the data was an iterative process in which the data was constantly revisited (Eisenhardt, 1989; Yin, 2008). NVIVO 10, a computer-aided text analysis (CATA) software program, was used for coding the interview data. Data coding was also an iterative process in which the research team searched the data for regularities and patterns and then recorded these key words and phrases to represent topics or themes which became the categories for further study (Bogdan & Biklen, 2007). It was our analysis of these themes that led us to focus on the internal and external factors which inhibit exploratory product development.

Reliability and Validity of the Findings

Checks for reliability are important because coding is subjective and therefore has the potential for rater bias. To ensure that our findings were reliable, interview data were first coded by one of the principal investigators to find patterns across interviews. Constructs emerged from these patterns. For consistency, a second coder was then employed to repeat the process. Cohen's Kappa, a statistic used to ensure inter-rater reliability, was calculated and results range from a low of 75% to a high of 87% which is well within the acceptable range (Landis & Koch, 1977).

Research suggests that the processes involved in analyzing qualitative data have motivated a change in the traditional frameworks that were used for ensuring the data validity (Erlandson, Harris, Skipper, & Allen, 1993). Specifically, to ensure validity, qualitative data must be checked against the criteria of credibility and transferability. In this study, data categories were identified across the nine firms to ensure data credibility. In addition, after each firm was interviewed, findings were sent to the interviewee as a way to ensure the validity of the findings. Data transferability was addressed by employing an interview protocol for collecting data that utilized questions that were primarily drawn from the existing literature. In relying on previous literature to ground our inquiry, future researchers examining project learning could potentially apply the interview protocol to their own studies.

The Interview Sites: Small and Medium Size Software Firms

The in-firm interview portion of this study was carried out in nine computer software firms. They were each chosen for their size, level of technology,
and type of business, as well as their need to make trade-offs between
exploration and exploitation innovation activities. The organizations
studied were all large enough to be differentiated into functional roles;
however, the firms were all small enough that strong personal ties within
the organization existed. For example, most employees were familiar with
management, and managers were all on a first name basis.

Each of the software firms was privately owned, and in each case the
ownership was shared between the company founders and external VC
firms. All of the firms were founded between 1995 and 2000, and most
employees had stock options. In five out of the nine software firms, the
company founders were in senior roles as either CEO or Chief Technology
Officer. Because the firms were private, exact firm size data is not available;
however, when asked, respondents indicated that the firm revenue range
was between $1 million for the smallest firm and up to $50 million for the
largest.

Each firm had a single main office location but in all but two firms,
remote salespeople worked from home. Every firm's place of business was
similar. Each firm was located in a ubiquitous office park with relatively
homogenous offices consisting of large rooms for each main department,
sectioned by cubicles. A few senior employees had offices with doors, and
conference rooms ringed the periphery. The largest space in each firm was
for R&D.

All the software firms were business-to business-focused; however, there
was variation in the target customer. Four firms developed software that
was industry-specific such as banking software or aviation logistic software.
Five firms produced more general purpose software that could be used at
most businesses such as data-base search, data management software, or
communications software. Therefore, their products ranged from modular
application packages for one market, to complex system configuration
software. Customization was avoided by all the firms. Customer requests –
which came often – were addressed by adding the change to the list of
features that were to be added into the standard product. In this way, it
would be included in development and become part of the upgrade for all
installations.

Customer profiles varied as some firms had a concentrated customer
base which consisted of a smaller number of large customers, while others

had hundreds of relatively equal sized customers. Customer acquisition and retention, however, had similar characteristics. Purchases would most often occur after a direct sales effort. A version of the product was usually given to a prospect as a free trial, and the selling effort was done by a combination of a sales person along with a technical field engineer. In all cases, a purchase meant that the customer was entering into a long-term relationship with the software provider. Installed software was anticipated to operate for years or decades with regular updates, upgrades, and new versions. Customers typically paid a yearly maintenance fee of 10−15% of list price for access to support and to obtain all future enhancements. In some instances, training was given to the end users, along with on-site assistance for the initial installation and to ensure the customer's computer platform was adequate for the new software program.

The products varied in importance to the end customer. For some of the software products, the software was important to the functioning of the customers' operations, and any downtime was considered a crisis. Every software firm expected to have regular contact with their customers every year.

All of the individuals interviewed for this inquiry were upper level managers. Specifically, we talked to either the Chief Executive Officer, or top managers such as the Vice President of Sales, the Vice President or Director of R&D, and the technical Product Manager. These respondents were all directly involved in decision-making concerning development plans, and so knew how priorities were set and changed in day-to-day operations.

All of the executives interviewed had strong opinions about the importance of new product development for the direction to the firm. Differences in emphasis, however, were consistent across firms. While the CEO was directly connected to development and actively involved in setting direction and priorities, they also each spent a great deal of time understanding the status of engineering tasks, the needs of the customers and the overall revenue profile. In contrast, engineering management discussed challenges around technology while sales management, emphasized the demands of the customers, and the need to meet those demands. Product managers would lament that they could never keep the plans on track long enough for engineers to finish anything. Nevertheless, all executives from CEO to product manager and in every firm seemed to believe that the "next release" would largely solve their respective problems.

In each firm, research and development worked on many projects simultaneously. While some subcontracting of development or license of specialty code might be done, the bulk of every product was created internally.

Normally, any one individual engineer spanned multiple projects, or was pulled into a project for a short duration in order to supply a narrow programming skill or subject expertise. Projects often consisted of a single developer. Much development time was spent on issues surrounding software architecture, scalability, and feature design. Actual coding of software was a lower level task. However, it was clear that management recognized the differences in the coding capabilities of individual software engineers.

VC Firms

In addition to interviewing software firms, we also talked with three venture finance organizations. These firms were chosen because each had specific expertise in investing in software ventures. We chose to target the investors because they had the potential to contribute insight into development decision making in software firms.

All individuals interviewed were experienced VC investors. Each VC interviewed was a partner and had both invested in and sat on, multiple boards of early stage, business-to-business, software firms. The venture firms included in the analysis varied in size and age, but each had over a decade of experience. Each firm tended to limit the geography in which it would invest to the greater Boston area, which included southern New Hampshire.

Beyond attending board meetings, interviewees spent much of their time fostering close working relationships with the senior managers of portfolio companies in an attempt to understand and help them with their businesses. Interviewees all expressed strong personal ties within members of the software firms they had oversight responsibility for; especially the CEO. Their ability and willingness to bring value to the firms was consistently discussed. The type of assistance they provided was generally in forming go-to-market strategy, recruiting executives, financing, customer introductions, and general problem solving.

FINDINGS AND DISCUSSION

Exploration and exploitation activities have been described as two fundamentally different directions which compete for limited organizational resources (March, 1991). Existing research suggests that, because firms are subject to organizational inertia, existing practices and processes obstruct more novel product development, causing firms to undertake an insufficient amount of explorative innovation (Benner & Tushman, 2003; Rosenkopf & Almeida, 2003). To remedy this, studies call for a balance between these two activities (e.g., He & Wong, 2004). This balance is an attempt to manage the tension between the need to compete in the existing market and the corresponding need to address new opportunities for future growth.

However, to date, little research has looked into the development phase of the project development process to see what happens to the planned balance between exploration projects and exploitation projects once planning ends and development proceeds. This was the initial objective of this inquiry. Our findings suggest that there is indeed a significant tension between these two types of innovation. This tension became evident when we looked at the disruption caused by shifting manpower and its subsequent impact on new product features and adherence to the original production schedule.

Moving from Exploration to Exploitation

The findings from our study indicate that firms change their mix of exploration/exploitation projects during the development phase, moving from exploration toward more short-term exploitative innovation. This manifests itself in the movement of manpower. Manpower refers to the amount of engineering resources available for R&D project development. Changes to the manpower allocated to a project impacts when the project will be completed and the number and intricacy of the features in the project. Findings from the interviews was consistent across all nine software development firms and suggests that when issues with a current revenue generating project arose, manpower, which was originally assigned to an explorative R&D project, was regularly diverted off that project to handle the immediate situation.

> That's not hard to recall [when an innovation had to be postponed due to an immediate customer demand], because it happened this morning. A customer decided not to buy unless we made changes. This was customer to sales and project manager. When the 23 item list came in, we had to just stop and do the list. Manager – Software Development

In addition to the disruption in the exploration project, moving manpower also has the effect of reducing the overall number and level of complexity of the new, exploration product features.

> What tends to occur is that things have dropped from the [new product] release. So the release may come out within a month of when it was projected to, but it might not have what was initially put into it. You're not going to push out the release date, you drop the stuff. Software Firm Board Member

Our findings also indicate that changes in manpower result in slipped exploration project schedules. In fact, exploration innovation was reported to be approximately 45% lower, on average across firms, than the firms had originally planned to produce. More specifically, interviewees consistently indicate that exploration projects were behind schedule more often than other project types; the start date for exploration projects was delayed; and the length of the overall project was typically significantly longer than planned for exploration projects versus planned exploitation projects.

> We don't hire more [engineers]. We only have so many [engineers] and we have only so many engineers. What gets pushed is anything that won't bring in revenue this year. Let's say you've got a release and the release includes some stuff that you've got to get to a customer, and it includes some innovation that can be pushed out another quarter, then you're going to push out the innovation and you're going to get the stuff to the customer on time. CEO – Software Development Firm

Our findings indicate that firms regularly change their mix of projects during the development stage, moving from exploration projects to projects which can be categorized as more exploitative. The shift manifests itself in the reallocation of manpower. Manpower reallocation is extremely disruptive for exploratory innovation projects. It results in significant delays or in a reduction in project features so that predetermined software release dates for current-product customers can be met. In sum, when resources are scarce, exploitive demands supersede exploratory innovations and exploratory innovation is postponed. This leads us to propose:

Proposition 1. During the development phase, manpower shifts from exploration projects to exploitation projects. This change results in fewer exploration projects, late projects, or projects with fewer features than originally planned.

At some point during our qualitative inquiry, our focus shifted from the baseline question that looked at the existence of a change in project priorities, to trying to develop a better understanding of the underlying reasons why the shifts from exploration to exploitation innovation occur. Our analysis of the data suggests two reasons; external forces in the form of resource dependences and internal forces in the form of agency influences. These are discussed below.

Changes in the Exploration/Exploitation Project Mix: The Role of Resource Dependencies

In resource dependency theory the external environment is the source of resources which are fundamental to the organization's performance, and these resources shape the structure, boundaries, and internal activity of the organization (Pfeffer & Salancik, 1978). The control of these valuable resources gives external firms power over the focal organization (*ibid.*). Resources can take different forms at different points on the value chain, from raw materials, to financial resources, to revenue.

Much of the empirical literature on resource dependence has looked at power dynamics in the context of mergers, acquisitions, and joint ventures (Hillman, Cannella, & Paetzold, 2000; Hillman, Withers, & Collins, 2009), boards of directors (Daily, McDougall, Covin, & Dalton, 2002), and customer–supplier relationships (Fink, Edelman, Hatten, & James, 2006). Little work has been undertaken using resource dependence theory to explain innovation. One exception to this is the work on disruptive technologies done by Christensen and Bower (1996). Using resource dependence logic, they argue that one of the principal reasons why most businesses fail to adopt disruptive technological changes is that they are dependent on their customers for short-term revenue, and in the early stages of a disruptive change, the emerging technology is typically not of the caliber to be adopted by existing customers. Hence, the firm's resource dependence, in terms of its dependence on an existing business model and corresponding revenue stream, lead the firm to make suboptimal innovation investment decisions.

While Christensen and Bower's (1996) research focused on large firms, SMEs are faced with similar trade-offs. Large prospects, customers, and partners are sources of prestige, validation, and revenue. The strong financial promise that these sources of revenue can generate assists firms in raising capital, increasing their valuation and potentially moving them closer to initial public offering (IPO).

> What things do they [venture capitalists and board members] think we need in order to get to exit? You have to show revenue traction. The company does not have to be profitable. You have to have the right type of clients. The Fortune 500 type, top brand names, customers and clients. CEO – Software Development Firm

However, marquee customers also generate regular demand to which the firm must respond; slowing exploration. Evidence from both the CEOs and the VCs interviewed was consistent: important customer demands retards exploration innovation.

Basically there are periods where – gotta do the big deal, gotta do the big deal, so product development slips. I mean, I can show you exactly how much the business development work accounts for a slip in our major product release – our new product release. VP Engineering – Software Development Firm

In sum, while high-status customers offer SMEs prestige, legitimacy, and potential revenue, they also place significant demands on small firms. These demands can lead to a shift in focus from exploration exploitation. Hence we propose:

Proposition 2. During the development phase, revenue resource dependencies lead SMEs to change their project mix from exploration to exploitation.

Agency Influences in the Change in the Exploration/Exploitation Project Mix
Agency theory is the study of the issues that arise from the agency relationship, particularly the situation where the principal and agent, while ostensibly working toward the same goal, may not always share the same interests (Jenson & Meckling, 1976). As both the principal and the agent navigate the agency relationship, agency costs are incurred (*ibid.*, 5). Much of the work on agency costs has focused on the costs incurred by the principal arising from asymmetric information and can lead to the agent acting opportunistically as well as the principal making suboptimal decisions. Specifically, researchers have focused on hidden actions and hidden information (Arrow, 1985). Hidden actions, more commonly known as moral hazard, lead to agency costs when the principal cannot directly observe the agent's actions. In this situation, the agent typically has more information than the principal, providing the agent with the incentive to act inappropriately, from the perspective of the principal. Adverse selection, also arising from "hidden information," leads to agency costs when the agent is better informed than the principal, and then uses this asymmetric information advantage for personal gain (Bromley, 1989). Both of these situations result in potential cost to the principal.

One important tenet of agency theory is goal incongruence. Goal incongruence is present when the goals or desires of the agent and principal diverge (Eisenhardt, 1989). Goal incongruity is manifested at all organizational levels through issues around delegation (Baumol, 1967; Jensen & Meckling, 1976). In the innovation literature, researchers have considered goal incongruence in relation to the performance of development projects (Eisenhardt, 1989; Jap & Anderson, 2003; Rossetti & Choi, 2008).

In the case of software development, interview data suggests that at every firm there were numerous situations of goal incongruence and opportunist behavior. Managers argued that the salespeople (agents) pursued enhancing personal compensation and that this activity was misaligned with management's innovation objective (principal). They reported that salespeople regularly requested exploitation projects with short-term positive revenue consequences receive special priority and be added to development. Thus the development plan, as originally set by the principal, could become skewed away from a balance between exploration and exploitation.

> They're [salespeople] trying to advance the features so they could accelerate a deal. But, the customer said, "I like your product. I'll wait for your feature, but I won't buy until next quarter — if you could accelerate the feature into this quarter, I will buy." So they [salespeople] will commit and then put the company over a barrel. So, if they feel they can do that and they can manipulate the system, they will do that. VP Sales — Software Development Firm

Bonding refers to the efforts of the agent to signal alignment with the principal (Jensen & Meckling, 1976). Bonding leads an agent to take action that would not normally be taken, with the express intent of demonstrating to the principal that their goals are aligned. Bonding behavior may lead CEOs (agent) to pursue marquee customers in order to signal the board (principal) that the young firm is a legitimate entity and that progress is being made.

> We share the good news [about specific customers with the board], it builds confidence in the business. So, we do it whenever we can. We'll brag about some of those things, or we'll talk about the big fish that we're working on. CEO — Software Development Firm

In sum, while the overall objective of agents and principals is to move the company forward, in all of the firms we investigated, hidden information led to opportunistic behavior on the part of the agent. This behavior skews the product mix away from longer-term exploratory research and toward more immediate customer-driven exploitative projects. Bonding behavior, designed to demonstrate the existence of goal alignment, may also serve to skew the product mix as prestigious customers' desires are seen as a top priority. Therefore we suggest the following:

Proposition 3. During the development phase, agency behavior, and specifically goal incongruence and bonding behavior, leads SMEs to change their project mix from exploration to exploitation.

LIMITATIONS, IMPLICATIONS, AND CONCLUSIONS

As global rivalry increases, the tension between short-term, customer facing exploitation, with its tangible and immediate payoffs will continue to challenge plans for longer-term, exploration innovation. However, research indicates that between 30% and 50% of firm sales and profits come from products introduced within the previous five years (Griffin, 1997; Hauser, Tellis, & Griffin, 2005). This suggests that despite the sirens of short-term exploitative development, to remain viable firms must pursue exploration innovation.

In this study we confirm that a shift during the development phase from exploration to exploitation innovation is occurring in SMEs, something that is not well documented in the literature to date. We then begin to explore the reasons for this shift in emphasis. We do this by interviewing high-level executives in nine Boston-based software development firms, and three venture capitalists who invest in software. Our findings suggest that the shift is driven by both internal and external forces. Externally, resource demands, specifically financial ones, drive resource constrained small and medium-sized enterprises to supersede longer-term, less revenue certain exploration research with shorter-term, revenue producing exploitative work. Internally, agency influences such as opportunism and bonding drive salespeople and top executives to emphasize their immediate personal successes. For salespeople, this takes the form of pressuring research and development to act upon immediate customer demands for short-term product improvements in order to secure new orders. For CEOs this takes the form of promoting the marquee customers and relationships to their board and other investors. However, no matter the form, opportunism, combined with asymmetric or hidden information allows the agent to promote short-term demands over longer-term, exploratory innovation, planned projects.

While this study explores product development trade-offs and suggests possible reasons for those trade-offs, it is not without limitations. Our inquiry was limited to New England based small and medium-sized software firms and venture capitalists who invest in those types of organizations. While we believe this to be an appropriate set of firms to learn about the trade-offs between exploration and exploitation innovation, it is a limited set of companies and our results must be interpreted with caution. Future research could build on this inquiry by conducting a more comprehensive investigation using a larger number of firms within the software industry or a more generalizable set of industries. In addition, while our initial conclusions point to agency and resource dependence explanations, there are likely to be other compelling rationales that were not investigated. Finally, this is an in-depth qualitative study of a small number of firms, but a larger, quantitative data collection effort, either focused on one industry or across industries would allow us to determine the generalizability of our findings across industries or populations.

Limitations notwithstanding, this inquiry begins to shed light on the balance of innovation that small and medium-sized software firms ultimately produce, and what drives the decisions behind the mix of exploration versus exploitation innovation. For scholars, this research suggests two well-regarded organization theories, resource dependence and agency, might explain how external and internal forces drive the innovation-type choices. For managers, this work starts to shed light on why their innovations mix changes. All firms need to respond to their customer's requests while at the same time planning for the future, and this study highlights the difficulty managers have balancing the tension between exploration and exploitation innovation.

ACKNOWLEDGMENT

The authors would like to acknowledge Scott Latham and Mike Hitt for their helpful comments on a previous version of this document.

REFERENCES

Aldrich, H. E., & Auster, E. R. (1986). Even dwarfs started small: Liabilities of age and size and their strategic implications. In B. M. Staw & L. L. Cummings (Eds.), *Research in organizational behavior* (Vol. 8, pp. 165–198). Greenwich, CT: JAI Press.

Arrow, K. J. (1985). The economics of agency. In J. W. Pratt & R. J. Zeckhauser (Eds.), *Principals and agents. The structure of business* (pp. 37–51).

Baumol, W. (1967). *Business behavior, value and growth*. New York, NY: Harcourt, Brace and World.

Benner, M., & Tushman, M. (2003). Exploitation, exploration, and process management: The productivity dilemma revisited. *The Academy of Management Review, 28*(2), 238–256.

Bogdan, R. C., & Biklen, S. K. (2007). Qualitative research for education: An introduction to theory and methods, *Boston, MA*: Pearson.

Bromley, D. (1989). *Economic interests and institutions: The conceptual foundations of public policy*. Oxford: Basil Blackwell.

Burgelman, R. A. (1991). Intraorganizational ecology of strategy making and organizational adaptation: Theory and field research. *Organization Science, 2*(3), 239–262.

Burgelman, R. A. (2002). Strategy as vector and the inertia of coevolutionary lock-in. *Administrative Science Quarterly, 47*(2), 325–357.

Christensen, C., & Bower, L. (1996). Customer power, strategic investment, and the failure of leading firms. *Strategic Management Journal, 17*(3), 197–218.

Cooper, R., Edgett, S., & Kleinschmidt, E. (2004). Benchmarking best NPD practices. *Research Technology Management, 1*, 31–43.

Cooper, R., & Kleinschmidt, E. (1986). An investigation into the new product process: Steps, deficiencies, and impact. *Journal of Product Innovation Management, 3*(2), 71–85.

Daily, C. P., McDougall, J., Covin, J., & Dalton, D. (2002). Governance and strategic leadership in entrepreneurial firms. *Journal of Management, 28*, 387–412.

Danneels, E. (2007). The process of technological competence leveraging. *Strategic Management Journal, 28*, 511–533.

Dooley, L., & O'Sullivan, D. (2001). Structuring innovation: A conceptual model and implementation methodology. *Enterprise and Innovation Management Studies, 2*(3), 177–194.

Eisenhardt, K., & Graebner, M. (2007). Theory building from cases: Opportunities and challenges. *Academy of Management Journal, 50*(1), 25–32.

Eisenhardt, K. M. (1989). Making fast strategic decisions in high-velocity environments. *Academy of Management Journal, 32*(3), 543–576.

Erlandson, D., Harris, B. L., Skipper, B. L., & Allen, D. S. (1993). Quality criteria for a naturalistic study. *Doing naturalistic inquiry*. Newbury Park, CA: Sage.

Fink, R., Edelman, L., Hatten, K., & James, W. (2006). Relational exchange strategies, performance, uncertainty and knowledge. *Journal of Marketing Theory and Practice, 14*(2), 139–153.

Garcia, R., Calantone, R., & Levine, R. (2003). The role of knowledge in resource allocation to exploration versus exploitation in technologically organizations. *Decision Sciences, 34*, 323.

Goktan, A., & Miles, G. (2011). Innovation speed and radicalness: Are they inversely related? *Management Decision, 49*(4), 533–547.

Griffin, A. (1997). PDMA research on new product development practices: Updating trends and benchmarking best practices. *Journal of Product Innovation Management, 14*, 429–458.

Gupta, A. K., Smith, K. G., & Shalley, C. E. (2006). The interplay between exploration and exploitation. *Academy of Management Journal, 49*(4), 693–706.

Hannan, M., & Freeman, J. (1984). Structural inertia and organizational change. *American Sociological Review, 49*(2), 149–164.

Hauser, J., Tellis, G., & Griffin, A. (2005). *Research on innovation: A review and agenda for marketing science*. Special Report No. 05-200f. Cambridge, MA: Marketing Science Institute.

He, Z., & Wong, P. (2004). Exploration vs. exploitation: An empirical test of the ambidexterity hypothesis. *Organization Science, 15*, 481–494.

Hillman, A., Cannella, A., & Paetzold, R. (2000). The resource dependence role of corporate directors: Strategic adaptation of board composition in response to environmental change. *Journal of Management Studies, 37*, 235–256.

Hillman, A., Withers, M., & Collins, B. (2009). Resource dependence theory: A review. *Journal of Management, 35*(6), 1404–1427.

Hoang, H., & Rothaermel, F. (2010). Leveraging internal and external experience: Exploration, exploitation, and project performance. *Strategic Management Journal, 31*(7), 734–758.

Jap, S., & Anderson, E. (2003). Safeguarding interorganizational performance and continuity under ex post opportunism. *Management Science, 49*(12), 1684–1701.

Jensen, M., & Meckling, W. (1976). Theory of the firm: Managerial behavior, agency cost and ownership structure. *Journal of Financial Economics, 3*, 305–360.

Kahn, K., Barczak, G., & Moss, R. (2006). Establishing an NPD best practices framework. *Journal of Product Innovation Management, 23*(2), 106–116.

Knox, S. (2002). The boardroom agenda: Developing the innovative organization. *Corporate Governance, 2*(1), 27–39.

Landis, J., & Koch, G. (1977). The measurement of observer agreement for categorical data. *Biometrics, 33*, 159–174.

Larson, E., & Brahmakulam, I. (2002). *Building a new foundation for innovation: Results of a workshop for the National Science Foundation.* Santa Monica, CA: RAND Corporation.

Lavie, D., & Rosenkopf, L. (2006). Balancing exploration and exploitation alliance formation. *Academy of Management Journal, 49*, 797–818.

Levinthal, D. A. (1997). Adaptation on rugged landscapes. *Management Science, 43*(7), 934–950.

Levinthal, D. A., & March, J. G. (1993). The myopia of learning. *Strategic Management Journal, 14*(S2), 95–112.

Li, C., Lin, C., & Chu, C. (2008). The nature of market orientation and the ambidexterity of innovations. *Management Decision, 46*(7), 1002–1026.

March, J. (1991). Exploration and exploitation in organizational learning. *Organization Science, 2*, 71–87.

Medcof, J. (1999). Identifying 'super-technology industries'. *Research-Technology, 42*(4), 31–36.

Medcof, J. (2010). Exploration, exploitation and technology management. *International Journal of Technology Intelligence and Planning, 6*(4), 301–316.

O'Neill, H., Pouder, R., & Buchholtz, A. (1998). Patterns in the diffusion of strategies across organizations: Insights from the innovation diffusion literature. *The Academy of Management Review, 23*(1), 98–114.

O'Reilly, C., & Tushman, M. (2008). Ambidexterity as a dynamic capability: Resolving the innovator's dilemma. *Research in Organizational Behavior, 28*, 185–206.

Parry, M., Song, M., Weerd-Nederhof, P., & Visscher, K. (2009). The impact of NPD strategy, product strategy, and NPD processes on perceived cycle time. *Journal of Product Innovation Management, 26*, 627–639.

Pfeffer, J., & Salancik, G. (1978, 2003). *The external control of organizations: A resource dependence perspective.* New York, NY: Harper and Row.

Rogers, E. (1995). *Diffusion of innovations.* New York, NY: The Free Press.

Rosenkopf, L., & Almeida, P. (2003). Overcoming local search through alliances and mobility. *Management Science, 49*, 751–766.

Rossetti, C., & Choi, T. (2008). Supply management under high goal incongruence: An empirical examination of disintermediation in the aerospace supply chain. *Decision Science, 39*(3), 369–386.

Sidhu, J., Commandeur, H., & Volberda, H. (2007). The Nature of exploration and exploitation: Value of supply, demand, and spatial search for innovation. *Organization Science, 18*, 20–38.

Siggelkow, N., & Levinthal, D. A. (2003). Temporarily divide to conquer: Centralized, decentralized, and reintegrated organizational approaches to exploration and adaptation. *Organization Science, 14*(6), 650–669.

Smith, W., & Tushman, M. (2005). Managing strategic contradictions: A top management model for managing innovation streams. *Organization Science, 16*(5), 522–536.

Stinchcombe, A. (1965). Social Structure and organizations. In J. G. March (Ed.), *Handbook of organizations* (Vol. 142). Chicago: Rand McNally.

Tushman, M. L., & Romanelli, E. (1985). Organizational evolution: Ametamorphosis model of convergence and reorientation. *Research in organizational behavior* (Vol. 7, pp. 171–222). Greenwich, CT: JAI Press.

Vermeulen, F., & Barkema, H. (2001). Learning through acquisitions. *Academy of Management Journal, 44*(3), 457–476.

Voss, G., Sirdeshmukh, D., & Voss, Z. (2008). The effects of slack resources and environmental threat on product exploration and exploitation. *Academy of Management Journal, 51*(1), 147–164.

Yin, R. (2008). *Case study research: Design and method.* Thousand Oaks, CA: Sage.

APPENDIX: INTERVIEW PROTOCOL

Software Firm Executives

How large is your largest customer − order/revenue?

How many people buy directly from you? What is an average order?

How large is the firm:

- Number of customers?
- Number of employees?

How long have you been in business?

What are the outside investors looking for? Why are they looking for this?

What is their time horizon?

What things − like company performance or technology − do they think they need to get there?

What about big names? Customers or partners? How important to the investors?

CEO: What is your vision for the company in two and five years? What is key to get there?

Do customers regularly ask for features or changes? How often?

Are these customers or prospects?
How do you decide which ones to do?

Who gives you information on it? (Support, Sales, Development, Marketing)
Can you tell me about a larger one?

What drives you to take deals with strings attached?

How big does the deal have to be to influence you? Is it because of the customer name?

Tell me about sales involvement?

How much does it matter if you are behind revenue plan at the end of the quarter?

How often do bugs flow in?

How often do they have a potential to impact revenue?

How do you decide which ones (bugs) to do?

Who gives you information on them? (Support, Sales, Development, Marketing)

How often do you have potential partners arise?

How often do partners who want you to do something to the product?

Are bugs accurately portrayed by sales when they affect one of their customers?

How often are things added to the development work load? Even minor things?

- Added and needs to be started immediately?
- Added and impacts existing projects and existing schedules?

What do these things tend to be?

- Bugs
- New features
- Customer specials
- Partner work
- Infrastructure

Why are they added?

- What's behind it
- Who's behind it? For example, CEO, VP Marketing, VP Sales, Direct from Customer to R&D

What is most disruptive to the schedule?
How much does just the fact that a change is made impact resources?

- Changing development environments
- Updating schedules
- Replanning, etc.

What is the effect on ongoing work? That is, compare the schedule with no interruptions, to the current schedule. What tends to slip?

Can you remember an incident where an innovation was pushed out because of a customer special or a large customer's bug had to be fixed, or a partner project?

How often (percent) do projects arrive after the initial plan schedule?

What would you say the average delay is (months)? As a percent of original time?

What is the biggest category of interruption?

Tell me about a significant project.

What percent of R&D is on innovation — new features or products not for a customer?

How often do releases have Features Missing?

How often do you need engineering to make changes to the product to get an order?

What is the impact on R&D from a change? Please provide an example?

How do promised orders compare with what you end up with? Are they sometimes smaller or bigger or later or earlier than promised?

How about the ones with special requests attached. Why is this?

What is Sales role in getting the company to respond to these offers? Please tell me about sales accuracy on this.

How are sales representatives compensated? — % commission and bonus? What are the repercussions of missing quota?

Owners and Board of Directors

What projects or customers do you bring up at board meetings?

How important is the "fame" to the outside investors, meaning important are marquis partners and marquis customers if there is no revenue benefit over an unknown name?

What are your goals for a typical investment? What do you want any given company to do when you decide to invest?

How important is a big name win in a prior fund for raising the next fund? What things — like company performance or technology — do they think they need to get there?

How often are partner meetings? How often are well known companies a part of your partner meeting to discuss your portfolio companies?

Is the list of larger names something you ask the CEO to give you?

Do you mention these wins in your updates to the investors?

CHAPTER 6

AMBIDEXTERITY AND ORGANIZATIONAL SURVIVAL: EVIDENCE FROM KOREAN SMEs

Guktae Kim and Moon-Goo Huh

ABSTRACT

Despite the theoretical assumption that balancing exploration and exploitation is important for long-term performance and survival, previous studies have provided few insights into these relationships because they have focused mainly on the short-term financial performance of organizations. In addition, balancing exploration and exploitation is a critical challenge for small- and medium-sized enterprises (SMEs) that lack the resources, capabilities, and experience necessary to achieving ambidexterity. In this regards, this study empirically explores the relationship between the exploration–exploitation balance and SMEs' longevity in order to address two important questions from the ambidexterity perspective: (1) How does the balance between exploration and exploitation influence organizational survival? (2) How is the appropriate balance between exploration and exploitation influenced by an organization's internal and external contexts?

An analysis of 1981–2012 data from the Korean SMEs in IT industry reveals an inverted U-shaped curvilinear relationship between the extent

Exploration and Exploitation in Early Stage Ventures and SMEs
Technology, Innovation, Entrepreneurship and Competitive Strategy, Volume 14, 123–148
ISSN: 1479-067X/doi:10.1108/S1479-067X20140000014003

*of exploratory innovation and organizational longevity, providing support
for the ambidexterity perspective. We further examine the moderating
effects of financial slack and environmental dynamism on the relationship
between exploratory innovation and organizational longevity. The results
indicate that financial slack moderated the exploration–longevity relationship and call for a contingency approach for a better understanding
of performance implications of the exploration–exploitation balance.*

Keywords: Exploration; exploitation; ambidexterity; organizational
longevity; contingency perspective; innovation

INTRODUCTION

With increasing competition and turbulence in the marketplace, organizations have paid increasing attention more to their survival in their industries
than their short-term financial benefits relative to their competitors. In
particular, organizational survival is more critical for small- and medium-
sized enterprises (SMEs) because they tend to lack resources and capabilities
necessary for responding sufficiently to rapidly changing environments.
According to Science and Technology Policy Institute (STEPI, 2008) report
based on a sample of 26,192 Korean venture firms, approximately 1,000
failed each year from 2002 to 2007. The average life span of these firms was
only 5.3 years.

This raises the question of how a firm can thrive over the long term.
A growing consensus among management scholars is that an appropriate
balance between exploration and exploitation can extend firms' longevity
(Burgelman & Creve, 2007; Levinthal & March, 1993; March, 1991).
Therefore, this study focuses on survival implications of balancing exploration and exploitation in the context of technological innovation because
innovation activity is a crucial factor influencing the survival of high-
tech firms. Baumol's (2002) assertion that "under capitalism, innovative
activity – which in other types of fortuitous and optional – becomes
mandatory, a life-and death matter for the firm (p. 1)."

Although several studies have empirically examined the effects of
exploration and exploitation on firm performance, few empirical studies
have considered survival implications of the twin concept. The theoretical
assumption is that balancing exploration and exploitation plays an important role in long-term performance and survival, but, most empirical studies

have focused on the short-term financial performance of organizations (e.g., He & Wong, 2004; Jansen, van den Bosch, & Volberda, 2006; Lubatkin, Simsek, Ling, & Veiga, 2006; Yamakawa, Yang, & Lin, 2011). In this vein, some scholars have highlighted the need for addressing how organizational ambidexterity can contribute to firms' long-term growth and survival (Lavie, Stettner, & Tushman, 2010; Raisch & Birkinshaw, 2008). On the other hand, an appropriate exploration—exploitation balance may quietly vary across firms because of their heterogeneity in terms of their resource endowments as well as differences in environmental dynamics. However, in investigating whether exploration or exploitation is more desirable for firms, only a few studies have considered the role of each firm's unique internal and external conditions such as environmental dynamism (Volberda, 1996), competitive intensity (Auh & Menguc, 2005), and absorptive capacity (Rothaermel & Alexandre, 2009). That is, various internal and external conditions of firms remain largely unexplored.

This study contributes to the literature by exploring the aforementioned issues. More specifically, the study addresses the following two research questions: (1) "How does the balance between exploration and exploitation influence organizational longevity?" (2) "How is a desirable balance between exploration and exploitation influenced by an organization's internal and external contexts?" The study hypothesizes a relationship between the extent of exploratory innovation, which implies the exploration—exploitation balance, and organizational longevity and argues that the effect of the extent of exploratory innovation on organizational longevity is moderated by the organization's organizational slack and environmental dynamism.

This study considers a sample of 255 SMEs in Korean IT-related industries for the 1981—2012 period. This sample provides this study with an appropriate context because IT-related SMEs are highly likely to fail and tend to place great emphasis on innovation activity for their survival.

By empirically testing the hypotheses, the study contributes to the current literature in several ways. First, the study provides clear empirical evidence that the exploration—exploitation balance plays an important role in the organizational longevity of SMEs. Previous studies have rarely paid attention to the relationship between the exploration—exploitation balance and SMEs' performance outcomes, and in addition, they have produced mixed results (e.g., Ebben & Johnson, 2005; Lubatkin et al., 2006; Voss & Voss, 2013). Second, empirical support for the hypotheses is expected to advance the contingency perspective in the ambidexterity literature. Although beneficial effects of the exploration—exploitation balance are widely accepted, the difference in the balance between exploration and exploitation for survival across firms is poorly understood. The results suggest a need for a good fit between a firm's emphasis on innovation activity and its distinct internal and external conditions. Overall, the study fills the gap between theoretical assumptions and empirical evidence in the organizational ambidexterity literature by examining the appropriate balance between exploration and exploitation based on patents and other objective data for a relatively long sample period (1981–2012).

LITERATURE REVIEW AND HYPOTHESES

Innovation as Exploration and Exploitation

March (1991) proposed that exploration and exploitation are two fundamentally different learning activities by defining exploration as "search, variation, risk-taking, experimentation, play, flexibility, discovery, and innovation" and exploitation as "refinement, choice, production, efficiency, selection, implementation, and execution" (p. 71). The notion of exploration—exploitation was subsequently refined and expanded in diverse ways in the literatures including organizational learning (e.g., Levinthal & March, 1993), organizational design (e.g., Tushman & O'Reilly, 1996), technological innovation (e.g., Greve, 2007; He & Wong, 2004), knowledge management (e.g., Katila & Ahuja, 2002; Wang & Li, 2008), and even strategic alliances (e.g., Yamakawa et al., 2011).

This study focuses on exploration and exploitation in terms of technological innovation. Based on previous research, we classify innovations as exploration and exploitation: (1) exploratory innovation is a form of radical innovation requiring new knowledge from existing knowledge to meet the needs of emerging customers or markets (Benner & Tushman, 2002; Levinthal & March, 1993). By contrast, (2) exploitative innovation is a form of incremental innovation that reinforces existing knowledge, skills, products, and processes to meet the needs of existing customers or markets (Abernathy & Clark, 1985; Benner & Tushman, 2003; Danneels, 2002).

A crucial issue in the conceptualization of exploration and exploitation entails the question "Are exploration and exploitation two ends of a continuum or two different and orthogonal aspects of organizational behavior?" (Gupta, Smith, & Shalley, 2006, p. 693). In view of continuity, exploration and exploitation compete for scarce organizational resources. This means that more resources devoted to exploration imply fewer resources for exploitation and vice versa (Gupta et al., 2006). On the other hand, in view of orthogonality, these two activities are independent, and therefore organizations can achieve high levels of both simultaneously (e.g., He & Wong, 2004; Katila & Ahuja, 2002).

Answering the question of continuity or orthogonality may depend on the level of analysis and the research context (Gupta et al., 2006). This study conceptualizes exploratory and exploitative innovation as the opposite ends of a continuum instead of orthogonal choices. Because firms' innovation activities compete for scarce R&D resources such as R&D investment, R&D manpower, and equipment, they have to decide on placing greater emphasis on exploration versus exploitation. In particular, it more reasonable for SMEs those are less likely to have separate domains for each innovation activity. In addition, this approach is fairly consistent with March's (1991) original assumption that "both exploration and exploitation are essential for organizations, but they compete for scarce resources" (p. 71) as well as with some recent studies considering exploration and exploitation as a continuum (e.g., Ebben & Johnson, 2005; Lavie & Rosenkopf, 2006; Lavie et al., 2010; Levinthal & Posen, 2008; Perretti & Negro, 2006; Rothaermel & Deeds, 2004; Uotila, Maula, Keil, & Zahra, 2009; Wadhwa & Kotha, 2006; Wang & Li, 2008; Yamakawa et al., 2011). Through this conceptualization of exploration and exploitation as a continuum, this study provides direct evidence supporting March's original assumptions about an appropriate balance between exploration and exploitation.

The Exploration−Exploitation Balance and Organizational Longevity

Exploitative innovation activities can lead to positive short-term performance by reducing variety, increasing efficiency, and improving adaptation to the current environment. However, excessive exploitation can reduce a firm's ability to discover new opportunities and respond to rapidly changing environmental conditions over time (Ahuja & Lampert, 2001; Raisch & Birkinshaw, 2008). That is, a firm's pursuit of short-term success can jeopardize its long-term success. Levinthal and March (1993) referred to this phenomenon as the "success trap." Exploitative innovation provides diminishing returns over time because of the obsolescence of existing technologies (Katila & Ahuja, 2002). In addition, excessive exploitative innovation may cause organizational rigidity. Firms exploiting only their existing knowledge and technologies can become susceptible to environmental changes (Levinthal & March, 1993).

To enhance their ability to respond to environmental changes and reduce the risk of obsolescence, firms need to engage in exploratory innovation activities that can facilitate the development of new knowledge and technologies (Uotila et al., 2009). However, compared with returns from exploitation, those from exploration are systematically less certain and more remote over time (March, 1991). Therefore, overexploration can lead to an endless cycle of searches and unrewarding changes, that is, the "failure trap" (Levinthal & March, 1993). In other words, because most exploratory innovation projects require a long time to be realized (Greve, 2003), firms pursuing only exploratory innovation may fail to maintain their existing viability.

Therefore, an organization's long-term survival and prosperity depend on its ability to "engage in sufficient exploitation to ensure its current viability and, at the same time, to devote enough energy to exploration to ensure its future viability" (Levinthal & March, 1993, p. 105). Although exploration and exploitation have a close trade-off relationship at any given point in time, exploratory innovation provides firms with opportunities that can be exploited over time. In turn, returns from exploitive innovation can support future exploration (Lavie et al., 2010). In this regard, March (1991) initially argued that organizations need to manage an appropriate balance between exploration and exploitation for their survival and long-term performance. In addition, several empirical studies have highlighted the benefits of balancing exploration and exploitation (Cottrell & Nault, 2004; He & Wong, 2004; Uotila et al., 2009; Wang & Li, 2008).

Based on the above theoretical argument and empirical evidence, this study proposes that organizations pursuing a balance between exploratory and exploitative innovation are more likely to survive than those placing excessive emphasis on only one of the two. This balance can be expressed as the extent to which a firm emphasizes exploration activities over exploitation ones, that is, the "extent of exploratory innovation." Therefore, organizational longevity may increase with the extent of exploratory innovation, but beyond a certain point, additional exploratory innovation can reduce longevity. In this regard, the following hypothesis is proposed:

Hypothesis 1. There is an inverted U-shaped curvilinear relationship between the extent of exploratory innovation and organizational longevity.

A Contingency Perspective on Ambidexterity

A key question concerns the appropriate balance between exploration and exploitation. For example, He and Wong (2004) suggested that organizations should maintain an equal proportion of exploratory and exploitative activities such that they can capture the balance as somewhere around the center of the exploration–exploitation continuum. However, should all firms achieve the same balance? Although there are alternative approaches to an appropriate balance, most scholars agree that a desirable balance depends on conditions of firms and industries (Gibson & Birkinshaw, 2004; Lavie et al., 2010; Raisch & Birkinshaw, 2008). In this vein, several empirical studies have examined the moderating effects of conditions of firms (e.g., Rothaermel & Alexandre, 2009) and industries (e.g., Auh & Menguc, 2005; Jansen et al., 2006; Wang & Li, 2008) on the relationship between the exploration–exploitation balance and performance outcomes, but various internal and external conditions of firms remain untested and mixed. In this regard, this study proposes two factors influencing a firm's appropriate balance between exploration and exploitation: its organizational slack and environmental dynamism.

Exploratory and exploitative innovation activities depend on the availability of sufficient resources (Raisch & Birkinshaw, 2008), and environmental dynamism reflects the risks and opportunities associated with a firm's innovation. Because firms are heterogeneous with respect to these conditions, which can influence benefits of each innovation activity, different organizations should emphasize different parts of a continuum reflecting exploratory and exploitative innovation for their long-term survival.

Moderating Role of Organizational Slack

Slack refers to a pool of resources within an organization beyond what is necessary for ordinary operations (Nohria & Gulati, 1996; Sharfman, Wolf, Chase, & Tansik, 1988). Slack and innovation activity are highly relevant. Slack facilitates and maintains innovation efforts by allowing for constant knowledge searches and protecting organizations from the uncertain success of some innovation activity (Levinthal & March, 1981; Nohria & Gulati, 1996). This study considers financial slack, which refers to the least absorbed form of slack and the easiest one to redeploy (Greve, 2003), such as cash on hand, among various forms of slack. Organizations are not constrained in their motivation to use financial slack and thus are willing to allocate financial slack to exploration to strengthen their long-term positions (Voss, Sirdeshmukh, & Voss, 2008).

An appropriate balance between exploratory and exploitative innovation may be contingent on the availability of sufficient resources (Raisch & Birkinshaw, 2008). An organization with a large amount of financial slack can deploy it for exploratory innovation without suffering a failure. Although returns from exploration are uncertain and distant, firms can continuously pursue exploratory innovation. Eventually, long-term intelligence and technologies from sustaining a sufficient level of exploratory innovation can provide organizations with opportunities that can be exploited in the future. In turn, exploitation can yield income that be used for future exploration (Lavie et al., 2010).

By contrast, it is better for an organization with a small amount of financial slack to preserve its slack to solidify ongoing activities and current viability than to use scarce resources for exploratory innovation. Pursuing exploratory and exploitative innovation simultaneously can reduce a firm's resources for the maintenance of current operations (Jansen et al., 2006). In addition, a small amount of slack may not be sufficient to maintain the consistency of exploratory innovation over time. Therefore, if a firm lacks sufficient slack resources, it may be better to place greater emphasis on exploitative innovation than on exploratory innovation for both maintaining current viability and accumulating sufficient resources for future exploratory innovation.

Based on the above discussion, this study proposes that the peak of the inverted U-shaped curvilinear relationship between the extent of exploratory innovation and organizational longevity, which indicates an appropriate balance between exploration and exploitation, moves toward the side of exploratory innovation with an increase in financial slack and vice versa. In this regard, the following hypothesis is proposed:

Hypothesis 2. Financial slack moderates the inverted U-shaped relationship between the extent of exploratory innovation and organizational longevity such that the higher the level of financial slack, the higher the extent of exploratory innovation at which organizational longevity peaks and vice versa.

Moderating Role of Environmental Dynamism
It is well known that external environments have considerable influence on the relationship between innovation and performance (e.g., Zahra, 1996; Zahra & Bogner, 1999). Environmental dynamism refers to the rate of change and the degree of instability in the environment (Dess & Beard, 1984). Dynamic environments may be characterized by changes in technologies, variations in customer preferences, and fluctuations in product

demand or the supply of materials (Jansen et al., 2006) and can make current products and services obsolete (Jansen, van den Bosch, & Volberda, 2005). Previous studies have suggested that environmental dynamism is likely to moderate the effects of exploratory and exploitative innovation on firm performance (Levinthal & March, 1993; Levinthal & Posen, 2008; Wang & Li, 2008).

In a stable environment, organizational viability tends to closely reflect how the firm best takes advantage of its existing knowledge, technologies, and products (Wang & Li, 2008). Therefore, a firm can increase its financial performance in the short term if it engages in exploitative innovation by focusing on its existing capabilities (Henderson & Cockburn, 1994). On the other hand, in such an environment, a firm is not likely to generate benefits from explorative innovation. Rather, excessive exploration can increase unnecessary risks and deplete scarce resources and capabilities necessary for exploitative innovation activities.

By contrast, in industries reflecting strong environmental dynamism, firms not only have more opportunities but also face the risk of their existing technologies becoming rapidly obsolete (Sørensen & Stuart, 2000). Exploitative innovation can make it difficult for a firm to adapt to rapidly changing environment. When a firm's industry is highly dynamic, its existing technologies may not be sufficient for addressing frequent changes in products and technologies (Anderson & Tushman, 1990, 2001; Sirmon, Hitt, & Ireland, 2007). On the other hand, Exploratory innovation can reduce the risk of obsolescence associated with existing technologies and products by developing a number of alternative technologies for responding to changes in the environment (Fleming, 2001; Fleming & Sorenson, 2001). In addition, the abundance of opportunities in a dynamic environment increases potential benefits from successful exploration (Uotila et al., 2009). This suggests that firms in dynamic environments may benefit from focusing more on exploration than on exploitation and vice versa.

Hypothesis 3. Environmental dynamism moderates the inverted U-shaped relationship between the extent of exploratory innovation and organizational longevity such that the higher the level of environmental dynamism, the higher the extent of exploratory innovation at which organizational longevity peaks and vice versa.

Based on the above discussion on the effect of the extent of exploration on organizational longevity and the moderating effects of slack and environments on this relationship, Fig. 1 summarizes the research model and hypotheses.

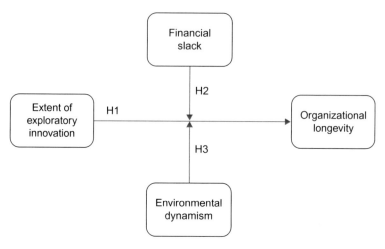

Fig. 1.   Research Model.

METHODS

Sample and Data

We collected data from 255 Korean SMEs in IT-related industries (manufacturers of electronic components, computers, and video/audio/ telecommunications equipment under the Korean Standard Industrial Classification) for 1981–2012 period. We constructed the sampling frame from the TS2000 database of the Korea Listed Companies Association (KLCA). This database provides financial as well as nonfinancial information on firms listed on the Korea Exchange since 1981. From total of 343 KOSDAQ firms in IT-related industries for the 1981–2012 period, we selected 255 SMEs, which employ fewer than 300 persons and/or which have a starting capital not exceeding 8 billion won. Among a total of 255 firms, 81 (34.9%) were delisted for reasons relevant to a firm's failure (capital erosion, unfavorable auditor opinions, and bankruptcy) during the 1981–2011 period, which provides support for the importance of the survival issue in these industries.

   We collected patent data from the WIPS database, including the patent number, the assignee name, the assignee number, the priority number, the filing year, the grant year, and International Patent Classification (IPC) codes. We considered both the registration and publication of patents because we focused not on innovation outcomes but on innovation processes and activities. To obtain historical patent data on survival periods, we tracked firms' name changes by using TS2000. In this way, we collected all patent data for survival periods by searching for all names in the WIPS database.

Measures

Dependent Variable: Organizational Longevity
We measured organizational longevity as the life span of each firm in IT-related industries. More specifically, we measured organizational longevity as the number of days from a firm's listing to its delisting from KOSPI. For firms with no delisting experience, we determined their longevity as the number of days from their listing to the observation date (December 31, 2012).

Independent Variables: Extent of Exploratory Innovation
We measured the extent of exploratory innovation by using the number of patents and the technology classification, because the number of patents is widely considered a good proxy for knowledge creation and innovation activity (Ramani & de Looze, 2002). In particular, IT firms compete based on advanced technologies and thus emphasize patents. Moreover, using patent data is virtually the only way to capture a firm's historical innovation activities. We measured exploratory innovation based on a two-step process.

First, we measured exploratory innovation as the proportion of patents in new technology fields, which was compared with that for existing technology fields of the focal firm during 5 years, on total patents. Previous studies have shown that the value of technologies for high-technology firms decreases sharply within about 5 years (Argote, 1999). We divided technological fields by using IPC codes for each patent. Based on the IPC subclass (four-digit level), if codes were the same, then we regarded the patents as belonging to homogeneous technology fields. One the other hand, we regarded different codes as belonging to heterogeneous ones. Previous studies categorizing technological fields through patents have generally employed IPC subclasses (Hu, 2012; Wagner, 2011). Second, we calculated the average of measured values of exploratory innovation on a yearly basis because we assumed the balance between exploration and exploitation to be not static but dynamic. That is, the exploration−exploitation balance can be achieved over time but not at any given point in time.

Moderating Variables

We measured *financial slack* by calculating the ratio of a firm's cash reserves to its total expenses (Voss et al., 2008). Based on previous research (e.g., Boyd, 1995; Dess & Beard, 1984; Keats & Hitt, 1988), we measured *environmental dynamism* by regressing the value of industry shipments over 11 years on time (1999–2009). We collected industry shipment dates for the 1999–2009 period from the Korea National Statistical Office (KNSO). Here 11 years were sufficient for capturing the dynamism of an industry. For example, Wang and Li (2008) identified industrial dynamism by using date data over a 5-year period. We used the standard error of the regression coefficient for a time dummy variable divided by the average value of an industry's shipments. This made it possible to capture the common environmental characteristics facing firms within a given industry (Boyd, 1995). Additionally, we considered alterative measurements such as the changes in average production capacity, operation ratio, and the number of participants in order to capture the dynamics in five Korean IT-related industries more precisely. We found no significant difference in the results. We subdivided IT-related industries into five industries: semiconductor manufacturers, electronic component manufacturers, computer and peripheral device manufacturers, telecommunications and broadcasting equipment manufacturers, and video and audio equipment manufacturers. Based on the regression results, we classified electronic component manufacturers (0.51), computer and peripheral device manufacturers (0.60), and telecommunications and broadcasting equipment manufacturers (0.41) as industries reflecting a high level of environmental dynamism and semiconductor manufacturers (0.28) and video and audio equipment manufacturers (0.26) as those reflecting a low level of environmental dynamism. This classification is consistent with widely held beliefs about these industries.

Control Variables

Based on previous research, we controlled for several factors. We controlled for *firm size* as the log of the number of employees because the difference in the level of resources based on firm size may impact a firm's innovation activity and survival (Autio, Sapienza, & Almeida, 2000). We controlled for *firm age* because this may be associated with the hazard rate of survival (Gilbert, 2005) and measured it as the number of days from a firm's founding to year t. We controlled for *R&D intensity* as the ratio of R&D expenses to total sales (Greve, 2003). We controlled for *the number of patents* because it entails the risk of overestimating the level of exploitation and measured it as the number of total patents during the survival period.

We controlled *the number of industry changes* that implies the number of industries to which a firm has belonged for its survival period. We found that some SMEs have moved across the Korean IT industries. In some cases, such a firm's movements across industries reflect the expansion and changes of the main products that may lead to the overestimation of the extent of exploration, in other cases, the possibility of failure in existing industry that may impact a firm's survival. Finally, there were differences in the average survival duration between *industries*. We subdivided IT-related industries into five industries and employed dummy variables. However, we did not use these dummy variables to test the hypothesis about environmental dynamism.

Analysis

To test the hypotheses, we used the Cox proportional hazard model for the following reasons: First, the Cox regression approach does not make any assumptions about the distribution of a dependent variable. In general, the survival function has a complex distribution, but the ordinary least squares method has difficulty handling this distribution. Second, the Cox regression approach is appropriate to use censoring data (Allison, 1995; Cox & Oakes, 1984). As in most event history analyses, a key concern in this study involved the censoring problem because the sample ended on December 31, 2011, but 44 firms maintained their listing after that. These firms correspond to right censoring. Third, in comparison with other survival analysis methods such as the life table and the Kaplan–Meier method, the Cox regression approach has certain strengths. The life table and the Kaplan–Meier method can analyze only categorical independent variables, whereas the Cox model can analyze all types of independent variables. Finally, in comparison with logistic regression, the Cox regression approach considers events as well as the time to a given event. Therefore, this model is substantially more robust than the aforementioned survival analysis models in the context of this study (Allison, 1995):

$$\lambda_i(t) = \lambda_0(t)\exp[x_i(t)'\beta]$$

where $\lambda_0(t)$ is the baseline hazard rate, which represents each firm's heterogeneity; $\lambda_i(t)$ is the hazard rate for firm i at time t; x_i is the covariate for firm i at time t; and β is the coefficient. The Cox proportional hazard model provides a method for estimating β without requiring the estimation of λ_0.

RESULTS

Table 1 gives the means, standard deviations, and correlations for the variables. Among the control variables, firm size had negative correlations with R&D intensity and the extent of exploratory innovation, indicating that the larger the firm, the lower the level of exploratory innovation as well as the level of R&D intensity. No correlations between the explanatory and control variables were high enough to indicate a serious multicollinearity problem.

Table 2 presents the results for the hypotheses. Model 1 included only the control variables for the regression, and Model 2 added the main effect. Hypothesis 1 predicted an inverted U-shaped curvilinear relationship between the extent of exploratory innovation and organizational longevity. The results for Model 2 show that exploratory innovation had a significant negative relationship ($p < 0.05$) with a firm's hazard rate and that its squared term had a significant positive relationship ($p < 0.05$), implying a U-shaped relationship between exploratory innovation and the hazard rate. That is, organizational longevity increased with an increase in the extent of exploratory innovation up to a certain point and then decreased, providing support for Hypothesis 1. Fig. 2(a) graphically summarizes the results for Model 2, which clearly demonstrate that firms were significantly more likely to survive if they maintained an appropriate balance between exploration and exploitation.

We employed Model 3 to assess the moderating effect of financial slack. Hypothesis 2 proposed that financial slack would moderate the relationship between exploratory innovation and organizational longevity. The results indicate that financial slack had a significant moderating effect on this relationship ($p < 0.05$). Fig. 2(b) clearly demonstrates the moderating effect by dividing the sample firms into two groups based on the median. Those firms with a large amount of financial slack were more likely to survive if they moved the exploration–exploitation balance to the right, that is, an increase in the level of exploration. For those with a small amount of financial slack, the opposite was true. These results provide support for Hypothesis 2.

We included Model 4 to examine the moderating effect of environmental dynamism. Hypothesis 3 predicted that environmental dynamism would moderate the relationship between the extent of exploratory innovation and organizational longevity. The results for Model 4 indicate a significant moderating effect ($p < 0.01$). However, as shown in Fig. 2(c), the moderating effect was inconsistent with our expectation. Fig. 2(c) demonstrates

Table 1. Descriptive Statistics and Correlations.

No.	Variable	Mean	SD	1	2	3	4	5	6	7	8	9
1	Longevity (number of days)	2862.016	1518.749									
2	Firm size (log)	2.043	0.237	0.00								
3	Firm age (number of days)	6161.859	3006.864	0.67***	0.10†							
4	R&D intensity	0.075	0.079	−0.08	−0.23***	−0.20***						
5	Number of patents	35.992	62.204	0.05	0.23***	−0.02	0.17**					
6	Number of industry changes	1.208	0.425	0.37***	−0.07	0.22***	−0.02	−0.05				
7	Extent of exploratory innovation	0.605	0.262	−0.01	−0.21***	0.05	−0.06	−0.44***	−0.02			
8	Financial slack	0.098	0.080	0.01	−0.19***	−0.10	0.29***	0.06	0.10	−0.16**		
9	Environmental dynamism	1.353	0.479	−0.06	−0.08	−0.12†	0.15*	0.10†	0.03	−0.10	0.15*	

†$p < 0.1$, *$p < 0.05$, **$p < 0.01$, ***$p < 0.001$.

Table 2.   Results of Cox Proportional Hazard Regression for Hazard Rate of Firm's Delisting.

Variables	Model 1	Model 2	Model 3	Model 4	Model 5
Firm size (log)	−0.04 (0.56)	0.01 (0.56)	−0.50 (0.59)	−0.37 (0.53)	−0.86 (0.57)
Firm age	0.00 (0.00)***	0.00 (0.00)***	0.00 (0.00)***	0.00 (0.00)***	0.00 (0.00)***
R&D intensity	−0.06 (1.66)	−0.20 (1.66)	0.40 (1.68)	−0.43 (1.56)	0.19 (1.59)
Number of patents	−0.03 (0.01)***	−0.02 (0.01)**	−0.02 (0.01)**	−0.02 (0.01)**	−0.02 (0.01)**
Number of industry changes	−0.68 (0.30)*	−0.70 (0.30)*	−0.58 (0.30)†	−0.61 (0.29)*	−0.43 (0.29)
Industry dummy	Incl.	Incl.	Incl.		
Extent of exploratory innovation		−2.91 (2.62)*	−9.71 (4.74)*	−3.99 (0.79)†	−10.99 (6.74)†
Extent of exploratory innovation squared		2.49 (1.95)*	7.56 (3.47)*	3.71 (0.73)*	8.66 (4.85)*
Financial slack			−27.72 (15.36)*		−24.15 (15.74*)
Environmental dynamism				0.38 (0.17)*	−0.28 (0.17)†
Extent of exploratory innovation × financial slack			76.56 (50.01)*		66.24 (51.05)*
Extent of exploratory innovation squared × financial slack			−58.62 (36.58)*		−51.01 (37.07)*
Extent of exploratory innovation × environmental dynamism				2.45 (0.77)*	2.10 (0.75)†
Extent of exploratory innovation squared × environmental dynamism				−2.01 (0.28)**	−1.64 (0.26)*
−2LL	728.800	726.523	712.082	734.918	722.823
χ^2	74.990***	84.115***	101.31***	76.994***	91.563***
Df	9	11	14	10	13
Delisting	89	89	89	89	89
N	255	255	255	255	255

( ) is the standard error. †$p < .1$, *$p < 0.05$, **$p < 0.01$, ***$p < 0.001$.

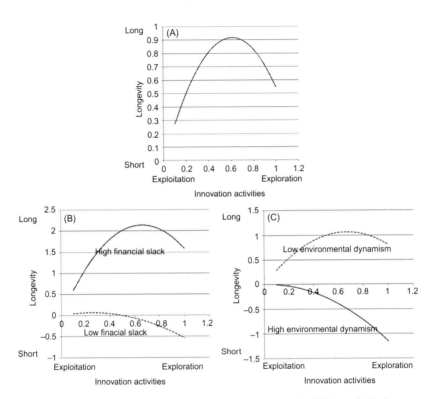

Fig. 2. Main Effect and Moderating Effects. (a) Main Effect of Exploratory Innovation Ratio. (b) Exploratory Innovation Ratio and Financial Slack. (c) Exploratory Innovation Ratio and Environmental Dynamism.

that those firms in a dynamic environment were more likely to survive if they moved the exploration–exploitation balance to the left, that is, a decrease in the extent of exploratory innovation. For those in a static environment, the opposite was true. Therefore, the results provide no support for Hypothesis 3, but raise an important question regarding the role of environmental conditions in the relationship between the firms' innovation activities and survival. In the discussion section, we provide a supplementary explanation about the results. The results for Model 5, which included all main and interaction effects, are generally consistent with those for other models.

DISCUSSION

This study has two objectives. First, the study addresses the question of how the balance between exploration and exploitation influences organizational survival. Second, the study further highlights the need for a contingency approach to the balance between exploration and exploitation by addressing the question of how an appropriate balance is influenced by organizational slack and environmental dynamism. To address these important questions about organizational ambidexterity, we examined the effects of the exploration−exploitation balance on organizational longevity by using data from Korean SMEs in IT-related industries for the 1981−2012 period. The results provide support for Hypothesis 1, indicating an inverted U-shaped curvilinear relationship between the extent of exploratory innovation and organizational longevity. In addition, the results provide the support for Hypotheses 2 asserting that slack plays an important role in achieving an appropriate balance between exploration and exploitation, but not for Hypothesis 3 about the environmental dynamism's role.

Theoretical Implications

This study makes several important contributions to the literature. First, the study provides clear empirical evidence that the exploration−exploitation balance plays an important role in organizational longevity of SMEs. Although the ongoing theoretical debate and common belief suggests that the exploration−exploitation balance plays a critical role in firms' long-term success, most empirical studies (e.g., He & Wong, 2004; Jansen et al., 2006; Rothaermel & Alexandre, 2009) have focused on the effects of exploration and exploitation on short-term financial performance, not on long-term performance. Except for Piao (2010), who investigated the longevity implications of exploration by considering manufacturers of hard drives for the 1980−1990 period, few studies have paid attention to survival implications of balancing exploration and exploitation, including how long a firm can survive based on this balance (Lavie et al., 2010; Raisch & Birkinshaw, 2008). In particular, previous studies more rarely take into account long-term performance implications of SMEs, and in addition, they have produced mixed results. For example, Ebben and Johnson (2005) suggested that small firms that pursue efficiency strategies or flexibility strategies outperform those that attempt to pursue both based on 114 U.S.

firms. By contrast, Lubatkin et al. (2006) argued that the joint pursuit of an exploration and exploitation positively affects performance based on survey data from 139 SMEs. This study fills the gap between theoretical beliefs and empirical evidence in the ambidexterity literature by examining the effects of an appropriate exploration—exploitation balance on organizational longevity based on patents and other objective data for a relatively long sample period (1981—2012).

Second, by conceptualizing them as the ends of a continuum, this study provides direct support for March's claims in context of firms' innovation activity. The results demonstrating an inverted U-shaped curvilinear relationship between the extent of exploratory innovation and organizational longevity provide support for March's (1991) original assumption that an appropriate level of balance can enhance long-term viability. In particular, this continuum perspective may be applicable to firms' innovation activities of SMEs because these two contradictory activities exert substantial pressure on the allocation of scare resources at the firm level.

Third, this study provides a contingency perspective on the exploration—exploitation balance. Although the beneficial effects of achieving a balance between exploration and exploitation are widely accepted, few studies have considered the organizational contexts that can influence the effectiveness of this balance (e.g., Jansen et al., 2006; Rothaermel & Alexandre, 2009). Because organizations generally face diverse internal and external conditions, this study contributes to the debate over how an appropriate balance between exploration and exploitation is influenced by internal and external organizational contexts. The results verify the moderating effects of financial slack on the relationship between the exploration—exploitation balance and organizational longevity. These results suggest that an appropriate exploration—exploitation balance is flexible, not fixed. In terms of internal fit, as Raisch and Birkinshaw (2008) argued, an appropriate balance may be contingent on the availability of sufficient resources. Our results highlight the importance of the fit between slack resources and innovation activities.

Finally, the results for Hypothesis 3 raise an important question regarding the role of environmental conditions in the relationship between the exploration—exploitation balance and organizational longevity. There are two dominant theoretical perspectives on environmental change and organizational adaptation: the adaptation view and the ecological approach. The former assumes that an organizational change has a positive effect on the likelihood of organizational survival, whereas the latter argues that attempts to respond to environmental changes tend to be associated with an increase in the likelihood of organizational death. In contrast to widely held beliefs and this study's hypothesis for adaptation view that environmental changes require a higher level of exploration, the results suggest that firms under a high level of environmental dynamism are more likely to survive when the level of exploratory innovation is lower. This provides support for the ecological perspective positing that potential changes in an organization's efforts are not commensurate with the rate of change in its environments (Hannan & Freeman, 1984; Levinthal & Posen, 2008). The population ecology perspective points out the liabilities of such changes (Amburgey, Kelly, & Barnett, 1993) and the possibility that the changes are not consistent with the rate of change in the environment (Hannan & Freeman, 1984). In their seminal study, Hannan and Freeman (1984) presented that organizations are highly inert because of organizational reliability and accountability. In population ecology theory, organizations are regarded as systems of highly elaborate structures reflecting the "sunk cost in plant, equipment, and personnel standards, … and exchange relations with other organizations" (Hannan & Freeman, 1984, p. 149). This structural inertia can hinder changes in the organization. Although a firm can sometimes manage to change its strategies and structures to accommodate new environments, this reorientation is rare and costly and can expose it to a much higher risk of death (Zuniga-Vicente & Vicente-Lorente, 2006). In a highly dynamic environment, organizations may anticipate and react only imperfectly to environmental changes. Therefore, increasing the extent of exploratory innovation may not be enough to enhance the ability to respond to environmental changes. Instead, increasing the extent of exploitative innovation may be a more attractive alternative for reducing the risk of shorter life spans for new technologies from exploratory innovation (Levinthal & Posen, 2008). Especially, in case of SMEs, it is harder to respond to rapidly changing environment because of their inadequate resources and capabilities than large companies. Fig. 2(c) visually indicates that firms belonging to a highly dynamic industry can survive longer by focusing on exploitation instead of maintaining a balance between exploration and exploitation.

Practical Implications

The results have important practical implications. Fig. 2 offers several important practical implications. First, Fig. 2(a) indicates not only that firms are likely to survive if they maintain an appropriate balance between exploration and exploitation but also that excessive exploitative innovation can be more dangerous than excessive exploratory innovation. This is inconsistent with previous argues that excessive exploration may explain the failure of many firms (Levinthal & March, 1993; March, 1991). It means that for SMEs or venture firms belonging to high-tech industries, radical innovation is more beneficial than incremental innovation. Therefore, managers should actively engage in exploratory innovation efforts for survival.

Second, when making decisions on innovation activities, managers should have a clear understanding of their available resources. The results in Fig. 2(b) indicate that the larger the slack, the longer the survival period. In addition, firms with a large amount of slack can extend their longevity by pursuing an appropriate exploration–exploitation balance. However, for those a small amount of slack, pursuing only one side (overexploitation) may be more beneficial than maintaining a balance between exploration and exploitation under certain conditions. Firms with a small amount of slack can first accumulate slack resources by engaging only in exploitative innovation activities and then allocating accumulated resources to future exploratory innovation activities.

Finally, managers can make better decisions by carefully assessing environmental changes. As shown in Fig. 2(c), firms in a stable environment may survive longer than those in a dynamic environment through aggressive exploratory innovation, and firms in a highly dynamic environment may survive longer through exploitative innovation than through exploratory innovation.

Limitations and Future Research Directions

This study has some limitations. First, we were not able to consider the changes in patent activity over time. To test the hypotheses about survival, we had to measure exploration and exploitation by using the aggregate number of patents. In this regard, future research should consider changes in innovation activity over time. For example, it should be interesting to capture the pattern of switches between exploration and exploitation because it may shed some insights into how an appropriate balance between exploration and exploitation can be achieved.

Second, we examined the moderating effects of environmental dynamism in terms of industrial demand volatility. We also considered the changes in average production capacity, operation ratio, and the number of participants. However, environmental dynamism includes many other dimensions, including technological and competitive changes. However, we did not consider other aspects of dynamism. Although demand dynamism is considered a key aspect of environmental dynamism and previous studies (e.g., Boyd, 1995; Simerly & Li, 2000; Wang & Li, 2008) have generally considered this dimension, it may be valuable to consider other aspects of environmental dynamism. In this regard, future research should examine the implications of different aspects of dynamism for this study's argument about environmental dynamism.

Third, this study's analysis of exploration and exploitation is limited to the domain of product innovation, and therefore future research should examine the survival implications of the exploration−exploitation balance for other domains. Fourth, this study's measures for the extent of exploratory innovation are based on patent application data. Therefore, it is difficult to apply this approach to industries that do not make active use of patents. Fifth, this study did not consider the specific variables for SMEs because of restrictions from objective database. For example, characteristics of CEO's leadership and managers' risk aversion and learning abilities can play important role in SMEs' ambidexterity. Finally, we examined the effects of the exploration−exploitation balance on organizational longevity only in the context of IT-related industries in Korea, and therefore future research should analyze a wider range of industries and countries for increased generalizability.

CONCLUSION

This study examines a fundamental question that has received insufficient empirical support from ambidexterity research: Do organizations pursuing the exploration−exploitation balance survive longer than those focusing only on one? The results demonstrate an inverted U-shaped curvilinear relationship between the extent of exploratory innovation and organizational longevity and thus give an affirmative answer. Further, the results call for a contingency approach for a better understanding of changes in survival implications of the exploration−exploitation balance. An appropriate balance between exploration and exploitation may vary widely according to the firm's unique internal and external conditions. We hypothesized that an appropriate balance between exploration and exploitation would be contingent on organizational conditions, including slack (which can enable innovation activities) and environmental dynamism (which reflects risks and opportunities associated with innovation activities). The results suggest that the fit between the exploration−exploitation balance and internal and external conditions is more important than the balance itself.

ACKNOWLEDGMENT

This work was supported by the National Research Foundation of Korea Grant funded by the Korean Government (NRF-2013S1A5A2A01018077) and by Kyungpook National University Research Fund, 2013.

REFERENCES

Abernathy, W. J., & Clark, K. B. (1985). Innovation: Mapping the winds of creative destruction. *Research Policy*, *14*, 3−22.

Ahuja, G., & Lampert, C. M. (2001). Entrepreneurship in the large corporation: A longitudinal study of how established firms create breakthrough inventions. *Strategic Management Journal*, *22*, 521−543.

Allison, P. (1995). *Survival analysis using the SAS system: A practical guide*. Cary, NC: SAS Publishing.

Amburgey, T., Kelly, D., & Barnett, W. P. (1993). Resetting the clock: The dynamics of organizational change and failure. *Administrative Science Quarterly*, *38*, 51−75.

Anderson, P., & Tushman, M. (1990). Technological discontinuities and dominant designs: A cyclical model of technological change. *Administrative Science Quarterly*, *35*, 604−633.

Anderson, P., & Tushman, M. (2001). Organizational environments and industry exit: The effects of uncertainty, munificence and complexity. *Industrial and Corporate Change*, *10*(3), 675−711.

Argote, L. (1999). *Organizational learning: Creating retaining and transferring knowledge*. Boston, MA: Kluwer Academic.

Auh, S., & Menguc, B. (2005). Balancing exploration and exploitation: The moderating role of competitive intensity. *Journal of Business Research*, *58*, 1652−1661.

Autio, E., Sapienza, H. J., & Almeida, J. (2000). Effects of age at entry, knowledge intensity and limitability on international growth. *Academy of Management Journal*, *43*, 909−924.

Baumol, W. J. (2002). *The free-market innovation machine: Analyzing the growth miracle of capitalism*. Princeton, NJ: Princeton University Press.

Benner, M., & Tushman, M. (2002). Process management and technological innovation: Longitudinal study of the photography and paint industries. *Administrative Science Quarterly*, 47, 676−706.

Benner, M. J., & Tushman, M. L. (2003). Exploitation, exploration, and process management: The productivity dilemma revisited. *Academy of Management Review*, *28*, 238−256.

Boyd, B. K. (1995). CEO duality and firm performance: A contingency model. *Strategic Management Journal, 16*, 301–312.

Burgelman, R. A., & Creve, A. S. (2007). Let chaos reign, the reign in chaos-repeatedly: Managing strategic dynamics for corporate longevity. *Strategic Management Journal, 28*, 965–979.

Cottrell, T. & Nault, B. R. (2004). Product variety and firm survival in the microcomputer software industry. *Strategic Management Journal, 25*, 1005–1026.

Cox, D. R., & Oakes, D. (1984). *Analysis of survival data.* London: Chapman and Hall.

Danneels, E. (2002). The dynamics of product innovation and firm competences. *Strategic Management Journal, 23*, 1095–1121.

Dess, G. G., & Beard, D. W. (1984). Dimensions of organizational task environment. *Administrative Science Quarterly, 29*, 52–73.

Ebben, J. J., & Johnson, A. C. (2005). Efficiency, flexibility, or both? Evidence linking strategy to performance in small firms. *Strategic Management Journal, 26*, 1249–1259.

Fleming, L. (2001). Recombinant uncertainty in technological search. *Management Science, 47*, 117–132.

Fleming, L., & Sorenson, O. (2001). Technology as a complex adaptive system. *Research Policy, 30*, 1019–1039.

Gibson, C. B., & Birkinshaw, J. (2004). The antecedents, consequences, and mediating role of organizational ambidexterity. *Academy of Management Journal, 47*(2), 209–226.

Gilbert, C. G. (2005). Unbundling the structure of inertia: Resource vs. routine rigidity. *Academy of Management Journal, 48*, 741–763.

Greve, H. R. (2003). A behavioral theory of R&D expenditures and innovations: Evidence from shipbuilding. *Academy of Management Journal, 46*, 685–702.

Greve, H. R. (2007). Exploration and exploitation in product innovation. *Industrial and Corporate Change, 16*(5), 945–975.

Gupta, A. K., Smith, K. G., & Shalley, C. E. (2006). The interplay between exploration and exploitation. *Academy of Management Journal, 4*, 693–706.

Hannan, M. T., & Freeman, J. H. (1984). Structural inertia and organizational change. *American Sociological Review, 49*, 149–164.

He, W. L., & Wong, P. K. (2004). Exploration vs. exploitation: An empirical test of the ambidexterity hypothesis. *Organization Science, 15*, 481–494.

Henderson, R., & Cockburn, I. (1994). Measuring competences? Exploring firm effects in pharmaceutical research. *Strategic Management Journal, 15*, 63–84.

Hu, M. C. (2012). Technological innovation capabilities in the thin film transistor-liquid crystal display industries of Japan, Korea, and Taiwan. *Research Policy, 41*, 541–555.

Jansen, J. J. R., van den Bosch, F. A. J., & Volberda, H. W. (2005). Exploratory innovation, exploitative innovation, and ambidexterity: The impact of environmental and organizational antecedents. *Schmalenbach Business Review, 57*, 351–363.

Jansen, J. J. R., van den Bosch, F. A. J., & Volberda, H. W. (2006). Exploratory innovation, exploitative innovation, and performance: Effects of organizational antecedents and environmental moderators. *Management Science, 52*, 1661–1674.

Katila, R., & Ahuja, G. (2002). Something old, something new: A longitudinal study of search behavior and new product introduction. *Academy of Management Journal, 45*, 1183–1194.

Keats, B. W., & Hitt, M. A. (1988). A causal model of linkages among environmental dimensions, macro organizational characteristics, and performance. *Academy of Management Journal, 31*, 570–598.

Lavie, D., & Rosenkopf, L. (2006). Balancing exploration and exploitation in alliance formation. *Academy of Management Journal, 49*, 797–818.

Lavie, D., Stettner, U., & Tushman, M. (2010). Exploration and exploitation within and across organization. *Academy of Management Annals, 4*, 109–155.

Levinthal, D., & March, J. (1993). Myopia of learning. *Strategic Management Journal, 14*, 95–112.

Levinthal, D. A., & March, J. G. (1981). A model of adaptive organizational search. *Journal of Economic Behavior, 2*, 307–333.

Levinthal, D. A., & Posen, H. E. (2008). Bringing context to the exploration-exploitation trade-off: Considering the impact of selection and turbulent environments. Woking Paper, Ann Arbor 1001, 48109-1234.

Lubatkin, M. H., Simsek, Z., Ling, Y., & Veiga, J. F. (2006). Ambidexterity and performance in small- to medium-sized firms: The pivotal role of TMT behavioral integration. *Journal of Management, 32*, 1–17.

March J. G. (1991). Exploration and exploitation in organizational learning. *Organization Science, 2*, 71–87.

Nohria, N., & Gulati, R. (1996). Is slack good or bad for innovation? *Academy of Management Journal, 39*, 1245–1264.

Perretti, F., & Negro, G. (2006). Filling empty seats: How status and organizational hierarchies affect exploration versus exploitation in team design. *Academy of Management Journal, 49*, 759–777.

Piao, M. (2010). Thriving in the new: Implication of exploration on organizational longevity. *Journal of Management, 36*, 1529–1554.

Raisch, A., & Birkinshaw, J. (2008). Organizational ambidexterity: Antecedents, outcomes, and moderators. *Journal of Management, 34*, 375–409.

Ramani, S. W., & de Looze, M. A. (2002). Using patent statistics as knowledge base indicators in the biotechnology sectors: An application to France, Germany and the U.K. *Scientometrics, 54*, 319–346.

Rothaermel, F. R., & Alexandre, M. T. (2009). Ambidexterity in technology sourcing: The moderating role of absorptive capacity. *Organization Science, 20*, 759–780.

Rothaermel, F. T., & Deeds, D. L. (2004). Exploration and exploitation alliances in biotechnology: A system of new product development. *Strategic Management Journal, 25*, 201–221.

Sharfman, M. P., Wolf, G., Chase, R. B., & Tansik, D. A. (1988). Antecedents of organizational slack. *Academy of Management Review, 13*, 601–614.

Simerly, R. L., & Li, M. (2000). Environmental dynamism, capital structure and performance: A theoretical integration and an empirical test. *Strategic Management Journal, 21*, 31–50.

Sirmon, D. G., Hitt, M. A., & Ireland, R. D. (2007). Managing firm resources in dynamic environments to create value: Looking inside the black box. *Academy of Management Review, 32*, 273–292.

Sørensen, J. B., & Stuart, T. E. (2000). Aging, obsolescence, and organizational innovation. *Administrative Science Quarterly, 45*, 81–112.

STEPI. (2008). *Analysis of ventures' survival factors.* Seoul: STEPI.

Tushman, M. L., & O'Reilly, C. A. (1996). Ambidextrous organizations: Managing evolutionary and revolutionary change. *California Management Review, 38*, 8–30.

Uotila J., Maula, M., Keil, T., & Zahra, S. A. (2009). Exploration, exploitation, and financial performance: Analysis of SandP500 corporations. *Strategic Management Journal, 30*, 221–231.

Volberda H. (1996). Toward the flexible form: How to remain vital in hypercompetitive environments. *Organization Science, 7*, 359–374.

Voss, G. B., Sirdeshmukh, D., & Voss, Z. G. (2008). The effects of slack resources and environmental threat on products exploration exploitation. *Academy of Management Journal, 51*, 147–164.

Voss, G. B. & Voss, Z. G. (2013). Strategic ambidexterity in small and medium-sized enterprises: Implementing exploration and exploitation in product and market domains. *Organization Science, 24*, 1459–1477.

Wadhwa, A., & Kotha, S. (2006). Knowledge creation through external venturing: Evidence from the telecommunications equipment manufacturing industry. *Academy of Management Journal, 49*, 1–17.

Wagner, M. (2011). To explore or to exploit? An empirical investigation of acquisitions by large incumbents. *Research Policy, 40*, 1217–1225.

Wang, H., & Li, J. (2008). Untangling the effects of overexploration and overexploitation on organizational performance: The moderating role of environmental dynamism. *Journal of Management, 34*, 925–951.

Yamakawa Y., Yang, H., & Lin, Z. J. (2011). Exploration versus exploitation in alliance portfolio: Performance implications of organizational, strategic, and environmental fit. *Research Policy, 40*, 287–296.

Zahra, S. A. (1996). Technology strategy and financial performance: Examining the moderating role of the firm's competitive environment. *Journal of Business Venturing, 11*, 189–219.

Zahra, S. A., & Bogner, W. C. (1999). Technology strategy and software new venture's performance: Exploring effect of the competitive environment. *Journal of Business Venturing, 15*, 135–173.

Zuniga-Vicente, J. A., & Vicente-Lorente, J. D. (2006). Strategic moves and organizational survival in turbulent environments: The case of Spanish banks (1983–97). *Journal of Management Studies, 43*, 485–519.

CHAPTER 7

EXPLORATION AND EXPLOITATION FROM START-UP TO SALE: A LONGITUDINAL ANALYSIS THROUGH STRATEGY AND MCS PRACTICES

M. Laura Frigotto, Graziano Coller and
Paolo Collini

ABSTRACT

Exploration and exploitation comprise one of the most well-known constructs in management and organization studies. However, there are three gaps in the extant literature on this topic. First, these studies focus mainly on large organizations and neglect small and medium-sized enterprises (SMEs) and new ventures. Second, when adopting a longitudinal perspective, the research typically consists of cross-sectional studies that fail to capture evolution. Third, the research focuses more on the role of antecedents and mediators of strategies that pursue exploration and exploitation than on the practices that embody such goals. In this chapter, we address these three gaps and complement the previous literature with a study of the growth of an SME from start-up to sale over

Exploration and Exploitation in Early Stage Ventures and SMEs
Technology, Innovation, Entrepreneurship and Competitive Strategy, Volume 14, 149–179
Copyright © 2014 by Emerald Group Publishing Limited
All rights of reproduction in any form reserved
ISSN: 1479-067X/doi:10.1108/S1479-067X20140000014004

a 19-year period (1993–2011). We depict the evolution of exploration and exploitation over time through an analysis of management system practices that employs a longitudinal perspective. We analyze the different roles that management systems have played in various stages of the growth paths of the organization. We show that the role of management systems in shaping exploration and exploitation only loosely depends on the design of these systems. The same management systems can fulfill an explorative function in one stage and an exploitative function in another, depending on how such systems are used. Conversely, across stages, the role of management systems typically changes from exploration to exploitation.

Keywords: Exploration and exploitation; SME; management control systems; practice; longitudinal analysis

INTRODUCTION

Exploration and exploitation have been – and remain – two of the most appealing concepts in management and organization studies and have served as the framework for numerous studies. Thanks to the work of a number of scholars, the original conception in March's work (1991) has been adapted, extended and articulated in several ways. Theoretically, the core of the debate on exploration and exploitation is built around two contrasting positions. On the one hand, the ambidexterity perspective claims that it is possible to simultaneously pursue exploitative and explorative targets through either a combination of organizational structures (Tushman & O'Reilly, 1996) or through contexts in which beliefs, processes, and systems sustain both (Gibson & Birkinshaw, 2004). On the other hand, the trade-off perspective claims the necessity of balancing exploration and exploitation, which are otherwise irreconcilable (Gupta, Smith, & Shalley, 2006), by alternating explorative and exploitative time periods. Notwithstanding the large number of contributions to both views, this literature does not constitute an organic body of knowledge where the two perspectives are confronted. Satellite concepts have been added (Nosella, Cantarello, & Filippini, 2012), numerous definitions within contrasting perspectives have been offered and diverse phenomena have been "re-badged" as pertaining to exploration and exploitation (O'Reilly & Tushman, 2013). As a result, these studies seem to have increased confusion (Nosella et al., 2012), excessively broadened the focus of the discourse (Lavie, Stettner, & Tushman, 2010) and added complexity (Raisch & Birkinshaw, 2008).

It is possible to identify three gaps in this broad literature that motivate our research and position our contribution. First, exploration and exploitation are addressed mainly by reference to large organizations that have reached a certain stability. In such cases, exploration and exploitation involve keeping pace with market changes and innovating to sustain competitive advantage. Of course, there are exceptions. On the one hand, small and medium-sized enterprises (SMEs) are considered in studies of size that investigate the role of resource availability in exploration and exploitation (Voss & Voss, 2013). On the other hand, SMEs are studied to address the quality of information exchange, collaborative behavior, and joint decision making in top management teams (Lubatkin, Simsek, Ling, & Veiga, 2006). However, SMEs are an important part of our economy and deserve attention per se. They are organizations whose internal mechanisms and dynamics of external impact are particular. In fact, knowledge regarding large organizations can only be applied to SMEs on a limited basis, and research that focuses on SMEs, in particular, is required.

Second, despite several contributions analyzing exploration and exploitation over time (e.g., Hess & Rothaermel, 2011; Lavie, Kang, & Rosenkopf, 2011; Lavie & Rosenkopf, 2006; Lin, Yang, & Demirkan, 2007), most studies adopt a cross-sectional approach. However, cross-sectional studies are unable to capture the evolution of exploration and exploitation intended as the *practice* of reconfiguration and adaptation to both external changes and internal tensions that continuously arise (Nosella et al., 2012). The lack of a longitudinal perspective with a focus on practice is, in our view, paradoxical for studies on exploration and exploitation. In fact, this literature is based on the conception of organizations as adaptive systems that continuously interact with and adapt to their environments. Nosella et al. (2012) suggest that this is what builds organizations' dynamic capabilities. However, more attention to the continuous reconfiguration of organizational activities and designs in pursuing exploration and exploitation is still required.

Third, a consistent stream in the literature addresses exploration and exploitation in terms of strategies for incremental or radical innovation. This line of research typically measures exploration and exploitation in terms of innovation in products, markets, and technologies. In addition, research questions address both the impact of exploration and exploitation on performance and the internal and external antecedents and mediators that explain exploration and exploitation (see Lavie et al., 2010, for a review). At the organizational level, there is particular attention directed at understanding the role of organizational structures (Jansen, Van den Bosch, & Volberda, 2006; Tushman & O'Reilly, 1996) and alliances (Lavie et al., 2011) and subgroups (Fang, Lee, & Schilling, 2010) in particular. Absorptive capacity, slack resources, organizational culture, identity, age, and size complete the set of organizational antecedents considered (Lavie et al., 2010). Gibson and Birkinshaw (2004) include management systems as "administrative mechanisms that foster certain behaviors in employees" (Gibson & Birkinshaw, 2004, p. 212) in their analysis of organizational antecedents. They include under management systems what is known in the accounting literature as management control systems (MCS) (as in Malmi & Brown, 2008): human resource (HR) management (including recruiting, training, incentives, and rewards); organizational identity (OI); management information systems (MIS) (collecting information and giving feedback); and production systems (PS). Gibson and Birkinshaw (2004) relate MCS to exploration and exploitation, depending on whether MCS are used in practice for adaptability or alignment. Building on an established typology of MCS developed by Simons (1994), McCarthy and Gordon (2011) specify the association between types of MCS and exploration and exploitation. However, they fail to account for MCS uses and practices and define the link only with respect to the characteristics of MCS design. Although such studies are helpful because they address MCS as a crucial element for exploration and exploitation, they fail to capture how exploration and exploitation are actually pursued daily through MCS practices. Therefore, we believe that a deep understanding of the role of MCS must extend beyond the influence of systems design in the previous literature and must explicitly include an understanding of management in practice.

In this chapter, we address these three gaps and respond to the call for research. We complement the studies on exploration and exploitation in three ways. First, our research focuses on SMEs. Addressing different stages of growth (from small to medium dimensions) and the life cycle (from start-up to maturity), we add to the previous research that focuses on large, well-established organizations. Second, we adopt a practice perspective on longitudinal data that fosters an understanding of how exploration and exploitation are deployed through the "activities of individuals and organizations who are working to effect those events and achieve that outcome" (Lawrence & Suddaby, 2006, p. 10). Third, this research combines an analysis of exploration and exploitation strategies with an analysis of the use of MCS. We investigate the role of MCS in directing action toward exploration and exploitation and in deploying exploration and exploitation in practice. Furthermore, building upon the literature, we contextualize this role within environmental (external factors), organizational, and managerial antecedents (internal factors).

Our main research question is the following: How are exploration and exploitation deployed along an SME's typical growth path? To answer this question, we define a set of second-order questions as follows: How does the relative importance of exploration and exploitation evolve over time? What is the role of changes in external factors (such as markets or competition) or internal factors (such as size and managerial preferences) in the evolution of the exploration and exploitation balance? What is the role of MCS practices in supporting exploration and exploitation by organizations?

To address these questions, we study the evolution of exploration and exploitation in an Italian firm operating in the information technology (IT) industry from its entrepreneurial birth until its sale to a competitor. We employ narrative observations, interview, and archival data of the company's history. Our analysis covers 19 years (1993–2011) and is presented as a case study. We focus our research on an SME as a privileged context. The small–medium size dimension simplifies the observation of both strategies and practices and offers a rich field in which to understand how exploration and exploitation are deployed in organizational life. In practice, SMEs exhibit little separation between strategic decisions and operational action. As Lubatkin et al. (2006) note, senior managers in SMEs play both operational and strategic roles: they "not only rectify and direct their firm's strategy, as do their counterparts in larger firms, but they also participate more directly in the day-to-day implementation of those strategies, as do the operating managers in larger firms" (Lubatkin et al., 2006, p. 649).[1]

Our research contributes to the ambidexterity literature by drawing attention to MCS and the different functions MCS may assume in its evolution through practice. We show that the explorative or exploitative role of MCS and strategies may vary depending on their use in practice and that, over time, their function typically changes from exploration to exploitation. Thus, we illustrate the "essence of organizational ambidexterity" that seeks to "leverage existing assets and capabilities from the mature side of the business to gain competitive advantage in new areas" (O'Reilly & Tushman, 2013, p. 18).

The chapter is structured as follows. In the next section, we position our work in the broad literature on exploration and exploitation. In the third section, we describe our data and methods. In the fourth section, we describe our case study; in the fifth section, we discuss how the empirical evidence on the evolution of exploration and exploitation adds to the extant literature. The sixth section contains our conclusions.

LITERATURE

Defining and Measuring Exploration and Exploitation

Conceptually, it is possible to classify contributions on exploration and exploitation by distinguishing (see Gupta et al., 2006, for a framework) whether exploration and exploitation should be deployed at distinct times, as in a punctuated equilibrium (e.g., Burgelman, 2002), or whether they may be pursued simultaneously. The literature on ambidexterity (Tushman & O'Reilly, 1996) supports the latter view, and such combinations are mainly achieved through the coexistence of structures with different goals and orientations either within organizations or across them. From this perspective, Gibson and Birkinshaw (2004) conceive of exploration and exploitation as a compound rather than a combination that flourishes in an organizational context. This context is defined as the mix of "the systems, processes, and beliefs that shape individual-level behaviors in an organization" (Gibson & Birkinshaw, 2004, p. 212) toward exploration and exploitation. Contextual ambidexterity "involves creating an organizational context and the organizational stimuli that inspire, guide, and reward people to act in a certain way" (McCarthy & Gordon, 2011, p. 241) that fosters exploration and exploitation behaviors. In this view, unpacking the components of the context to classify them as either exploration or exploitation would hinder capturing the overall effect.

Opposing positions about whether an organization can pursue both exploration and exploitation "depend crucially on whether these two tasks are treated as competing or complementary aspects of organizational decisions and actions" (Gupta et al., 2006). On the one hand, exploration and exploitation are understood as mutually exclusive; on the other hand, they can be combined. The answer to the question is related to the definition of the two concepts. However, far beyond pure definitional issues, the resolution of this point affects the robustness of the field and the comparability of contributions through homogeneous empirical measures.

Much of this divergence is explained by whether the distinction between exploration and exploitation is a matter of "degree" or "kind" (Lavie et al., 2010, p. 114). On the one hand, some scholars claim that exploration and exploitation are two extremes of the same nature and argue for continuous measures (Lavie et al., 2010). On the other hand, others understand exploration and exploitation as separate constructs and activities and argue for separate measures (Birkinshaw & Gupta, 2013; O'Reilly & Tushman, 2013).

Recent works (Gupta et al., 2006; Lavie et al., 2010; O'Reilly & Tushman, 2013) emphasize the need for systematic definitions of exploration and exploitation. In fact, they are crucial for building a robust body of knowledge and for deriving operationalizations that are consistent with them.

In the original definition from March (1991, p. 71), exploration and exploitation refer to change, i.e., "refinement" for exploitation and "experimentation" and "discovery" for exploration. Although there seems to be consensus on the content of exploration, which is learning and innovation, it is not settled whether exploitation means the deployment of past knowledge or whether it also refers to the pursuit and acquisition of new knowledge (Gupta et al., 2006).

A proper understanding of change implies a "definition of sameness" (Fontana, 2001, p. 1). This task would be simple if change did not concern knowledge that typically is a "cluster concept"[2] (Pigliucci, 2008, p. 888). In fact, there are two properties of knowledge that provide particular complexity and confusion to this definitional effort. First, knowledge is a multidimensional construct. Scholars may focus on its different aspects and come to different conclusions: knowledge can be investigated from several perspectives and change can be read on some but not on others. Second, it is hardly possible to reproduce knowledge without producing change because there is always some refinement and adaptation in reproduction. In other words, the mere deployment of previous knowledge has been considered exploitation (Vermeulen & Barkema, 2001). Less broadly, others have understood that the core of exploration and exploitation is the knowledge *base* (Cohen & Levinthal, 1990; Levinthal & March, 1993); thus, they do not contemplate the deployment of previous knowledge as causing change.

A second reason for low convergence in the literature on exploration and exploitation concerns operationalizations. Measuring exploration and exploitation is surely a "challenge" (Lavie et al., 2010) for scholars who have adopted several potential solutions (O'Reilly & Tushman, 2013), including separate measures (e.g., Auh & Menguc, 2005), the sum or absolute difference (e.g., He & Wong, 2004) and the product of the two values (e.g., Lubatkin et al., 2006) of the same measure. As a result, our understanding of exploration and exploitation in organizations is limited by the divergent operationalizations, by the low degree of comparability of contributions and by the typical mono-dimensional representation of exploration and exploitation that most studies employ (Rosenkopf & McGrath, 2011).

Exploration and Exploitation Through MCS Practices

The literature on exploration and exploitation pays particular attention to the relation of exploration and exploitation to performance. Studies distinguish between short- and long-term performances and investigate antecedents that range from variables related to the environment, to the organization and to the top management team (Lavie et al., 2010). The perspective adopted has typically been static and punctual in time even in the rare cases that concern time series (Nosella et al., 2012). Cross-sectional studies fail to adopt a practice perspective that understands the evolution of the tension between exploration and exploitation over time. Moreover, in this stream of literature, exploration and exploitation are typically identified as outcomes of an explorative or exploitative strategy. Widely adopted operationalizations associate entry into new markets and the introduction of new products with exploration, whereas exploitation is associated with old markets and products.

Extending the set of organizational antecedents under consideration, Gibson and Brikinshaw (2004) included MCS as the backbone of contextual ambidexterity. They note both the organizational micro-level and the role of MCS in directing and adjusting behaviors that foster explorative or exploitative outcomes. McCarthy and Gordon (2011) focus on managerial systems that support the pursuit of such goals and outcomes, in contrast to the previous stream of research that focuses on exploration and exploitation as strategic goals and operationalizes them as strategic outcomes.

McCarthy and Gordon (2011) define MCS as the "formal, information-based routines and procedures used by managers to maintain or alter patterns in organizational activities" (Simons, 1994, p. 170). They build a normative correspondence between MCS types and exploration or exploration. In particular, adopting the typology of MCS proposed by Simons (1994), McCarthy and Gordon (2011) associate boundary systems and diagnostic systems with exploitation and associated interactive systems and belief systems with exploration. These associations are based on an analysis of the design of each MCS type: rule-based MCS (i.e., MCS that specify what to do or not to do or that measure outcomes) are associated with exploitation, whereas principle-based MCS (i.e., MCS that establish broader principles for directing action) are associated with exploration. However, these connections have not been validated empirically.

There remains a research gap addressing the biunivocal relationship between MCS types and exploration or exploitation; however, the extant empirical studies indicate that when such relations are defined on the basis of MCS design, they may be misleading. In fact, studies on culture (Ravasi & Schultz, 2006; Sidhu, Volberda, & Commandeur, 2004) show that rule-based systems do not necessarily advocate refinement (exploitation). Moreover, the literature on contextual ambidexterity notes the existence of equifinality, i.e., that there are different ways to pursue exploration and exploitation depending on the heritage of an organization or its people's characteristics (Gibson & Birkinshaw, 2004). Thus, exploration and exploitation resolution may take the form of diverse combinations of management systems. Collini and Frigotto (2013) argue that the same MCS may serve exploration or exploitation because it is not important whether a particular system is more or less strict in listing rules, indicators, and rewarding targets. Instead, whether the system advocates refinement or experimentation is important. Consistent with the foregoing, Gibson and Birkinshaw (2004) analyze the general scope of MCS and show a relationship between MCS and exploration when advocating adaptation as well as a relationship with exploitation in the case of alignment.

Although these studies address MCS as one of the organizational antecedents that explain exploration or exploitation, observing *how* MCS are used in practice (instead of analyzing their design properties) may help clarify their role in the pursuit of exploration and exploitation. In our argument regarding MCS, we echo Orlikowski (2000, p. 407) regarding technology: "while users can and do use [MCS] *technologies* as they were designed, they also can and do circumvent inscribed ways of using the [MCS] *technologies* — either ignoring certain properties of the [MCS] *technology*, working around them, or inventing new ones that may go beyond or even contradict designers' expectations and inscriptions."[3]

Although at first glance these systems may be associated with exploration or exploitation on the basis of how much discretion they provide the organization *by design*, a more careful look reveals that the way in which these systems are used *in practice* may display a more grounded association with exploration and exploitation. Thus, instead of a one-to-one correspondence of each system with exploration or exploitation, the way in which these systems are used plays an important role. In fact, these systems make sense through practice, and only the observation of how they are used allows us to understand their role in exploration and exploitation.

Therefore, we adopt a conception of MCS that both builds on a practice theory perspective (Ahrens & Chapman, 2007, 2005; Hopwood & Miller, 1994; Jørgensen & Messner, 2010; Miller, 2001) and addresses the complete system of rules, practices, values, and other activities management establishes to direct employee behavior (Malmi & Brown, 2008). In this view, the MCS concept is further broadened from Simons's (1994) definition and includes goals and operational directions for action, financial and nonfinancial control, HR rewards, compensation and incentive systems, organizational design and structures, governance structures (accountability), and procedures (how tasks are to be performed or not performed), which include the MIS. As such, MCS form "a package" (Malmi & Brown, 2008) rather than a set of separate systems; more precisely, they are "the complete set of practices in place" (Grabner & Moers, 2013, p. 410). Moreover, the association with exploration and exploitation of MCS depends on the use that is made of them, not on their design. This implies a focus on how exploration and exploitation is pursued in MCS practice, rather than on the design of MCS that is pursuing them. This conception is consistent with the longitudinal perspective of the analysis of exploration and exploitation. In fact, even within the stability of MCS design, it accounts for different uses of the same MCS over time that may support exploration in some phases and exploitation in others.

METHOD, DATA, AND ANALYTICAL FRAMEWORK

Our research is based on the case study research method, in accordance with Yin (1994), and Siggelkow (2007). Yin defines the method as "an empirical inquiry that investigates a contemporary phenomenon within its real-life context; when the boundaries between phenomenon and context are not clearly evident; and in which multiple sources of evidence are used" (Yin, 1994, p. 23). This method is consistent with the research question because it allows us to answer a "how question" regarding the ways in which exploration and exploitation are deployed along the typical growth path of an SME. Moreover, the research question targets exploration and exploitation and their changes over time. To analyze the role of strategies and practices in terms of building exploration and exploitation, their scope and meaning within a detailed picture of the context must be understood. The case study method, by combining a variety of data, allows us not only to gather this complexity but also to produce evidence that answers the research question.

The object of our research is a primary player in the Italian IT market for the production and distribution of computers and electronics in addition to web-based services and solutions such as Internet connectivity, e-learning, web hosting, web housing, and networking. For privacy purposes, we call this company "SMIT" (Small–Medium Information Technology). Founded in 1993, SMIT reached €10 million in sales within 3 years and nearly €82 million sales in 10 years; it grew from a company operating out of a garage in a local market to a nationwide player. In 2010, SMIT's core business was sold and the organization began anew with the launch of a new business.

We chose SMIT for our analysis for several reasons. First, SMIT represents an entrepreneurial venture that grew into both a successful company and a main player in the market. Several experiences in the broad population of successful SMEs resemble SMIT's growth. In fact, SMIT offers a story that is both specific in its details and general in depicting the evolution of entrepreneurial start-ups into the medium-sized dimension. Second, SMIT reflects the Italian culture of entrepreneurial SMEs, in which an entrepreneur leads a company and his/her entrepreneurial attitude spreads among the members of the management team. In fact, SMIT's management team consists of people who started young at the company and never abandoned it (the company's turnover is close to zero). Third, SMIT provided extensive and generous access over time, which made it possible to conduct a longitudinal analysis that involved intense data gathering.

Our study combines archival data with interviews and direct observation. Archival data includes press reviews (2000–2009), documents for external communications, financial statements of the group's companies (1996–2011), consolidated financial statements (2002–2011), notes on the financial statements (1996–2011), annual reports on operations (2000–2011) and official records on ownership structure and governance (1995–2011). We conducted 11 interviews for a total of 22.5 hours. We interviewed the president and CEO (1 interview) at company headquarters and the management control director (4 interviews). At the distribution network, we interviewed two store managers for each governance category (company owned (CO), franchisees, and selling-corners) for a total of 6 interviews. We observed selling activities and performed related data entry into the company's information system at six shops. A set of queries on the company's database and reported production was observed at the head office.

The following outlines the analytical framework that we adopted for the analysis of the case study.

First, as suggested by the literature (Lavie et al., 2010), we considered a number of environmental antecedents for exploration and exploitation with the purpose of contextualizing the analysis (Exhibit 1), including sector life cycle phase and structure, distribution of knowledge, competitive intensity, and appropriability regimes.

Second, organizational elements were considered as potentially relevant to the exploration and exploitation analysis if they provided changes in the knowledge base. Consistent with the literature, we addressed strategy outcomes, such as the introduction of new products or entry into new markets. Moreover, we analyzed MCS as HR systems, OI, MIS, and as a production system (PS) to explore how exploration and exploitation were deployed into day-to-day practice.

Third, strategies and MCS were classified as belonging to exploration or exploitation. The criterion for classification was whether a particular strategy or system provided a change in terms of refinement rather than discovery and experimentation. With respect to strategies, the classic association of new products and markets with exploration and old products and markets with exploitation was adopted. With respect to management systems, we associated them with exploration or exploitation according to the manner in which they were used in practice, without regard to previous classifications in the literature, e.g., McCarthy and Gordon (2011). The results are displayed in Exhibit 2.

CASE STUDY

In this section, we introduce SMIT,[4] a medium-sized Italian IT company, and we present our analysis of its evolution from 1993 to 2011 across exploration and exploitation. We identify five stages in SMIT's life, in addition to a stage zero (1990–1993) that contextualizes SMIT's birth. Each stage is characterized by a specific market situation that is reported in Exhibit 1. We devote the next subsection to a brief illustration of the market conditions and of SMIT's growth in each stage (see Exhibit 1 for data on sales and distribution coverage) and we contextualize them within the market environment. In the section "Exploration and Exploitation Over Time Through Strategy and Management Control Systems," we describe our analysis of exploration and exploitation over time, which is defined in terms of strategies and management practices (see Exhibit 2).

Market Conditions and SMIT's Evolution

Stage 0 (Early 1990s) — Professionals in a "Knowledge-Driven Market"
In the early 1990s, SMIT's founder (later president and CEO) was working as an independent IT consultant. The market was characterized by a large

		Stage 0			Stage 1				Stage 2			Stage 3				Stage 4				Stage 5			
		1990	1991	1992	1993	1994	1995	1996	1997	1998	1999	2000	2001	2002	2003	2004	2005	2006	2007	2008	2009	2010	2011
MARKET	Distinguishing feature	Knowledge based market "the power of knowledge"			Economy of specialization "the power of producer"				Downstream integration "the power of distributors"			Market expansion "the power of demand"				Market maturity "the power of customers"				Commoditization "the power of competition"			
	Driving force	Consultant driven supply chain			Producers (assemblers) driven supply chain				Distribution driven supply chain			Mass market - Fast market growth				Customer driven supply chain				Size of distribution chain			
	Description	IT consultants are the main players in identifying customers' needs, designing computers and assembling them. The integration between producers and consultants is the key element.			Assemblers are serving the needs of consultants. Production is a specialized function.				Distributors control the market. A consumer market is emerging.			Economy of scale are becoming more important in distribution.				The market stops growing and there is distribution overcapacity.				The product is a commodity, competition is on price. Due to lower margins on products, the minimum efficient scale for operating a distribution network is bigger.			
SMIT	Organizational life cycle	Background			Start-up				Growth			Consolidation				Maturity				Reconfiguration			
	Business model				Sell at day, make at night				Let the sales go			Open and set a queue				Reduce costs				Sell & restart			
	Sales in € millions					n.a	3,522	10,032	12,610	17,811	33,711	61,015	77,425	76,140	81,789	73,678	71,721	75,075	71,378	60,882	62,320	73,885	32,556
	Number of stores					1	2	4	13	21	38	52	66	74	80	92	96	91	78	81*	81*	89*	0
	Area coverage				Local				North/Centre + Online			Nation wide + Online				Nation wide + Online				Nation wide + Online			

n.a. = not available   * = including selling-corners

Exhibit 1. Market Conditions at Each Development Stage of SMIT's Life.

number of independent professionals who were able to translate customer needs into IT requirements. Customers were able to express their needs in terms of functionality but not in terms of product characteristics. Consultants played a fundamental role in identifying product characteristics and acted to interface with computer manufacturers. In general, the IT market was primarily a business-to-business market. In fact, consumer "end users" were only a small fraction of the demand. Knowledge was concentrated in the hands of a small number of IT consultants who operated locally and whose businesses boomed in the early years. Later (1993), the number of IT consultants outstripped demand, and market shares and margins began to decline.

Stage 1 (1993–1996) – Leveraging the Economy of Specialization
In 1993, building on connections with hardware producers developed while working as a consultant and small producer, SMIT's founder decided to move into the hardware supply business and set up a small production shop in a garage in which he assembled computers for other consultants.

SMIT's business model was simple and powerful: computers were built to order (BTO) and delivered within a few days. The rationale was to minimize inventory and reduce capital investment in hardware components. The market appreciated the idea of customized computers, production costs were low due to economies of scale in production and purchasing (as compared with other small producers), demand was high and sales grew rapidly.

In 1995, SMIT moved from the 17-square-meter garage in which the business had started to a shop measuring 200-square-meters with a store open to individual customers. The same year, SMIT opened its first two franchises in nearby cities. In 1996, following a competitor, SMIT decided to open a new store in a town 100 kilometers from its headquarters and hired local staff to manage it.

Stage 2 (1997–1999) – Growing in an Expanding Market
In the following years, SMIT developed a distribution network through CO and franchised stores. In stage 2, SMIT's distribution network and sales grew quickly, benefitting both from the market's overall growth and from a special governmental program that funded entrepreneurs opening new franchises. Moreover, to further support sales in stores, an online store was started. With the store network growing rapidly, a PC assembly shop floor was created. In addition, a division between the distribution network and the strategic management department was created through

the establishment of the headquarters in a separate building from the historical first shop. SMIT's founder stopped working as a salesperson at his store and began working at the headquarters.

Stage 3 (2000–2003) – The Dawn of Market Maturity
In stage 3, the market was still growing fast and to find a line at the counter, it was sufficient merely to open a store. However, the consumer electronics market was changing: a few big players were entering the market with large stores who engaged in price competition. Customized PC hardware became expensive compared with newly available, commodity-like PCs.

From 2000 to 2003, SMIT increased the number of stores in its network from 52 to 80. In 2003, sales peaked at €81.7 million, but the market had just entered a maturity phase in which personal computers had become a mass product and margins were shrinking.

Stage 4 (2004–2007) – Facing Market Maturity
From 2004 to 2007, sales stagnated at approximately €70 million. Competition among big players was based on high volumes with low prices and slim margins. SMIT tried to offer complementary services such as in-store counseling and after-sale (repair and maintenance) services.

Stage 5 (2008–2011) – Facing the Commoditization of IT
In 2008, SMIT's sales dropped to €60 million. IT commoditization was occurring, and large-scale retailers were gaining market share by reducing prices. In 2007, sales of computers increased by 13.1% in volume and only 5.5% in value throughout the entire Italian market. SMIT was competing in a commodity market, margins on products were low, and the minimum efficient scale for operating a distribution network had grown larger. With the aim of pushing hardware sales, SMIT decided to further enlarge its distribution network through a new "light" franchising agreement called the "selling-corner." At the end of 2010, SMIT decided to sell its entire distribution network and PC assembly factory to a competitor. From 2011 on, SMIT focused its business on the B2B market, providing e-learning, web, and IT rental services. A new online store was established with a wide range of products that were still high-tech (PC, PC components, accessories, and technological gadgets), but did not include BTO personal computers. Company headquarters were maintained and nationwide B2B services were offered by extending the supply chain. In 2009, SMIT started a completely new business in LED production; however, in 2011, SMIT's core business was still focused on IT and the B2B services.

Exploration and Exploitation Over Time Through Strategy and MCS

Our discussion of the explorative and exploitative nature of SMIT's strategies and management system practices focuses on the period between 1993
and 2011 (from stage 1 through stage 5). In Exhibit 2, we identify SMIT's
major strategies and management system practices at each stage and categorize those strategies and practices according to their explorative and/or
exploitative natures. We distinguish those strategies related to product
portfolio (dotted line boxes) from those related to market expansion
(dashed line boxes). We identify four major management systems (solid line
boxes) that merit attention: the OI, HR management, the MIS, and the PS.
We intend that these management systems make up the MCS package
(Malmi & Brown, 2008).

Strategy − Markets
Throughout its life, SMIT gradually expanded to change its market. Early
in stage 1, SMIT customers were mainly IT consultants who required
customized PCs. The target market was local. In 1995, SMIT opened a
200-square-meter store and served every person who was willing to buy a
customized PC. During those years, the geographical scope of the target
market expanded through the first two franchisees and another CO store.
The four stores were located in central Italy; three were located in cities
that were close to one another. The drive to expand the business through
the franchising formula emerged from the initiative of two loyal customers.
Impressed by the success of SMIT's business, they resigned from their jobs
and invested their severance pay in franchises located in nearby towns. The
choice to open the franchised stores in nearby cities was encouraged by
SMIT's founder's interest in maintaining a type of monopoly in his own
town.
    Later in its life, SMIT decided to explore the opportunity to increase
sales by expanding the number of stores over a wider geographical area,
including northern and central Italy in stage 2 and nationwide in later
stages. SMIT controlled the evolution of the distribution network, granting
a type of "local monopoly" for each new store. In practice, the rule was to
impose a minimum distance between stores, with a preference for stores
located downtown in big cities. To further support sales and reach all
potential customers, an online store was created. The opening of new stores
was a key success factor. In the eyes of SMIT's founder, there were no
differences between CO stores and franchisees. All stores were equally
important in SMIT's strategy, and the wholesale price list for each store

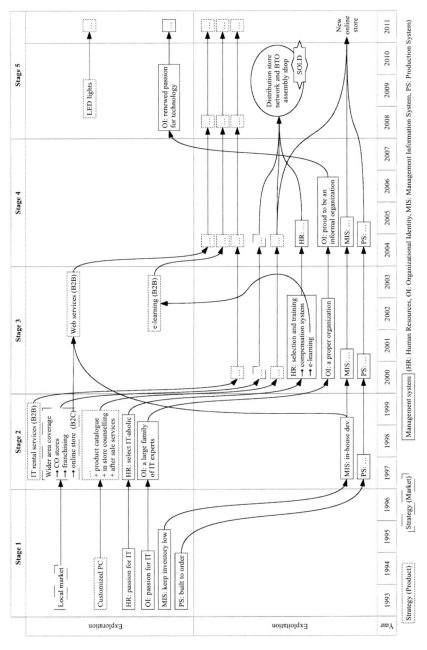

Exhibit 2. Exploration and Exploitation at SMIT from 1993 to 2011.

was the same. We might say that the CO stores were a type of franchise. Franchisees had to buy 80% of their products from SMIT and pay a franchise fee to receive services from SMIT's headquarters, such as the use of SMIT's software and advertising at the national and local levels (in collaboration with headquarters). All stores were forced to accept both price lists and temporary promotions that were determined by company headquarters. MIS played a crucial role in fostering the franchise strategy: profit margins for products sold through CO stores and franchises were the same, and franchises were less problematic by far in terms of management. In stage 3 and the stages that followed, SMIT exploited the franchising formula and opened various CO stores. MIS became the only way to make sense of the overall sales force. Feeding the system with daily data become a priority that led to shortening the daily schedule of stores. This allowed employees to fulfill end-of-day requirements. MIS was playing an unpredicted role in designing boundaries that later appeared to be inconsistent with the idea of implementing a service strategy (for which closing a store earlier in the evening is clearly nonsensical).

In 2008, a new form of "light franchising" was introduced to further expand the distribution network, which was intended to introduce SMIT-branded selling-corners in independent stores (i.e., stores not owned by SMIT) in smaller cities. Compared with standard franchising agreements, "light" franchising required a much lower fee but allowed the franchisee access to the entire SMIT catalogue and services (e.g., delivery within a few days). Given the commoditization of the market and competition with large-scale retailers, many franchisees either asked for franchise fee reductions or switched to the light franchising option. In 2010, the entire distribution network was sold to a competitor. SMIT then abandoned the production of customized hardware and started a new online store.

Strategy – Products
From its start-up until 2011, SMIT's core business consisted of producing and distributing IT to consumers (B2C). Over the course of its organizational life, SMIT expanded its product range, including products such as IT rental services, web services, and e-learning. In addition, SMIT developed a completely new business in the production of LED light solutions.

Beginning at stage 2, SMIT introduced a large set of products through its catalogue. In fact, after its success with the zero-stock approach that it adopted in its operations, SMIT exploited the same approach to expand its product range without increasing its investment. Moreover, by using MIS, it was possible to quickly analyze dispatched orders and learn customers' preferences. By keeping its product range as broad as possible, SMIT could explore the market by understanding its customers' needs. Only after a period of learning was SMIT able both to standardize its stores' product stock and improve its product offerings in the areas that consumers preferred. In this later stage, SMIT's product range supported the exploitation of knowledge that it had previously accumulated.

Web services such as housing, hosting, and construction of e-commerce and e-procurement systems were introduced in 1998. SMIT developed its e-commerce and MIS in-house. The company realized that it could explore a new business opportunity by customizing and selling its in-house-developed systems to a B2B audience. SMIT's online store was initially set up to cover a wider geographical area without opening new stores (in this sense, the online store was an exploration tool). Later, the store became a tool with which SMIT could exploit the market by supporting local store sales with in-store delivery.

In 1999, SMIT started an IT rental service. The service consisted of both leasing IT products and ensuring on-site maintenance. Rental periods could be short (e.g., providing computers and Internet connectivity to conferences) or long (e.g., entering into operating leases for IT and office-automation products). This type of service exploited SMIT's nationwide store distribution network: services were directed by SMIT's headquarters but delivered with the support of a local store.

Exploring a new "service strategy" was motivated by the decreasing profitability of selling products and the decreasing margins in the distribution (stores). This natural effect of moving toward industry maturity could have led to a number of possible solutions. However, managers were stuck on the idea of looking for high unit profit, and MIS was the way to get there. With this perspective, exploring servitization as a way to achieve these goals was the natural next step.

Driven by the need to efficiently manage its distribution network and the BTO process, SMIT demonstrated an unusual ability to develop innovative e-procurement and e-commerce solutions. Because it developed hardware and software solutions in-house, SMIT was able to adapt and offer these services, thus establishing a new business area.

In 2002, e-learning services were started, including training courses with certifications for using the software and hardware products of major IT players. SMIT's ability to provide that training through classes and an e-learning platform was driven by the need to train its employees and franchisees in the distribution network. As with the development of e-commerce and e-procurement solutions, SMIT could offer the same training courses to a wider business audience, which became a business opportunity to explore and exploit.

In 2009, SMIT explored another business opportunity that was not strictly related to IT. Although LED light production was not IT-related, it was a clear technological breakthrough in lighting as IT had been a techno-logical breakthrough for computers and networks in the 1990s. SMIT's founder and current CEO, the IT-aholic person who drove SMIT's growth, decided to explore this new technology.

During its evolution from a small entrepreneurial business to medium-sized IT firm, SMIT explored new business opportunities that were rooted in its previous experience and practice. Web services and e-learning activities (see Exhibit 2) grew out of SMIT's attempt to offer a service that consisted of certain management practices (or a combination of them) that were developed internally to exploit its core business.

Management Systems – HR System and OI
In stage 1, SMIT was a small organization with little complexity. PC assembly was personally undertaken by SMIT's founder in the store's workshop. With two CO stores and two franchisees, organizational struc-ture was minimal and informal. SMIT's founder led a group of enthusiastic entrepreneurs who were willing to make the business work. Coordination among members was easy because they shared the same mindset: a genuine passion for technology. There was no "HR selection" in SMIT's founder's intentions; the company's HR shared a genuine passion for IT, which was enough for him. The company's employees were "IT-addicted" and "computer-aholics," i.e., in the words of SMIT's founder, "they were the kind of IT addicts that nowadays are almost extinct; they were really fond of computers and loved fiddling with them."

In stage 2, during SMIT's initial growth, the criterion for employee selection continued to be a genuine passion for IT and technological inno-vation. Moreover, the choice of whether to hire a person to work in a store or to propose that they start a franchise was driven by opportunism, not by deliberate preference. If the "right" person showed an entrepreneurial attitude, he or she would open a franchise; otherwise, that employee would open a CO store.

SMIT's OI during this period was that of a "large family of IT experts." To build the community, an e-mail-based discussion forum for the distri-bution network was started. All stores, whether COs or franchises could directly communicate with one another and with headquarters. The CEO personally read and posted messages. The issues discussed on the forum ranged from technical support to advertising policy at the national and local levels, and they addressed critical points of the organization and its overall strategy, in addition to the particular needs of local markets. Moreover, an annual employee meeting was organized to build the community. Several technical training courses were organized at company headquarters and attaining advanced technical certifications for hardware and software products was strongly supported.

In stage 3, with a growing number of CO stores (14 in 2004) and franchises (96 in 2005), SMIT tried to become a "proper organization," i.e., formal, structured, and rational. A managing director was hired to support all of the CO stores and to "build a bridge" between SMIT and its network of CO stores. The managing director was in charge of monitoring and supporting staff activities in all CO stores. An incentivized compensation system for sales employees in all CO stores was set up. MIS played a fundamental role in monitoring stores' activities and supporting all in-store procedures. The substantial effort to create structure and formalize activities was mainly directed at governing increasing complexity. The number of stores in the distribution network was rapidly growing, and success was taken for granted; during that period, the company needed only to open its doors to have a line at the counter.

This transformation into a "proper organization" never occurred in practice. SMIT was "proud to be an informal organization." Moreover, this "informal organization" was able to reduce costs and recover agility, which was necessary given market conditions. From 2004 to 2007, the market was entering its maturity stage and price competition from large retailers was increasing. Margins on services were still higher than margins on hardware; however, CO store employees cared less about store profitability than entrepreneurs (franchisees). The profitability of the CO store network was shrinking, and a need for cost reduction emerged. MIS was showing profitability by product or by store, but there was no knowledge about customers' profitability that could have supported the validity of a CO distribution system to foster the firm-to-customer relationship. These factors drove the decision to emphasize franchising over CO stores. The distribution system was considered without any distinction between CO stores and franchising. The profitability analysis did not show any value in the overall distribution network. Its strategic value was totally neglected. Indeed, some CO stores were closed (after 2 consecutive years of losses), and the number of employees was reduced at the remaining stores. The hours at CO stores' were reduced to allow employees to perform end-of-day data entry without overtime. Reward mechanisms based on sales targets were abandoned because they conflicted with the company's "large family" values. The managing director of CO stores resigned and was never replaced. SMIT decided to group CO stores and franchises together under one network and distribution manager.

An opportunity to expand the distribution network came from a governmental program supporting young entrepreneurs. Financial support (low-interest-rate loans and free grants) was offered to help young entrepreneurs start their businesses. Young entrepreneurs selected for this program were not "IT-aholic" people; thus, they were outsiders in the large family of IT experts that SMIT was trying to preserve. The result was a failure, and these franchises closed just a few years later.

In stage 5, after the sale of the distribution network to a competitor, all of SMIT's personnel worked at headquarters. A renewed passion for technology characterized SMIT's OI. SMIT no longer competed in large-scale distribution and focused instead on e-commerce (both B2C and B2B) by providing high-value services to business customers.

Management Systems – Management Information System
As described in the previous sections, MIS played a central role in a number of strategic decisions regarding the growth of SMIT's distribution development and its product range. Such a role was not designed nor planned and derived from the actual use of the system.

As previously mentioned, in 1993 and 1994, the "keep inventory low" rule was easily enforced by collecting orders "by day" and assembling computers "by night." However, in the following years (1995 and 1996), with two franchisees and two CO stores, SMIT needed a way to manage large numbers of orders; therefore, SMIT's founder developed a web-based MIS to automatically record orders. The choice to develop the MIS in-house was explained by SMIT's founder: "In the 90s, very few professional software-based information systems were available, no one was sufficiently efficient and affordable for our needs and many small software houses were producing unreliable software, so we decided on in-house production." Using the software, any store in the network could easily and correctly match hardware components to create a customized personal computer and send the order to SMIT's headquarters. New stores could easily be added to the system at no cost, and new products could be easily added to the catalogue and made immediately available for sale at all stores.

In-house development allowed SMIT to adapt its MIS to the specific needs of headquarters. In particular, all stores were forced to follow all procedures defined by headquarters: all product-related activities (orders, shipments, billing, in-shop availability, etc.) were managed by the MIS. Because in-house development of the software was time consuming, SMIT tried to replace the "old" MIS with an ERP software package in stage 2. However, the ERP software was not designed for SMIT's needs, and changing it was expensive, slow, and problematic. After a short period of time, SMIT's CEO decided to go back to in-house development of MIS. In the words of SMIT's CEO, "We tried to buy ERP software and stop in-house development, but adopting the new ERP would have forced us to change our procedures and we did not want to adapt to the software. We wanted software that could adapt to our needs."

Thanks to the MIS, SMIT was able to explore the BTO opportunity in stage 1 and to exploit it in later stages with the growth of the company's distribution network. It was time consuming to implement any change to the MIS, but the MIS could change according to SMIT's needs and procedures. Furthermore, the experience gained while developing the software allowed SMIT to add a new business to its portfolio. In fact, the web-service platform introduced in stage 3 and aimed at a business audience (B2B) was an evolution of the in-house-developed MIS. The ability to adapt the software to its internal needs (exploitation) allowed SMIT to offer the same service to a new audience (exploration).

Management Systems – Production System
In stage 1, the BTO approach was forced by the need to reduce the company's investment in expensive components. As stated by SMIT's CEO, "We were forced into BTO production because we did not have much money to buy hardware components." The market appreciated the idea of on-demand production of customized computers, and sales grew rapidly: "We were working 15 hours per day: during the day we were selling computers, during the night we were assembling them." In later stages, BTO production became SMIT's natural way of conducting business. When the market grew rapidly due to consumers' demand for tailor-made personal computers, SMIT was able to exploit its BTO PS by offering counseling and after-sale services to inexperienced customers. In 1993 and 1994, the BTO system could employ the practice of collecting orders "by day" and assembling computers "by night." By 1995, when the first franchise opened, and in 1996, with two franchisees and two CO stores, it was necessary to find a way to manage large numbers of orders.

In later stages, with a growing store network, the "keep inventory low" rule was enforced through the MIS developed by SMIT's founder. Company inventory and the BTO PC assembly line were located at SMIT's headquarters; each store could place orders and receive products within a few days. The "keep inventory low" approach was also extended to all products in the catalog. Special agreements with product providers allowed SMIT to keep zero inventory for most products in its catalog: orders were placed with providers only after the product was sold to a final customer. These agreements, together with SMIT's ability to deliver products to stores within a few days from the order, allowed the company to offer a wide range of IT products without huge inventory investments. Only a few products – primarily low-value items such as print cartridges and computer accessories – were immediately available in SMIT's stores. All the other products in the company's catalog were available on demand. This approach allowed SMIT to offer a wider catalog than its competitors.

EXPLORATION AND EXPLOITATION ALONG ORGANIZATIONAL EVOLUTION

In this chapter, we analyze the evolution of an organization from an entrepreneurial one-man venture to a business and explain how exploration and exploitation were balanced along the organization's growth path. We consider both exploration and exploitation strategies (intended as decisions to work in new or old markets and to introduce new products or focus on old ones) and exploration and exploitation practices (intended as exploration and exploitation conveyed through the use of MCS). We consider changes to these strategies and practices and contextualize them in both internal and external conditions. Although there is only one company in our sample, we believe that this case typifies both issues and growth of entrepreneurial ventures to SME size; thus, we may draw certain conclusions from this case that may broaden our understanding of the exploration and exploitation phenomenon and prompt further research for testing and generalizing.

First, our study was undertaken with the question of how the relative weight of exploration and exploitation evolves over an organization's life. From the overall analysis of SMIT's evolution, it is possible to find the main trend that moves from exploration to exploitation. In fact, the organization was already being developed in the start-up phase. Because the organization started from a position with no experience in the business, exploration was at its maximum: there were no specific resources, a customer base had to be constructed, and investments had to be made. In the early years of an organization, the combination of operational and strategic roles that characterize SMEs is found in an extreme form in the entrepreneur: both the business and the job of leading it are learned every day through trial and error. This learning cannot be categorized as refinement because there is no ready-to-use base from which to start. As a company gains market success and acquires a leading position among its competitors, it also increases its size, resulting in increased operational burden. In these later stages, with few exceptions, an organization's strategies focus on refining its product range and geographical presence along established channels of operating. As for the practice conveyed through MCS, the main focus is exploitation, in terms of focus and efficiency. This overall trend is consistent with the literature that acknowledges both the assets (March, 2010) and the liabilities of newness (Stinchcombe, 1965), in addition to the growing inertia that is associated with establishing an organization (Hannan & Freeman, 1984). Building on this evidence, we emphasize that entrepreneurial ventures are typically misbalanced toward exploration at their beginning because they start from blurry business ideas that become clear when they are realized. Next, the main trend moves from exploration to exploitation in the leading role. However, there are also changes from exploitation to exploration.

The balance changes from exploitation to exploration in rare cases, given that established organizations that are characterized by inertia "encounter difficulties in keeping up with technological advancements" and "become dependent on established routines and skills" (Lavie et al., 2010, p. 123). The evidence shows that the transformation from exploitation to exploration concerns competencies enabled in MCS that have reached a high rate of refinement and are offered as new services on the market. The web-services and e-learning service platform displayed this experimental nature when they were conveyed to the market, whereas their underlying competencies and skills were highly defined and mainly focused on internal needs. This evidence shows the cross-link between practice and strategy and responds to the literature that has requested studies showing "the ability of the organization to leverage existing assets and capabilities from the mature side of the business to gain competitive advantage in new areas" (O'Reilly & Tushman, 2013, p. 18). Within MCS, there have been attempts to introduce some form of exploration after the exploitative focus has been assimilated. These attempts concern interactive forms of discussion, such as the e-mail-based discussion forum or the annual meeting where store managers shared their experience of the market and their ideas for innovation and further improvement. Nevertheless, such initiatives were isolated and did not reflect a general organizational orientation toward exploration. Instead, they constituted a quiet attempt to maintain the balance between exploration and exploitation in the face of a strong, clear prevalence for exploitation.

A second line of inquiry is to understand the role of external factors (such as market dimension or competitive intensity) and internal factors (such as size and managerial preferences) in the evolution of the exploration and exploitation balance. With respect to external conditions, profitability conditions changed with MCS. When margins fell, SMIT tried the efficiency solution by adopting MCS displaying both the rigidity and clarity of a rule-based system. Boundaries to organizational action were set – for instance, CO stores were closed after 2 years of losses. Performance measurement was enhanced, and incentives and rewards were introduced. SMIT tried to become a textbook-archetypal "proper organization" with everything set in formal systems. However, the organization did not react as expected: "We tried, but we are not like that." The organization understood that internal conditions follow an evolutionary path that reflects but is not strictly determined by external conditions. This shows that adaptation is possible only within the plasticity of existing systems and that radical transformation is difficult.

Concerning internal conditions, considerations of OI are the other side of the coin of the coevolution described above and can be derived accordingly. We may add instead a comment on the relevance of managerial antecedents such as risk preferences and learning abilities in deploying explorative or exploitative strategies and practices. In the initial stages of SMIT, participants in the organization either adhered to an entrepreneurial project or were entrepreneurs themselves who started franchises. They were inclined to accept risk and were eager to learn from experience. In later stages, the organization involved different types of participants who displayed opportunistic behaviors in some cases that typified those that thought they had joined a big-enough, safe "elephant" organization. In addition to these considerations of the properties of the participants, particularities of the repeated processes also pushed toward exploitation. Indeed, the recurrent use of actions associated with positive feedback typically leads to a change in managerial preference toward reliable outcomes and risk aversion. Both internal and external conditions play a prominent role in the evolution of exploration and exploitation. First, both sets of conditions change their reactions to one another as exogenous elements and, second, these conditions both display an endogenous source of change. The distinction can be captured by the changes that occurred in OI in our case study: growth in the dimension and complexity of operations first required a change from a "large family" to a "proper organization," whereas the change from the "proper organization" to the "informal organization" took place largely as a reaction to the first change. As a result, there are several drivers of change that operate simultaneously, but the evidence provided in our case did not allow us to identify clear, causal patterns in such a complex source of change. We interpret this result as consistent with evidence for the equifinality of diverse components and paths to exploration and exploitation, which may advocate for the same exploitative or exploratory targets (Gibson & Birkinshaw, 2004). Organizational experience and heritage account for which components and paths occur in the evolution of an organization and how much they can be adapted to coevolve with other factors.

As a third point, we address the role of MCS in supporting exploration and exploitation in organizations. Typically, the literature on exploration and exploitation considers such systems to play a neutral role, i.e., they provide the function and finality for which they were designed (McCarthy & Gordon, 2011). In this line of research, MCS types have been associated with exploration or exploitation for normative purposes. Our case shows the various roles that management systems play during the evolution of an organization, despite their design. A clear example is provided by the product catalog, i.e., the list of products that can be sold. Building on McCarthy and Gordon's (2011) categorization, this is a tool designed to support exploitation because it clearly defines the boundaries of what can and cannot be done. In fact, in stages three and four this was the case. However, in the previous stage, the product catalog was a system that supported the exploration of customers' preferences because it was large enough to allow customers to reveal their preferences with no constraints on the availability of products. We argue that this shows that MCS are not neutral in conveying, supporting or simply deploying exploration and exploitation. However, their role in the pursuit of exploration and exploitation reflects the use that is made of them, rather than their design.

Over the life cycle, MCS assume essential and primitive forms in the start-up phase. Our interpretation is that this is the case because these MCS are defined through practice rather than design, and the typical emergent development of the entrepreneurial venture in our case allows that to emerge. One example of this phenomenon is the BTO production approach. Moreover, in several cases, when MCS are introduced into a managerial practice, they provide general direction for action, but their primary function is explorative. Nevertheless, this evidence can only be considered in a limited manner because we have a low variety of MCS entry periods in the exploration area. Indeed, alternative hypotheses may explain this effect. On the one hand, this could be an effect of the start-up phase in which they were introduced: by definition, people are more inclined to experimentation and adapt any system to this attitude despite its design. On the other hand, this could also be caused by the exploratory attitude around a new system that is necessary to build a new practice and that weakens once a practice is established. Future studies are required to clarify this point.

CONCLUSION

In this chapter, we conducted a longitudinal analysis of the balance of exploration and exploitation in organizational evolution. We addressed the typical growth path of an entrepreneurial one-man venture until it became a stable and fully shaped business. We have three main findings. First, exploration plays a prominent role in the start-up phase because practices and strategies are shaped while being realized and there is a substantial openness to experimentation. Conversely, as an organization enjoys market success and grows in size and organizational complexity, exploitation becomes the main focus. Second, there is a coevolution of changes in the exploration and exploitation balance with external factors (such as market dimension and competitive intensity) and internal factors (such as size and managerial preferences). Third, MCS practices, not MCS design, account for the role of MCS in exploration and exploitation in organizations.

This study contributes to the ambidexterity literature by expanding our understanding of the role of management systems in supporting exploration and exploitation in organizations. We draw attention to MCS and the different functions that it may assume through practice and along evolution. In fact, we show that in each stage of organizational evolution, exploration and exploitation are simultaneously pursued through MCS and product or market strategies. However, the explorative or exploitative role of MCS and strategies may vary depending on their use in practice. Further, across stages, MCS practices and strategies typically change their role from exploration to exploitation; however, there are cases in which competencies accumulated through exploitation are used to explore new areas of business.

Despite the fact that our findings arise out of a one-firm sample, given that our case represents the typical growth of an entrepreneurial venture that achieves both the size and acquires the issues of an SME, we take these considerations as valid for broadening our understanding of the exploration and exploitation phenomenon. Indeed, we invite further research for testing and generalization.

NOTES

1. They debate, decide, and fulfill exploration and exploitation. We found this to be particularly true in our case study, probably because the senior managers of SMEs frequently are the entrepreneurs.

2. According to Wittgenstein (1973), a "cluster concept" is one that "is defined by a weighted list of criteria, such that no one of these criteria is either necessary or sufficient for membership, but nonetheless meaningful" (Pigliucci, 2008, p. 888).

3. MCS and emphasis added. Replacing the emphasized terms with "MCS" conveys our intended meaning.

4. For confidentiality reasons, the actual name of the firm is omitted. SMIT is a fictitious acronym that stands for "Small−Medium Information Technology." All details about the firm and the data collected are available from our archive upon request.

REFERENCES

Ahrens, T., & Chapman, C. S. (2005). Management control systems and the crafting of strategy: A practice based view. In C. S. Chapman (Ed.), *Controlling strategy: Management, accounting and performance measurement*. Oxford: Oxford University Press.

Ahrens, T., & Chapman, C. S. (2007). Management accounting as practice. *Accounting, Organizations and Society, 32*, 1−27.

Auh, S., & Menguc, B. (2005). Balancing exploration and exploitation: The moderating role of competitive intensity. *Journal of Business Research, 58*(12), 1652−1661.

Birkinshaw, J., & Gupta, K. (2013). Clarifying the distinctive contribution of ambidexterity to the field of organization studies. *Academy of Management Perspectives, 27*(4), 287−298.

Burgelman, R. A. (2002). Strategy as vector and the inertia of coevolutionary lock-in. *Administrative Science Quarterly, 47*(2), 325−357.

Cohen, W. M., & Levinthal, D. A. (1990). Absorptive capacity: A new perspective on learning and innovation. *Administrative Science Quarterly, 35*(1), 128−152.

Collini, P., & Frigotto, M. L. (2013). Management control systems for exploration? A paradox and a challenge for research. *Management Control, 2*, 15−41.

Fang, C., Lee, J., & Schilling, M. A. (2010). Balancing exploration and exploitation through structural design: The isolation of subgroups and organizational learning. *Organization Science, 21*, 625−642.

Fontana, W. (2001). *Novelty in evolution, Green Paper for Bioevolutionary Concepts for NASA, BEACON*. Retrieved from http://tuvalu.santafe.edu/~walter/Papers/beacon.pdf. Accessed on December 29, 2013.

Gibson, C. B., & Birkinshaw, J. (2004). The antecedents, consequences, and mediating role of organizational ambidexterity. *Academy of Management Journal, 47*(2), 209–226.

Grabner, I., & Moers, F. (2013). Management control as a system or a package? Conceptual and empirical issues. *Accounting, Organizations and Society, 38*, 407–419.

Gupta, A. K., Smith, K. G., & Shalley, C. E. (2006). The interplay between exploration and exploitation. *Academy of Management Journal, 49*(4), 693–706.

Hannan, M. T., & Freeman, J. (1984). Structural inertia and organizational change. *American Sociological Review, 49*(2), 149–164.

He, Z., & Wong, P. (2004). Exploration vs. exploitation: An empirical test of the ambidexterity hypothesis. *Organization Science, 15*(4), 481–494.

Hess, A. M., & Rothaermel, F. T. (2011). When are assets complementary? Star scientists, strategic alliances, and innovation in the pharmaceutical industry. *Strategic Management Journal, 32*(8), 895–909.

Hopwood, A., & Miller, P. (1994). Cambridge studies in management. *Accounting as social and institutional practice* (Vol. 24). Cambridge, UK: Cambridge University Press.

Jansen, J. P., Van den Bosch, F. A., & Volberda, H. W. (2006). Exploratory innovation, exploitative innovation and performance effects: Effects of organizational antecedents and environmental moderators. *Management Science, 52*, 1661–1674.

Jørgensen, B., & Messner, M. (2010). Accounting and strategising: A case study from new product development. *Accounting, Organizations and Society, 35*, 184–204.

Lavie, D., Kang, J., & Rosenkopf, L. (2011). Balance within and across domains: The performance implications of exploration and exploitation in alliances. *Organization Science, 22*, 1517–1538.

Lavie, D., & Rosenkopf, L. (2006). Balancing exploration and exploitation in alliance formation. *Academy of Management Journal, 49*, 797–818.

Lavie, D., Stettner, U., & Tushman, M. L. (2010). Exploration and exploitation within and across organizations. *The Academy of Management Annals, 4*(1), 109–155.

Lawrence, T. B., & Suddaby, R. (2006). Institutions and institutional work. In S. R. Clegg, C. Hardy, T. B. Lawrence, & W. N. Nord (Eds.), *The Sage handbook of organization studies*. London: SAGE Publications Ltd.

Levinthal, D., & March, J. (1993). The myopia of learning. *Strategic Management Journal, 14*, 5–112.

Lin, Z. J., Yang, H., & Demirkan, I. (2007). The performance consequences of ambidexterity in strategic alliance formations: Empirical investigation and computational theorizing. *Management Science, 53*(10), 1645–1658.

Lubatkin, M. H., Simsek, Z., Ling, Y., & Veiga, J. F. (2006). Ambidexterity and performance in small-to medium-sized firms: The pivotal role of top management team behavioral integration. *Journal of Management, 32*(5), 646–672.

Malmi, T., & Brown, D. A. (2008). Management control systems as a package – opportunities, challenges and research directions. *Management Accounting Research, 19*(4), 287–300.

March, J. G. (1991). Exploration and exploitation in organizational learning. *Organization Science, 2*(1), 71–87.

March, J. G. (2010). *The ambiguities of experience*. Ithaca, NY: Cornell University Press.

McCarthy, I. P., & Gordon, B. R. (2011). Achieving contextual ambidexterity in R&D organizations: A management control system approach. *R&D Management, 41*(3), 240–258.

Miller, P. (2001). Governing by numbers: Why calculative practices matter. *Social Research*, *68*, 379–396.

Nosella, A., Cantarello, S., & Filippini, R. (2012). The intellectual structure of organizational ambidexterity: A bibliographic investigation into the state of the art. *Strategic Organization*, *10*(4), 450–465.

O'Reilly, C. A., & Tushman, M. L. (2013). Organizational ambidexterity: Past, present and future. *Academy of Management Perspectives*, *27*(4), 324–338.

Orlikowski, W. J. (2000). Using technology and constituting structures: A practice lens for studying technology in organizations. *Organization Science*, *11*(4), 404–428.

Pigliucci, M. (2008). What, if anything, is an evolutionary novelty? *Philosophy of Science*, *75*(5), 887–898.

Raisch, S., & Birkinshaw, J. (2008). Organizational ambidexterity: Antecedents, outcomes, and moderators. *Journal of Management*, *34*(3), 375–409.

Ravasi, D., & Schultz, M. (2006). Responding to organizational identity threats: Exploring the role of organizational culture. *Academy of Management Journal*, *49*(3), 433–458.

Rosenkopf, L., & Mcgrath, P. (2011). Advancing the conceptualization and operationalization of novelty in organizational research. *Organization Science*, *22*(5), 1297–1311.

Sidhu, J., Volberda, H., & Commandeur, H. (2004). Exploring exploration orientation and its determinants: Some empirical evidence. *Journal of Management Studies*, *41*, 913–932.

Siggelkow, N. (2007). Persuasion with case studies. *Academy of Management Journal*, *50*, 20–24.

Simons, R. (1994). How new top managers use control systems as levers of strategic renewal. *Strategic Management Journal*, *15*(3), 169–189.

Stinchcombe, A. L. (1965). Social structure and organizations. In J. G. March (Ed.), *The handbook of organizations* (pp. 142–193). Chicago, IL: Rand McNally & Co.

Tushman, M. L., & O'Reilly, C. A. (1996). The ambidextrous organization: Managing evolutionary and revolutionary change. *California Management Review*, *38*, 1–23.

Vermeulen, F., & Barkema, H. (2001). Learning through acquisitions. *Academy of Management Journal*, *44*(3), 457–476.

Voss, G. B., & Voss, Z. G. (2013). Strategic ambidexterity in small and medium-sized enterprises: Implementing exploration and exploitation in product and market domains. *Organization Science*, *24*(5), 1459–1477.

Wittgenstein, L. ([1953] 1973). *Philosophical investigations*. New York, NY: Macmillan.

Yin, R. (1994). *Case study research: Design and methods*. Thousand Oaks, CA: Sage.

CHAPTER 8

A HEIGHT–DISTANCE VIEW ON EXPLORATION AND EXPLOITATION

Anna Sabidussi

ABSTRACT

This chapter investigates how small- and medium-sized enterprises and large firms decide the sourcing strategies to explore and exploit. This study adopts a qualitative methodology and reports on the insights derived from interviews with 35 companies and 2 experts. A series of propositions are derived, and these propositions are used to propose a height–distance view of exploration and exploitation. The implications for theory and managerial practice are presented in the concluding remarks.

Keywords: Innovation; exploration; exploitation; height; distance; external sourcing

INTRODUCTION

Companies' ability to develop existing competencies and create new ones lies at the heart of the strategic management debate and of firms'

Exploration and Exploitation in Early Stage Ventures and SMEs
Technology, Innovation, Entrepreneurship and Competitive Strategy, Volume 14, 181−210
Copyright © 2014 by Emerald Group Publishing Limited
All rights of reproduction in any form reserved
ISSN: 1479-067X/doi:10.1108/S1479-067X20140000014005

sustainable competitive advantage (Benner & Tushman, 2003; Teece, Pisano, & Shuen, 1997). The seminal work by March (1991) made it clear that exploration and exploitation are essential. Exploration is associated with experimentation and discovery, whereas exploitation refers to refinement, efficiency, and implementations.

In the context of technological innovation, the literature has linked explorative innovation to entry into novel product-market areas and has linked exploitation to the enhancement of current product-market positioning (Greve, 2007; He & Wong, 2004). Additionally, because exploitation is central to improving firms' current activities, increasing efficiency and routines, and improving existing processes may be considered a form of exploitation. Similarly, experimenting with new ways of doing and novel processes may be linked to exploration.

The issue of how exploration and exploitation can be organized remains a driving question in continuous research endeavors. As briefly noted by O'Reilly and Tushman (2013), certain firms excel in developing new capabilities through external sourcing but not in developing them internally, and vice versa. In their explorative and exploitative endeavors, organizations can rely on developing innovation internally or (partially) sourcing innovation externally. The present research examines how companies decide to pursue exploration and exploitation using external or internal sourcing modalities. This topic is at the core of organizations' strategic orientation. How does a propensity to use specific sourcing modalities arise in managerial practice? Addressing these challenges answers the call for more qualitative studies investigating how managers allocate resources to exploration and exploitation (O'Reilly & Tushman, 2013).

Our current understanding of the phenomenon is not complete, particularly with respect to the potential differences and similarities between small- and medium-sized enterprises (SMEs) and large companies. Previous studies analyzing the performance, growth, and innovation of SMEs clarify the specific conditions of SMEs compared to larger firms. SMEs are generally at a disadvantage in terms of resource availabilities and capabilities compared to large companies, which is relevant for the pursuit of exploration and exploitation. For instance, March-Chorda, Gunasekaran, and Lloria-Aramburo (2002) have noted that the costs associated with innovation constitute a barrier particularly for SMEs. Compared to larger firms, SMEs have less access to financial resources (Serrasqueiro & Maçãs Nunes, 2008). Large companies benefit from economies of scale and typically have more diversified businesses, allowing them to spread risk over more business units (Serrasqueiro & Maçãs Nunes, 2008), whereas small companies tend to limit their exposure to risky situations (Lensink, Steen, & Sterken, 2005; Serrasqueiro & Maçãs Nunes, 2008). However, SMEs are favored by less rigid and less formal organizational structures, a factor that may potentially enhance their flexibility and response to new opportunities (Serrasqueiro & Maçãs Nunes, 2008). These elements represent ways in which SMEs and large firms differ. Understanding the similarities and differences in how differently sized companies pursue exploration and exploitation may provide a deeper understanding of the key strategic phenomenon of ambidexterity.

The present research investigates the managerial practices that drive the external sourcing decision for exploration and exploitation in SMEs and large firms. The current literature does not provide a clear framework to address the above issue because it has focused mainly on large and established organizations, dedicating limited attention to SMEs.

Answering the "how" question and gathering the perspectives of informants is the domain of qualitative research (Pratt, 2009). The present study adopts a qualitative methodology and integrates both deductive and inductive approaches. Deductive methods refer to the empirical validation of conceptual constructs derived from theory. Inductive research is the opposite process and refers to the development of conceptual constructs from the data to create new or refine existing theoretical approaches. Inductive approaches are complementary to deductive, hypotheses-testing methods (Eisenhardt & Graebner, 2007). The combination of deductive and inductive approaches is referred to as the hybrid method, which uses insights derived from the existing literature as well as patterns and themes from raw data (Fereday & Muir-Cochrane, 2006).

In the next section, the relevant literature for the study is introduced. Next, the methodology and data collection are illustrated. Finally, insights from the qualitative research are presented and discussed. Potential avenues for further research are proposed in the concluding remarks.

THE LITERATURE

Exploration and Exploitation

Exploration and exploitation are key corporate tasks that have attracted the attention of both scholars and practitioners. These concepts were originally defined in broad terms by March (1991, p. 71), who associates exploration with "search, variation, risk taking, experimentation, play, flexibility, discovery, innovation" and exploitation with "refinement, choice, production, efficiency, selection, implementation, execution."

As noted by Lavie, Stettner, and Tushman (2010) in their review, the interpretation of exploration and exploitation has been restricted in the subsequent work by Levinthal and March (1993) to the development of new knowledge (exploration) or the utilization of existing knowledge (exploitation). Further developments have extended the definitions beyond their initial boundaries to a vast range of phenomena (Lavie et al., 2010).

As noted by O'Reilly and Tushman (2013), studies have found that the pursuit of both exploration and exploitation (ambidexterity) is beneficial for performance. Despite the advantages, exploration and exploitation are driven by inherently contradictory logics, which creates tension between the two activities. The literature has dedicated considerable attention to the ways in which ambidexterity may be balanced. As O'Reilly and Tushman (2013) conclude, all the balancing modes are valid, and organizations can balance the trade-offs by organizing ambidexterity sequentially (temporally separating exploration and exploitation), structurally (separating the units in which exploration and exploitation are performed), or contextually (separating exploration and exploitation in the activities of individuals).

One of the areas in which the ambidexterity focus has been applied is the external sourcing mechanisms that can be used to pursue exploration and exploitation. For example, Rothaermel and Deeds (2004) found that innovation and the new product process benefit from an explorative–exploitative alliances strategy. Lavie and Rosenkopf (2006) fostered understanding of why and how companies balance exploration and exploitation in alliance formation. Their findings showed that companies exploit and explore over time and across domains. Recently, Stettner and Lavie (2013) investigated the advantages of balancing exploration and exploitation by using distinct interorganizational forms (e.g., exploring with one mode and exploiting with another mode). From this literature stream, it may be noted that external sourcing strategies and cooperation can effectively contribute to the pursuit of exploration and exploitation objectives.

The Causes of External Sourcing

The pursuit of exploration and exploitation can be supported by internal efforts and by external relationships. As noted by March (1991), exploration and exploitation are two distinct activities with specific characteristics. Compared to exploitation, exploration is associated with the creation of new knowledge and is therefore more risky and uncertain, with benefits that are potentially more distant in time. Companies that engage in exploration endeavors may expect greater exposure to higher costs, risks, and a longer time-to-market span due to the complexity associated with developing novel knowledge and entering new markets. As noted by Veugelers and Cassiman (1999), factors such as risks, costs, and the appropriability of innovation do not deter the decision to innovate but rather determine the innovation sourcing strategies that a firm adopts. Therefore, it may be speculated that the relevance of specific motives differs when the innovation objective is exploration or exploitation and that this influences the sourcing decision.

The literature on how firms determine their boundaries and use open innovation practices provides useful insights into the general benefits companies seek from external relationships (e.g., Parmigiani, 2007; Poppo & Zenger, 1998; Van de Vrande, de Jong, Vanhaverbeke, & de Rochemont, 2009; Yasuda, 2005). Hagedoorn (1993) has provided an extensive list of these external relationship motives by following the linear progression of innovation from basic research to market introduction. From basic or applied research beginnings, companies may engage in external relationships to monitor technological developments and share costs and uncertainty. Monitoring is relevant because it may provide valuable insight into novel developments in the technology field (Duysters & De Man, 2003). Additionally, companies may rely on external partners to limit their own exposure to uncertain technological advancements or market developments (Folta, 1998; Van de Vrande, Lemmens, & Vanhaverbeke, 2006). Sharing risk is one of the key motivations for sourcing innovation externally (Tethler, 2002). Uncertainty may refer to the unclear outcomes of innovation efforts or to the fact that the results may be achieved at a higher cost or later than expected (Bayona, Garcia-Marco, & Huerta, 2001). Sharing costs is also recognized as an important driver. A recent report from the Boston Consulting Group (Andrew, Sirkin, Haanaes, & Michael, 2007) indicated that reducing costs through cooperation rather than performing the work in-house contributes to an increase in returns on innovation investments. Together with sharing the costs of innovation, reducing the time-to-market is a relevant motive for engaging with external partners (Hynes & Mollenkopf, 2008; Manders & Brenner, 1995; Sakakibara, 1997). In Hagedoorn's (1993) classification, time-to-market and gaining access to others' knowledge are part of improving the overall efficiency of the innovation process. With respect to market access, internationalization, and shaping market structure, partnerships can be used to enter into new, unknown markets or to internationalize portions of corporate activity (Hagedoorn, 1993). In case of government or legislative constraints, entrance to the market may be facilitated by a link with an external partner (Contractor & Lorange, 2004; Vilkamo & Keil, 2003). Partners may be beneficial because they hold specific knowledge about the target market or are already active in it (Bayona et al., 2001). All of the above-mentioned aspects play different roles when exploration or exploitation is the objective of the innovative endeavor. However, the way that companies make decisions about their external sourcing activities when aiming at exploration and exploitation is an issue that has not received a clear answer in previous studies.

SMEs and Large Firms

In the current literature, it remains unclear how large firms and SMEs allocate their choices about external partnerships when aiming at exploratory or exploitative objectives. Firms' size characteristics (and the associated resource availability) may endorse a different modality in the pursuit of solutions for exploration versus exploitation. In the literature on ambidexterity, there is no clear consensus about the role of organizational aspects such as size, and conflicting views still coexist, as noted by Csaszar (2013). Csaszar noted that according to Beckman, Haunschild, and Phillips (2004), exploration is favored by large firms, whereas according to Rothaermel and Deeds (2004), the opposite is true. Smaller firms may be expected to dispose of less slack resources compared to larger firms. Slack resources are resources in "excess of the minimum necessary to produce a given level of organizational output" (Nohria & Gulati, 1996, p. 1246). There are opposing views in the literature about the impact of slack resources on exploration (Lavie et al., 2010). The conciliation seems to come from the view that slack resources have a curvilinear relationship with innovation: too little does not allow for experimentation, and too much creates a lack of discipline, whereas both experimentation and discipline are needed for innovation (Nohria & Gulati, 1996).

The literature has also not provided clear guidance from either a theoretical or empirical viewpoint about the role of size in the sourcing decision process. Here, too, contradictory arguments coexist (Bayona et al., 2001). For example, it has been argued that small firms have learned to remove obstacles when innovating by making proper use of external relationships (Narula, 2004). Ali, Krapfel, and LaBahn (1995) showed that being fast to market is beneficial for SMEs because it allows them to recover their initial investment sooner. The specific issues noted above may represent an incentive for engaging in external relationships. It has been observed, however, that a lack of resources and internal innovation capacity constrains firms' abilities to engage in partnerships. This limit to the propensity for external collaboration is especially severe in SMEs (Bayona et al., 2001).

Overall, it may be concluded that shedding light on the way that large firms and SMEs allocate resources to external partnerships for exploration and exploitation can contribute to our current understanding of ambidexterity.

A QUALITATIVE APPROACH

The present study adopts a qualitative method. The next section illustrates how the research has been structured to investigate the way that management elaborates the decision to use external versus internal sourcing for explorative or exploitative scopes.

Sample

In qualitative studies, three approaches may be adopted: convenience sampling, judgment sampling, and theoretical sampling (Marshall, 1996). According to the classifications provided by Marshall (1996), judgment sampling can be further specified on the basis of the criteria adopted. For example, a researcher may be interested in following outliers or a broad range of respondents (maximum variance), critical cases, or specific expertise (key informant). Following Marshall (1996), the present research adopted a judgment approach and identified the most appropriate and competent subjects (key informants) to address the issue under investigation.

The companies were identified based on three main key characteristics: their high performance as innovators, the geographical location of their headquarters, and the sector of activity. First, companies had to be actively involved in advanced technologies, and their innovation success had to be confirmed by secondary sources of information. Second, the companies' headquarters had to be located in Europe or the United States. Third, a multisector approach was adopted because sampling across multiple sectors met the need for variance in the industries considered by the study.

To ensure a high response rate, the present study used direct contacts or intermediaries to initialize communication with the target organizations.

Of all the contacts made, only two potential respondents (one expert and one biotech firm) did not reply to the invitation to participate in the study.

In total, interviews were performed with representatives of 35 companies and two industry experts from consultancy firms.[1] The selection included both large and small companies with headquarters in nine different countries in Europe and in the United States. The sample of companies included various sectors: Biopharmaceuticals (27%), Food and Chemistry (11%), Energy (8%), Materials (21%), Mechanics (19%), and Electronics (3%). The sample was well balanced in terms of size: 54% were large companies (>250 employees), and 46% were small companies (<250 employees). The sample included fourteen world leader companies (companies in the top ten for market share in the specific, worldwide sector of reference at the time of the interview) and eight best-in-class companies (top three worldwide in their sector of reference at the time of the interview) with a recognized record in innovation performance. Table 1 contains the baseline descriptions of the participating companies.

Because the purpose of the research was to capture a view of managerial practice, the respondents were selected based on their decision power within

Table 1. Baseline Description of Interviewed Companies.

Baseline of interviewed companies: SMEs companies (n = 17)

Employees	From 2 to less than 150
R&D personnel	From 2 to 35
Countries	Europe/USA
Sectors	Bio-pharma 47%, Materials 35%, Food/Chemistry 12%, Electronics 6%
Innovation sourcing (average)	68% Internal, 32% External (SD 22%)

Baseline of interviewed companies: large companies (n = 18)

Employees	From 900 to less than 350.000
R&D personnel	From 70 to less than 5.000
Countries	Europe/USA
Sectors	Mechanics 39%, Food/Chemistry 17%, Bio-pharma 11%, Energy 22%, Materials 11%
Innovation sourcing (average)	70% Internal, 30% External (SD 22%)

Baseline of interviewed companies: best-in-class companies (n = 8)

Employees	From 5000 to less than 350,000
R&D personnel	From 110 to less than 25,000
Countries	Europe/USA
Sectors	50% Mechanics, 12.5% Food, 12.5% Materials, 12.5% Bio-pharma, 12.5%, Energy
Innovation sourcing (average)	79% Internal, 21% External (SD 10%)

Table 2. Overview of Job Classes of Interviewed Respondents.

Interviewed decision makers: SMEs (n = 17)	
CEO/Board	81%
Vice President	13%
Director	0%
Corporate Innovation Manager	6%
Interviewed decision makers: large companies (n = 18)	
CEO/Board	30%
Vice President	12%
Director	29%
Corporate Innovation Manager	29%
Interviewed decision makers: best-in-class companies (n = 8)	
CEO/Board	12%
Vice President	25%
Director	25%
Corporate Innovation Manager	38%

the organization; they were involved in strategic innovation decisions for their organizations. The interviewees can be divided into four job description classes: (1) CEOs, managing directors, and board members (54%); (2) CTOs and vice presidents (11%); (3) directors (14%); and (4) corporate innovation managers (16%). Table 2 provides an overview of the interviewees.

The Interview Process

The data collection phase was organized as semi-structured interviews with representatives of top management from innovative companies. Semi-structured interviews have the advantage of facilitating comparisons among the respondents' answers by following a common interview guideline but leaving freedom for the respondents to express their thoughts in a flexible and open way (Horton, Macve, & Struyven, 2004). A qualitative methodology allows the researcher to obtain "the perspective of the players" (Dodourova, 2009, p. 833). The procedure was designed to gather insights about both the explicit priorities that the executives recognize and the implicit considerations and unconscious knowledge that may underlie their decisions (Dienes, 2008; Größler, Rouwette, & Vennix, 2008).

The interviews were performed by telephone, with the exception of nine cases in which face-to-face meetings were organized. The conversations took place in English with a few exceptions (French and Italian). The interview protocol included both closed-form and semi-open questions. The closed-form questions were sent to the respondents prior to the interview, and the respondents were asked to write their answers. The goal of the closed questions was to facilitate discussion during the interview phase. During the conversation, respondents were asked to comment and explain their choices.

Because innovation represented the focus of the discussion, to ensure that all respondents referred to the same concept, innovation was clearly defined in the text that was sent prior to the conversation, and its definition was stated at the beginning of each interview. Specifically, in this study, the concept of innovation referred to a novel idea applied to products and/or processes that are introduced into the market. This clarification ensured the homogeneity and comparability of the information obtained from the interviewees.

Data about each individual company were collected from public sources (corporate websites or newspapers). In the first part of the interview, the respondents were asked to provide (or to confirm, when initial information was gathered from the above-mentioned secondary sources) a profile of their company's characteristics in terms of the number of employees, markets of operations, and so forth. Next, the discussion moved to an investigation of the relevance of innovation for their company's corporate competitive success, the company's strategic orientation (e.g., from "follower"to "ahead of competition"), and the perceived level of competition intensity. To understand the relevance of external relationships and internal efforts for innovation, the interviewees were asked to distinguish between the proportion of innovation derived from internal and external sources.

Overall, the first phase of the interview aimed to gather key information about the organizations, managers' strategic attitudes toward innovation, and their main innovation modalities.

The second phase of the discussion focused on understanding the use of internal and external resources for purposes of exploration and exploitation. The respondents were asked to rank the relative importance of each item on a list of motives that were mainly derived from this study's literature review. Although the overall approach of the research can be considered inductive, the existing literature on the causes of external sourcing was used to draft a general preliminary list, which can be qualified as deductive. In this sense, the present study combined inductive and deductive approaches. During the conversation, the respondents had the opportunity to discuss any additional drivers that they would have considered relevant that were not included in the options provided. The discussion offered the opportunity to gather comments and observations about the association between certain motives and the specific type of objectives.

To gain a deeper understanding of how the above-mentioned motives serve the purposes of innovation, managers' functions in the decision process received additional attention. The third phase of the interview was structured as a journey into the considerations of decision makers when undertaking different types of innovation projects and deciding on the use of external and/or internal sources.

The interview approach was partially inspired by the logic of experiment-based research approaches and "think aloud" methods (e.g., Nees, 1983; Someren, Barnard, & Sandberg, 1994). In experiment-based research, the respondents imitate a process to clarify the decision mechanisms involved in real-life experiences (Nees, 1983). Think aloud methods refer to saying one's thoughts aloud when solving a specific problem and are especially useful for gathering insights on cognitive processes (Someren et al., 1994). Think aloud approaches may avoid misleading information that can be obtained, for example, by asking managers to recall their thoughts when they were confronted with a similar problem in the past. Memory may be easily altered by errors or (mis)interpretation (Someren et al., 1994). The approach of the present study was derived from the logic underlying the above techniques.

During the interview, a hypothetical case (simulation experiment) was presented to the interviewees, and they were asked to explicitly state their reflections (think aloud) when deciding whether to use external or internal sourcing for exploration and exploitation.

In the decision simulation process, respondents may clarify the reasons for developing innovation internally and the changes they would make in their decision depending on the goal (exploration and exploitation) under various conditions. During the third phase of the interview, the respondents were asked about their logic, or the factors they consider when deciding between engaging in external relationships or undertaking in-house development when they aim to exploit, (improve an existing product). Information was provided about the technology, the market, and the availability of an existing partner. In the case of an external partnership, the interviewee was asked about the reasons for choosing a specific governance modality (strategic alliance, acquisition) and a specific type of partner (customer, supplier, competitor).

The initial conditions under which the decision was initially formulated were progressively altered, and the respondents were asked to consider the impact of these changes on their previous choices. The changes in conditions were based on the key drivers used in the first part of the interview.

In particular, the respondents were invited to consider first exploitation and then exploration as an innovation goal, and they were asked to explicitly state the rationale driving their choices. Overall, two endeavors of an explorative nature (new product and new market) and two endeavors of an exploitative nature (improvement of an existing product and process innovation) were considered. The appendix presents the version of the interview protocol guidelines adopted in this study.

Data Processing

Before starting the conversation, the respondents were asked if they would permit the interview to be recorded to derive scripts and notes from the discussion. With the exception of one case in which notes had to be taken during a telephone interview, all respondents agreed to allow their interviews to be recorded.

The interview scripts and/or notes were elaborated in all cases in which explicit authorization was provided by the respondents. In the case in which permission was not granted, only the notes taken during the conversation were used.

To allow an efficient analysis, the information collected during each interview was entered into a database. An entry was created for each individual company and for each individual item measured. Some of the items profiling the organization were quantitative in nature (e.g., proportion of innovation driven by alliances, acquisitions, internal R&D, number of employees). Other items, although more qualitative in their interpretation (e.g., the importance of motives for partnering), were collected by inviting the respondents to assign a score to their perceived importance and to discuss the assignments during their judgment. This approach allowed us to obtain information reflecting the views of the interviewees and to limit any potential interpretation bias from the researcher. The qualitative answers that were provided and those that were coded (e.g., type of strategic orientation) were included in the database.

The insights were aggregated by clustering them into two groups: large firms and SMEs. It is worth repeating that the present study is qualitative in nature, and numerical or coded data were used only to more easily navigate the information offered by the interviews.

The notes of the simulation were also imported into software designed for text analysis. In particular, this software was used to perform word count analyses. Word count methods are used in qualitative research to identify word patterns that are expected to reflect the most important concepts expressed by respondents during interviews (e.g., Leech & Onwuegbuzie, 2007).

In the next section, the findings are presented in the form of propositions. Where appropriate, particularly relevant citations from the conversations are provided.

INSIGHTS FROM THE INTERVIEWS

For the sample under observation, innovation was confirmed to be essential for competitive success (average of 6.8 on a 7-point scale; SD 0.7). The relative distributions of external and internal sources of exploration and exploitation were similar for small and large companies. Small companies used 32% external sourcing and 68% internal sourcing, whereas large companies used 30% external sourcing and 70% internal development. Interestingly, among large companies, the top performing (best-in-class) companies relied less on external partners than on internal efforts (on average, 79% of their innovation came from internal development, and 21% came from external relationships).

Forty percent of our respondents reported that their organization was ahead of the competition. However, among both SMEs and large firms, only 28% perceived their performance to be at the maximum level (7 on our scale). As clearly indicated by the respondents from large firms, being ahead of the competition cannot be achieved easily by multi-business organizations. For small firms, pursuing absolute leadership in their market approach is more feasible as long as they operate in a single, specific niche market. The above findings are confirmed by the fact that small firms perceived lower levels of competition compared to large firms, which typically compete in several markets simultaneously.

With respect to strategic orientation, operational excellence, customer intimacy, and product leadership (Treacy & Wiersema, 1995), SMEs and large firms differed. Large firms considered all three approaches relevant, whereas small companies tended to privilege customer intimacy and were less oriented toward operational excellence.

External Sourcing for Exploration and Exploitation

With respect to the motives for engaging in external relationships, the six main motivations that were derived from previous studies (acquiring novel knowledge, monitoring technological developments, access to new markets, sharing risks,[2] costs, and reducing time-to-market) were listed. Monitoring technological developments, sharing risks and costs, reducing time-to-market are equally applicable to exploration and exploitation activities. Acquiring novel knowledge and entering new markets may be more directly associated with explorative intents.

Time-to-market seems to be relevant for large companies. SME respondents explained that when they needed to accelerate the innovation process, they preferred to intensify internal efforts. As reported by one of the respondents, finding a suitable partner and arranging a deal was considered a time-consuming process. In the words of one of our respondents from a small company, "I am sitting on top of it, and I can steer it. If I have to find a partner who can do it and settle an agreement, then it takes time." Being first to the market seems to be perceived by SMEs as the competitive domain of large organizations. A respondent explained, "A new market for us generally is an existing market for a bigger company. So I can never be there first."

For large firms, reducing uncertainty in their core area is not perceived as relevant. One of the respondents from a large firm argued that large firms are competent to manage any uncertainties encountered in technological innovation on their own. Partnering, in itself, is not important for reducing uncertainty, unless the desired technology lies outside the company's range of expertise (as in the case of expanding into a new market, for example). In this case, external sourcing can help to diminish risks.

Proposition 1. Faster time-to-market is associated with internal development for SMEs and with external sourcing for large firms.

For both large firms and SMEs, access to novel knowledge was identified as the key factor for engaging in external relations. In an increasingly complex technological context, this seems to be an important reason for external sourcing.

Entering new markets is similarly relevant for SMEs and large firms. It is perceived as a costly and time-consuming activity that might be simplified by external relationships. One respondent commented, "Finding the right market is more problematic than developing a new product," and another added, "To transform knowledge into value, you need a market."

Similarly, monitoring external developments was identified as a relevant advantage of engaging in external partnerships.

Interestingly, when the best-in-class companies are considered separately from the other large companies, a remarkable consideration emerges. For world champion companies, monitoring technological opportunities and developments is of crucial importance. The ability to remain constantly alert to potential opportunities distinguishes the companies that are excellent. One respondent explained, "We work with people outside our company to know what is going on out there," and another commented, "I want to have access to all kind of new opportunities, and yes, I may lose some knowledge or I may have to share something with others, but at least I take my part." In the words of yet another respondent, "We can do everything we want. We have the knowledge and the resources to do that, but we have to be open to opportunities that come from outside." Thus, monitoring seems to be a distinguishing feature of companies that excel in innovation.

Proposition 2. Monitoring external knowledge is a distinguishing feature of the most successful large firms.

Once the opportunity for engaging in an external relationship has been identified, various relationship forms are available, such as alliances and acquisitions. For SMEs, unlike large firms, cost sharing and trust are the most relevant motives for choosing alliances for their innovative initiatives. Particularly with respect to trust, a respondent from a large firm explained, "You work better if you know each other, but this does not have to limit us … we do not want to limit ourselves to what we know and what we have." Another said, "We want to have the best partner, the most competent in the field." Large companies choose a cooperation partner primarily to expand their competence and reduce the uncertainty associated with entering new technological areas, and these drivers emerge as the two most important reasons to engage in alliances.

When considering other governance modalities, such as acquisitions, large firms are mainly driven by the willingness to expand their core competences and maintain control over their knowledge. Remarkably, expanding core competences is also the driver for acquiring other business for SMEs. Large companies seem to consider acquisitions and internal development to be two faces of the same coin. Indeed, the main driving force for internal development is the same as the driving force for engaging in acquisitions: developing competences and securing control over the knowledge. In the case of SMEs, relying on internal development is by far the most important tool for reducing the time-to-market.

Proposition 3a. For SMEs and large firms, acquisitions are considered a form of internalizing external knowledge and are driven by the desire to maintain control in areas that are perceived as core.

Proposition 3b. When engaging in alliances, SMEs are especially driven by trust and cost sharing, whereas large firms are driven by risk reduction and the partner's expertise and excellence (when moving in novel areas).

To perform a preliminary exploration of the text of the simulation portion of the interviews, the comments and/or notes from the interviews with managers of SMEs and large firms were analyzed using word count software. For both SMEs and large firms, the most recurrent word was "market." This result suggests that organizations pay special attention to the commercial impact of their innovation initiatives. The second most cited word for SMEs was "product," whereas for large firms, it was "technology." The above findings are consistent with the fact that SMEs tend to be limited to a few products in one technology arena, whereas large firms, which typically have a much broader portfolio of products, tend to be active in multiple technologies. Overall, the market/technology/product matrix dimensions appear to be at the center of the strategic decisions of organizations.

Proposition 4. Technology, markets, and products are key dimensions that organizations use to define their strategic and operational landscape.

With regard to the decision process, the considerations highlighted by both large firms and SMEs seem to be comparable. The process begins with the definition of the strategic objectives to be achieved and the analysis of what is available and feasible internally. In the words of one of our respondents, "If you do not have the expertise or the capacity in-house, then you will work with an external partner … . We try to do everything ourselves … if we cannot, then we have to decide how to proceed."

Internal efforts appear to be the first preference in innovation regardless of the type of innovation objective that is pursued. Indeed, the above finding seems to apply to both explorative and exploitative innovation. For exploitative innovation, the closer the innovation type is to the organization and its core expertise (e.g., process innovation), the stronger the inclination is to use internal resources. This preference is also mentioned for explorative innovation purposes (e.g., radically new products) as long as the organization perceives that the underlying technology is not too distant from the company's knowledge base. A respondent illustrates this point explicitly: "If I can do it by myself, I will do it." Another said, "If … you have the confidence that you can do it on your own … then you just want to do it yourself." Another respondent explained, "With radical new products, it is the same if you have the expertise in-house." Respondents from both SMEs and large firms noted that if full control over the new technology is needed, internal development is preferable. Some of our respondents commented on this preference: "Having control over the new technology is the main benefit of internal development." "It is the control over the developed technology that is very important." Another added, "The corporate culture is such that we must give priority to internal development for reasons of control and secrecy." In particular, technologies that are considered core to the company's business tend to be developed in-house.

Proposition 5. Internal development is the first choice for developing exploration and exploitation as long as companies perceive that the innovation objective is within their reach.

The greater the distance from the organization's comfort area (e.g., entering a completely new market), the higher the need for and propensity to use external relationships. When a need arises that cannot be fulfilled by internal efforts, companies use external sourcing. One respondent said, "The reason for sourcing innovation externally is that we do not have the knowledge in-house. What is core to the company is done in-house; what is not core is done externally." Another respondent, referring to the opportunity to engage with external partners for a radically new product, stated, "If I can do this alone, I will try to do this alone. It is your first choice, but normally, if we talk about really radical innovation, you might be forced to look for a partner who already has the technology more or less running."

Proposition 6. For SMEs and large firms, the further out of reach of the firm's competencies the innovation objective is considered, the more probable external sourcing is considered as a solution.

Some issues emerged from the discussion that seem to be of specific relevance for SMEs. For example, when engaging in partnerships, SMEs are sensitive to intellectual property (IP) rights that are not defended by patents. In particular, when intellectual assets are defended by secrecy (and not by patents), cooperation may pose threats that must be carefully balanced against opportunities. In such a case, previous experiences with the partner are of great importance for engaging in external relationships. A respondent from a small company commented, "It is risky to be so close to a competitor." In terms of business partners' profiles, large companies are more open than SMEs to partnering with competitors, unless legislative restrictions (e.g., antitrust regulations) apply. Cooperation with competitors is considered especially valuable by large firms if the aim is to influence the adoption of industry technology standards.

Another sensitive issue that is especially relevant for SMEs is the relative size difference with respect to the potential partner. A power imbalance in the relationship due to size differences limits small firms' willingness to cooperate. A respondent said, "We have to worry, especially with respect to relationships with large companies. They can overcome us easily. If they get interested in something, they can put many more people to work on it than we can." The cautious approach adopted by SMEs has some potential downsides. SMEs have a more limited vision about what others are doing, especially competitors, and this may prevent them from identifying early signs of change in their environments. In particular, SMEs seem to operate with "lower radar" vision compared to large firms with respect to external contacts. SMEs tend to privilege trust and repeated contacts, whereas large firms are oriented toward identifying the best partner for a specific goal. Guided by the fear of knowledge leakage and often limited by the financial resources required to protect their IP by means of law enforcement (e.g., costly trials), SMEs may tend to make more extensive use of secrecy. As one of the interviewed experts noted, SMEs' limited exchange of information with other players may contribute to explaining why SMEs tend to overestimate the novelty of their own innovations. This misperception of SMEs is recognized in the literature (Amara, Landry, Becheikh, & Ouimet, 2008). Compared to large companies, SMEs also face higher information barriers and suffer from higher information asymmetry when deciding to engage in an external relationship. Especially when attempting to assess the potential contribution of new partners, a balanced and realistic perception of the relative advantage of the parties involved is crucial.

> **Proposition 7.** More limited competences (as may occur in the case of SMEs) tend to be associated with a less extended vision of the technology, market, and product developments.

Overall, the findings indicate that SMEs and large firms seem to display similar schemes for engaging in external relationships for exploration and exploitation. The main difference does not appear in the process itself. In the next section, I will reflect on the findings and propose some insights for further development.

> **Proposition 8.** Differences between SMEs and large firms in the use of external sourcing for exploration and exploitation depend on their specific resources and competencies and the strategic objective for which they aim.

A HEIGHT–DISTANCE VIEW

The insights proposed in this section illustrate the elements that have emerged as key factors in the way that external sourcing is chosen for exploration and exploitation. An organization aims to achieve a specific innovation function that may be either exploration or exploitation (new or improved technologies or products and new or expanded markets). The landscape is defined along the dimensions presented in Proposition 4. In their innovative endeavors, companies envisage reaching a frontier on the horizon that is a certain distance from their current status. Distance refers to the space or time separating the organization's current position and its target position in the future. The greater the distance is, the more explorative the endeavor is. Distance is a multidimensional concept and refers to technology as well as product and market aspects.

To achieve their goals, companies use and develop their internal resources as much as possible. Beyond a certain threshold, however, the organization cannot stretch its own competencies quickly or efficiently enough. If the distance between the current condition of the firm and the projected goal cannot be covered by internal efforts, a threshold has been reached. The perception of the existence of the above-mentioned limit represents an external sourcing trigger. For further advancement toward the innovation goal, external sources are perceived as necessary to reduce the distance between the current status and the desired position. This consideration is derived from the interpretation of Propositions 5 and 6. It should be noted that the distance is always specific to an individual company; it depends on the firm's unique resources and capabilities and how ambitious the prospective goal is. Indeed, Proposition 1 suggests that each of a company's characteristics influences the leverage points that are preferred.

In line with Propositions 3a and 3b, external resources can be obtained either by M&As (thus expanding the set of internal competencies) or through collaboration with partners. The partner or the acquisition target is considered capable of "filling the gap" and thus is considered appropriate for supporting the company ambitions. The external partner does not necessarily have superior resources or qualities; rather, the partner is perceived as having resources with a lower relative distance to the original company's innovation target.

By examining the research results, especially Proposition 8, it may be noted that large firms and SMEs have comparable decision processes. The main difference between these two groups of firms is their vision/resources.

ANNA SABIDUSSI

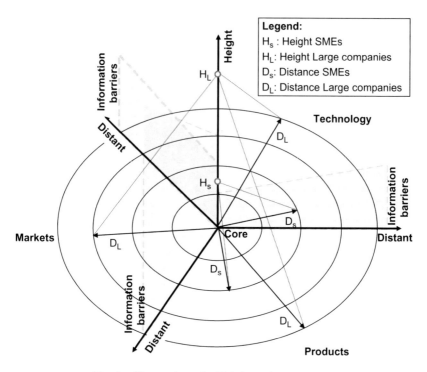

Fig. 1. Illustration of a Height–Distance View.

SMEs have more limited vision of what happens in the world compared to large firms. For large firms, monitoring the technological and competitive environment is essential. Compared to SMEs, large firms have a more panoramic view because they are positioned at a greater height. These considerations are in line with Propositions 7 and 2. Height refers to the extension of the firm's managerial competencies and knowledge.

Fig. 1 illustrates the proposed view.

DISCUSSION AND CONCLUSION

The insights derived from the present study indicate that the sourcing modality seems to depend on the height/distance positioning of the company and the exploration/exploitation objective for which the company aims. The presented approach provides a coherent framework for interpreting the explorative and exploitative endeavors of a firm. Exploration and exploitation may be classified based on the distance from the current market, technology, or product position and the prospective target point on the horizon. The greater the distance from the core competencies is, the more explorative the endeavor is.

Beyond a certain threshold, reducing the distance between a company's current status and target position requires not only increasing the company's existing resources through internal development but also making use of external resources. By considering the height at which firms operate, the proposed view allows us to present a framework that can be applied to organizations with diverse levels of vision.

From a theoretical viewpoint, the model resonates with the resource-based view (Barney, 1991) and dynamic capabilities (Teece et al., 1997) approaches. From an RBV viewpoint, the resources, competencies, and capabilities of an organization are the components of its competitive advantage. The organization mobilizes and expands these resources to reach its objectives. In a dynamic capabilities context, internal resources and capabilities are recombined and integrated with external ones to achieve the goals of the organization. By proposing the concept of distance, the present model highlights an aspect that has remained implicit but unexpressed in previous conceptual approaches. How advanced an organization currently is with respect to its future goals is the essential driver for activating internal resources, gathering new resources, and integrating them in a dynamic process. The model also proposes the concept of height, which is connected to the logic at the core of both RBV and dynamic capabilities. "How high" the organization (and its vision) is refers to the firm's existing competencies and capabilities. The height of the firm contributes to defining where the company intends to go. A panoramic view allows the company to better understand what is happening in its environment, seize opportunities, and identify threats. Ultimately, this view allows the company to make (more) informed decisions about the paths to sustain competitive advantage by selecting potential partners and identifying new technological developments or market changes. A height–distance view resonates with the theoretical perspectives of RBV and dynamic capabilities.

The present work also contributes to managerial practice. The height–distance view provides a dynamic approach to the evolution of companies in time and their increased ability to monitor fields in areas beyond their immediate adjacencies. The concept of distance provides a strategic notion of exploration–exploitation positioning in terms of strategic goals in the market, technology, and product arenas for the company. The ability to discern positioning beyond the obvious business vicinity requires a set of managerial and financial competencies that provide reach to the corporation. The different heights of large companies and SMEs lead to differences in the exploration–exploitation distance. Large firms monitor their environments and aim farther than do SMEs. Another consequence of the height–distance view is that the means and motivations for exploration–exploitation differ depending on company size. Large firms can better profit from a higher height (in terms of monitoring reach and financial and managerial capabilities) to identify exploration–exploitation opportunities that are farther from their core areas. Large firms have a portfolio of tools (M&A, CVC, and so on) with which to internalize or assimilate external knowledge, and this internalization increases the height of the acquiring firm. This increased height provides a strategic learning capability that, if properly used, can support competitive advantage. Previous research (Sabidussi, 2009; Sabidussi, Bremmers, Duysters, & Omta, 2011) has shown that organizations view sourcing strategies from a portfolio perspective, in which synergies play an important role.

There is one important type of synergy between large firms and SMEs. The former have greater reach in monitoring opportunities in both exploration and exploitation but lack the agility of SMEs. SMEs, which are more limited in their height–distance capabilities, need to have greater focus. The natural synergy of broader scope and faster execution make external sourcing of dissimilarly sized companies a way to capitalize on the exploration–exploitation complementarities that the height–distance view highlights.

Overall, the height–distance view presented here contributes to the development of a conceptual framework for interpreting sourcing strategies for exploration and exploitation. It is an initial seed intended to stimulate debate within the academic and business communities. This discussion is intended to pave the way for further expansions, refinements, and a formal model elaboration. A fruitful avenue would be to empirically test the proposed framework with quantitative approaches. These points serve as recommendations for future research endeavors.

NOTES

1. All interviews were conducted in the summer of 2009 by the author, with the exception of four interviews that were collected by a master's student. The interviews with the experts took place at the beginning and the end of the interview period.

2. Formally, uncertainty and risk are not the same. In business language, however, they are considered overlapping concepts. The two terms have been used interchangeably in the present chapter because this usage reflects corporate managerial views and language.

ACKNOWLEDGMENT

The author thanks Alejandro Sanz, Harry Bremmers, Onno Omta, Hans Schenk, Victor Lascano, Paul Arts, Anjo Steen, the interviewees and gratefully acknowledges the constructive comments of the editors and the reviewers on earlier versions of this work.

REFERENCES

Ali, A., Krapfel, R., Jr., & LaBahn, D. W. (1995). Product innovativeness and entry strategy: Impact on cycle time and break-even time. *Journal of Product Innovation Management, 12*(1), 54–69.

Amara, N., Landry, R., Becheikh, N., & Ouimet, M. (2008). Learning and novelty of innovation in established manufacturing SMEs. *Technovation, 28*(7), 450–463.

Andrew, J. P., Sirkin, H. L., Haanaes, K., & Michael, D. C. (2007). "Innovation 2007," BCG Senior management survey, BCG report.

Barney, J. B. (1991). Firm resources and sustained competitive advantage. *Journal of Management, 17*(1), 99–120.

Bayona, C., Garcia-Marco, T., & Huerta, E. (2001). Firms' motivation for cooperative R&D: An empirical analysis of Spanish firms. *Research Policy, 30*, 1289–1307.

Beckman, C. M., Haunschild, P. R., & Phillips, D. J. (2004). Friends or strangers? Firm-specific uncertainty, market uncertainty, and network partner selection. *Organization Science, 15*(3), 259–275.

Benner, M. J., & Tushman, M. L. (2003). Exploitation, exploration, and process management: The productivity dilemma revisited. *Academy of Management Review, 2*, 238–256.

Contractor, F. J., & Lorange, P. (2004). Why should firms cooperate? The strategy and economics basis for cooperative ventures. In J. J. Reuer (Ed.), *Strategic alliances: Theory and evidence* (pp. 19–47). Oxford: Oxford University Press.

Csaszar, F. A. (2013). An efficient frontier in organization design: Organizational structure as a determinant of exploration and exploitation. *Organization Science, 24*(4), 1083–1101.

Dienes, Z. (2008). Subjective measures of unconscious knowledge. In R. Banerjee & B. K. Chakrabarti (Eds.), *Models of brain and mind: Physical, computational and psychological approaches* (Vol. 168, pp. 49–64). Amsterdam: Elsevier.

Dodourova, M. (2009). Alliances as strategic tools. A cross-industry study of partnerships planning, formation and success. *Management Decision, 47*(5), 831–844.

Duysters, G., & de Man, A. P. (2003). Transitory alliances: An instrument for surviving turbulent industries? *R&D Management, 33*(1), 49–58.

Eisenhardt, K. M., & Graebner, M. E. (2007). Theory building from cases: Opportunities and challenges. *Academy of Management Journal, 50*(1), 25−32.

Fereday, J., & Muir-Cochrane, E. (2006). Demonstrating rigor using thematic analysis: A hybrid approach of inductive and deductive coding and theme development. *International Journal of Qualitative Methods, 5*(1), 80−92.

Folta, T. B. (1998). Governance and uncertainty: The trade-off between administrative control and commitment. *Strategic Management Journal, 19*(11), 1007−1028.

Greve, H. R. (2007). Exploration and exploitation in product innovation. *Industrial and Corporate Change, 16*(5), 945−975.

Größler, A., Rouwette, E. & Vennix, J. (2008). Unconscious processing of information in dynamic decision-making − An experimental approach. *26th international conference of the system dynamics society*, Athens, Greece. Retrieved from http://www.systemdynamics.org/conferences/2008/proceed/papers/GROES363.pdf. Accessed on July 20−24, 2008.

Hagedoorn, J. (1993). Understanding the rationale of strategic technology partnering: International modes of cooperation and sectorial differences. *Strategic Management Journal, 14*(15), 371−385.

He, Z., & Wong, P. (2004). Exploration vs. exploitation: And empirical test of the ambidexterity hypothesis. *Strategic Management Journal, 21*, 961−979.

Horton, J., Macve, R., & Struyven, G. (2004). Qualitative research: Experiences in using semi-structured Interviews. In C. Humphrey & B. Lee (Eds.), *The real life guide to accounting research: A behind-the-scenes view of using qualitative research methods* (pp. 339−358). London: Elsevier.

Hynes, N., & Mollenkopf, D. (2008). Capturing strategic alliance outcomes: An analysis of motives, objectives and outcomes. *International Journal Technology Management, 43*(1−3), 194−211.

Lavie, D., & Rosenkopf, L. (2006). 'Balancing exploration and exploitation in alliance formation. *Academy of Management Journal, 49*(4), 797−818.

Lavie, D., Stettner, U., & Tushman, M. (2010). Exploration and exploitation within and across organizations. *The Academy of Management Annals, 4*(1), 109−155.

Leech, N. L., & Onwuegbuzie, A. J. (2007). An array of qualitative data analysis: A call for data analysis triangulation. *School Psychology Quarterly, 22*(4), 557−584.

Lensink, R., Steen, P., & Sterken, E. (2005). Uncertainty and growth of the firm. *Small Business Economics, 24*, 381−391.

Levinthal, D. A., & March, J. G. (1993). The myopia of learning. *Strategic Management Journal, 14*, 95−112.

Manders, A. J. C., & Brenner, Y. S. (1995). Make or buy: The potential subversion of corporate strategy-The case of Philips. *International Journal of Social Economics, 22*(4), 4−11.

March, J. G. (1991). Exploration and exploitation in organizational learning. *Organization Science, 2*, 71−87.

March-Chorda, I., Gunasekaran, A., & Lloria-Aramburo, B. (2002). Product development process in Spanish SMEs: An empirical research. *Technovation, 22*(5), 301−312.

Marshall, M. N. (1996). Sampling for qualitative research. *Family Practice, 13*, 522−525.

Narula, R. (2004). R&D collaboration by SMEs: New opportunities and limitations in the face of globalization. *Technovation, 24*, 153−161.

Nees, D. B. (1983). A complementary method for research on strategic decision-making processes. *Strategic Management Journal, 4*(2), 175−185.

Nohria, N., & Gulati, R. (1996). Is slack good or bad for innovation? *Academy of Management Journal, 39*(5), 1245−1264.

O'Reilly III, C. A., & Tushman, M. L. (2013). Organizational ambidexterity: past, present and future, Research Paper No. 2130. Research Paper Series, Stanford Graduate School of Business.

Parmigiani, A. (2007). Why do firms both make and buy? An investigation of concurrent sourcing. *Strategic Management Journal, 28*, 285–311.

Poppo, L., & Zenger, T. (1998). Testing alternative theories of the firm: Transaction cost, knowledge-based, and measurement explanations for make-or-buy decisions in information services. *Strategic Management Journal, 19*(9), 853–877.

Pratt, M. G. (2009). For the lack of a boilerplate: Tips on writing up (and reviewing) qualitative research. *Academy of Management Journal, 52*(5), 856–862.

Rothaermel, F. T., & Deeds, D. L. (2004). Exploration and exploitation alliances in biotechnology: A system of new product development. *Strategic Management Journal, 25*(3), 201–221.

Sabidussi, A. (2009). Governance choices for external sourcing in innovation: Towards a portfolio of strategic alliances and mergers & acquisitions. Wageningen University and Research Center, PhD Thesis, ISBN: ISBN978-90-8585-532-3.

Sabidussi, A., Bremmers, H., Duysters, G., & Omta, O. (2011). Value enhancing in the governance decision process: A portfolio perspective on strategic alliances and mergers and acquisitions. In T. K. Das (Ed.), *Strategic alliances for value creation*. City University of New York: Information Age Publishing Inc.

Sakakibara, M. (1997). Heterogeneity of firm capabilities and cooperative research and development: An empirical examination of motives. *Strategic Management Journal, 18*, 143–164.

Serrasqueiro, Z. S., & Maçãs Nunes, P. (2008). Performance size: Empirical evidence from Portuguese SMEs. *Small Business Economics, 31*, 195–217.

Someren, M. W., Barnard, Y. F., & Sandberg, J. A. C. (1994). *The think aloud method. A practical guide to modelling cognitive processes*. London: Academic Press.

Stettner, U., & Lavie, D., (2013). Ambidexterity under scrutiny: Exploration and exploitation via internal organization, alliances, and acquisitions. *Strategic Management Journal.* Available at SSRN: http://ssrn.com/abstract=2328338.

Teece, D. J., Pisano, G., & Shuen, A. (1997). Dynamic capabilities and strategic management. *Strategic Management Journal, 18*, 509–533.

Tether, B. (2002). Who co-operates for innovation, and why? An empirical analysis. *Research Policy, 35*(6), 947–967.

Treacy, M., & Wiersema, F. (1995). *The discipline of market leaders: Choose your customers, narrow your focus, dominate your market*. Cambridge: Perseus Books.

Van de Vrande, V., de Jong, J. P. J., Vanhaverbeke, W., & de Rochemont, M. (2009). Open innovation in SMEs: Trends, motives and management challenges. *Technovation, 29*, 423–437.

Van de Vrande, V., Lemmens, C., & Vanhaverbeke, W. (2006). Choosing governance modes for external technology sourcing. *R&D Management, 36*(3), 347–363.

Veugelers, R., & Cassiman, B. (1999). Make and buy in innovation strategies: Evidence from Belgian manufacturing firms. *Research Policy, 28*, 63–80.

Vilkamo, T., & Keil, T. (2003). Strategic technology partnering in high-velocity environments: Lessons from a case study. *Technovation, 23*(3), 193–204.

Yasuda, H. (2005). Formation of strategic alliances in high-technology industries: Comparative study of the resource-based theory and transaction cost theory. *Technovation, 25*(7), 763–770.

APPENDIX: INTERVIEW PROTOCOL GUIDELINES

Definitions:

Innovation is defined as products and/or processes that are new to the firm and/or new to the market and that are introduced to the market

Portfolio refers to all the business-to-business relationships in which the firm is involved

---

General Questions:

What has been the experience with innovation in the last three years?

How many employees do you have (in fte)?

How many R&D-E personnel do you have (in fte)?

On a scale from 1 to 7, where 7 = very important, 4 = neutral and 1 = not important, how would you define the importance of innovation for your competitive success?

On a scale from 1 to 7, where 7 = ahead of competition, 4 = neutral and 1 = follower, how would you define the strategic orientation of your firm?

What is the importance of the following strategic orientations for your company?

− operational excellence
− customer intimacy
− product leadership

Are your sales:

a. Regional
b. National
c. Continental
d. Global

Are your competitors:

a. Regional
b. National
c. Continental
d. Global

On a scale from 1 to 7, where 7 = very high, 4 = neutral, and 1 = very low, how would you categorize the competition levels in the industry in which your company operates?

How much of your innovation in percentage terms comes from:

In-house R&D	%
Internal development*	%
Nonequity alliances	%
Joint ventures	%
M&As	%
	100%

*Engineering

From 1 (the most important) to 6 (the least important), how would you rank the following motives for sourcing innovation externally:

Motives		Ranking (1–6)
A	Increased complexity of technology developments and access to new knowledge	
B	Reducing uncertainty in internal development	
C	Reducing costs in internal development	
D	Monitoring environmental changes/technological opportunities	
E	Entry into new product markets/internationalization	
F	Reducing the time-to-market	

Does your company have alliances, joint ventures, and M&As for reasons other than innovation? Please, mention.

From 1 to 8, how would you rank the relevance of the following motives to innovate internally (**R&D**), to have alliances, mergers or acquisitions (1 is the most important, 8 is the least important):

	Ranking Order for Choice	Internal Development	Alliances	M&A
A	Control over the developed technology/new knowledge			
B	Strategic importance/expertise related to the technology (core to the company)			
C	Uncertainty/risk connected to the technology (product/process)			
D	Uncertainty/risk connected to the market (product differentiation/business model)			
E	Cost reduction			
F	Time-to-market			
G	Past experiences and/or trust with respect to the partner			
H	Existing portfolio of external sources of technology modalities			

On a scale from 1 to 7, where $7 = $ continuously, $4 = $ sometimes, and $1 = $ on demand, how often do you monitor/rebalance the composition of business relationships?

Simulation Hypothetical Decision Case

(A) Suppose you want to modify and improve an existing product. You already have a level of expertise with respect to the technology that has to be applied because it is a technology that is already known or you have already developed it, so you are confident about the technological success. The market acceptance of the product is relatively certain. You can introduce it to a geographical or product market that is already familiar to your company. An existing business partner can contribute. The possibility of using a partner refers to joining forces for the technological/product improvement or for subsequent introduction of the incrementally new product in the market.

Under which conditions would you develop exclusively in-house (and reject the external partner)? Please think aloud step-by-step about the logic, the arguments that you elaborate and the factors you would consider when making your decision.

Suppose that you accept that the external partner would enter into an alliance, joint venture or acquisition? Please give your argumentation about the elements supporting your decision.

Is your choice influenced by other existing alliances/joint ventures/ acquisitions you already have? How?

What would change in your decision if the technology was not well known to you (higher technology risk)? In what way?

What would change in your decision if the market success was highly uncertain?

Would the nature of the potential partner – (1) supplier or a (2) customer or a (3) competitor – change your decision? How?
What would change in your decision if your partner was already involved with one of your competitors? Do you verify the portfolio of your partner before taking a decision?

What would change in your decision if you did not have previous experience with the potential business partner?

(B) How would the above answers change if you were developing a radical new product with respect to the in-house versus external decision, and with respect to the partnering modalities decision (for each of the arguments you have pointed out)?

How would the above answers change if you were entering a new market with an existing product with respect to the in-house versus external decision, and with respect to the partnering modalities decision (for each of the arguments you have pointed out)?

How would the above answers change if you were developing a new process with respect to the in-house versus external decision, and with respect to the partnering modalities decision (for each of the arguments you have pointed out)?

How would the above answers change if the development costs were substantial with respect to the in-house versus external decision, and with respect to the partnering modalities decision (for each of the arguments you have pointed out)?

How would the above answers change if you needed to reduce time-to-market with respect to the in-house versus external decision, and with respect to the partnering modalities decision (for each of the arguments you have pointed out)?

CHAPTER 9

INNOVATION IN THE AUSTRALIAN SPATIAL INFORMATION INDUSTRY

Sukanlaya Sawang, Roxanne Zolin, Judy Matthews and Meriam Bezemer

ABSTRACT

Business literature reveals the importance of generating innovative products and services, but much of the innovation research has been conducted in large firms and not replicated in small firms. These firms are likely to have different perspectives on innovation, which means that they will probably behave differently to large firms. Our study aims to unpack how firms in Spatial Information perceive and engage in innovation as a part of their business operation.

To investigate these questions we conduct 20 in-depth interviews of top management team members in Spatial Information firms in Australia.

We find that small firms define innovation very broadly and measure innovation by its effect on productivity or market success. Innovation is seen as crucial to survival and success in a competitive environment. Most firms engage in product and/or service innovations, while some also mentioned marketing, process and organisational innovations. Most

Exploration and Exploitation in Early Stage Ventures and SMEs
Technology, Innovation, Entrepreneurship and Competitive Strategy, Volume 14, 211–236
Copyright © 2014 by Emerald Group Publishing Limited
ISSN: 1479-067X/doi:10.1108/S1479-067X20140000014006

innovations were more exploitative rather than exploratory with only a few being radical innovations. Innovation barriers include time and money constraints, corporate culture and Government tendering practices. Our study sheds a light on our understanding of innovation in an under-researched sector; that is Spatial Information industry.

Keywords: Innovation; small firms; Australia; exploitative innovation; Spatial Information

INTRODUCTION

Business literature reveals the importance of generating innovative products and services (e.g. Branzei & Vertinsky, 2006; Xerri & Brunetto, 2011), making innovation a widely discussed topic in business, information technology, engineering and public development contexts (Unsworth, Sawang, Murray, Norman, & Sorbello, 2012). However much of the innovation research has been conducted in large firms, leaving small- and medium-size firms (SMEs) largely unstudied (Hoffman, Parejo, Bessant, & Perren, 1998). Recent research calls for investigation of the innovation-performance among SMEs in particular, because they differ from large firms (Rosenbusch, Brinckmann, & Bausch, 2011). SMEs are likely to have different perspectives on innovation, with different resource constraints, and may carry out innovative activities differently to large firms. Overall, our research question explores how firms in Spatial Information (SI) perceive and engage in innovation as a part of their business operation.

To investigate this research question, we conduct a study of the SI Industry in Australia. The SI firms are considered as the backbone of our national infrastructure from surveying and mapping to geographic information systems (GIS) and location-based services. An estimate of income is approximately $926 million (Australian Bureau of Statistics, 1999) and a total of around 93,000 people are directly involved in SI services in industry and government. Given a limited study of this sector, an implication of innovation literature may not fully reflect the nature of this sector. For example, while innovation is heavily gauged by production innovation and/ or research and development investment (as a proxy), SI firms, which are mostly small to medium enterprises, heavily focus on service provision by utilising an existing technology/product (rather than inventing a new wheel). Thus, it is important to understand how SI firms define innovation and what current innovation engagement is. Our study aims to provide a preliminary framework of innovation practice in this specific sector through this exploratory view.

The remainder of this chapter is organised as follows. In the literature review we report variations in the definitions of innovation, what we know about the importance of innovation in SI firms (mainly small firms), and how small firms differ from large firms. Then we describe our methodology and report our findings. We conclude with a discussion of our contributions to SME and innovation literatures, the limitations of our study and suggestions for future research.

LITERATURE REVIEW

In this section we report variations in the definitions of innovation, what we know about the importance of innovation in SI firms and how small firms differ from large firms.

How Do We Define Innovation?

Innovation has been described as a multidimensional phenomenon that is notoriously ambiguous and lacking either a single definition or measure (Adams, Bessant, & Phelps, 2006). In the following section we provide a short overview of the different views on the definition of innovation from the literature to provide dimensions for investigation in our study.

Innovation is Understood as both a Process and an Outcome
There is general consensus among innovation scholars that innovation encompasses something novel. A recent literature review describes innovation as either a process or an outcome (Crossan & Apaydin, 2010). Some scholars believe that the newness is in the process (Acs, Anselin, & Varga, 2002; Avermaete, Viaene, Morgan, & Crawford, 2003; Garcia & Calantone, 2002; Huggins & Johnston, 2009; Katila & Chen, 2008), whereas others believe innovation to be the outcome of a process (Camisón-Zornoza, Lapiedra-Alcamí, Segarra-Ciprés, & Boronat-Navarro, 2004; Huse, Neubaum, & Gabrielsson, 2005). Process scholars believe innovation to be a complex series of various actions (Gopalakrishnan & Damanpour, 1994) that ultimately aim at introducing something new at the organisational level

(Avermaete et al., 2003). Therefore their research stream focuses on the question of what facilitates this process, such as learning, applying knowledge, exploration and championing of individuals (Cho & Pucik, 2005; De Jong & Kemp, 2003; Katila & Chen, 2008) or social mechanisms such as networks and organisational culture (Brunetto & Xerri, 2011; Obstfeld, 2005).

Outcome scholars describe innovation as a relatively new manufactured product (Parthasarthy & Hammond, 2002) or merely the attempt to commercialise newly discovered methods or materials (Freeman & Soete, 1997), albeit others believe there is no innovation unless the new results are economically successful (Bucic & Ngo, 2012; Çakar & Ertürk, 2010; Denti, 2012; Hipp & Grupp, 2005). Others see innovation as the result of a process that can even have negative consequences, such as overturning a firm's existing competencies, skills and know-how (Gatignon, Tushman, Smith, & Anderson, 2002). Outcome scholars focus on studying factors that might lead to innovation results, such as public subsidies (Albors-Garrigos & Barrera, 2011) or R&D cooperation (Becker & Dietz, 2004).

Innovation as New to the Industry, New to the Firm and New to the World
Scholars defining innovation as a new outcome of a process emphasise different locations of this newness. Some believe innovations are by definition (relatively) new to the industry or market (Parthasarthy & Hammond, 2002; Salavou, Baltas, & Lioukas, 2004), yet many scholars think that the newness of the innovation itself is less relevant than the newness for the innovator (Bos-Brouwers, 2010; Hill & Rothaermel, 2003; Howell, Shea, & Higgins, 2005; Souitaris, 2001).

Another way scholars deal with innovation newness is by differentiating between radical and incremental innovation. Radical innovations involve the use of new technology or knowledge (Cardinal, 2001; Chandy & Tellis, 2000; Goktan & Miles, 2011; Leifer, O'connor, & Rice, 2001) and are perceived new to the industry (Johannessen, Olsen & Lumpkin, 2001). These innovations involve substantial technical risks, time and costs (Roussel, Saad, Erickson, & Little, 1991). In contrast, incremental innovations are the result of a continuing process of improvement (Goktan & Miles, 2011), based on existing knowledge (Cardinal, 2001) or technology (Gatignon et al., 2002). They are new to a certain firm but not to the industry in general (Johannessen, Olsen, & Lumpkin, 2001). The difference between radical and incremental innovations may seem strict, yet Baumol (2002) argues that most new products fall somewhere in between these two categories.

Additionally, scholars differentiate between firms that generate (radical or incremental) innovations themselves and those that rather adopt those innovations that were developed elsewhere (Damanpour & Wischnevsky, 2006). The majority of firms adopt rather than generate innovation (Pérez-Luño, Wiklund, & Cabrera, 2011) and this is particularly the case for smaller firms (Verhees & Meulenberg, 2004).

Various Definitions but What the Innovation is for SI Firms?

Although the need for more innovations is widely recognised, there is no commonly accepted view of what innovation means across industry sectors (Sawang & Unsworth, 2011). The word of innovation is entering conversations everywhere, whether talking technology or the world economy. Whereas some studies do not differentiate at all between the different innovation types (Chassagnon & Audran, 2011; De Jong & Kemp, 2003; Denti, 2012; O'Cass & Weerawardena, 2009) many scholars see innovation mainly as the development of new products (Cooper, 2011; Laforet, 2008), while other studies differentiate between product, process and service innovations (Acs et al., 2002; Parthasarthy & Hammond, 2002; Thornhill, 2006). According to previous literature, there are no clear-cut definitions, as there is no general agreement on the exact differences between these concepts. Therefore, it is important to understand how firms, especially in under-researched sector such as SI, define innovation and engage with it. Product innovation, for instance, is defined as a new product that a firm produces (Goktan & Miles, 2011). Among SI firms, which are service orientation, one may argues that the definition of innovation as product should be excluded. Yet, product innovation can be defined broader as the development of both new products and/or services (Armbruster, Bikfalvi, Kinkel, & Lay, 2008; Huse et al., 2005; Rundquist, 2012). Therefore, SI firms may perceive innovation as a new product such as a new service plan for customers.

The same lack of clarity can be found with regard to service innovations. Some scholars believe service innovations are distinctively different from product or process innovations; others think they are very similar, and again others argue a synthesis approach (Coombs & Miles, 2000). More agreement is present on the definition of process innovations, that is mostly defined as altering and improving the technical systems or production processes for product innovation (Camisón-Zornoza et al., 2004; Garcia & Calantone, 2002; Goktan & Miles, 2011; Huse et al., 2005).

Other forms of innovation that are generally distinguished in the literature are managerial innovations, which involve changes in an organisation's
structure and administrative processes (Madrid-Guijarro, Garcia, & Van
Auken, 2009), marketing innovations which involve changes in marketing
to potential or existing customers (Halpern, 2010) and market innovations,
the exploitation of new markets and the penetration of new market
segments within existing markets (Avermaete et al., 2003). The natures of SI
firms are small and limited resources. Therefore, the degree of marketing
innovation may be fewer comparing to product/service innovation. Yet,
it can be argued vice versa, thus an in-depth exploration of how SI firms
perceive and engage in innovation is important. For the purpose of this
study, we define innovation very broadly as ideas, systems, technologies,
products, processes, services or policies that are new to the adopting organisation (Sawang & Unsworth, 2011; Zaltman, Duncan, & Holbek, 1973) so
we do not exclude any of these factors that SI firms might include in their
definition of innovation.

Why is Innovation Important to SI Firms?

There is a wealth of research stressing the importance of innovation for
both countries and industries as individual firms. Firstly, innovation is
believed to be the main driver of economic growth (Bos-Brouwers, 2010).
Its resulting new processes and products contribute to productivity
improvement for the economy as a whole, thereby increasing the basis for
economic growth and rising living standards (OECD, 2004). Therefore,
many government policies aim at increasing innovation to boost their
economy (Baer & Frese, 2003; Forsman, 2009). Secondly, innovation has
been found to benefit SI firms, which are small and medium sizes, in several
ways, most importantly as a vital factor for developing and sustaining competitive advantage (Branzei & Vertinsky, 2006; Parida, Westerberg, &
Frishammar, 2012; Xerri & Brunetto, 2011). Being innovative helps SI firms
to stand out from competitors, establish temporal monopolies, compete
with established larger incumbents, grow and generate new quality jobs
(Mazzarol & Reboud, 2008; Rosenbusch et al., 2011). The learning that
takes place during the innovation process further generates absorptive
capacity (Rosenbusch et al., 2011), the skill to recognise external knowledge,
assimilate and apply new knowledge that firms need to survive (Jansen,
Van Den Bosch, & Volberda, 2005). The literature illustrates a number of

benefits for SI firms to be innovative, therefore promoting innovation practices within this sector is important.

How to Promote Innovation in SI Firms

SI firms, which are mainly small, may innovate differently from other large companies (Bos-Brouwers, 2010; Dodgson & Rothwell, 1991) and therefore we will now discuss common factors that have been found to influence innovation in SI firms. Research on factors that facilitate or impede innovation in small firms can broadly be divided into three groups: firm characteristics, internal and environmental factors.

Firm Factors
Results regarding firm characteristics enhancing or inhibiting innovation appear contradictory: studies have found that mid-size (Van De Vrande, De Jong, Vanhaverbeke, & De Rochemont, 2009) or larger (Branzei & Vertinsky, 2006) firms are more innovative than others, but also that firm size has no significant effect on innovativeness (Camelo-Ordaz, Fernández-Alles, Ruiz-Navarro, & Sousa-Ginel, 2012) and that innovation is mainly triggered by the firm's environment rather than from within firms (Barrett & Sexton, 2006).

Internal Factors
Quite a number of studies have found several firm internal factors that might facilitate or impede small firms' innovation. Firstly, there is the crucial role of people, since small firms are often people oriented rather than system oriented (McAdam, Reid, & Gibson, 2004). Firms with an owner-CEO are found to be more innovative than others (Souitaris, 2001). Owners have the power to make quick decisions and pursue innovation activities (Barrett & Sexton, 2006). but when the CEO has a dominant role without the necessary vision, he can constrain innovative activity (Barrett & Sexton, 2006). Small firm managers, for instance, can increase firm innovation by supporting innovative behaviour (Brophey & Brown, 2009) and being favourable to risk taking (Souitaris, 2001). However, their perceptions of issues related to costs (Madrid-Guijarro et al., 2009) or failure to provide enough support for innovation (Xerri & Brunetto, 2011) can hamper it. Also, an intrapreneur's organisational tenure, business background, age and educational level all have a negative influence on innovation (Camelo-Ordaz et al., 2012).

Secondly, organisational culture is of importance for a firm's innovativeness. A low power distance and little bureaucratic surroundings (Çakar & Ertürk, 2010) or a climate for initiative and psychological safety (Baer & Frese, 2003) can foster innovation, whereas tensions related to ownership issues, control and management (Van Es & Van Der Wal, 2012) or systems based more on rules and procedures and uncertainty avoidance (Çakar & Ertürk, 2010) negatively affect innovation. This can also be said about a firm's day-to-day delivery pressures imposing time constraints on staff to work on ideas (Brophey & Brown, 2009) and about a firm's financial constraints (Madrid-Guijarro et al., 2009) or lack of resources (McAdam et al., 2004).

Thirdly, firm policies can matter to SME innovation. Prioritising human resource (HR) development increases innovation (Barnett & Storey, 2000), whereas a lower HR commitment can be a barrier for innovation (Madrid-Guijarro et al., 2009). Firm proactiveness and scanning (Khan & Manopichetwattana, 1989), technology sourcing (Parida et al., 2012), R&D intensity accompanied by a higher level of functional integration (Parthasarthy & Hammond, 2002) and the inclusion of new technology plans in the business strategy (Souitaris, 2001) have all been found to positively affect innovation.

Finally, networks are an important enabler of firm innovation. Relationships with clients (Ceci & Iubatti, 2012), technical interaction with other professionals (Khan & Manopichetwattana, 1989) and using external advice (Higón, 2012) are important tools to generate innovation. The more heterogeneous and stronger a firm's networks are, the more the SME can obtain the advantages of a larger size firm, whose resources, skills and capabilities lead to a greater innovation breath (Gronum, Verreynne, & Kastelle, 2012).

Environmental Factors
Customers are an important trigger to innovation (Barrett & Sexton, 2006). Van Es and Van der Wal (2012) contend that innovative small firms' behaviour is usually based on customer input. Other environmental triggers are presented in the form of new legislations, spurring companies into action (Avermaete et al., 2003, Brophey & Brown, 2009). Moreover, research has shown that the more dynamic (Khan & Manopichetwattana, 1989), challenging (Madrid-Guijarro et al., 2009) or uncertain (Uzkurt, Kumar, Kimzan, & Sert, 2012) an SMEs environment is, the more innovative they are, as they are challenged to respond to this by constantly finding new solutions for their business. External factors that have been found to hinder

innovation are an industry's preference for the status quo (Brophey & Brown, 2009) and shareholders who are focussed on short-term profits (Van Es & Van Der Wal, 2012).

Based on literature review of firm characteristics, internal and environmental factors, which can influence innovation practices, our study will therefore employ the three elements as framework in qualitative analysis of the data.

METHOD

In this study, we examine innovation activities in a specific industry that is the SI sector firms that are classified as Surveying and Mapping Services according to the latest Australian and New Zealand Standard Industrial Classification code. The SI sector has been recognised as a discrete sector in Australia since 2001. The industry is mainly small firms with a few large firms for comparison. SI is also a good industry for our study because it has two clear segments; the traditional surveying industry using mature technology (our low tech segment), and SI firms using new technologies, such as Global Positioning Systems technology (our high tech segment).

We conducted semi-structured interviews with the top management team members of a theoretically selected sample of 20 SI firms in Australia. Samples for qualitative studies are generally much smaller than those used in quantitative studies. To determine the sample size in qualitative study, we should follow the concept of saturation (Glaser & Strauss, 1967). Our study found that at 15th firm, the information became saturated and collecting five new firms did not shed any further light on our research questions.

Given that SI firms are small and often service focused, it is important to understand how these firms conceptualise innovation and how they integrate the innovation aspect into their operations. The following section describes our sample selection.

Organisation Cases and Participants

A guided non-representative sample was created from the a list of organisations in the spatial industry business association (SIBA) members list, including surveying and other spatial firms with different sizes on both the east and west coast of Australia. The SI is a rapidly growing industry that consists of companies offering a wide range of geographic-related services such as surveying, remote sensing, location-based services, photogrammetry, mapping, aerial imagery, land development, environmental management, GIS, web services and Global Positioning Systems (GPS) amongst others. The SI industry contributes approximately $12.5 billion annually to Australia's gross domestic product. This industry includes a diversity of firms; some with a history of surveying and other spatial service firms more focused on the application of information technology. Some small firms are family businesses while medium sized firms are partners in international collaborations.

We have included four firms in Queensland, four in New South Wales, five in Western Australia, six firms in Victoria and one in the Australian Capital Territory. We began with a list of companies obtained from Spatial Industries Business Association (SIBA), and contacted companies to request their participation in face-to-face semi-structured interviews with one member of the research team. We updated existing information from information provided and ascertained through company information on the web and phone conversations who would be the appropriate personnel with direct involvement with innovation. Table 1 is a list of key informants.

Due to the different firm activities within SI industry, it is appropriate to cluster SI firms into three groups: *Category A*: Predominantly Surveying firms; *Category B*: Predominantly Spatial Sciences firms and *Category C*: Combination of Surveying and Spatial Sciences firms. Category A firms' primary activities are measuring, assembling and assessing land and geographic-related information to be used for land planning and implementing the efficient administration of the land and the structures thereon, for example engineering and mining surveyors or boundary surveyors. These firms predominantly use mature technologies. Category B firms consist of SI users and information technology firms that manage and analyse data that has geographic, temporal and/or spatial context. This category also includes development and management of related information technology tools, such as aerial and satellite remote sensing imagery, GPS, and computerised GIS. These firms predominantly use new and emerging 'high tech' technologies.

Procedure

An interdisciplinary research team was used for data collection, in accordance with the methodology described. A team of three researchers and

Table 1. Key Informants for Our Interview Study.

Firm Code	Interviewee's Function	Firm Category	Firm Size	Firm Location
A1	Director	Category A	Small	NSW
A2	Managing Director	Category A	Small	NSW
A3	Director	Category A	Medium	NSW
A4	Registered cadastral Surveyor, Owner	Category A	Small	QLD
A5	Office Manager	Category A	Medium	QLD
A6	General Manager; Operational Manager	Category A	Small	WA
B1	Chief Executive Officer	Category B	Medium	ACT
B2	Managing Director, Owner	Category B	Small	NSW
B3	Survey Manager	Category B	Large	QLD
B4	Managing Director	Category B	Small	QLD
B5	Manager	Category B	Small	VIC
B6	Managing Director, Geo spatial systems developer	Category B	Small	VIC
B7	Client executive	Category B	Large	VIC
B8	Managing Director	Category B	Medium	VIC
B9	Managing Director, Chief Executive Officer	Category B	Medium	VIC
B10	R&D Manager	Category B	Medium	WA
B11	Managing Director	Category B	Medium	WA
B12	Chief Executive Officer	Category B	Medium	WA
C1	GIS Coordinator	Category C	Small	VIC
C2	Business Development Manager	Category C	Medium	WA

one graduate student with strengths in innovation, entrepreneurship, strategy, marketing, history, technology management, and organisational behaviour worked on this project. This disciplinary breadth enabled a multi-perspective, interactive examination of the phenomenon of interest. The diverse perspectives of the multidisciplinary research team shaped the development of the interview protocols for the semi-structured interviews, the data collection and data analysis, generating rich discussions and insights. The interview protocols were also discussed with industry experts to ensure appropriate terminology and language were used in the data collection phase.

An interview protocol developed from in-depth discussion of the different dimensions of the research questions was trialled during the first few interviews and the modifications developed were used throughout the project. Semi-structured face-to-face interviews that on average lasted approximately 1—1.5 hours were employed to explore the activities and orientation of 20 firms structured interviews. The interview protocol was much broader than the information presented in this chapter, given the comprehensive nature of the overall research programme. We developed question areas investigating aspects of business strategy, innovative activities, organisational interfaces, processes, skills, metrics, culture and leadership. We used semi-structured interviews to have comparability across firms and used these interviews to obtain better ideas about issues of importance to them.

All interviews were recorded and transcribed and interviewers also took field notes. Both transcribed interviews and the field notes were used in the data analysis. In addition to the face-to-face interview and company observations with each company during the site visits, follow-up phone calls or emails were used to seek clarification or greater depth in particular areas.

FINDINGS

Our study aimed to answer 'how do firms in SI perceive and engage in innovation as a part of their business operation?' Based on thematic analysis, we identified three main themes, that is innovation perceptions, innovation engagement and innovation facilitators/impediment. We also identified five sub-themes for innovation engagement (measurement, roles, activities, exploration–exploitation and beneficial gains) and three sub-themes for innovation facilitators/impediment (firm characteristics, internal and external factors).

Innovation Perceptions

In order to gain insights into the firms' understanding of innovation, we enquired of the interviewees how they define innovation. Fig. 1 provides an overview of their responses, highlighting that there is no broadly prevailing definition of innovation. The most frequently mentioned factor from more than half of the participants was that innovation was something new, usually to enable an increase in efficiency or problem solving. Examples are:

> I would say it is solving a problem in a unique way (B1).

> Innovation on is how you do surveys, and how you deliver surveys (A1).

Other interviewees referred to the use of new technologies, software or instruments (mentioned by almost one third of participants) and to

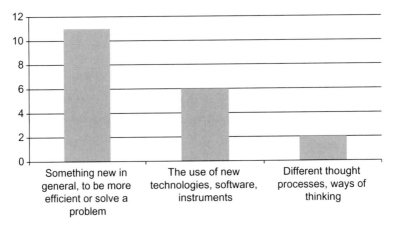

Fig. 1. Interviewee's Definitions of Innovation.

different ways of thinking and approaching issues that arise in firms (mentioned by two participants). Examples are:

It's the new thought process. Bringing in fresh ideas, new ideas (C1).

(Our) innovation is in the laser scanning environment ... it is 3D modelling, visualization (C2).

Fig. 1 illustrates that SI firms define innovation in very broad terms. Most described innovation as something new in general, to be more efficient or to solve a problem. One could use the saying 'Faster, better, cheaper'.

Proposition 1. SI firms are more likely to perceive innovation as new to the firms rather than new to the industry or to the world.

Proposition 2. SI firms are more likely to perceive innovation as ways to increase their work efficiency which then turn into business growth.

Innovation Engagement: Measuring Innovation
Most interviewees suggested measuring changes in productivity or market success, while fewer interviewees suggested measuring changes in firms' R&D expenditure or in their efficiency. (Fig. 2). Examples are:

Find out how much of a company's revenue stream came from the same product they were offering last year (B6).

I would look at ROI (return on investment) ... we spent $100K on a piece of equipment, we want to attribute $200K worth of work on that equipment in that year (C3).

It would be speed and accuracy and the cost of acquiring those products (A4).

A lot of the improvement is coming about through IT, you know, speed of processes and that sort of thing, you could measure the amount of time it would have taken to do a certain area in you know, in different times, you know in five year increments (B8).

Several other interviewees referred to a broad range of answers, such as the number of developed software products or client satisfaction. As shown in Fig. 2, most respondents measure innovation by its effect on either productivity or market success.

Proposition 3. SI firms are more likely to measure innovation through changes in productivity or market growth rather than typical R&D investment.

Innovation Engagement: Innovation Roles
Because participants clearly had various perceptions of the concept of innovation, they were provided with the researchers' innovation definition,[1] to ensure uniformity across interviewees regarding the same concept of innovation in the subsequent question. Our enquiry into the role that participants ascribed to innovation in their firms found that many firms identified significant changes and improvements regarding how the firm was now carrying out its business, compared to the recent past.

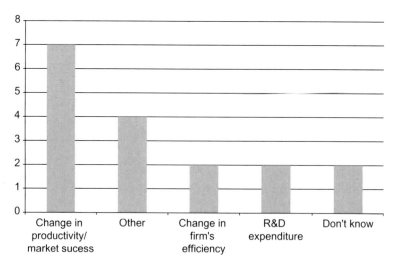

Fig. 2. Interviewees' Views on Measuring Innovation.

Out of the 17 participants who answered this question, only one firm said that innovation does not play a very great role in their company. Nine interviewees, however, stated that innovation is (very) important for their company (Fig. 3).

It has been the absolute critical foundation of this company's success and continued success, has been and will be – innovation (B12).

The main (important) thing is to improve your efficiency or your bottom line (A4).

It (innovation) is a huge role (B5).

Firms described the importance of innovation in their firms in multiple ways. Firstly, more than one company stated that innovation is crucial to their existence. The manager of a small Category B company, for instance, said that without their investments in innovations, they 'would not exist'. Secondly, innovation is described as a way to stay ahead of their competitors and growth. Examples are:

Being a service oriented company in a competitive environment, we need to continually look for innovation to improve the product and the service delivery. The clients won't stay with the same product, if someone else comes out and says oh you know, my widget has got a whistle for the same price, then they will go with that, even if they don't want a whistle, they will just say oh well, I'm getting more why wouldn't I want one with a whistle (B5).

Our business is in a growing stage, so managing a growing business requires innovative ideas. Going by your definition we are introducing ... systems and processes, so that

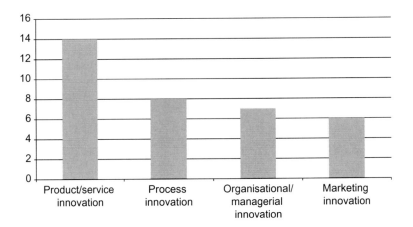

Fig. 3. Reported Innovations by Interviewees.

you are able to manage that growth and also compete. So it is not just about competing in the marketplace, but also about how you are growing the business (C1).

Proposition 4. SI firms that focus on business survival and competitive advantage are more likely to highly value innovation.

Innovation Engagement: Activities
Subsequent to investigating respondents' views on innovation, we examined the innovations that had actually taken place in their firms during the past year. Many firms did not describe themselves as innovative. However, during the interviews, most firms described continuous improvements, and many interviewees reported one or more innovations in their firm during the past year. Out of the 20 interviewed companies, 14 mentioned one or more product or service innovations during the last year. Six firms mentioned one or more marketing innovation, eight firms mentioned one or more process innovation and seven firms mentioned organisational innovations. Fig. 4 provides an overview of the reported innovations.

The wide range of innovative activities, with product or service innovation being the most frequently mentioned are shown in Fig. 4. Product innovations included, for example, a natural language search engine, the sales of new technology and the use of sophisticated graphs for image pattern recognition. Examples of marketing innovations included the use of social media and the introduction of several new marketing concepts. Process innovations included new manufacturing techniques and new

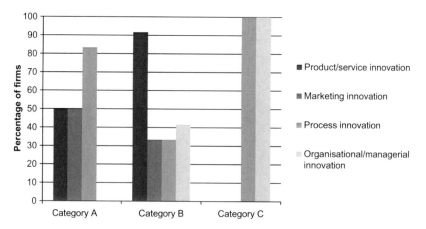

Fig. 4.   Innovation Types by Firm Type.

processes to draw up plans, and organisational innovations included going public and the introduction of new management teamwork strategies.

Remarkably, relatively few of the interviewed Category A firms mentioned organisational or managerial innovations, while almost all Category B firms mentioned one or more product or service innovations. Firm size does not seem to have an effect on the type of reported innovations. Fig. 5 provides an overview of the mentioned innovations per firm type.

As shown in Fig. 5, Category A firms mentioned process innovation most frequently followed by product/service and marketing innovations. Almost all Category B firms mentioned marketing innovation with the other forms of innovation mentioned by fewer than half. All Category C firms mentioned both Process and Organisational/managerial innovation. Thus it seems that High Tech and Low Tech SI firms have different preferences for the types of innovation.

Proposition 5. SI firms are more likely to engage in product and service innovations rather than other type of innovations.

Innovation Engagement: Exploration or Exploitation?
Exploratory innovation offers new designs, creates new markets and develops new channels of distribution. Conversely, exploitative innovation broadens existing knowledge and skills, improves established designs and expands existing products and services, and increases the efficiency of production (Liao & Hu, 2007). Thus, the concept of exploratory innovation is

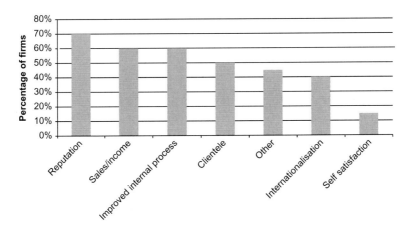

Fig. 5. Reported Benefits of Innovation.

akin to radicalness while exploitative innovation is relatively associated with incremental changes. We found that 13 firms reported that their innovations were new to the firm or industry, while 7 firms were reported as new to the world. Not surprisingly, most firms mentioned one or more innovations that were new to the firm. More surprising was the number of reported innovations that were new to the world. The new to the world innovations were all reported by the Category B firms, both small and medium/large firms. There was also a strong relationship between firm age and this type of innovation: all new to the world innovations were reported by firms founded after 1997, while firms in our sample that were founded before 1997 reported no new to the world innovations. Most innovations (18 firms) were incremental innovations.

Proposition 6. Innovation activities in SI firms are more likely to be exploitation rather than exploration.

Innovation Engagement: Beneficial Gains
Apart from these innovation outcomes, most interviewees alluded to several other benefits their firm has gained from innovation. A large majority of interviewees referred to innovation as a key factor to increase their reputation, followed by sales or income, improved internal process and clientele, among other benefits. Examples are:

> No doubt reputation improves; people like to see innovative companies. Customers don't always like to pay, but they like to think they are dealing with something new, sexy and good (B17).

> [Innovation] has built our reputation; it is wholly responsible for our reputation (B12).

Another big Category B company claimed they have become market leader due to their innovation. An additional benefit from innovation reported by many firms is the improvement of the firm's internal processes, such as time efficiency. Many of the interviewees further reported that their innovations have helped them to attract new customers or to gain recurring customers. One large Category C firm reported that customers stay with the firm because of 'our innovative approach to doing it and our solutions are technically superior to the others'. The benefits of innovation included market expansion and 8 of the 20 interviewees reported that their innovations contributed to their firm's internationalisation.

Proposition 7. SI firms are more likely to associate innovation benefits with market expansion, including internationalisation.

Facilitation and Impediment of Innovation Engagement: Firm Characteristics
Time and monetary constraints proved to be the greatest barrier for the interviewed companies. The necessity to maintain their cash flow is especially important for small firms: eight out of nine small firms reported this as an innovation barrier, while only five out of thirteen medium to large firms considered this as a concern. One of the interviewees described this as following:

> Internally we might slow things down on the innovation if cash flow becomes an issue; then we concentrate more on client work (B6).

Time and money constraints obstructed innovation equally in Category A and Category B firms: four out of six Category A firms, seven out of twelve Category B firms and both Category C firms described this as an innovation barrier.

Facilitation and Impediment of Innovation Engagement: Internal Factors
While respondents mentioned their corporate culture as an important factor to enable innovation, a firm's corporate culture can also form a hindrance to innovate. Several firms mentioned opposition to the use of new technology or procedures in their firm as a barrier to innovate. A large Category A formulates the issue concisely as the old 'we've always done it that way' (A3). This resistance to change is reported as coming from staff, but also from a company's management, who were not easily persuaded to try innovative and new techniques.

Not only new technology, but also uncertain outcomes can cause resistance to innovation. Examples are:

> Sometimes we get discouraged from pursuing the building of a completely different product because we're not sure how it is going to be received in the marketplace (A3).

> If you invest in something and it ends up being a waste of time you are shyer the next time around, even though it might better, you are shyer. So your corporate memory sometimes causes issues, and that is why we have probably had about a four year gap where we haven't been that innovative, and it is only now we are starting to get back into it (B6).

Facilitation and Impediment of Innovation Engagement: External Factors
Seven respondents referred to government as a barrier to innovation: two Category A, one Category C and four Category B firms,. Three were small firms, while four were medium to large. One of their concerns regarded government 'attitude' in general, such as government's focus on mining and

little investment in the commercialisation of innovation. A large Category B company (B1), for instance, calls the government 'conservative and tardy', which is an important barrier to innovation, because he feels that for the government, 'process becomes more important than the result' (B7).

Perceptions of excessive paperwork or procedures are also reported; a small Category A firm for instance refers to the 'requirements for tendering as a massive process that discourages small operators' (A4). In some cases, government regulations could be perceived as a barrier. A small Category A firm (A2) referred to the Surveyor's Act, which prescribes the presence of a second person while using GPS instruments for safety regulations. He judged this to be sensible in cities with much traffic, but not in a paddock. Also reported was a local council initially opposing a small Category A's innovative approach (A1). One large Category C firm stated that government internal processes and procurement were a barrier to competition.

Other Internal and External Factors

In addition, other issues were mentioned by firms. Three firms reported having had various technical issues when developing or introducing their innovation. One large and two small companies refer to the company's size as a barrier; in the case of the small firm, the interviewees referred to a lack of internal skills. Other examples include outsiders not believing in the innovation or cooperating with a big foreign company with their own procedures. Further, a respondent mentioned tight customer requirements:

> I notice people are getting quite prescriptive now about how they want things done and sometimes you don't get much leeway to improve the process. You need to follow what they prescribe (B8).

Despite being the greatest enhancer for innovation, some customers can also hamper innovation, which makes them an influential factor for innovation within this industry.

Proposition 8. Firms size, organisational culture and government regulations are important factors to influencing innovation among SI firms.

DISCUSSION AND CONCLUSIONS

Our examination of innovation activities in the SI firms revealed how firms perceive and engage in innovation as a part of their business operation.

While innovation is understood as both a process and an outcome (Crossan & Apaydin, 2010), nonetheless, the distinction between process and outcome of innovation are not clear cut, according to the authors. These authors synthesised past studies of innovation mostly based on large organisations and described that organisations viewed innovation as to 'how to' innovate and 'what to' innovate. SI firms compete in a fast changing market where increasingly sophisticated technology, thus creating new ways of working, new ways of solving problems and faster, more accurate and more efficient solutions driving innovation activities within this sector.

Our qualitative findings suggest that SI firms typically define innovation more broadly and towards product/service as a process innovation in terms of something new to increase efficiency or solve a problem. This finding perhaps could impact how SI firms, especially small firms, report a number of innovation activities. For example, we conducted a follow-up survey with additional 64 SI firms, asking number of innovation activities (based on the UK innovation survey). The innovation activities which are most mentioned product and/or service innovations. Some mentioned marketing innovations, such as the use of social media. Process innovations mentioned included new manufacturing techniques and organisational innovations included going public and new teamwork strategies. As can be expected, smaller SI firms had the lowest innovation activities, comparing to larger SI firms.

We found that most of our case firms tended to view innovation as a process, that is how to innovate in order to improve internal processes and clientele, among other benefits. This is akin to Crossan and Apaydin's (2010) study where innovation is also viewed not only as an outcome but also as a process. Recent research on the approach of small- and medium-sized firms to their environment and situation suggest that 'fostering an innovation orientation has more positive effects on firm performance than creating innovation process outcomes such as patents or innovative products or services' (Rosenbusch et al., 2011).

Our findings also confirm Choi and Shepherd's (2004) findings that small firms are more likely to exploit opportunities when they perceive more knowledge of customer demand for the product and more fully developed technologies. The firms in this study ascribed much of their success as being related to their closeness to customers and knowledge of customer's concerns and demands. Our study provides some indication that firm level entrepreneurial attitudes and behaviours are strongly linked to the innovative activities initiated by firms to maintain or improve their business performance.

Our study needs to be interpreted with consideration given to the limitations of the research. Our samples were drawn from a specific industry, and thus generalisability cannot be claimed. Nonetheless, our study contributes to our knowledge of innovation by highlighting the differences size makes in approaches to innovation and the importance of treating SMEs different than large corporations. We also highlight the potential differences between High and Low Tech firms in their approaches to innovation. This study used an inductive qualitative approach to generate ideas for future studies. All of our findings provide opportunities for further research into innovation in High and Low Tech SMEs, in other industries and in other countries.

NOTE

1. Innovation refers to a new idea or behaviour, including a product, service, system, program, device, process, or practice to an organisation or an organisational sub-unit. This may include an invention, an improvement or diffusion of something pre-existing elsewhere.

REFERENCES

Acs, Z. J., Anselin, L., & Varga, A. (2002). Patents and innovation counts as measures of regional production of new knowledge. *Research Policy, 31*, 1069–1085.

Adams, R., Bessant, J., & Phelps, R. (2006). Innovation management measurement: A review. *International Journal of Management Reviews, 8*, 21–47.

Albors-Garrigos, J., & Barrera, R. R. (2011). Impact of public funding on a firm's innovation performance: Analysis of internal and external moderating factors. *International Journal of Innovation Management, 15*, 1297–1322.

Armbruster, H., Bikfalvi, A., Kinkel, S., & Lay, G. (2008). Organizational innovation: The challenge of measuring non-technical innovation in large-scale surveys. *Technovation, 28*, 644–657.

Australian Bureau of Statistics. (1999). ABS Annual Report (Cat. No. 1001.0), ABS, Canberra.

Avermaete, T., Viaene, J., Morgan, E. J., & Crawford, N. (2003). Determinants of innovation in small food firms. *European Journal of Innovation Management, 6*, 8–17.

Baer, M., & Frese, M. (2003). Innovation is not enough: Climates for initiative and psychological safety, process innovations, and firm performance. *Journal of Organizational Behavior, 24*, 45–68.

Barnett, E., & Storey, J. (2000). Managers' accounts of innovation processes in small and medium-sized enterprises. *Journal of Small Business and Enterprise Development, 7*, 315–324.

Barrett, P., & Sexton, M. (2006). Innovation in small, project-based construction firms. *British Journal of Management, 17*, 331–346.

Baumol, W. J. (2002). Entrepreneurship, innovation and growth: The David–Goliath symbiosis. *The Journal of Entrepreneurial Finance & Business Ventures, 7*(2), 1–10.

Becker, W., & Dietz, J. (2004). R&D cooperation and innovation activities of firms – Evidence for the German manufacturing industry. *Research Policy, 33*, 209–223.

Bos-Brouwers, H. E. J. (2010). Corporate sustainability and innovation in SMEs: Evidence of themes and activities in practice. *Business Strategy and the Environment, 19*, 417–435.

Branzei, O., & Vertinsky, I. (2006). Strategic pathways to product innovation capabilities in SMEs. *Journal of Business Venturing, 21*, 75–105.

Brophey, G., & Brown, S. (2009). Innovation practices within small to medium-sized mechanically-based manufacturers. *Innovation: Management, Policy & Practice, 11*, 327–340.

Brunetto, Y., & Xerri, M. J. (2011). The impact of the perceived usefulness of workplace social networks upon the innovative behaviour of SME employees: A social capital perspective. *International Journal of Innovation Management, 15*, 959–987.

Bucic, T., & Ngo, L. V. (2012). Examining drivers of collaborative inbound open innovation: Empirical evidence from Australian firms. *International Journal of Innovation Management, 16*, 1250017–1250041.

Çakar, N. D., & Ertürk, A. (2010). Comparing innovation capability of small and medium-sized enterprises: Examining the effects of organizational culture and empowerment. *Journal of Small Business Management, 48*, 325–359.

Camelo-Ordaz, C., Fernández-Alles, M., Ruiz-Navarro, J., & Sousa-Ginel, E. (2012). The intrapreneur and innovation in creative firms. *International Small Business Journal, 30*, 513–535.

Camisón-Zornoza, C., Lapiedra-Alcamí, R., Segarra-Ciprés, M., & Boronat-Navarro, M. (2004). A meta-analysis of innovation and organizational size. *Organization Studies, 25*, 331–361.

Cardinal, L. B. (2001). Technological innovation in the pharmaceutical industry: The use of organizational control in managing research and development. *Organization Science, 12*, 19–36.

Ceci, F., & Iubatti, D. (2012). Personal relationships and innovation diffusion in SME networks: A content analysis approach. *Research Policy, 41*, 565–579.

Chandy, R. K., & Tellis, G. J. (2000). The incumbent's curse? Incumbency, size, and radical product innovation. *The Journal of Marketing, 64*, 1–17.

Chassagnon, V., & Audran, M. (2011). The impact of interpersonal networks on the innovativeness of inventors: From theory to empirical evidence. *International Journal of Innovation Management, 15*, 931–958.

Cho, H. J., & Pucik, V. (2005). Relationship between innovativeness, quality, growth, profitability, and market value. *Strategic Management Journal, 26*, 555–575.

Choi, Y. R., & Shepherd, D. A. (2004). Entrepreneurs' decisions to exploit opportunities. *Journal of Management, 30*, 377–395.

Cooper, R. G. (2011). Perspective: The innovation dilemma: How to innovate when the market is mature. *Journal of Product Innovation Management, 28*, 2–27.

Coombs, R., & Miles, I. (2000). Innovation, measurement and services: The new problematique. In J. S. Metcalfe & I. Miles (Eds.), *Innovation systems in the service economy* (Vol. 18, pp. 85–103). Springer US.

Crossan, M. M., & Apaydin, M. (2010). A multi-dimensional framework of organizational innovation: A systematic review of the literature. *Journal of Management Studies, 47*, 1154–1191.

Damanpour, F., & Wischnevsky, J. D. (2006). Research on innovation in organizations: Distinguishing innovation-generating from innovation-adopting organizations. *Journal of Engineering and Technology Management, 23*, 269–291.

De Jong, J. P., & Kemp, R. (2003). Determinants of co-workers' innovative behaviour: An investigation into knowledge intensive services. *International Journal of Innovation Management, 7*, 189–212.

Denti, L. (2012). Leadership and innovation in organizations: A systematic review of factors that mediate or moderate the relationship. *International Journal of Innovation Management, 16*(3), 1240007-1-1240007-20.

Dodgson, M., & Rothwell, R. (1991). Technology strategies in small firms. *Journal of General Management, 17*, 45–55.

Forsman, H. (2009). Improving innovation capabilities of small enterprises: Cluster strategy as a tool. *International Journal of Innovation Management, 13*, 221–243.

Freeman, C., & Soete, L. (1997). *The economics of industrial innovation*. Cambridge, MA: The MIT Press.

Garcia, R., & Calantone, R. (2002). A critical look at technological innovation typology and innovativeness terminology: A literature review. *Journal of Product Innovation Management, 19*, 110–132.

Gatignon, H., Tushman, M. L., Smith, W., & Anderson, P. (2002). A structural approach to assessing innovation: Construct development of innovation locus, type, and characteristics. *Management Science, 48*, 1103–1122.

Glaser, B., & Strauss, A. (1967). *The discovery of grounded theory: Strategies for qualitative research*. New York, NY: Aldine Publishing Company.

Goktan, A. B., & Miles, G. (2011). Innovation speed and radicalness: Are they inversely related? *Management Decision, 49*, 533–547.

Gopalakrishnan, S., & Damanpour, F. (1994). Patterns of generation and adoption of innovation in organizations: Contingency models of innovation attributes. *Journal of Engineering and Technology Management, 11*, 95–116.

Gronum, S., Verreynne, M. L., & Kastelle, T. (2012). The role of networks in small and medium-sized enterprise innovation and firm performance. *Journal of Small Business Management, 50*, 257–282.

Halpern, N. (2010). Marketing innovation: Sources, capabilities and consequences at airports in Europe's peripheral areas. *Journal of Air Transport Management, 16*, 52–58.

Higón, D. A. (2012). The impact of ICT on innovation activities: Evidence for UK SMEs. *International Small Business Journal, 30*, 684–699.

Hill, C. W., & Rothaermel, F. T. (2003). The performance of incumbent firms in the face of radical technological innovation. *Academy of Management Review, 28*, 257–274.

Hipp, C., & Grupp, H. (2005). Innovation in the service sector: The demand for service-specific innovation measurement concepts and typologies. *Research Policy, 34*, 517–535.

Hoffman, K., Parejo, M., Bessant, J., & Perren, L. (1998). Small firms, R&D, technology and innovation in the UK: A literature review. *Technovation, 18*, 39–55.

Howell, J. M., Shea, C. M., & Higgins, C. A. (2005). Champions of product innovations: Defining, developing, and validating a measure of champion behavior. *Journal of Business Venturing, 20*, 641–661.

Huggins, R., & Johnston, A. (2009). Knowledge networks in an uncompetitive region: SME innovation and growth. *Growth and Change, 40*, 227–259.

Huse, M., Neubaum, D. O., & Gabrielsson, J. (2005). Corporate innovation and competitive environment. *The International Entrepreneurship and Management Journal, 1*, 313–333.

Jansen, J. J., Van Den Bosch, F. A., & Volberda, H. W. (2005). Managing potential and realized absorptive capacity: How do organizational antecedents matter? *Academy of Management Journal, 48*, 999−1015.

Johannessen, J., Olsen, B., & Lumpkin, G. T. (2001). Innovation as newness: What is new, how new, and new to whom? *European Journal of Innovation Management, 4*(1), 20−31.

Katila, R., & Chen, E. L. (2008). Effects of search timing on innovation: The value of not being in sync with rivals. *Administrative Science Quarterly, 53*, 593−625.

Khan, A. M., & Manopichetwattana, V. (1989). Innovative and noninnovative small firms: Types and characteristics. *Management Science, 35*, 597−606.

Laforet, S. (2008). Size, strategic, and market orientation effects on innovation. *Journal of Business Research, 61*, 753−764.

Leifer, R., O'connor, G. C., & Rice, M. (2001). Creating game changers in mature firms: The role of radical innovation hubs. *Academy of Management Executive, 15*, 102−113.

Liao, S.-H., & Hu, T.-C. (2007). Knowledge transfer and competitive advantage on environmental uncertainty: An empirical study of the Taiwan semiconductor industry. *Technovation, 27*, 402−411.

Madrid-Guijarro, A., Garcia, D., & Van Auken, H. (2009). Barriers to innovation among Spanish manufacturing SMEs. *Journal of Small Business Management, 47*, 465−488.

Mazzarol, T., & Reboud, S. (2008). The role of complementary actors in the development of innovation in small firms. *International Journal of Innovation Management, 12*, 223−253.

McAdam, R., Reid, R. S., & Gibson, D. A. (2004). Innovation and organisational size in Irish SMEs: An empirical study. *International Journal of Innovation Management, 8*, 147−165.

Obstfeld, D. (2005). Social networks, the tertius iungens orientation, and involvement in innovation. *Administrative Science Quarterly, 50*, 100−130.

O'Cass, A., & Weerawardena, J. (2009). Examining the role of international entrepreneurship, innovation and international market performance in SME internationalisation. *European Journal of Marketing, 43*, 1325−1348.

OECD. (2004). *Effective policies for small business*. Paris: OECD.

Parida, V., Westerberg, M., & Frishammar, J. (2012). Inbound open innovation activities in high-tech SMEs: The impact on innovation performance. *Journal of Small Business Management, 50*, 283−309.

Parthasarthy, R., & Hammond, J. (2002). Product innovation input and outcome: Moderating effects of the innovation process. *Journal of Engineering and Technology Management, 19*, 75−91.

Pérez-Luño, A., Wiklund, J., & Cabrera, R. V. (2011). The dual nature of innovative activity: How entrepreneurial orientation influences innovation generation and adoption. *Journal of Business Venturing, 26*, 555−571.

Rosenbusch, N., Brinckmann, J., & Bausch, A. (2011). Is innovation always beneficial? A meta-analysis of the relationship between innovation and performance in SMEs. *Journal of Business Venturing, 26*, 441−457.

Roussel, P. A., Saad, K. N., Erickson, T. J., & Little, A. D. (1991). *Third generation R&D: Managing the link to corporate strategy*. Boston, MA: Harvard Business School Press.

Rundquist, J. (2012). The ability to integrate different types of knowledge and its effect on innovation performance. *International Journal of Innovation Management, 16*.

Salavou, H., Baltas, G., & Lioukas, S. (2004). Organisational innovation in SMEs: The importance of strategic orientation and competitive structure. *European Journal of Marketing*,
38, 1091–1112.

Sawang, S., & Unsworth, K. L. (2011). Why adopt now? Multiple case studies and survey
studies comparing small, medium and large firms. *Technovation*, *31*, 554–559.

Souitaris, V. (2001). Strategic influences of technological innovation in Greece. *British Journal
of Management*, *12*, 131–147.

Thornhill, S. (2006). Knowledge, innovation and firm performance in high-and low-technology
regimes. *Journal of Business Venturing*, *21*, 687–703.

Unsworth, K., Sawang, S., Murray, J., Norman, P., & Sorbello, T. (2012). Understanding
innovation adoption: Effects of orientation, pressure and control on adoption intentions. *International Journal of Innovation Management*, *16*, 1250004–1250039.

Uzkurt, C., Kumar, R., Kimzan, H. S., & Sert, H. (2012). The impact of environmental uncertainty dimensions on organisational innovativeness: An empirical study on SMEs.
International Journal of Innovation Management, *16*(2), 1250015–1250038.

Van De Vrande, V., De Jong, J. P., Vanhaverbeke, W., & De Rochemont, M. (2009).
Open innovation in SMEs: Trends, motives and management challenges. *Technovation*,
29, 423–437.

Van Es, R., & Van Der Wal, H. (2012). Innovation in SMEs: A race with no finish line.
International Journal of Innovation Management, *16*, 1250027–1250048.

Verhees, F. J., & Meulenberg, M. T. (2004). Market orientation, innovativeness, product
innovation, and performance in small firms. *Journal of Small Business Management*, *42*,
134–154.

Xerri, M. J., & Brunetto, Y. (2011). The impact of the perceived usefulness of workplace
social networks upon the innovative behaviour of SME employees: A social capital
perspective. *International Journal of Innovation Management*, *15*, 959–987.

Zaltman, G., Duncan, R., & Holbek, J. (1973). *Innovations and organizations*. New York, NY:
John Wiley.

CHAPTER 10

SUSTAINING COMPETITIVENESS IN THE ECONOMIC RECESSION: EXPLORATION AND EXPLOITATION IN TWO SMALL- AND MEDIUM-SIZED ENTERPRISES IN A DEVELOPING ECONOMY

Peiran Su and Shengce Ren

ABSTRACT

We link the exploration−exploitation framework of organizational learning to small- and medium-sized enterprises (SMEs) in a developing economy. SMEs in a developing economy generally lack abundant resources and capabilities because of an evolving set of industrial and environmental regulations. Studying two SMEs in China, we argue that their approaches to balancing exploration and exploitation depend on the development stages of the SMEs and their industrial and environmental contexts. In particular, we propose a four-stage framework that unfolds

Exploration and Exploitation in Early Stage Ventures and SMEs
Technology, Innovation, Entrepreneurship and Competitive Strategy, Volume 14, 237−262
ISSN: 1479-067X/doi:10.1108/S1479-067X20140000014007

via initiation, innovation, transformation, and expansion. In this frame-work, SMEs balance exploration and exploitation by adopting temporal separation and organizational separation sequentially. We also find that SMEs may benefit from exploring a narrow scope of products and exploiting them in a wide market scope.

Keywords: Small- and medium-sized enterprises (SMEs); developing economy; exploration and exploitation; temporal separation; organizational separation

INTRODUCTION

The tension between exploration and exploitation in organizational learning is at the heart of strategic renewal (Crossan, Lane, & White, 1999). March (1991) defines exploration as "things captured by terms such as search, variation, risk taking, experimentation, play, flexibility, discovery, innovation" and exploitation as "things such as refinement, choice, production, efficiency, selection, implementation, execution" (March, 1991, p. 71). Levinthal and March (1993) define exploration as "the pursuit of new knowledge, of things that might come to be known" and exploitation as "the use and development of things already known" (Levinthal & March, 1993, p. 104). Some argue that firms need to maintain both exploration and exploitation to achieve superior performance (Cao, Gedajlovic, & Zhang, 2009; He & Wong, 2004). Others suggest that balancing exploration and exploitation may not necessarily relate to superior performance; thus, firms may need to focus on either exploration or exploitation (Lavie, Kang, & Rosenkopf, 2011). Various modes of balancing approaches have emerged as solutions to this issue, such as contextual ambidexterity (Gibson & Birkinshaw, 2004), temporal separation (Duncan, 1976), organizational separation (Benner & Tushman, 2003), and domain separation (Lavie & Rosenkopf, 2006). There is little discussion in the literature about which balancing mode a firm chooses first and whether a firm can switch from one mode to another.

SMEs face inherent constraints in resources and capabilities when they explore and exploit, challenging our understanding of the balance of exploration and exploitation. SMEs are easily affected by environmental and external changes as well as internal factors (Cope, 2003; Dodgson, 1993; Zhang, Macpherson, & Jones, 2006). Successful product innovation is important for the survival of SMEs in the long term because innovative products provide SMEs with opportunities to generate market share, enhance cash flows, and increase their external visibility (De Jong & Vermeulen, 2006; Tellis, Prabhu, & Chandy, 2009). SMEs in a developing economy are further limited in their potential because of an evolving set of economic, financial, and legal regulations. The innovation, organizational learning, and firm growth of SMEs in a developing economy have attracted increasing attention in recent years. Despite a substantial increase in the volume of research on SMEs in developing economies, we lack understanding of their approaches to exploration and exploitation and the performance implications of their product innovation strategies.

The aim of this study is to investigate how SMEs in a developing economy balance exploration and exploitation in their product innovation strategies. We use an integrated model of small firm growth to analyze the internal and external factors that affect two SMEs in China from their establishment in the late 1990s or early 2000s to 2012. The integrated model, developed by Wiklund, Patzelt, and Shepherd (2009), uses four dimensions to analyze small firm growth: strategic orientation, resources, industry, and environment. One of the SMEs was selected from a high-technology industry and the other from a non-high-technology industry in Shanghai, China.

We find that the balancing approaches the SMEs used to build firm-level resources and capabilities depended on the developmental stage of the SMEs and their industrial and environmental contexts. We also find that the SMEs started with temporal separation, which requires a lower level of resource endowment than organizational separation. Furthermore, the two SMEs did not remain permanently in a mode of separation. They switched from temporal separation to organizational separation. The findings of this study also suggest that SMEs may benefit from exploring a narrow scope of products and exploiting these products in a wide scope of customers.

Contributions

The elucidation of a nonlinear process of exploration and exploitation in the product innovation of an SME in a developing economy contributes to the understanding of various approaches to balancing exploration and exploitation in organizational learning. Firms may switch between exploration and exploitation. Firms may also change their mode of balancing exploration and exploitation from temporal separation to organizational separation. These changes depend on the stages of firm development, the firm's resources and capabilities, and the firm's environment.

Choosing a developing economy as the context for this study contributes to the current literature beyond studies on SMEs that have largely focused on developed economics (Wiklund & Shepherd, 2005). We contribute to the understanding of SMEs' growth in developing economies by providing empirical evidence of SMEs that initially lack resources and capabilities and later transform from local to international players.

Our study also adds to the understanding of the strategy and competitiveness of Chinese SMEs. The Chinese economy is large and growing rapidly. The evolving set of industrial and environmental regulations in the country implies uncertainty in resource reallocation among firms. Large firms that can compete internationally or that have the potential to do so generally have easier access to resources than do SMEs. The two cases in this study demonstrate a route to gaining firm-level resources and capabilities in a Chinese context.

We begin by discussing theory development through the multiple case method. We then describe the data and the findings drawn from the cases. We conclude by tying these findings to the broader agenda of exploration, exploitation, and firm growth in SMEs.

THEORY

Two Modes of Balancing Exploration and Exploitation

Two modes of balancing exploration and exploitation are temporal separation and organizational separation. Temporal separation involves cycles of exploration and exploitation (Lavie, Stettner, & Tushman, 2010). In temporal separation, organizations balance exploration and exploitation by shifting from one to the other over time (Duncan, 1976). Temporal separation enables organizations to avoid the conflicting pressures of simultaneous exploration and exploitation (Lavie & Rosenkopf, 2006).

In organizational separation, exploratory and exploitative units are loosely integrated in organizations. Organizations simultaneously perform exploration and exploitation, balancing them within organizational boundaries (Jansen, Tempelaar, Van Den Bosch, & Volberda, 2009). Organizational separation enables organizations to develop innovation options internally without relying on spinouts or venture capital (Lavie et al., 2010).

Temporal separation and organizational separation require different organizational resources and capabilities. When organizations lack sufficient resources and capabilities to pursue exploration and exploitation simultaneously, they can use temporal separation to focus on one at a certain stage and later switch to the other. Hence, temporal separation may require a lower level of resources and capabilities than does organizational separation.

The Context of a Developing Economy: China

China strongly supports the development of its SMEs. The government introduced the SME Promotion Act in 2002. SMEs played an important role in the Chinese economy by contributing to employment and economic growth. SMEs provided eight million jobs in China in 2010. By September 2011, there were more than nine million registered SMEs in China, accounting for 3.7 trillion US Dollars. Over the last decades of reform in China, SMEs accounted for 75% of the gross domestic product (GDP) and provided 80% of all jobs in China.

Some existing Chinese studies support different relationships between entrepreneurial orientation and firm performance than those found in developed economies. Firms with low or high levels of entrepreneurial orientation tend to have lower levels of performance than other firms do, forming an inverted curvilinear relationship between entrepreneurial orientation and firm performance (Tan & Tan, 2005; Tang, Tang, Marino, Zhang, & Li, 2008). The Chinese economy is generally considered a transitional economy that is reforming its economic system from centralized state planning to a market economy. Firms in this economy need to change their strategic orientations accordingly and to respond competitively to market forces and customer demands (Zhao, Li, Lee, & Chen, 2011).

Among Chinese SMEs, small firms have unique features. They are followers with low levels of technology in the market. Their entrepreneurs are relatively young and receive little higher education. Their managers are conservative. Small firms focus on short-term goals and profits. The senior managers we interviewed at the two SMEs shared these characteristics. Generally, small firms do not have sufficient resources and suffer from increasing costs, and they tend to exit the market at a young age. However, small firms have advantages: they are active, rapid in decision making, and flexible in investment.

An Integrative Model of SME Growth

Wiklund et al. (2009) combine five perspectives to develop an integrative model of small firm growth. Based on 413 incorporated Swedish small businesses in knowledge-intensive manufacturing, labor-intensive manufacturing, professional services, and retail sectors, their model suggests the influence of entrepreneurial orientation, environmental characteristics, industrial characteristics, firm resources, and managers' personal attitudes on small firm growth (Wiklund et al., 2009). In this study, we apply Wiklund et al. (2009) model to SMEs. In particular, we are interested in four dimensions of SME growth based on the integrative model: strategic orientation, resources, industry, and environment.

Entrepreneurial orientation refers to a firm's strategic orientation, reflecting how a firm operates (Lumpkin & Dess, 1996). Entrepreneurial firms create and introduce new products and services, generating economic performance (Mcgrath, Tsai, Venkataraman, & Macmillan, 1996). Generally, entrepreneurial orientation has a positive effect on small firm growth. The complexity of entrepreneurial processes implies that small firm growth can depend on a number of factors beyond entrepreneurial orientation, such as the industry growth rate (Audretsch & Mahmood, 1994), market maturity (Baldwin & Gellatly, 2003), and location (Cooper, Gimenogascon, & Woo, 1994). Wiklund et al. (2009) propose that environmental dynamism has a direct negative effect and an indirect positive effect through entrepreneurial orientation on small firm growth. They also propose that the industry context has a direct effect on small firm growth.

Small firms generally lack abundant resources and capabilities. The resource-based view suggests that valuable, rare, inimitable, and non-substitutable resources can be a source of sustainable competitive advantage for a firm (Barney, 1991). Wiklund et al. (2009) propose that financial capital and human resources have positive effects on small firm growth through entrepreneurial orientation. Financial capital is the most general type of resource and can be converted into other types of resources. Human resources have knowledge, skills, and experience that impact the overall resources of the firm and contribute to small firm growth.

METHODS

To answer our research question of how SMEs balance exploration and exploitation in a developing economy, we studied two Chinese SMEs.

The case study method is appropriate for exploring a complex, nonlinear process. The two Chinese firms selected were J Mechanic in the packaging industry and S Wireless in the telecommunications industry. Both firms are leading private SMEs that were ranked in the top 10 in sales revenues in their respective industries at the end of 2012.

J Mechanic was founded in 1998. It is a small, professional manufacturer in the packaging industry specializing in designing, manufacturing, and marketing coil-packaging machinery and orbital packaging. J Mechanic provides customized packaging systems mainly for the iron and steel industry. Their products include machines for pipe wrapping, pre-stress wire wrapping, steel coil wrapping, steel wire wrapping, automatic pallet stretch packing, box shrinking packing, rotate arm wrapping, and coil tilters. By virtue of its technical capabilities, the company holds a leading position in the packaging industry in China. J Mechanic entered the international market in 2005. As of August 2012, J Mechanic's sales revenue had reached 44.17 million US Dollars, with foreign markets accounting for 40% of the firm's overall sales revenue.

A senior manager at J Mechanic described the challenges that the firm experienced as follows:

> At J Mechanic, we have a number of constraints. We do not have sufficient capital investment in innovation. Over the years, similar to numerous private small businesses, we have struggled to "survive in a crack". The fact is that you may see clearly the market prospects of a project, but it is so difficult to get money from the bank. Small businesses have to bear more risk than large enterprises do. ... Even if we get money, we lack creative people. The fast growth in the last two years has caused a shortage of technical staff. [As a result,] the team often works overtime, and the work pressure is huge. ... One of our most pressing issues is to improve the environment for product innovation. ... We need more [time] to reach a balance between market research, service, technological development, manufacturing, and supply.

S Wireless, founded in 2002, is a medium-sized firm in the telecommunication industry. It is a professional manufacturer of wireless communication modules. The company has multiple platforms for the design and manufacturing of second, third, and fourth generation (2G, 3G, and 4G, respectively) wireless communication modules in Global System for Mobile Communications (GSM), General Packet Radio Services (GPRS), Enhanced Data Rates for GSM Evolution, Wideband Code Division Multiple Access (W-CDMA), Time Division Synchronous Code Division Multiple Access (TD-SCDMA), and High-Speed Downlink Package Access. By virtue of its technical capabilities, it holds a leading position in the Chinese telecommunications industry. Wireless communication modules produced by S Wireless are widely used in remote data transmission and monitoring in various areas, such as vehicle positioning, pollutant emissions, aquaculture production and management, and meter reading. The firm incorporated with third parties to provide customized solutions for machine-to-machine, wireless local loop, mobile computing, and global positioning system technologies.

The two case studies follow replication logic (Eisenhardt, 1989; Yin, 2003). This design is justified by the fact that the two firms represent two critical cases for testing and extending theories on SMEs' exploration and exploitation. Both firms are in industries that experience rapid development and severe competition and are located in the region of Shanghai that is at the forefront of the Chinese economy. The difference between them is that S Wireless is a high-technology firm, whereas J Mechanic is not. We selected a high-tech and non-high-tech firm to determine whether the findings could be replicated. The two cases were treated as two independent experiments that confirm or disconfirm conceptual insights.

We aimed to investigate how SMEs explore and exploit over time. Both case studies are longitudinal. Longitudinal case studies can achieve this goal of revealing the processes and dynamics by which firms innovate (Van De Vean & Huber, 1990). The information we collected covers over 10 years of each firm's history since its establishment. We collected evidence from a number of sources, including documentary evidence (i.e., newspaper and web information), archival records (i.e., organizational records), direct observations, and interviews. We conducted a series of interviews with one senior manager for each SME over the period of research. Accordingly, we were able to consult the interviewees repeatedly at different stages of our research and to convey our findings to the insiders. The content of the conversations between the interviewers and the interviewees evolved alongside the development of our theoretical framework. Data triangulation was realized not only using cross-sectional evidence but also via longitudinal efforts. J Mechanic was not listed on any stock market. S Wireless appeared on the Hong Kong Stock Market in 2005.

The underlying logic of the research presented here is grounded theory building, which involves inducting insights from field-based case data (Glaser & Strauss, 1967). A grounded theory-building approach is likely to generate novel and accurate insights into the phenomenon under study. The analytic technique in this study is explanation building (Yin, 2003). The goal of explanation building is to analyze the case study data by building an explanation about the case. As is typical in inductive research, our analysis involved triangulating the data and comparing across individual case studies to construct a conceptual framework (Miles & Huberman, 1984; Yin, 2003). Once the individual case studies were complete, we used a cross-case analysis to develop the conceptual insights. Rather than developing an a priori hypothesis, we compared the cases to identify common dilemmas and to refine the unique aspects of each particular case.

FINDINGS

The findings have two parts. In the first part, we present a model of the innovation strategies adopted by J Mechanic in the firm's product exploration and exploitation. The model unfolds via four stages: initiation, innovation, transformation, and expansion. Generally, each stage exhibits features of strategic orientation, resources, industry, and environment that are different from those of the other stages. Table 1 summarizes the main findings based on our study of J Mechanic. In the second part, we follow replication logic (Yin, 2003) and examine our findings for S Wireless.

J Mechanic

Stage One: Initiation (Exploitation in Temporal Separation, 1998–2001)

During its early years, J Mechanic was a buy-and-sell firm, purchasing products cheaply and reselling them for a profit. The products that J Mechanic purchased and resold were simple packaging machinery. The firm did not have the necessary resources or capabilities to innovate, and it did not have a target market. The buy-and-sell strategy lowered the firm's investment, financial risk, and skill requirements. A senior manager of J Mechanic said,

> [In this industry,] market confusion in the early years brought J Mechanic into a brutal price competition without rules. [There were] disputes between dealers and agents, between manufacturers and distributors. [There were] no rules. In this competitive environment of disorder, J Mechanic cultivated a most critical flexibility and adaptability and a keen sense of the market.

The buy-and-sell strategy also brought disadvantages to J Mechanic. The firm did not make the products itself and did not control product quality. It had to rely on external parties to provide after-sales service and to resolve problems associated with the products. The firm's human resources were involved in broad distribution of product service.

At this stage, the Chinese packaging industry was in its early development. The industry has a weak base because China's industrialization

Table 1. J Mechanic: Four Stages of Firm Development.

Balancing Approach	Temporal Separation		Organizational Separation	
	Exploitation	Exploration	Exploration Focused	Exploitation Focused
Name of stage	Initiation	Innovation	Transformation	Expansion
Period of stage	1998–2001	2001–2005	2005–2008	2008 and onwards
Strategic orientation	The firm pursued a buy-and-sell strategy.	The firm focused on product innovation in the enwind packaging market.	The firm focused on producing nonstandard, customized products.	The firm offered solutions to customized, auto-packaging nationally and internationally.
Resources	The firm had too few resources and capabilities to innovate. Buy-and-sell business made the firm spend resources on service.	Sales grew. The firm could start its product innovation.	The firm had early-mover advantages, established reputation, innovative capabilities, technological and market knowledge, and experienced human resources.	The firm took advantage of e-commerce. It strengthened its reputation in developing economies.
Industry	The industrial base was weak. Firms in the industry imported foreign technologies and could not make profitable use of them.	A few firms manufactured enwind packaging machine. Profit margins were high.	The general enwind packaging market matured. Many firms became OEMs, increasing production capacity at low price.	Many firms experienced decrease in their sale revenue because of the economic recession.
Environment	China's industrialization was in its infancy. The Company Act and the SME Promotion Act were launched.	China joined WTO. WTO brought opportunities for international trade and challenges of foreign products.	China made strategies on industrialization and sustainable development, encouraging the development of machinery and equipment manufacturing.	The economic recession began and lasted for years.

process was in its infancy. The early development of the industry depended on foreign technologies introduced from developed countries, including Japan and some European countries. These foreign technologies were so advanced that they did not align well with the existing equipment and materials of the industry. J Mechanic experienced not only price competition but also tensions among dealers, manufacturers, and distributors.

However, the transformation to a market economy in China accelerated industrial growth and spurred the demand for products in the packaging industry. The Chinese government introduced the Company Act. As a major outcome of this regulation, firms stopped price competition and began a period of rational planning and specifications in their strategies and production. The Company Act not only built a legal basis for the establishment of norms and regulations but also stated firms' responsibilities, duties, and rights. Following the Company Act, firms improved their organizational structures and established clear and detailed rules and instructions for their development.

The Chinese government also introduced the SME Promotion Act. The purpose of this Act is to implement nationwide, proactive support policies for the creation and development of SMEs. The Chinese National SME Development also established a special fund to provide timely assistance and services for SMEs, such as counseling, credit guarantees, technological innovation, and market development.

Stage Two: Innovation (Exploration in Temporal Separation, 2001–2005)
J Mechanic obtained basic resources, especially financial resources, during the initiation stage. The firm made a historic, strategic decision to innovate. The firm planned to transform its focus from buy-and-sell to manufacturing. Its first product targeted the enwind packaging market. The firm started with imitations of similar advanced products and became a professional manufacturer of an enwind packaging machine. In October 2001, J Mechanic's first enwind packaging machine passed its performance test right before the machine was exhibited at the International Industry Fair in Shanghai, China. A senior manager of the firm explained,

> There were few enwind packaging machine manufacturers in China. The competition was [relatively] stable. Customers were high-end ones. It was easy to regulate the business and its related operations. Because of this, profit margins were higher [than other products]. Our product was at an excellent point of its life cycle.

This type of enwind packaging machine was welcomed by many export-oriented enterprises. During this period, China maintained a stable, export-oriented economy with a promising market and much room for development. However, despite the demands, there were few enwind packaging manufacturers in the industry. The competition was rational, and the profit was high. The enwind packaging machine was at an ideal point of the product life cycle. Based on the success of its enwind packaging machine, J Mechanic built a large number of high-quality customer groups, entering the high-end market of the packaging industry. J Mechanic's new strategic orientation changed the firm's resource endowments.

During this stage, China joined the World Trade Organization (WTO). The country strengthened its foreign trade partnerships with other countries. On the one hand, the international business brought the Chinese packaging industry opportunities for technological exchanges and improvement in research and development (R&D). On the other hand, foreign packaging manufacturers entered the Chinese packaging market with their products. These products generally had advanced technologies and met the needs of sophisticated customers. The experienced new comers challenged the competitiveness of Chinese firms that were still building their innovation capabilities.

In this stage of innovation, J Mechanic experienced a number of attempts while building its innovative capabilities. One example is the successful innovation of a plastic coil-packaging machine. Most plastic coil manufacturers at that time relied on manual packaging, which was cost efficient but raised concerns about time efficiency and workers' safety. A plastic coil manufacturer was attracted by a series of upright packaging machines that J Mechanic introduced to the iron and steel industry in 2003 and contacted J Mechanic.

Although J Mechanic did not have experience in lightweight packaging, the firm decided to take the opportunity and the challenge. Following technological exploration and market analysis, J Mechanic made its first plastic coil-packaging machine based on its series of upright packaging machines. The successful test of the machine served as a perfect advertisement for J Mechanic's product innovation. The product soon found its market in leading firms of the Chinese plastics industry in Guangdong, Hubei, Liaoning, and Zhejiang. By the end of 2012, the sales of upright packaging machines accounted for 56% of J Mechanic's sales of stand-alone packaging machines. A senior manager of the firm commented,

Differentiation is shown in the upgrading capacity of a firm's product innovation capabilities. The newness of your product, the popularity of the demand, the influence of your product on the industry, and customers are the main factors [of product innovation capabilities].

A second example is the innovation of an automatic packaging machine. In early 2004, a leading Chinese motorcycle manufacturer in Chongqing asked J Mechanic to make an automatic pallet wrapping line. The motorcycle manufacturer planned to use the wrapping line as part of its production line imported from Italy. The wrapping line should completely replace manual packaging in the integration of offline product packaging. At that time, most firms used semiautomatic wrapping machines and were reluctant to invest in automatic wrapping machines because of low labor costs. A few large manufacturing enterprises used a similar product made in Italy, which cost around 30 million US Dollars.

J Mechanic was in the forefront of the manufacturing of stand-alone pallet wrapping machines. Because an automatic wrapping line consists of a number of pieces of stand-alone pallet wrapping machines, J Mechanic did not see significant technical difficulties in making its first automatic wrapping line. The firm signed the contract with the motorcycle manufacturer. However, difficulties arose throughout the entire process of product innovation. First, J Mechanic did not have experience in automatic controlling systems. Their existing controlling system did not align with the automatic wrapping machine. Second, making the machine requires the processing of precision parts, and the existing equipment on the market could not meet the requirement for accuracy.

Overcoming these difficulties, J Mechanic delivered the automatic wrapping line successfully. Although the price of a set of automatic wrapping line machines made by J Mechanic was approximately 10% of the price of a similar product made in Italy, few domestic enterprises were interested in this equipment because of the relatively high price. By the end of 2012, J Mechanic sold nine sets of the automatic wrapping line in China. A senior manager said,

> It is hard to say that such product innovation had no value. It might have offered J Mechanic invaluable experience in product innovation but did not achieve the economic income that the firm expected. The problem was that before the implementation of the project, we did not find out about the real market demand. Temporary needs of individual users, if they do not bring universal demands, cannot produce market players.

Stage Three: Transformation (Exploration in Organizational Separation, 2005–2008)

In late 2005, the market of conventional pallet wrapping machines was about to mature. Significant growth and innovation were absent, and profits were low. Many manufacturing firms in the packaging industry attempted to win market share by offering low prices. They chose low-cost routes and became original equipment manufacturers (OEMs) to increase their production capacity.

J Mechanic refused to be an OEM. The firm gained its leading position in the packaging industry with an established reputation, early-mover advantages, and innovative capabilities. More importantly, J Mechanic had a group of entrepreneurial employees with technical expertise and innovative capabilities. However, J Mechanic did not stop here. The strategic goals of J Mechanic at this stage were twofold: J Mechanic explored how to improve product design and quality management in its manufacturing as well as the market for special and nonstandard equipment, meeting the growing needs of highly experienced customers.

To revitalize and upgrade the equipment manufacturing industry, China launched a number of acts to support the development of machinery and equipment manufacturing industries, including the packaging industry, as part of the country's industrialization and sustainable development. For instance, in 2005, the Chinese State Council introduced policies for Accelerating the Revitalization of the Equipment Manufacturing Industry. These regulations were also part of the major initiatives in the Tenth Five-Year Plan for Chinese national economic and social development.

Stage Four: Expansion (Exploitation in Organizational Separation, 2008 Onwards)

J Mechanic maintained its innovation strategies and did not become an OEM for international companies. This decision made it difficult for J Mechanic to compete in the market and to gain short-term profits. The firm decided to take advantage of rapidly growing electronic commerce (e-commerce) to compete in the international market. J Mechanic established a collaboration with the Alibaba Group, a private-owned group of Internet-based e-commerce businesses.

Eventually, J Mechanic established a stable market, providing customized automatic packaging systems for domestic and international enterprises mainly in the iron and steel industry. J Mechanic's customers included a number of leading firms in this industry and their subsidiaries in China, India, and South Korea. The firm made significant progress in product innovation and technology management. Commenting on the firm's development in this period, a senior manager said,

> We planned for our long-term goals. [...] When international buyers were seeking OEM cooperation, short-term interests did not attract us. We kept a clear head, understood [the firm's] strengths and weaknesses, and maintained [the firm's] innovation and strategic

direction. … Companies do not "hibernate". We increased valuable input, sought the maximization of customer value, instead of maximizing profits. The firm endeavored to win customer loyalty and to defend its market, […] improved its skills, improved the process [of production], upgraded management, and prepared for the economic recovery.

Due to the differences in general trading conditions between developing economies and developed ones, the Chinese packaging industry exported product mainly to developing countries, focusing on the Southeast Asian market. Eighty percent of J Mechanic's exports went to developing countries, of which half were in Southeast Asia. Meanwhile, J Mechanic noticed a growing demand in African countries and increased its exports to Africa. During the recent economic recession, when global financial and debt crisis hit the developed economies, J Mechanic was able to double its sales revenues. Fig. 1 depicts the increase of J Mechanic's sales revenue.

S Wireless

Following replication logic, we altered the industry context and studied S Wireless in the telecommunications industry. This industry is generally considered a high-technology industry in China.

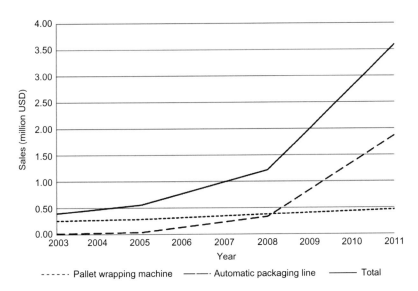

Fig. 1. J Mechanic: Sales Revenue (USD). *Source*: J Mechanic's Annual Reports of 2003, 2005, 2008, and 2011.

S Wireless was founded in 2002 as part of a group of businesses from which the firm received its first resources. Because of this, S Wireless had a brief initiation stage. Adopting the mode of temporal separation at the beginning, S Wireless started with exploration followed by exploitation. Therefore, the firm's first stage was innovation, or exploration in temporal separation, which lasted for approximately two years. By the end of the first stage, S Wireless launched its first self-designed module of GSM/GPRS in 2004. During the period from 2004 to 2006, S Wireless switched to exploitation in its product strategies. Its wireless module products successfully entered the Asia-Pacific and Eastern European markets.

S Wireless adopted the model of organizational separation from 2007 onwards. The firm balanced exploration and exploitation simultaneously during this period. The firm explored the market of 3G mobile telecommunications technology and made its wireless modules for the market in 2007. The firm launched various 3G modules of W-CDMA and TD-SCDMA. The firm's production increased to 10 million wireless modules. At the same time, S Wireless expanded its global market for its certified, quality products. In 2009, the GSM Association (GSMA[1]) certified the firm's W-CDMA 3G wireless module. In 2010, S Wireless' GSM module was certified by AT&T in the United States, Vodafone in the United Kingdom, and Organge in France. The firm's W-CDMA 3G module received the certification of AT&T in 2011. In 2012, S Wireless passed the TS16949 quality test of the International Organization for Standardization (ISO).

In contrast to the increase in S Wireless' production between 2005 and 2012, its sales decreased from 2009. Fig. 2 depicts the changes in S Wireless' production and sales revenue. Although S Wireless reached its production peak and had its key products certified internationally, the economic recession began, and S Wireless' sales revenue began to fall. S Wireless and J Mechanic experienced similar processes from temporal separation to organizational separation, but they differed in financial performance during the economic recession.

J Mechanic undertook specialized product innovation after adopting the mode of organizational separation to balance exploration and exploitation. S Wireless did not specialize in a particular product and became an OEM of leading multinational enterprises. S Wireless entered the 3G wireless market, which was expanding because of the growing popularity of 3G technologies in wireless telecommunications. These strategic choices may be associated with the increases in S Wireless' production and sales revenue but may not have benefitted the firm during the economic recession.

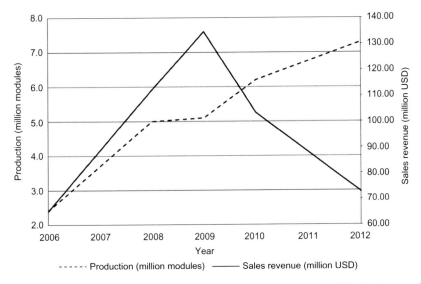

Fig. 2. S Wireless: Production and Sales Revenue. *Source*: S Wireless' annual reports of 2006, 2008, 2009, 2010, and 2012.

We find that specialization in product innovation may be associated with positive financial performance when the firm adopts the mode of organizational separation to balance exploration and exploitation.

DISCUSSION

Aiming to understand SMEs' exploration and exploitation in a developing economy, we studied how two Chinese private SMEs strategized their product innovation and balanced exploration and exploitation via temporal separation and organizational separation. We identified a four-stage framework of balancing exploration and exploitation in SMEs' product innovation in a developing economy. SMEs adopted the mode of temporal separation in the first two stages, namely, initiation and innovation. Depending on the resource endowment that an SME had when it was established, the firm pursued either exploitation or exploration in the first stage, followed by either exploration or exploitation in the second stage. The firm adopted the mode of organizational separation in the next two stages, namely, transformation and expansion. We also found that specialization was important to financial performance in a firm's transformation and expansion. While J Mechanic balanced exploration and exploitation in organizational separation, it undertook specialized product innovation intensively and expanded its market extensively. The findings suggest that in the mode of organizational separation, specialization strategy in product innovation is associated with an increase in a firm's financial performance, especially during an economic recession.

Theoretical Implications

Nonlinear Approach to Balancing Exploitation and Exploration
The two SMEs exhibited a nonlinear process for balancing exploration and exploitation in their product innovation over time. This nonlinear process is depicted in Table 2, where the mode of temporal separation is followed by the mode of organizational separation. The former allows the firm to switch between exploration and exploitation, whereas the latter requires the firm to explore and exploit simultaneously. The adoption of temporal separation in the early years of an SME may be the strategic choice because of the limited resources and capabilities of the SME. The adoption of organizational separation may require higher levels of resources and capabilities. Similarly, domain separation may require the highest levels of resources and capabilities among the four modes of balancing approaches because domain separation allows exploration and/or exploitation in multiple domains within an organization.

Table 2. A Nonlinear Approach for Balancing Exploration and Exploitation in SMEs.

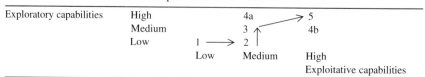

Note: Initiation: 1–2 (exploration in temporal separation).
Innovation: 2–3 (exploitation in temporal separation).
Transformation: 3–4a–5 (exploration in organizational separation).
Expansion: 3–4b–5 (exploitation in organizational separation).

Product Innovation and Catching-up in Developing Economies
Researchers have examined the determinants of product innovation success (De Jong & Vermeulen, 2006; Freel & Robson, 2004). However, little attention has been paid to the effects of environmental factors and industrial resources on product innovation success. For SMEs' growth in a developing economy, exporting products may be an important path because of the lack of opportunities in their domestic markets (Boso, Cadogan, & Story, 2013). Our case studies support this point and show evidence of SMEs exporting to foreign markets to sustain their competitiveness in the domestic market. Both J Mechanic and S Wireless had a substantial proportion of their sales from exportation.

One of the differences between the two SMEs' exported products is that J Mechanic provided customized nonstandard products, whereas S Wireless provided high-quality standard products. This difference may have implications for SMEs attempting to catch up in a developing economy. To survive, many SMEs choose to become OEMs of multinational enterprises. S Wireless was one of these SMEs. Although its production increased, this seemingly successful strategic orientation may have been fatal because it made S Wireless a follower of technologies developed by leading players in the industry. We suggest that SMEs in a developing economy should catch up but not "follow up." SMEs need to catch up by developing their own specializations instead of continuing or repeating what leading firms have done. This argument provides logical support for the association between SMEs' specialization in product innovation and their financial performance.

Practical Implications

Product Innovation and Differentiation
J Mechanic provided nonstandard solutions to its customers. Requests from firms in other industries helped J Mechanic expand its market. Developing successful innovative products is important for long-term business success because novel products provide SMEs with the opportunity to generate early-mover advantages, gain cash flows, increase external visibility, and sustain competition (Langerak, Hultink, & Robben, 2004; Tellis et al., 2009). J Mechanic was able to upgrade its competitiveness in the packaging industry by introducing new products to the industry and introducing existing products to a broader market. This capability brought the firm the advantage of product differentiation. Product differentiation

reflects the tension between customers' demand and manufacturers' supply. Faced with a new field, most managers of SMEs may be conservative and hesitate to innovate. The case of J Mechanic suggests that managers may value the organizational learning provided by product innovation initiatives even when the resulting product is not a great success. If J Mechanic had not agreed to try new solutions, it would not have gained experience in providing customized solutions.

Product differentiation requires a firm to know the market well and to recognize the common needs of individual users. This is not easy for an SME, which may not be able to conduct market research. An SME may not have a "big picture" of the industry. For instance, when J Mechanic decided to design and produce the automatic packaging line for the motorcycle manufacturer, it did not realize the precision parts and accuracy that would be required by an automatic packaging line. Furthermore, J Mechanic may not have perceived the potential market of an automatic packaging line in a developing economy, where semiautomatic packaging systems assisted by manual packaging would be cheaper. Product differentiation requires both enthusiasm and rationality. Rationality in product innovation is especially important to SMEs because they may have difficulties with financial resources and human resources. As a senior manager put it,

> Generally, the degree of automation of production lines in the manufacturing enterprises was relatively low. With the help of a semi-automatic machine, it was convenient and did not cost much. Why not [produce in this way]? Complete automation requires an integrated system with high levels of device speed, precision, safety, space, and other requirements. [Chinese] domestic enterprises could not choose [complete automation machine], so this project was a failure. The firm was blinded, anxious, [depending on] enthusiasm to innovate, [and] ultimately failed to realize the market value of the product. On the other hand, if this type of innovative project was implemented, it would consume the innovative efforts of our small team. The team would be then forced to do something they should not do at that time. Especially for small businesses, whose innovation was very often subject to financial and human capitals, more homework should be done before project implementation.

Product differentiation requires time. It took J Mechanic 15 years to become a leading firm in the Chinese packaging industry as well as an international provider of customized nonstandard solutions. If J Mechanic had chosen to be an OEM and gained short-term interests, it would not have achieved what it has achieved.

Product differentiation creates barriers for competitors to enter the market. J Mechanic's competitors need to meet customers' technology requirements and to earn customer loyalty, both of which are difficult. J Mechanic experienced a number of trials and errors before achieving its innovative capabilities. This was a process of learning from experience. After years of innovating, J Mechanic developed customer groups that were satisfied with the firm's products and were reluctant to pay the switching costs they would incur if they changed their suppliers.

Product Innovation and Intellectual Property

The packaging industry was an emerging industry that had not established a set of industrial standards and norms. This situation resulted in different levels of technologies in the product market. J Mechanic grew rapidly at the forefront of the industry. Many of its products were not addressed by current industry standards. The firm had to refer to its own standards to design and make products. Its technologies were not patented and hence were not protected, and other firms easily imitated J Mechanic's products at lower costs. These imitations not only damaged the innovator's motivation but also shortened product life cycles. It is important for policy makers to anticipate and prevent problems associated with SMEs' development.

As an emerging industry, the packaging industry lacks technological exchanges within the country and across countries. The communication platforms of the Chinese packaging industry are mainly exhibitions, web sites, and magazines. International counterparts in developed countries create technical barriers to protect their advanced equipment. To catch up, SMEs in a developing economy need to develop their own technologies and solutions. For instance, more than 50% of J Mechanic's products were customized and nonstandard. Hence, the pricing of the customized products did not depend on what the firm's competitors made but rather on their design and cost of production. These customized solutions served as an effective way of protecting J Mechanic's intellectual property.

Limitations

Scholars often argue that empirical studies rely on biased samples that have undergone a selection process that identifies successful examples, not failures (Denrell, 2003). Therefore, the generalizability of findings may be limited. In our study, the two SMEs survived a selection process in the vibrant environment of a developing economy. Our observations may explain why the SMEs succeeded, but they cannot explain why they did not fail.

Reasons for failure or "non-failure" may be more vital than reasons for success. Future studies may benefit from investigating failed SMEs.

Catching-up processes can vary from industry to industry and from economy to economy. The findings of our study may thus elucidate a process experienced by a limited number of SMEs in certain industries. There may be industrial or institutional effects in our findings. For instance, pharmaceutical firms in India chose to grow via duplicative imitation followed by creative imitation to move up the value chain of pharmaceutical R&D (Chataway, Kale, & Wield, 2007; Simonetti, Archambault, Cote, & Kale, 2007). Strategies chosen by an SME matter; however, what matters more may be the firm's industry or institutional environment. An industry or an economy may play a moderating role, shaping the process of an SME's product innovation and firm growth. For example, regulatory changes play an important role in the creation of dynamic capabilities in Indian pharmaceutical firms (Athreye, Kale, & Ramani, 2009). In China, scholars have found government effects on Chinese firms' growth and entrepreneurial activities (Jing & Tylecote, 2005; Millar, Choi, & CHU, 2005).

The selection of two SMEs from two industries affects the generalizability of the findings of this study. What we observed in the SMEs' strategic choices and firm performance might be an outcome of various features of the two industries. However, the negative influence of this limitation may be reduced by the fact that the two SMEs were leading SMEs in their industries and hence faced similar environments of a developing economy. Success for other SMEs might require similar strategic choices and innovative activities. We recommend that future studies should overcome this limitation and control for the industry effect.

Areas for Future Research

The process model requires quantitative, longitudinal evidence. Similar research was conducted in product development, examining product development through exploration and exploitation alliances (Rothaermel & Deeds, 2004). This type of research rarely appears in the literature on organizational transformation and firm growth, nor does research on the complex, nonlinear process of balancing exploration and exploitation via two approaches. Future research should apply this process model to longitudinal, quantitative data to determine if one period of exploration or exploitation in the process predicts the next. Future research could also investigate moderating and mediating factors that affect the process of firms' product innovation and strategic decisions.

Comparative studies on SMEs may be expected between technology-intensive and non-technology-intensive firms; between firms in two developing economies, such as China and India; and between firms in a developing economy and those in a developed economy. Comparative studies could consider the organizational level, the industrial level, and the national level.

CONCLUSION

The two case studies reveal a nonlinear process model of balancing exploration and exploitation in SMEs' product innovation in a developing economy. The process has four stages: initiation, innovation, transformation, and expansion. Depending on an SME's resources and capabilities, it may choose temporal separation followed by organizational separation. The case studies also reveal the importance of specialization in product innovation, especially when an SME adopts organizational separation to balance exploration and exploitation.

The complexity in the industrial and environmental contexts that SMEs face in a developing economy challenges SMEs' innovation strategies and international competitiveness. Policy makers, managers, and researchers need to collaborate to improve the business environment for SMEs' growth.

NOTE

1. GSMA was the world's largest association in the telecommunications industry, and its members included AT&T, KT, O2, TIM, and Vodafone.

ACKNOWLEDGMENTS

We thank Anya Xu and Yueqi Yang for their help in collecting information about the firms. We thank the editors and an anonymous reviewer for their insightful comments.

REFERENCES

Athreye, S., Kale, D., & Ramani, S. V. (2009). Experimentation with strategy and the evolution of dynamic capability in the Indian pharmaceutical sector. *Industrial and Corporate Change, 18*, 729–759.

Audretsch, D. B., & Mahmood, T. (1994). Firm selection and industry evolution: The post-entry performance of new firms. *Journal of Evolutionary Economics, 4*, 243–260.

Baldwin, J., & Gellatly, G. (2003). *Innovation strategies and performance in small firms*, Cheltenham, UK: Edward Elgar.

Barney, J. (1991). Firm resources and sustained competitive advantage. *Journal of Management, 17*, 99–120.

Benner, M. J., & Tushman, M. L. (2003). Exploitation, exploration, and process management: The productivity dilemma revisited. *Academy of Management Review, 28*, 238–256.

Boso, N., Cadogan, J. W., & Story, V. M. (2013). Entrepreneurial orientation and market orientation as drivers of product innovation success: A study of exporters from a developing economy. *International Small Business Journal, 31*, 57–81.

Cao, Q., Gedajlovic, E., & Zhang, H. P. (2009). Unpacking organizational ambidexterity: Dimensions, contingencies, and synergistic effects. *Organization Science, 20*, 781–796.

Chataway, J., Kale, D., & Wield, D. (2007). The Indian pharmaceutical industry before and after trips. *Technology Analysis & Strategic Management, 19*, 559–563.

Cooper, A. C., Gimenogascon, F. J., & Woo, C. Y. (1994). Initial human and financial capital as predictors of new venture performance. *Journal of Business Venturing, 9*, 371–395.

Cope, J. (2003). Entrepreneurial learning and critical reflection – Discontinuous events as triggers for 'higher-level' learning. *Management Learning, 34*, 429–450.

Crossan, M. M., Lane, H. W., & White, R. E. (1999). An organizational learning framework: From intuition to institution. *Academy of Management Review, 24*, 522–537.

De Jong, J. P. J., & Vermeulen, P. A. M. (2006). Determinants of product innovation in small firms – A comparison across industries. *International Small Business Journal, 24*, 587–609.

Denrell, J. (2003). Vicarious learning, undersampling of failure, and the myths of management. *Organization Science, 14*, 227–243.

Dodgson, M. (1993). Organizational learning – A review of some literatures. *Organization Studies, 14*, 375–394.

Duncan, R. (1976). The ambidextrous organization: Designing dual structures for innovation. In Kilman, R. & Pondy, L. (Eds.), *The management of organizational design*. New York, NY: North Holland.

Eisenhardt, K. M. (1989). Building theories from case-study research. *Academy of Management Review, 14*, 532–550.

Freel, M. S., & Robson, P. J. A. (2004). Small firm innovation, growth and performance – Evidence from Scotland and northern England. *International Small Business Journal, 22*, 561–575.

Gibson, C. B., & Birkinshaw, J. (2004). The antecedents, consequences, and mediating role of organizational ambidexterity. *Academy of Management Journal, 47*, 209–226.

Glaser, B. G., & Strauss, A. L. (1967). *The discovery of grounded theory: Strategies for qualitative research*. London: Weidenfeld and Nicholson.

He, Z. L., & Wong, P. K. (2004). Exploration vs. exploitation: An empirical test of the ambidexterity hypothesis. *Organization Science, 15*, 481–494.

Jansen, J. J. P., Tempelaar, M. P., Van Den Bosch, F. A. J., & Volberda, H. W. (2009). Structural differentiation and ambidexterity: The mediating role of integration mechanisms. *Organization Science, 20*, 797–811.

Jing, C., & Tylecote, A. (2005). A healthy hybrid: The technological dynamism of minority-state-owned firms in China. *Technology Analysis & Strategic Management, 17*, 257–277.

Langerak, F., Hultink, E. J., & Robben, H. S. J. (2004). The impact of market orientation, product advantage, and launch proficiency on new product performance and organizational performance. *Journal of Product Innovation Management, 21*, 79–94.

Lavie, D., Kang, J., & Rosenkopf, L. (2011). Balance within and across domains: The performance implications of exploration and exploitation in alliances. *Organization Science, 22*, 1517–1538.

Lavie, D., & Rosenkopf, L. (2006). Balancing exploration and exploitation in alliance formation. *Academy of Management Journal, 49*, 797–818.

Lavie, D., Stettner, U., & Tushman, M. L. (2010). Exploration and exploitation within and across organizations. *Academy of Management Annals, 4*, 109–155.

Levinthal, D. A., & March, J. G. (1993). The myopia of learning. *Strategic Management Journal, 14*, 95–112.

Lumpkin, G. T., & Dess, G. G. (1996). Clarifying the entrepreneurial orientation construct and linking it to performance. *Academy of Management Review, 21*, 135–172.

March, J. G. (1991). Exploration and exploitation in organizational learning. *Organization Science, 2*, 71–87.

Mcgrath, R. G., Tsai, M. H., Venkataraman, S., & Macmillan, I. C. (1996). Innovation, competitive advantage and rent: A model and test. *Management Science, 42*, 389–403.

Miles, M. B., & Huberman, A. M. (1984). *Qualitative data analysis: A source book of new methods*. Beverly Hills: Sage Publications.

Millar, C., Choi, C. J., & CHU, R. T. J. (2005). The state in science, technology and innovation districts: Conceptual models for China. *Technology Analysis & Strategic Management, 17*, 367–373.

Rothaermel, F. T., & Deeds, D. L. (2004). Exploration and exploitation alliances in biotechnology: A system of new product development. *Strategic Management Journal, 25*, 201–221.

Simonetti, R., Archambault, E., Cote, G., & Kale, D. (2007). The dynamics of pharmaceutical patenting in India: Evidence from USPTO data. *Technology Analysis & Strategic Management, 19*, 625–642.

Tan, J., & Tan, D. (2005). Environment-strategy co-evolution and co-alignment: A staged model of Chinese SOEs under transition. *Strategic Management Journal, 26*, 141–157.

Tang, J. T., Tang, Z., Marino, L. D., Zhang, Y. L., & Li, Q. W. (2008). Exploring an inverted u-shape relationship between entrepreneurial orientation and performance in Chinese ventures. *Entrepreneurship Theory and Practice, 32*, 219–239.

Tellis, G. J., Prabhu, J. C., & Chandy, R. K. (2009). Radical innovation across nations: The preeminence of corporate culture. *Journal of Marketing, 73*, 3–23.

Van De Vean, A. H., & Huber, G. P. (1990). Longitudinal field research methods for studying processes of organizational change. *Organization Science, 1*, 213–219.

Wiklund, J., Patzelt, H., & Shepherd, D. A. (2009). Building an integrative model of small business growth. *Small Business Economics, 32*, 351–374.

Wiklund, J., & Shepherd, D. (2005). Entrepreneurial orientation and small business performance: A configurational approach. *Journal of Business Venturing, 20*, 71–91.

Yin, R. K. (2003). *Case study research: Design and methods.* Thousand Oaks, CA: Sage Publications.

Zhang, M., Macpherson, A., & Jones, O. (2006). Conceptualizing the learning process in SMEs – Improving innovation through external orientation. *International Small Business Journal, 24*, 299–323.

Zhao, Y., Li, Y., Lee, S. H., & Chen, L. B. (2011). Entrepreneurial orientation, organizational learning, and performance: Evidence from China. *Entrepreneurship Theory and Practice, 35*, 293–317.

CHAPTER 11

RESOURCE ACQUISITION IN HIGH-TECH START-UP GLOBAL STRATEGIES

Noriko Taji

ABSTRACT

The global strategies of high-tech start-ups fall into two types. One is characteristic of knowledge-based firms; the other is characteristic of knowledge-intensive firms. We present two propositions related to timing of globalization and resource acquisition for each type and examine four case studies from the region around Cambridge University in the United Kingdom.

Knowledge-based start-ups target global markets from the very beginning, aiming at rapid market penetration. From the start they are highly globalized in acquiring core technology and financial and human resources.

In contrast, knowledge-intensive start-ups start in local markets and initially restrict acquisition of core technology and financial and human resources to those markets. Only at a later stage, when the local business

Exploration and Exploitation in Early Stage Ventures and SMEs
Technology, Innovation, Entrepreneurship and Competitive Strategy, Volume 14, 263–287
Copyright © 2014 by Emerald Group Publishing Limited
ISSN: 1479-067X/doi:10.1108/S1479-067X20140000014008

is solidly established, do they gradually expand their businesses to global markets.

Keywords: High-tech start-up; globalization; resource; knowledge-based; knowledge-intensive

RESEARCH OBJECTIVES

March (1991) considered exploitation and exploration fundamentally incompatible. However, in Levinthal and March (1993), they admitted that a well-balanced combination of them is effective for organizations. They defined such organizations' ability as "to engage in enough exploitation to ensure the organizations' current viability and to engage in enough exploration to ensure future viability." Subsequent studies clarified that exploitation and exploration can be done simultaneously (Auh & Menguc, 2005; Katila & Ahuja, 2002).

The ability to deal with both innovations is called ambidexterity. These organizations can achieve high performance. This topic is investigated by Gibson and Birkinshaw (2004) and Tushman and O'Reilly (1996).

However, ambidexterity tends to bring complexity to the business model and plural product lines. Large companies can pursue it, but start-ups or small firms cannot handle it easily.

In particular, start-ups, because they lack management resources, cannot help focusing on a solo product in the early phase. As a result, is it even possible that most start-ups choose exploitation, which involves refinement, efficiency, selection, implementation, and execution? No, they do not always choose exploitation. Start-ups sometimes choose exploration, which involves search, variation, risk-taking, experimentation, discovery and innovation. And some start-ups can accomplish exploration and succeed in globalization.

This chapter clarifies the growing trend, in start-ups that intend to globalize, toward a process of analyzing procurement of key resources (core technology, financing, management teams, alliances, and client networks). The process will be diversified into two types: exploitation and exploration.

Please see previous studies that cover globalization and entrepreneurship.

Entrepreneurship has been defined as a mechanism by which entrepreneurs discover and exploit opportunities to recombine existing resources to enhance wealth (Kirzner, 1973; Schumpeter, 1934). Entrepreneurial success depends on an entrepreneur's finding and utilizing an opportunity well (Shane & Venkataraman, 2000). Having to overcome numerous difficulties to achieve this goal is predictable. Today, however, the hurdles are higher than ever. With globalization affecting whole industries, small as well as large firms must compete in the global marketplace over country boundaries.

Companies that are globalized from the start have been labeled "born-global" (Bell, McNaughton, & Young, 2001; Bell, McNaughton, Young, & Crick, 2003; Chetty & Campbell-Hunt, 2004; Knight & Cavusgil, 1996; Madsen & Servais, 1997). From the very beginning, these companies aim to supply the global market with high-tech products in a specified domain.

The born-global model can be traced back to McDougall and Oviatt's "international entrepreneur." These authors defined as international entrepreneurs businesses that exhibit "a combination of innovative, proactive, and risk-seeking behavior that crosses national borders and is intended to create value in organizations" (McDougall & Oviatt, 2000).

The born-global model contrasts with the traditional "stage" model. In the traditional model, a company first develops a domestic market, with incremental expansion into the global market following at a later stage (Johanson & Vahlne, 1977; Johanson & Wiedersheim-Paul, 1975). In contrast, the born-global model seeks first-mover advantage through rapid creation of global niches from the outset (Bell et al., 2003; Chetty & Campbell-Hunt, 2004).

The research reported here focuses on born-global high-tech start-ups[1] whose growth is expected to fuel the emergence of whole new industries. These firms are launched as global companies and must thus, from the very beginning, consider how best to enter the global market and how best to position product development, manufacturing, and sales from a global (not domestic) perspective. Common strategies include R&D alliances with international partners, rapid product delivery, and taking advantage of the Internet to gather information.

This is, however, only an ideal image of international entrepreneurship. Start-ups often find it difficult to acquire the financial and human resources that global activities require. Silicon Valley has been an exception, in that these resources are concentrated and more easily accessible there. But what happens in other regions and countries? How do start-ups not based in Silicon Valley acquire the resources global growth requires? This chapter partially answers these questions. It proposes a theoretical model in which resource acquisition is dependent on global strategy and tests it by examining a small set of start-ups located in the region around Cambridge in the United Kingdom. Since all of the firms share the possibility of utilizing existing resources, output from university laboratories, alumni networks, angels, and VCs, all clustered around Cambridge University, we are able to control these factors and focus on the relationship between global strategy and resource acquisition.

PROPOSITION – TYPES OF GLOBAL STRATEGY

Types of Start-up Strategies

Previous research on international entrepreneurship and born-global companies divides high-tech firms into two categories: knowledge-intensive and knowledge-based.

Autio, Sapienza, and Almeida (2000) define knowledge intensity as the extent to which a firm depends on the knowledge inherent in its activities and outputs as a source of competitive advantage. Knowledge-intensive firms can exploit international growth opportunities more flexibly by combining explicit knowledge with fixed assets than can firms dependent on fixed assets alone. Knowledge-intensive firms are, however, sometimes constrained by competitors' ability to imitate explicit knowledge. In contrast, they define knowledge-based firms as possessing tacit knowledge whose replication is difficult. Varying degrees of replication may, however, be achieved via reverse engineering, hiring away employees, or surveying customers and suppliers.

Bell et al. (2003) note that we see many knowledge-based firms in emerging fields like biotech and ICT. These firms combine core competence and competitive edge. In contrast, knowledge-intensive firms improve productivity, introduce new methods of production, and improve service delivery – all incremental improvements to the original business model. Knowledge-based and knowledge-intensive firms also differ in speed of globalization. Knowledge-based firms are likely to globalize rapidly. Knowledge-intensive firms globalize more slowly with the pace of globalization dependent on whether they are innovators or adopters of new technology.

Building on these two examples of previous research, the research reported here starts from the premise that knowledge-based firms focus on developing new technology that competitors find difficult to imitate, while knowledge-intensive firms offer greater customer convenience by simplifying procedures and customizing development and support for client and region.

The former can be regarded as exploration and the latter can be regarded as exploitation, which were defined by March (1991). However, it would be difficult to differentiate into exploration or exploitation concretely. As previous studies pointed out, balancing of exploration and exploitation is desirable (Ancona, Goodman, Lawrence, & Tushman, 2001; Colbert, 2004; Lavie & Rosenkopf, 2006; Tushman & O'Reilly, 1996). Ambidexterity is a word describing the ability to simultaneously pursue exploration and exploitation, or incremental and radical innovation. It is proper that start-ups described in this chapter are requested to be ambidextrous. Therefore, I want to focus on core technology, which was the most important type of expertise guiding success, or which was knowledge that was a distinctive characteristic of product service. If core technology is explored, I call it knowledge-based. On the other hand, if it is exploited, I call it knowledge-intensive.

It suggests propositions related to the timing of globalization and the degree of global resource acquisition. While there are many previous studies on the timing of globalization and of resource acquisition from resource-based and organizational learning perspectives, they do not compare knowledge-based firms with knowledge-intensive ones. This study is the first comparative study regarding the timing of globalization and of resource acquisition.

Knowledge-Based Start-ups

Knowledge-based high-tech start-ups display the following characteristics:

1. Established expertise in a particular field
2. Commercialization of technology seeds owned by universities and large companies
3. Efficient R&D through licensing or collaborative research with existing companies

Established expertise in a particular field equals "a pursuit of a new thing," which is defined by March (1991). These characteristics can be precisely related to exploration. Furthermore, it is reasonable for universities to play important roles in providing technology seeds. As previous studies have pointed out, alliances like licensing or collaborative research can push exploration forward (Chung, Singh, & Lee, 2000; Lavie et al., 2006).

The fields in which they operate are global niche markets. Their markets are not confined to individual countries. Clear product positioning makes it possible for these born-global firms to grow rapidly (Knight & Cavusgil, 1996, 2004; Madsen & Servais, 1997).

These are typically academic start-ups (Roberts, 1991), which use intellectual property from universities and national labs or spin-offs, which exploit technology whose development has been interrupted at the companies that own the seeds. As these start-ups require huge amounts of time and money to be able to supply concrete products or services, they must try to obtain funding through licensing or compensate for the lack of resources through collaborative research. By creating new intellectual property, they make themselves hard to imitate. We expect this kind of start-up to emerge in such cutting-edge technology fields as clean-tech, life science, and semiconductors.

Shane (2004) has suggested that there are seven characteristics of technology seeds that make them fundamental resources for academic start-ups. They are radical, tacit, early stage, versatile, high in customer value, dramatic advances in technology, and firmly protected by intellectual property rights. While technology seeds with these characteristics may spur the growth of large new markets in the future, the immature markets in which they appear allow immediate growth and offer room for new entrants.

These considerations suggest two propositions about the timing of globalization and resource acquisition:

Proposition 1. Knowledge-based start-ups initially target global markets and aim to penetrate rapidly.

Proposition 2. They are highly globalized in acquiring core technology, financial and human resources.

Regarding Proposition 1, if firms possess innovative technologies that are difficult to imitate, they can aim to rapidly penetrate the global market and become leaders there. In some cases, they immediately enter the global market to maximize business opportunities (Jones, 1999). Autio et al. (2000) provide evidence confirming that early entry into the global market accelerated the growth of the electronics industry in Finland.

Proposition 2 follows the lead of several previous studies that argue that globalizing firms need access to international finance markets, alliances with foreign partners, and the leadership of experienced entrepreneurs (Knight & Cavusgil, 1996; Madsen & Servais, 1997; McKinsey & Co., 1993). British data demonstrate that knowledge acquired through alliances with large clients enhances product development and heightens technological uniqueness (Yli-Renko, Autio, & Sapienza, 2001).

Knowledge-Intensive Start-ups

Knowledge-intensive start-ups display the following characteristics:

1. targeting niche products or market segments untapped by existing companies
2. agile and flexible response to customer needs
3. simplifying procedures; technology offer or payment
4. fast and secure commercialization through collaboration with lead users

That is to say, these characteristics are equal to exploitation, "the use and development of things already known," which is defined by March (1991).

These start-ups emphasize service tailored to customer needs or localization of product design instead of low price or high performance. Their product delivery and payment systems save their customers trouble and contribute to high convenience. For start-ups adopting these strategies, priority number one is to identify customer needs. Thus we see a pattern of commercialization that involves collaboration with lead users at the design stage. Building business models that offer high convenience, even without advanced technology, can provide these start-ups' competitive edge. Initial offerings are commonly commercialized in limited areas, with globalization following at a later stage. The limited areas in question are not always located in the domestic markets – a major difference from the traditional model in which the first target is always a domestic local market. We offer the following propositions about the timing of globalization and resource acquisition by knowledge-intensive high-tech start-ups:

Proposition 3. Knowledge-intensive start-ups initially target local markets, build their business model, and only then expand into global markets.

Proposition 4. These start-ups are not highly globalized in acquisition of core technology, financial and human resources.

Regarding Proposition 3, as these start-ups develop products to meet their lead user's needs, their initial target market is likely to depend on their users' location. As indicated in Proposition 4, one consequence is a low degree of globalization in acquisition of resources required to grow the business.

We now turn to relating Propositions 3 and 4 to Propositions 1 and 2. Jones (1999), a study that investigated high-tech start-ups in the United Kingdom, is a good place to begin. Jones compared knowledge-based and knowledge-intensive firms. Knowledge-based firms aimed to globalize from the start and began foreign market entry, international procurement and production within three years after their founding. These firms were eager to adopt foreign technology, signed technology-sharing agreements with overseas partners within one year, and engaged in outbound licensing and joint R&D with overseas partners within three years. In contrast, it was five years before knowledge-intensive firms entered foreign markets or acquired overseas resources. They did no outbound licensing or joint R&D with overseas partners.

In the next section, we turn to four case studies that allow us to examine more closely our four propositions. Here the approach differs from that of Autio et al. (2000) for whom the limitations of their quantitative survey made it impossible to separate knowledge-based from knowledge-intensive firms, and that of Bell et al. (2003) who proposed two conceptual models but left them ungrounded in empirical data.

FOUR CAMBRIDGE START-UPS

The research reported here investigated entrepreneurship in the Cambridge region of the United Kingdom, where many independent high-tech start-ups are clustered. This region was chosen for the diversity of the start-ups found there, which allows us to test our propositions across a variety of industries.

Field research in this region was conducted seven times between 2004 and 2010. It confirmed that knowledge-based start-ups with original technology sought alliance with foreign companies quite early on. These firms also recruited their management teams from individuals with long experience and large global networks in Europe or the United States. Life sciences-related start-ups were conspicuous in this group, but knowledge-based firms in other fields were not unusual. This research also identified many knowledge-intensive start-ups with businesses launched in domestic markets in the United Kingdom or Europe, which later expanded to include markets in Asia and the United States. The four cases described below were selected from that sample because they had all reached the exit stage with an IPO or buyout, and thus provided rich pools of information on strategy, management team recruitment, and resource acquisition during prior stages of business development. The four firms in our sample are in the life sciences, semiconductor, and ICT fields (Tables 1 and 2).[2]

Regarding collecting data, technology and business models were revealed on their website. In the case of CDT, Abcam, and Bango, as they were listed companies, financial data and business performance were easily acquired. Though Astex was not a listed company, it disclosed capital procurement, number of employees, partners, management team, and scientific boards on the website. Besides, there are many articles about technology in academic journals and in industrial magazines. As a primary source, I was able to contact three companies. I had interviews with a CEO, two senior executives, and a president of the Japanese subsidiary of Abcam in 2010, with a CEO of Bango in 2010, and with an executive of the parent company of CDT in 2011.

All four firms were clearly either knowledge-based or knowledge-intensive firms. They were founded by alumni of Cambridge University or grown from technological seeds owned by the university. All had access to the same entrepreneurial infrastructure concentrated in the region around the university.

Cambridge Display Technology (Semiconductors)

Cambridge Display Technology (CDT) develops materials and produces devices using polymer organic light-emitting diodes (P-OLEDs). This core technology has raised high expectations since the 1990s as a possible replacement for liquid-crystal display. The year 2011 saw electronics manufacturers begin test production of large screen displays using this technology. CDT was founded in 1989 using the research results of Cambridge University professor Richard Friend and researcher Jeremy Burroughes. In 2004 it was listed on NASDAQ, and in 2007 was bought out by Sumitomo Chemical. In 2006, the last year for which sales figures were disclosed, total sales had reached US$8 million, and the company's employees numbered 120.

(1) Core Technology
    P-OLEDs have a good contrast ratio and are visible from wide angles. P-OLEDs can be fabricated as thin as an LCD without backlight, that is to say, P-OLEDs have lower overall power consumption.
(2) Capital Procurement
    CDT was launched with university funding, then looked for ways to develop the business and fund production through connections with

Table 1. Overview of Two Cases (Knowledge-Based Firms).

	Semiconductor	Life Science
Name	CDT	Astex
Spin-off type	Academic start-up	Academic start-up
Technology seeds	Founders were professors and researchers at Cambridge University	Founders were professors and researchers at Cambridge University
Product & service	Developing material and devices of PLEDs	Offering a drug discovery tool & developing a new drug
Founded	1989	1999
Raised capital before exit	$360M (estimated)	£70M (estimated)
Initial investor	Cambridge University, Local VC	Abingworth Management (UK), Oxford Biosciences Partners (US), Cambridge University
Main investors	Lord Young of Grafham (UK)Intel (US)	Other ten private VCs in US & UK
Exist	Listed in NASDAQ in 2004, Sold to Sumitomo Chemical in 2007	Sold to an American company in 2011
Alliance partners	Sumitomo Chemical (Japan), Philips, Seiko Epson (Japan)	AstraZeneca, Pfizer, GlaxoSmithKline, Janssen Research Foundation, Fujisawa Pharma, Mitsubishi Pharma (Japan)
Alliance content	Licensing, R&D Collaboration	Analytical tools, R&D collaboration, commissioned research
Connection	Alliance partner	Alliance partner
Founders	Cambridge University professor and postdoctoral fellow	Two Cambridge University professors,Former big pharma CEO. VC
Academic degree and position	Science adviser (Ph.D.), CTO (Ph.D.)	CEO (Ph.D.), Science adviser (Ph.D.)
Management team	Former CEO of an American chemical company, former Phillips and Dow Corning employees, former CFO of start-ups that had gone public	Ph.D., big pharma professionals, former CFO of start-ups that had gone public
Recruitment channels	Related industry and VC	Academy, VC, founder network

Table 2. Overview of Two Cases (Knowledge-Intensive Firms).

	Life Science	ICT
Name	Abcam	Bango
Spin-off type	Academic start-up	Third start-up
Technology seeds	Cambridge University postdoctoral fellow (founder & CEO)	Developed after founding
Product & service	Antibody development and procurement	Mobile charge and payment system
Founded	1998	1999
Raised capital before exit	£250K	Unknown
Initial investor	Famous angel (founder), local angels	Local VC, local investment bank
Main investor	Angels	ET Capital, Herald Ventures (UK)
Exist	Listed in AIM in 2005 (£15.5M raised)	Listed in AIM in 2005 (£6.2M raised)
Alliance partner	Universities	–
Alliance content	Procurement by academic labs	–
Connections	University labs, National labs, Biotech company	Broadcasting and mobile communication companies (Discovery Channel, Yahoo, MTV, NTT Docomo, etc.)
Founders	Cambridge University professor & postdoctoral fellow, famous angel	Cambridge University alumni
Academic degree and position	CEO (Ph.D.), Chairman (Ph.D.), Non-executive director (Ph.D.)	CEO (B.S.)
Management team	VP (Ph.D. of Cambridge or alumni)	CFO & Chairman (start-up experts), VP invited from US, Part-time director selected by VC
Recruitment channels	Founder networks	Former co-workers, related industry networks

local angels. Since it came to require large sums for those purposes, however, the company's strategy changed to supplying technology to other
firms. In 1996, a CEO was recruited from Siemens and in 1997, on the
strength of success in supplying technology to Philips, it was able to raise
US$9.7 million from one of the United Kingdom's largest venture capital
firms, Lord Young of Grafham, and to secure additional funding from
Intel's investment arm. That was followed by a joint venture with Seiko
Epson to develop inkjet technology for printing polymer-OLEDs on
fabrics. Then, in 1999, an additional capital infusion of $133 million was
received from US investment funds Kelso Investment and Hillman
Capital Management. These funds were used to build the firm's R&D
center and to buy out other start-ups. In 2004, CDT was listed on
NASDAQ, and in 2005 an energy-saving technology project was begun
with Sumitomo Chemical. That project led to Sumitomo Chemical's
acquisition of CDT in 2007 (for an estimated $360 million).

(3) Alliances

Besides the firms mentioned above, CDT's business partners also
include Matsushita Electric, Dai Nippon Printing, and Delta
Optoelectronics, to all of which CDT supplies technology. CDT technology is used in products ranging from mobile phones and miniature
cameras to MP3 players.

(4) Management Team and HR

The inventor-professor has become an advisor on technology. The
other inventor, after working for Toshiba for six years, became Chief
Technology Officer (CTO) in 1997. In 1999, anticipating the need for
large-scale investment, David Fyfe took over as CEO. A Cambridge
University Ph.D. in electronics, he had previously been CEO of a large
American chemical company. Two vice-presidents are specialists in
OLED technology with experience at large electronics or chemical
firms. The CFO had experience supporting other listings on the
London and NASDAQ stock exchanges. The management team is,
thus, composed of top professionals in their fields from both inside and
outside the United Kingdom.

Astex Therapeutics (Life Science)

Astex Therapeutics has combined X-ray crystallography and magnetic
resonance imaging to develop a drug development support technology for
drug design using fragment-based analysis of molecular structures, a

technology that makes possible more efficient isolation of promising new pharmaceuticals. It both supplies this technology to other pharmaceutical firms and develops its own new drugs, constantly aiming to maintain a full pipeline. Founded in 1999, Astex had, in its first decade, produced numerous new drug candidates that reached stage 1 clinical testing.

Astex is an academic start-up whose founders include Sir Tom Blundell, head of the biochemistry department at Cambridge University, Chris Abell, a professor in the same department, Harren Jhoti, who was both a former chair of Glaxo Wellcome and chair of the UK Structural Biology Association, and Robert Solari from Abingworth, the first VC to invest in the firm. Sales figures are unavailable, but as of 2010, the firm had 75 employees. In 2011, Astex was bought out by US-based Supergen and renamed Astex Pharmaceuticals.

(1) Core Technology

The very high sensitivity of a drug design tool affords a detailed understanding of the fragment's binding environment at an atomic level. These structural insights support a very efficient chemistry optimization process. As a result, drug candidates are designed to have lower molecular weight, reduced metabolic liability, improved target selectivity, and ease of chemical synthesis.

(2) Capital Procurement

One of Astex's founding partners was Abingworth Management, a private-sector VC with an office in Cambridge. (Its headquarters are in London.) Seed money was procured from Abingworth Management and Boston-based Oxford Biosciences Partners. Two years later, Astex raised 28 million British pounds from five entities in a private placement. Estimates suggest that Astex had procured a total of 70 million British pounds as of 2007.

Astex's aggressive approach to capital procurement reflected not only a desire to develop and sell systems that would shorten the lead time for new drug development, but also its intention to discover and develop drugs itself, a goal for which large amounts of capital were needed. It was also necessary to raise funds to buy out a German bioventure, in order to expand its pipeline. Apart from Cambridge University, where two of the founders were employed, all funds were raised from VCs specializing in life science and investing globally.

(3) Alliances

The year after Astex was founded, it reached an agreement with Janssen Biotech, followed the year after that by an agreement with

AstraZeneca. In addition to technology-licensing agreements with some 20 pharmaceuticals companies and research foundations, Astex also participates in joint and commissioned research projects. Partners in these projects include most of the world's largest pharmaceuticals companies, including many based in Japan.

(4) Management Team and HR

Examining Astex's efforts to strengthen its management team during the decade after its founding, we identify three distinct periods: from founding to 2003, when the company was focused on developing and testing its basic technology, a middle period when it actively developed alliances on the basis of that technology, and a third period during which it was focused on preparation for an IPO. During the first, technology-oriented period, it recruited experts in computational chemistry, proteins, high-throughput screening, and NMR to join its executive team. The focus during this period was on talent that could help create new drug development technologies and accelerate their use in drug discovery. During the middle period, the focus shifted to lawyers and individuals experienced with clinical trials, to support internal drug development efforts. Then, in 2006, it added a CFO with IPO experience in anticipation of the IPO. The successful timing of these efforts can be attributed to the founders' stature as leaders in their fields in the United Kingdom, their networks of connections through academic associations and with pharmaceutical industry firms, and the global reach of their VCs, which facilitated recruitment, in particular in the United States.

Abcam (Life Science)

Abcam was founded in 1998 by three men who shared a common vision: to use the Web to market antibodies worldwide. The first was Jonathan Milner, a postdoctoral fellow at Cambridge University, the second his academic mentor, and the third an angel investor, David Cleevely, famous for his contributions to growing a telecommunications business. Abcam was founded in the same year as Google. As the Internet became more pervasive, Abcam grew by expanding its web-based catalog. As of 2010, annual sales had reached 72 million British pounds, operating profit was 35%, and the company's employees numbered 250 worldwide.

(1) Core Technology

The basic online catalog is supplemented by up-to-date detailed technical information. This is derived from the company's own testing and research, as well as customers' enquiries and feedback from using the products. Over time, each product builds up a substantial set of relevant background information that helps inform the purchasing decisions of researchers searching for reagents.

(2) Capital Procurement

Seed money and Series A funding were provided by angels, including one of the founders, who was already well known in Cambridge for investing in start-up businesses. The initial seed money was only 250,000 British pounds. A business that required only the procurement of antibodies and the announcement on the Web that they were available for sale did not require a heavy investment. Like Google, which was founded in the same year, Abcam grew along with the Internet. It was unable to procure additional capital from VCs, but, instead, accumulated profits from successful sales in North America. Its 2005 IPO raised 15.5 million British pounds, which were used to develop new businesses in Japan and Hong Kong.

(3) Alliances

Basic research on antibodies is conducted in university and government laboratories. Applied research is typically joint research involving universities and biotech companies, and the resulting antibodies are used in pharmaceutical company laboratories. Abcam sales are 48% to universities, 24% to biotech companies and government laboratories, and 23% to pharmaceutical companies. Its suppliers include many university and government laboratories; in all, Abcam does business with 250 companies. Only 4% of the antibodies it sells are produced near Abcam's headquarters. Its initial customers were in the United Kingdom, but it has gradually expanded to reach a global customer base.

Five years after the company's founding, it set up an office in Cambridge, Massachusetts, in the United States, followed by offices in Japan and Hong Kong. Its online catalog lists more than 60,000 items. Because the amounts supplied are small, only a few cubic centimeters (cc), global purchasing, storage, and shipping costs are low. Speedy delivery and technical support that ensures that the antibodies supplied are optimized for the customer's research are the strengths of the Abcam business model. Sales are now 44% to North America, 30% to Europe, 9% to Japan, 8% to the United Kingdom, and 5% to China.

(4) Management Team and HR

Besides the founders, the managers in charge of business development, logistics, and Web system design all have doctorates in biochemistry or pathology from Cambridge. They do not feel uncomfortable in being responsible for areas outside their R&D specialties. They joined the firm in their twenties, were in their thirties at the time of the IPO, and have reached the rank of general manager or vice president. Most other employees, especially those involved in R&D, are graduates of Cambridge University.

Bango (ICT)

Bango provides billing, payment, and analytics solutions for the mobile Internet. Founder Ray Anderson is a serial entrepreneur. After graduating with a degree in computer science from Cambridge University, he founded and managed several start-ups, which he then sold to other companies. He founded Bango in 1999. Co-founder Anil Malhotra had been in charge of tie-ups and licensing for Anderson's second start-up. As of 2010, Bango's annual sales were approximately 26 million British pounds, with operating profit at 10% and 50 employees.

(1) Core Technology

Payment platforms can provide consumers with an easy payment process via WiFi, Blackberry, and iPhone, etc. Analytics platforms record the most accurate information about mobile visitors to customers' websites and analyze mobile traffic in real time.

(2) Capital Procurement

The bulk of the seed money for Bango's founding was capital gains from the sale of the two founders' previous start-ups. Following the company's IPO, the three managing directors continue to own more than 30% of its shares. Subsequent efforts to raise funds did not go as well as expected, and the founders have ended up continuing to own a high proportion of the shares. Partners in two local VCs, ET Capital, and Electric and General Investment Trust, serve as non-executive directors of Bango and have also invested personally in the firm. Herald Ventures and Chase Nominees Ltd., two local VCs, are the only corporations that hold more than 5% of the firm's shares. The 6.2 million British pounds raised by the 2005 IPO were used to set up the firm's data center.

(3) Alliances

Bango has two types of customers: content providers and mobile telecoms. To solidify its position in the European market, the firm opened offices in Germany and Spain. Then, entering the larger US market, it developed services for US-based broadcasters (Discovery Channel, Yahoo, MTV). The firm now has a bipolar structure, with European operations concentrated in London and US operations concentrated on the East Coast.

(4) Management Team and HR

Founders Ray Anderson and Anil Malhotra have continued to be in charge after the IPO. Five years after the founding, they added an experienced CFO whose background included serving as managing director in charge of finance for a large corporation in the same industry. The company's ability to attract two highly experienced vice-presidents from Silicon Valley to manage sales and administration was rooted in the fact that the CEO had lived in the United States following the sale of a previous start-up to an American corporation. The network he built during that time made it possible to construct an international management team and develop business in the United States. All of the firm's management team had global experience and substantial achievements in telecommunications, electronic trading, or software, and were able to contribute to the expansion of Bango's business.

RESULT – EXAMINING THE PROPOSITIONS

Of the four firms described in Part 3, Astex and CDT are among the knowledge-based firms; Abcam and Bango are, instead, among the knowledge-intensive firms. Since Astex and Abcam are both life-science-related businesses, they provide a good contrast. Let us review briefly the evidence for these classifications. We can confirm that core technology is established by exploration or exploitation, as follows.

Astex's drug-screening tools support drug design using fragment-based drug discovery. By making it possible to analyze interactions between fragments of larger molecules, its technology makes it possible to analyze the structures of proteins more accurately, in a clear departure from existing tools. The seeds of CDT's technology have been featured in the prestigious scientific journal *Nature*, and it has been a major player in OLED development. Both companies' technologies are based on cutting-edge science and are extremely distinctive, corresponding to "a pursuit of new knowledge" (Levinthal & March, 1993). That is to say, it is exploration. In contrast, Abcam is involved in developing and marketing antibodies, a business with a much lower threshold. It has secured its present position by being the first mover in putting its catalog on the Web. Bango's mobile Internet billing and payment services compete in a market where the spread of mobile devices has led to ferocious competition. Its edge is maintained by carefully tailored customization. These two companies have succeeded by offering superior customer convenience, corresponding to "the use and development of things already known." In other words, it is exploitation.

Starting from this classification, let us turn now to Propositions 1–4.

Proposition 1. Knowledge-based start-ups initially target global markets and aim to penetrate rapidly.

Both Astex and CDT build on core technologies based on discoveries by Cambridge University faculty members. Aiming to commercialize these discoveries, they are classic examples of academic start-ups. From the beginning, both looked for joint research partners and customers worldwide.

If we look at the nationalities of the firms with which Astex has tie-ups, we find that its first joint-research tie-up was with Janssen Biotech, a firm based in Belgium. Next came UK-based AstraZeneca, followed by Mitsubishi Well Pharma (Mitsubishi Tanabe Pharma since 2007) in Japan. CDT first licensed its technology to Philips and Uniax, companies based in the Netherlands and the United States. Both Astex and CDT have aimed to establish their own technologies as the global default standards as quickly as possible. That both used the exit strategy of a buyout by major corporations outside their home country was a demonstration of the value put on their highly sophisticated advances, which have, in fact, been accepted as global standards.

Proposition 2. They are highly globalized in acquiring core technology, financial and human resources.

While still at the growth stage, both firms formed numerous alliances. While participating in joint research and undertaking commissioned research, they supplied development tools and know-how. In the process, they were able to integrate a variety of component technologies and strengthen their core technologies. Astex is on public record as a participant in 26 joint research projects and technology-licensing agreements. Its partners include pharmaceuticals companies and laboratories scattered across Europe, the United States and Japan. CDT is on public record as having entered into tie-ups with nearly 10 electronics and printing equipment manufacturers, most of which are Japanese companies. It also bought out a local start-up that specialized in development of component technology for OLEDs.

Turning to capital procurement, we see that, from the seed money stage through subsequent rounds of financing, Astex procured funds from multiple VCs, including some American sources. CDT's seed money came only from local VCs, but following its success with licensing, it succeeded in procuring additional capital from Intel and a US-based investment fund. We can confirm that exploration can be accelerated by alliances, which provide learning and knowledge from outside, as previous studies have suggested.

On the HR front, both firms have sought out the best possible members for their management teams, from the United Kingdom, Europe, or even the United States. Their ability to fill CEO and CFO slots with individuals who brought with them deep industry experience depended on introductions from globally active VCs and the management team's own personal networks. Their ability to recruit talented engineers may also reflect the global networks of Cambridge University and the academic societies to which their founders belong.

Thus, we can confirm that, at least in these two cases, these unique technology start-ups adopted from the very beginning a highly globalized approach to procuring the resources they needed, including core technologies, capital, and talent.

The critical point is that two of the start-ups owned technology seeds with high potential, which attracted global VC, large companies, and highly experienced talent for management. This put them in a different class from start-ups that did not own their own seeds. The difference between the knowledge-based and knowledge-intensive development start-ups was clear.

Proposition 3. Knowledge-intensive start-ups initially target local markets, build their business model, and only then expand into global markets.

During the start-up phase, Abcam's suppliers and customers were confined to the United Kingdom, primarily the region around Cambridge. As the business grew, it expanded its market to Europe, the United States, and Asia. Global expansion was possible because customers could place orders on the Web and because the small size of shipments minimized shipping costs. It has also opened branches in the United States, Japan, and Hong Kong to improve the efficiency of both product procurement and distribution.

Since Bango's business is IT services provided via the Internet, global expansion incurred no additional shipping or delivery costs. The CEO's business experience had been in the United States, but the firm's first target was Europe. Only later did it enter the larger US market. At that point, recruiting American vice-presidents spurred success in the global market.

Here we glimpse the necessity for globalization, even in customer convenience-oriented businesses.

Thus we can confirm that in both these cases, the initial target market was local. Global expansion came later.

Proposition 4. These start-ups are not highly globalized in acquisition of core technology, financial and human resources.

With respect to core technologies, Abcam began by selling antibodies developed by the founder, a Cambridge University postdoc, and the researchers with whom he worked, then it gradually expanded the range of products it handled. It was a start-up dependent on strong local ties. Antibodies provided by Abcam were not an extraordinary type. However, they could be convenient in the online catalogue. The core technology was developed on the basis of already existing knowledge. Bango's core technology consisted of the skills built up by its founders through the experience of founding two earlier locally-based start-ups. To sum up, core technologies were brought in by exploitation.

On the capital procurement front, both firms secured capital only from domestic sources. Bango was started with funds from the buyout of the two founders' previous start-up, supplemented by an investment by a local VC. As one of the founders explained, they tried to procure capital globally but found it difficult (even from the United States, where they had hoped to attract investors). Abcam was started with capital procured from its founder chairman, who was also an angel investor. The firm received no funding from VCs. Since buying and selling antibodies required only a small amount of additional research expense to achieve solid earnings, the company did not need to seek large amounts of external funding.

On the HR front, these two firms differ somewhat. The members of Abcam's management team almost all hold either doctorates or master's degrees in biochemistry or pathology from Cambridge University. They have been recruited via alumni associations or local networks. In this case, recruitment is very local. In contrast, Bango's CEO was able to use his personal connections built while living in the United States to recruit two Americans as vice-presidents for sales and administration. That would have been very difficult to do without the CEO's overseas experience and personal networks, because it had not received investments from overseas VCs, who would have been able to tap their global networks for introductions to capable individuals.

Thus, in both these cases, the degree of globalization in procurement of core technologies and capital was low, if not completely local. On the HR front, globalization of recruitment would also have been low, had there not been special circumstances in one of the two cases.

Several previous studies also point out that globalization is accelerated by top management teams whose members have broad international experience (Madsen & Servais, 1997; Reuber & Fischer, 1997). However, we suspect knowledge-intensive firms may be able to recruit highly-experienced global talent. This situation is totally different from that in knowledge-based firms. The CEO of Bango was a serial entrepreneur who had accumulated business experience in the United States while running a previous start-up. In the knowledge-intensive case, entrepreneurs can acquire global management skills through serial entrepreneurship. Choosing a knowledge-intensive strategy and seeking early exit, then starting a new business, is a realistic strategy for these entrepreneurs.

LIMITATIONS AND FURTHER RESEARCH

This chapter proposes a tentative classification of high-tech start-up globalization strategies and considers several propositions relating to the timing of globalization and global resource procurement. Confining the case studies to firms based near Cambridge in the United Kingdom, it controls for differences due to geographical, social, economic, or political conditions. It remains only the first step in a larger project. The next step will be to examine more start-ups from the Cambridge region that fit the proposed classification, to see how the propositions hold up.

In this concluding section, we consider ten cases for which public information is available (Table 3). The start-ups in these cases are in the IT, materials, electronics, and semiconductor industries. All have received support from Cambridge Enterprise, a wholly-owned subsidiary of Cambridge University that promotes technology transfer and new business start-ups using intellectual property developed at and owned by Cambridge University. From the firms in the larger initial sample, we chose only those whose websites provide the information required for our analysis. We did not include life science companies because their long R&D process precludes adequate assessment of growth based on public data alone.

Of the ten firms examined here, three out of the four knowledge-based firms procure resources from Europe and the United States and are, thus, judged to be highly globalized in resource acquisition. Of the six knowledge-intensive firms, four are less globalized in resource acquisition

Table 3. Academic Start-ups from Cambridge University.

Founded	Name	Field	Category	Core Technology Capital, Management Team	Resource Acquisition
1994	Granta	IT	Knowledge-intensive	Academic seeds, No VC investment, CEO from UK	Weakly globalized
1995	Cambridge Mechatronics	Electronics	Knowledge-based	Academic seeds, Licensing to overseas, CEO from the US	Strongly globalized
2000	Polatis	Electronics	Knowledge-based	R&D collaboration with foreign university, American VC, CEO with experience in the US	Strongly globalized
2001	Teraview	Semiconductor	Knowledge-based	Academic seeds, Domestic VC, Founder is CEO	Weakly globalized
2003	Zinwave	IT	Knowledge-intensive	Academic seeds, European VC, CEO from Canada & CTO from Europe	Gradually globalized
2004	Q-Flo	Materials	Knowledge-intensive	Academic seeds, Overseas R&D collaboration, domestic licensing, CEO from UK	Weakly globalized
2004	Light Blue Optics	Electronics	Knowledge-intensive	Academic seeds, European VC, CEO from East Asia	Gradually globalized
2004	Ion Scope	Electronics	Knowledge-intensive	Academic seeds, Domestic VC, CEO from UK	Weakly globalized
2008	Cambridge CMOS Sensor	Semiconductor	Knowledge-intensive	Academic seeds, Subsidy, Founder is CEO	Weakly globalized
2010	Sphere Fluidics	Materials	Knowledge-based	Academic seeds, Subsidy, CEO with experience in the US	Moderately globalized

and two are gradually globalizing, but do not acquire resources from the United States. These results appear to support our propositions. We now need to contact individuals involved in these start-ups and explore their growth in greater detail.

Simply increasing the size of our sample in the region around Cambridge will not, however, be sufficient to ensure the validity of the propositions. More countries and regions need to be included, and future research will include cases from Europe, the United States, and Japan.

There are also new directions we intend to pursue: the influence on the speed of growth of the timing of globalization and the path-dependence of resource acquisition. Following the lead of Mathews and Zander (2007), we also intend to explore how strongly the entry point in global economy affects survival and performance. We are particularly interested in the extent to which delay in entering the global market makes it difficult for knowledge-intensive firms to survive or forces them to change their strategies. Even if a firm begins to globalize simultaneously with its competitors, its speed of growth may be influenced by the path-dependence of resource acquisition via an entrepreneur's personal network or that of a VC or partner. These issues also need to be addressed in future research.

This chapter focuses on primary products, especially at the starting and early stages of the growing process. It does not focus on diversifying products when the exit is approaching or has passed. At such a later stage, firms would be able to perform ambidexterity, achieving a balance between exploration and exploitation. Then, they would change their alliance partners. Lavie and Rosenkopf (2006) pointed out that function domain (R&D alliances or marketing alliances) and structure domain (prior alliance partners or new alliance partners) depend on exploration or exploitation. Change in alliances equals change in the path of resource acquisition, which this chapter argues. Thus, in future research focusing on a later stage, the relationship between the exploration-exploitation balance and resource acquisition would have to be discussed. This point was emphasized in several previous studies (Lavie, Stettner, & Tushman, 2010; Raisch & Birkinshaw, 2008).

NOTES

1. Definitions of high-tech start-ups are taken from David J. Ben Daniel, the Don and Margi Berens Professor of Entrepreneurship at Cornell University, and the US Department of Commerce. According to the Department of Commerce, high-tech

firms are those that spend twice as much as other firms on R&D (Shanklin, W. L., & Ryans, J. K. Jr, 1984). John Nesheim quotes Ben Daniel's description of Apple during its start up phase, where he describes Apple as a small firm that had latent within it the power to create an economic foundation for future growth, generate employment, propagate technological change, and create a distinctive corporate culture that would influence management everywhere (Nesheim, 1997).

2. For more information on the four case studies, see Taji and Tsuyuki (2010) and Tsuyuki (2009). Information used here was taken from the four firms' websites. The founders and alliance partners were interviewed between 2010 and 2011.

REFERENCES

Ancona, D. G., Goodman, P. S., Lawrence, B. S., & Tushman, M. L. (2001). Time: A new research lens. *Academy of Management Review*, *26*, 645–663.

Auh, S., & Menguc, B. (2005). Balancing exploration and exploitation: The moderating role of competitive intensity. *Journal of Business Research*, *58*, 1652–1661.

Autio, E. H., Sapienza, J., & Almeida, J. G. (2000). Effects of age at entry, knowledge intensity, and imitability on international growth. *Academy of Management Journal*, *43*(5), 902–906.

Bell, J., McNaughton, R., & Young, S. (2001). "Born-again global" firms: An extension to the "born global" phenomenon. *Journal of International Management*, *7*(3), 173–189.

Bell, J., McNaughton, R., Young, S., & Crick, D. (2003). Towards an integrative model of small firm internationalization. *Journal of International Entrepreneurship*, *1*(4), 339–362.

Chetty, S., & Campbell-Hunt, C. (2004). A strategic approach to internationalization: A traditional versus a "born-global" approach. *Journal of International Marketing*, *12*(1), 57–81.

Chung, S., Singh, H., & Lee, K. (2000). Complementarity, status similarity and social capital as drivers of alliance formation. *Strategic Management Journal*, *21*, 1–22.

Colbert, B. A. (2004). The complex resource-based view: Implications for theory and practice of strategic human resource management. *Academy of Management Review*, *29*(3), 341–358.

Gibson, C. B., & Birkinshaw, J. (2004). The antecedents, consequences and mediating role of organizational ambidexterity. *Academy of Management Journal*, *47*, 209–226.

Johanson, J., & Vahlne, J.-E. (1977). The internationalization process of the firm. *Journal of International Business Studies*, *8*(Spring–Summer), 23–32.

Johanson, J., & Wiedersheim-Paul, F. (1975). The internationalization of the firm-four Swedish cases. *Journal of Management Studies*, *12*(3), 305–322.

Jones, M. V. (1999). The internationalization of small UK high technology based firms. *Journal of International Marketing*, *7*(4), 15–41.

Katila, R., & Ahuja, G. (2002). Something old, something new: A longitudinal study of search behavior and new product introduction. *Academy of Management Journal*, *45*, 1183–1194.

Kirzner, I. (1973). *Competition and entrepreneurship*. Chicago, IL: University of Chicago Press.

Knight, G. A., & Cavusgil, S. T. (1996). The born global firm: A challenge to traditional internationalization theory. *Advances in International Marketing*, *8*, 11–26.

Knight, G. A., & Cavusgil, S. T. (2004). Innovation, organizational capabilities, and the born-global firm. *Journal of International Business Studies, 35*(2), 124−141.

Lavie, D., & Rosenkopf, L. (2006). Balancing exploration and exploitation in alliance formation. *Academy of Management Journal, 49*(4), 797−818.

Lavie, D., Stettner, U., & Tushman, M. L. (2010). Exploration and exploitation within and across organizations. *The Academy of Management Annals, 4*(1), 109−155.

Levinthal, D., & March, J. (1993). Myopia of learning. *Strategic Management Journal, 14*, 95−112.

Madsen, T. K., & Servais, P. (1997). The internationalization of born global: An evolutionary process? *International Business Review, 6*(6), 561−583.

March, J. G. (1991). Exploration and exploitation in organizational learning. *Organization Science, 2*, 71−87.

Mathews, J. A., & Zander, I. (2007). The international entrepreneurial dynamics of accelerated internationalization. *Journal of International Business Studies, 38*, 387−403.

McDougall, P. P., & Oviatt, B. M. (2000). International entrepreneurship: The intersection of two research paths. *Academy of Management Journal, 43*(5), 902−906.

McKinsey and Co. (1993). *Emerging exporters: Australia's high value-added manufacturing exporters.* Melbourne, Australia: McKinsey and Co., Australian Manufacturing Council.

Nesheim, J. L. (1997). *High tech startup: The complete handbook for creating successful new high tech companies.* New York, NY: The Free Press.

Raisch, S., & Birkinshaw, J. (2008). Organizational ambidexterity: Antecedents, outcomes and moderators. *Journal of Management, 34*(3), 375−409.

Reuber, A. R., & Fischer, E. (1997). The influence of the management team's international experience on the internationalization behaviors of SMEs. *Journal of International Business Studies, 28*(4), 807−825.

Roberts, E. B. (1991). The technology base of the new enterprise. *Research policy, 20*, 283−298.

Schumpeter, J. (1934). *Capitalism, socialism and democracy.* New York, NY: Harper & Row.

Shane, S. (2004). *Academic entrepreneurship: University spinoffs and wealth creation.* Northampton, MA: Edward Elger publishing.

Shane, S., & Venkataraman, S. (2000). The promise of entrepreneurship as a field of research. *Academy of Management Review, 25*(1), 217−226.

Shanklin, W.L., & Ryans, J.K., Jr. (1984). *Marketing hightechnology.* Lexington, MA: D.C. Heath.

Tushman, M. L., & O'Reilly, C. A. (1996). Ambidextrous organizations: Managing evolutionary and revolutionary change. *California Management Review, 38*, 8−30.

Yli-Renko, H., Autio, E., & Sapienza, H. (2001). Social capital, knowledge acquisition, and knowledge exploitation in young technology-based firms. *Strategic Management Journal, 22*(6−7), 587−613.

THE FOLLOWING ARE PRINTED IN JAPANESE

Taji, N., & Tsuyuki, E. (2010). *The strategy of high-tech startups − The sources of open innovation.* Toyokeiza publishing.

Tsuyuki, E. (2009). Academic startups in Cambridge, UK. *The Journal of Science Policy and Research Management, 23*(2), 91−100.

CHAPTER 12

EXPLORATION, EXPLOITATION, AMBIDEXTERITY, AND FIRM PERFORMANCE: A META-ANALYSIS

Blake D. Mathias

ABSTRACT

Since March (1991) presented his ideas on organizational learning, hundreds of empirical tests have been conducted on relationships among the activities of exploration, exploitation, ambidexterity, and firm performance. Despite continued interest in his ideas, there has not been a systematic assessment of extant research to reveal whether, and to what extent, these activities relate to firm performance. This study uses meta-analysis to take a next step by aggregating results of 117 studies from more than 21,000 firms. I find strong performance effects for exploration and exploitation, but contrary to received theory, I discover ambidexterity yields weaker effects than a focus on either exploration or exploitation. Thus, I leverage these findings to offer future research opportunities.

Keywords: Ambidexterity; exploitation; exploration; firm performance; meta-analysis

Exploration and Exploitation in Early Stage Ventures and SMEs
Technology, Innovation, Entrepreneurship and Competitive Strategy, Volume 14, 289–317
Copyright © 2014 by Emerald Group Publishing Limited
All rights of reproduction in any form reserved
ISSN: 1479-067X/doi:10.1108/S1479-067X20140000014009

INTRODUCTION

A central goal of strategic management inquiry is to understand why some firms outperform others (Meyer, 1991). Roughly twenty years ago, March (1991) theorized that two main organizational learning activities – exploration and exploitation – influence how organizations navigate their competitive environments, and correspondingly, perform. According to March (1991), exploration refers to experimentation with new alternatives; it helps organizations develop new knowledge via activities such as search, variation, risk-taking, and innovation. Exploitation refers to the refinement and extension of existing competencies; it helps organizations leverage extant knowledge through activities such as selection, implementation, production, and execution. March's ideas involving explorative and exploitative learning appear to be very influential. According to *Google Scholar*, March's (1991) seminal article has attracted over 9,000 citations, with over 4,000 coming in the past five years. These citations attest not only to the influence March's ideas have had to date, but also to their continued popularity.

Despite the influence and continued popularity of organization learning, empirical evidence examining relationships among organizational learning activities and performance has been mixed. While studies report results that exploration is positively related to performance (e.g., Ahuja & Lampert, 2001), other studies show that exploration is unrelated to performance (e.g., Hill & Birkinshaw, 2008), or negatively related to performance (e.g., Lechner & Floyd, 2012). Likewise, studies report results that exploitation is positively related to performance (e.g., Cho & Pucik, 2005), but others show that exploitation is unrelated to performance (e.g., Hess & Rothaermel, 2011), or negatively related to performance (e.g., Hmieleski & Baron, 2008).

One potential reason for these inconsistent findings is that focusing mainly on one learning activity without focusing on the other might not enhance performance. In particular, researchers suggest that organizations need to pursue ambidexterity, which is defined as a balanced pursuit of both exploration and exploitation activities (Gupta, Smith, & Shalley, 2006). Many scholars posit that ambidexterity yields even stronger performance than engaging in either exploration or exploitation alone (e.g., Cao, Gedajlovic, & Zhang, 2009). However, like the results involving exploration and exploitation activities, the results surrounding ambidexterity are also mixed, with studies indicating that it is both positively (Cao et al., 2009) and negatively related (Menguc & Auh, 2008) to performance.

Despite excellent reviews of organizational learning activities and performance, important questions remain. In their review of exploration and exploitation, Lavie, Stettner, and Tushman (2010, p. 137) conclude that, "The evidence in support of the performance implications of exploration and exploitation is relatively limited." Similarly, in Raisch and Birkinshaw's (2008, p. 393) review of the ambidexterity literature, they conclude that, "In sum, the empirical evidence of the organizational ambidexterity—performance relationship remains limited and mixed." Overall, this suggests that despite the influence and prominence of organizational learning ideas, the evidence is limited regarding whether organization learning activities matter, or to what extent they matter.

Although these reviews provide thorough summaries of extant inquiry, their conclusions (1) are based on whether there is statistical significance for theorized relationships instead of the size of the relationships and (2) do not statistically account for potential moderators that might be potentially important (Lavie et al., 2010). Fortunately, meta-analysis allows for the statistical aggregation of empirical findings to establish whether relationships exist and the extent to which they exist (Hunter & Schmidt, 2004). Meta-analysis provides at least three important benefits that might aid in understanding the performance implications of organizational learning activities. First, it provides an effect size estimate, or strength, of relationships of interest. Second, it allows researchers to account for statistical artifacts, such as sampling and measurement error, which might influence any single study's results (Hunter & Schmidt, 2004). Third, meta-analysis can help detect contextual factors (i.e., moderators) that explain variability across findings.

Given (1) the influence and popularity of organizational learning ideas and (2) that it is unknown whether and to what extent organizational learning activities relate to performance, a systematic assessment of the organizational learning literature appears both timely and warranted. As such, this study meta-analyzes 117 studies involving 21,252 firms. This study seeks to make three overarching contributions. First, I empirically examine key propositions set forth by March (1991) that related learning activities to performance. In so doing, I provide some resolution to the inconclusive learning—performance results by offering estimates of the extent to which organizational learning activities relate to performance. Second, this study offers evidence suggesting that the type of organizational learning — exploration, exploitation, or ambidexterity — substantively affects the learning to performance relationship. Specifically, I find evidence that challenges long-held claims regarding ambidexterity, and I build and extend work in this area by examining the role of measurement in the ambidexterity—performance relationship. Third, I investigate whether there are important moderators of these relationships, such as performance measurement, content variation in learning activities, geographical region, industry type, firm age, and firm size. Together, by examining the claims asserted in March's (1991) influential article and subsequent literature, I hope to offer increased clarity and new insights for the impact of organizational learning activities on firm performance.

THEORETICAL BACKGROUND AND HYPOTHESES

The notion that organizational learning is important is not new. Schumpeter (1934) cited "creative destruction" — the process of disruptive and transformative innovation by firms (i.e., exploration) — as the driving force that sustains long-term firm growth. Cyert and March (1963) identified success programs, goals, and decision rules as important modes of learning through routine (i.e., exploitation) that may benefit organizations. Duncan (1976) and Argyris and Schön (1978) provided further justification for how learning improves the process of organizational actions. Yet, it was when March (1991) theorized that firms can learn through the *exploration* of new possibilities and the *exploitation* of old certainties that ideas involving organizational learning gained considerable traction in strategy. Although debate exists as to whether exploration and exploitation operate on a continuum or as discrete choices (Gupta et al., 2006), most scholars agree that a firm can engage in both activities, and that both are vital aspects of organizational learning (Rothaermel & Deeds, 2004).

A key tenet within organizational learning research is that learning will enhance performance when an organization out-learns the competition (March, 1991). Scholars have theorized that organizational learning allows firms to improve upon their ability to continuously build and modify unique capabilities (Teece, Pisano, & Shuen, 1997), expand upon their range of strategic choices (Hedlund, 1994), and prevent their core capabilities from becoming core rigidities (Leonard-Barton, 1992). Organizational learning has also shown to exhibit positional advantages (Hult & Ketchen, 2001), better profitability (Cho & Pucik, 2005), and improved return on equity (Rothaermel, 2001) for firms.

Exploration is an important component of organizational learning. Firms must discover new knowledge and explore new opportunities to earn future economic gains (Lavie et al., 2010). Organizations that explore by launching novel technologies (Ahuja & Lampert, 2001), pursuing innovative strategies (Lichtenthaler, 2009), establishing an entrepreneurial culture (Li, Wei, & Liu, 2010), or developing expansive ties and alliances (Hess & Rothaermel, 2011) enhance their performance. For example, Toms Shoes' novel "One for One" business model, which involves donating a pair of shoes for every purchased pair, struck a chord with many consumers and fostered great success, both financially and socially (Taylor, 2012). Especially in today's increasingly dynamic environment, organizations must be flexible and adaptive in the way they conduct business (D'Aveni, 1994; Jansen, Van Den Bosch, & Volberda, 2005). Explorative learning allows firms to incorporate new information and transform it into the products and services of the future. Thus, I predict:

Hypothesis 1. Exploration is positively related to firm performance.

Exploitation is also an important facet of organizational learning and a necessary step in creating a successful business (Choi & Shepherd, 2004). Many exploration activities eventually transform into exploitation exercises, as firms build routines and repetitive processes that allow for enhanced efficiency and productivity (Zollo & Winter, 2002). For example, consider McDonalds' experience in hamburgers. Over the years, the hamburger has remained largely unchanged, yet McDonalds has continuously improved the production process over previous methods, allowing them to become increasingly efficient and profitable in making hamburgers. If organizations fail to leverage existing knowledge, then they may struggle to develop core competencies (Leonard-Barton, 1992). The notion of core competencies implies that firms must (1) find what they excel at and (2) exploit those areas. By understanding and appropriately applying extant knowledge, organizations further develop their core competencies, and in turn, enhance their performance (Peteraf, 1993; Prahalad & Hamel, 1990). As such, exploitative learning is vital to the health and well-being of organizations; it allows firms to concentrate on certain activities and refine them into lucrative proficiencies. Accordingly, theory suggests that:

Hypothesis 2. Exploitation is positively related to firm performance.

Exploration and exploitation involve tensions and trade-offs (Lavie et al., 2010) — firms typically choose between exploring new possibilities and exploiting old certainties. To achieve balance, firms must engage in the processes of variation and selection (Hannan & Freeman, 1984). While the development of organizational routines and practices is essential to firm survival, so too is the advancement of new technologies and processes. For example, O'Reilly and Tushman (2007) describe how IBM strategically and profitably integrates mature (pre-existing) business assets and resources with their Emerging Business Organizations. This strategy has fostered constant innovations and new technologies for IBM, while allowing them to refine their core software and consulting competencies (O'Reilly & Tushman, 2007). Thus, many researchers (cf. He & Wong, 2004; O'Reilly & Tushman, 2004; Raisch, Birkinshaw, Probst, & Tushman, 2009) assert that a balance between exploration and exploitation (i.e., ambidexterity) is a driving factor in firm survival and prosperity. As such, theory suggests:

Hypothesis 3a. Ambidexterity is positively related to firm performance.

The logic supporting organizational ambidexterity rests on the notion that balancing exploration and exploitation enhances performance more than focusing mainly on one activity. On the one hand, a one-sided focus on exploration activities for a given firm may (1) prevent the firm from developing and refining core capabilities and (2) offer highly risky and uncertain payoffs (Uotila, Maula, Keil, & Zahra, 2009). On the other hand, a one-sided focus on exploitation activities may (1) force the firm into a competency trap in which it is unable to adapt to shifts in the environment (Leonard-Barton, 1992; Levitt & March, 1988; Raisch & Birkinshaw, 2008) and (2) offer little opportunity for long-term growth (Clarysse, Wright, & Van de Velde, 2011; Gedajlovic, Cao, & Zhang, 2012; Hmieleski & Baron, 2008). Accordingly, from a theoretical standpoint, most researchers agree that firms must balance their learning by engaging in explorative activities that offer growth potential, and exploitative activities that build core competencies, and in turn, the opportunity for profit potential. In other words, received theory suggests firms that pursue both exploration and exploitation are better off than those with a single focus (Andriopoulos & Lewis, 2009; O'Reilly & Tushman, 2007; Raisch et al., 2009). Thus, received theory suggests:

Hypothesis 3b. The positive relationship between ambidexterity and firm performance is stronger than for exploration or exploitation and firm performance.

March (1991) also asserted that exploration and exploitation might impact different types of performance measures differently. Firm growth is one of the key dimensions of firm performance (Combs, Crook, & Shook, 2005; Richard, Devinney, Yip, & Johnson, 2009), and often considered one of the primary variables of interest in the strategic management and entrepreneurship literatures (Ireland, Hitt, Camp, & Sexton, 2001). Growth can encompass a variety of measures, such as increases in sales, market share, or employment. Although growth does not provide a complete picture of organizational performance, it is highly indicative of how well a firm performs (cf. Combs et al., 2005). Research indicates that firm growth is often achieved through the introduction of new products and services or expansion into new markets − activities synonymous with exploration (Cho & Pucik, 2005; March, 1991). Organizations that consistently produce innovative and pioneering products may be "rewarded" by customers through increased sales.

Conversely, exploitation encompasses a focus on refinement and execution in learning processes (Baum, Li, & Usher, 2000). As such, exploitative activities, such as selection and implementation, are often associated with enhanced operational performance, such as incremental process improvements (Martins & Kambil, 1999), incident and performance variation reductions (Baum & Dahlin, 2007; March, 1991), and alignment and efficiency gains (Bontis, Crossan, & Hulland, 2002; Gibson & Birkinshaw, 2004). Unlike exploration, which is geared toward growth, exploitation is geared toward overall improvement and efficiency in processes (March, 1991). Thus, I expect:

Hypothesis 4. The positive relationship between exploration and firm growth is stronger than the relationship for exploitation and firm growth.

Hypothesis 5. The positive relationship between exploitation and operational performance is stronger than the relationship for exploration and operational performance.

Although learning and knowledge may help make performance more reliable, exploration is a risky business (March, 1991). Many firms strive to create, innovate, and discover new products and technologies, yet engaging in these activities offers uncertainty (Lin, Peng, Yang, & Sun, 2009). A firm may design an unpopular product, incur research and development costs far beyond budget, or launch into a new market unsuccessfully. As such, trying new things can introduce increased uncertainty than would normally arise from "doing the same old thing" (Lewin, Long, & Carroll, 1999). Therefore, explorative processes, such as experimentation and discovery, are often associated with fostering greater performance variation (Andriopoulos & Lewis, 2009), increasing ambiguity (Lin et al., 2009), and heightening risk (Rothaermel & Deeds, 2004).

Alternatively, exploitation offers stability, but relies on inertia (March, 1991). Exploitative learning largely assumes that what has worked in the past will work in the future. Accordingly, exploitation can prevent exposure to understanding changing trends and market demands (Rothaermel & Deeds, 2004), foster rigid and linear thinking patterns (Kang & Snell, 2009; Leonard-Barton, 1995), prevent product differentiation (Delacroix, Swaminathan, & Solt, 1989), and lead to intellectual and technological traps (Levitt & March, 1988; Rosenkopf & Nerkar, 2001).

Given what is known from modern portfolio theory (Markowitz, 1952; Markowitz, Todd, & Sharpe, 2000), investing in relatively uncertain investments (e.g., high-tech stocks) may be risky in the short-term. For this reason, finance scholars and practitioners often advocate that investment decisions should often be made with a relatively long time horizon. Similarly, investing in relatively certain investments (e.g., certificates of deposit) may provide clear short-term returns, but offers little flexibility if sudden changes, such as drastic changes in interest rates, occur.

Scholars posit that exploration and exploitation may provide similar outcomes. Like stock investing, exploration may offer highly uncertain rewards in the short-term, but higher returns in the long-term (Lavie et al., 2010; March, 1991). On the other hand, performance outcomes from exploitation are far more proximate (Gupta et al., 2006). Like a certificate of deposit (CD), exploitation may offer relatively certain short-term returns, but prevent organizations from reacting to sudden changes in the environment (Ahuja & Lampert, 2001; Leonard-Barton, 1992). Firms that rely too heavily on exploitation may struggle when competitive actions or industry shifts – an almost assured phenomenon in today's dynamic environment – occur (Benner & Tushman, 2003; Hannan & Freeman, 1984; Lewin et al., 1999).

Taken together, whereas exploration likely leads to performance outcomes that are often distant, and may not be discerned if performance is measured in the short-term, exploitation offers more proximate returns, which may evaporate if performance is measured in the long-term. Thus, I predict:

Hypothesis 6. The positive relationship between exploration and long-term firm performance is stronger than the relationship for exploitation and long-term performance.

Hypothesis 7. The positive relationship between exploitation and short-term firm performance is stronger than the relationship for exploration and short-term performance.

METHOD

Sample and Coding

The study's aim is to capture the comprehensive set of studies that investigated the relationships of interest and reported the requisite effect size statistics. The search began in 1991 because this was the year of March's seminal article in which he spelled out the importance of organizational learning activities, and specifically, exploration and exploitation. I searched *Google Scholar* and *Business Source Premier* databases for studies containing the keywords "organizational learning," "exploration," "exploitation," or "ambidexterity." I also checked the reference sections of articles that have reviewed aspects of organizational learning (i.e., Gupta et al., 2006; Lavie et al., 2010; Raisch & Birkinshaw, 2008) to identify studies that were not captured in the search. This initial screening resulted in roughly 202 studies. I then more carefully inspected each of the papers to ensure that their theory, constructs, and measures met the criteria for inclusion. That is, the studies (1) matched definitionally with each of March's (1991) learning constructs, (2) reported the requisite effects, (3) were conducted at the firm level of analysis, and (4) contained cross-sectional or lagged performance measures. The final sample of studies, listed in Table 1, includes 117 studies with 119 samples representing 21,252 firms.

The author, along with a research assistant, coded the first 10 studies to develop a final heuristic for the coding scheme. This effort resulted in 92 percent agreement of initial codes; all discrepancies were resolved via discussion. This final coding scheme was then applied to the remaining 107 studies by the author. To code for Hypotheses 1−3a, I identified the organizational learning activity described in the study as (1) exploration, (2) exploitation, or (3) ambidexterity, and captured the reported effects between the specific activity and firm performance. Following Hunter and Schmidt (2004), if studies reported multiple relationships between different measures of an organizational learning activity and performance (e.g., two separate exploration activities), I averaged across those relationships to produce one estimate per study. Where multiple primary studies appeared to rely on the same sample, the average of the correlations and sample sizes across the multiple studies was used as input into the meta-analysis (Hunter & Schmidt, 2004). Table 2 lists the key constructs along with example measures.

Table 1.   Studies Used in the Meta-Analysis.

Author	Year	Journal	Author	Year	Journal
Ahuja and Lampert	2001	*SMJ*	Lavie and Rosenkopf	2006	*AMJ*
Arnold et al.	2011	*JAMS*	Lechner and Floyd	2012	*SMJ*
Atuahene-Gima	2005	*JM*	Lechner et al.	2010	*AMJ*
Atuahene-Gima et al.	2005	*JPIM*	Lee et al.	2010	*LRP*
Audia et al. (Sample 1)	2000	*AMJ*	Levitas and McFayden	2009	*SMJ*
Audia et al. (Sample 2)	2000	*AMJ*	Li et al.	2010	*IMM*
Auh and Menguc	2005	*JBR*	Li et al.	2010	*JOMS*
Baker and Sinkula	2007	*JPIM*	Lichtenthaler	2009	*AMJ*
Barkema and Drogendijk	2007	*JIBS*	Lin et al.	2009	*SMJ*
Baum and Dahlin	2007	*OS*	Lin, Yang, and Demirkan	2007	*MS*
Beck et al.	2011	*FBR*	Lisboa et al.	2011	*IMM*
Beckman	2006	*AMJ*	Lubatkin, Simsek, Ling, and Veiga	2006	*JOM*
Beckman et al.	2004	*OS*	Lumpkin and Dess	2001	*JBV*
Belderbos et al.	2010	*JPIM*	Luo (Sample 1)	2002	*OS*
Bell et al.	2010	*JAMS*	Luo (Sample 2)	2002	*OS*
Bierly and Daly	2007	*ETP*	Luo and Peng	1999	*JIBS*
Bierly et al.	2009	*JOMS*	Makino et al.	2002	*JIBS*
Bingham et al.	2007	*SEJ*	Makri, Lane, and Hitt	2010	*SMJ*
Bontis et al.	2002	*JOMS*	Marsh and Stock	2006	*JPIM*
Burpitt	2009	*JBAM*	Martins and Kambil	1999	*AMJ*
Calantone and Rubera	2011	*JPIM*	McGrath	2001	*AMJ*
Cao et al.	2009	*OS*	Menguc and Auh	2008	*IMM*
Cegarra-Navarro	2007	*JSBM*	Menguc and Auh	2010	*IMM*
Cegarra-Navarro and Dewhurst	2011	*MD*	Morgan and Berthon	2008	*JOMS*
Cegarra-Navarro et al.	2007	*IJHRM*	Parke et al.	2002	*AMJ*
Cepeda-Carrion et al.	2010	*BJOM*	Patel et al.	2012	*JOPM*
Chandrasekaran et al.	2012	*JOPM*	Perretti and Negro	2006	*AMJ*
Cho and Pucik	2005	*SMJ*	Piao	2010	*JOM*
Clarysse et al.	2011	*JOMS*	Prieto and Santana	2012	*HRM*
Coombs, Deeds, and Ireland	2009	*SEJ*	Rosenkopf and Nerkar	2001	*SMJ*
Cui and Kumar	2011	*JBR*	Rothaermel	2001	*RP*
Dai and Lia	2009	*IBR*	Rothaermel	2001	*SMJ*
Dencker et al.	2009	*OS*	Rothaermel and Alexandre	2009	*OS*
Dröge et al.	2003	*DS*	Rothaermel and Deeds	2004	*SMJ*
Dunlap-Hinkler et al.	2010	*SEJ*	Russo and Vurro	2010	*EMR*
Durand et al.	2008	*SMJ*	Rust et al.	2002	*JM*
Faems et al.	2005	*JPIM*	Salge and Vera	2011	*BJOM*
Fernhaber and Patel	2012	*SMJ*	Sapienza et al.	2004	*JBV*
Fiss	2011	*AMJ*	Sarkees	2007	*D-U.Pitt*
Friesl	2011	*BJOM*	Sarkees et al.	2010	*JSM*
Gedajlovic et al.	2012	*JBV*	Sethi and Sethi	2009	*JPIM*
Gibson and Birkinshaw	2004	*AMJ*	Sidhu et al.	2007	*OS*
Greve	2007	*ICC*	Su et al.	2011	*APJM*

Table 1. (*Continued*)

Author	Year	Journal	Author	Year	Journal
Halebian et al.	2006	*AMJ*	Subramani	2004	*MIS*
Han and Celly	2008	*CJAS*	Tsai and Huang	2008	*JHTMR*
Hayward	2002	*SMJ*	Venkatraman, Lee, and Iyer	2007	*WIP*
He and Wong	2004	*OS*	Vorhies et al.	2011	*JAMS*
Henard and McFadyen	2005	*JPIM*	Voss et al.	2008	*AMJ*
Henderson and Stern	2004	*ASQ*	Voss and Voss	2013	*OS*
Hess and Rothaermel	2011	*SMJ*	Wadhwa and Kotha	2006	*AMJ*
Hill and Birkinshaw	2008	*JBV*	Wang	2008	*ETP*
Hmielski and Baron	2008	*SEJ*	Wang and Li	2008	*JOM*
Hoang and Rothaermel	2010	*SMJ*	Wu and Shanley	2009	*JBR*
Hughes et al.	2007	*BJOM*	Wulf et al.	2010	*WIP*
Isobe et al.	2008	*APJM*	Yamakawa et al.	2011	*RP*
Katila and Ahuja	2002	*AMJ*	Zahra and Hayton	2008	*JBV*
Katila and Chen	2008	*ASQ*	Zhan and Chen	2010	*APJM*
Kim and Atuahene-Gima	2010	*JPIM*	Zhan and Luo	2008	*MIR*
Kristal et al.	2010	*JOPM*	Zhao et al.	2009	*ETP*
Kyriakopoulos and Moorman	2004	*IJRM*			

Journals are abbreviated as follows: Academy of Management Journal (AMJ); Asia Pacific Journal of Management (APJM); Administrative Science Quarterly (ASQ); British Journal of Management (BJOM); Canadian Journal of Administrative Sciences (CJAS); Dissertation (D); Decision Sciences (DS); European Management Review (EMR); Entrepreneurship Theory and Practice (ETP); Family Business Review (FBR); Human Resource Management (HRM); International Business Review (IBR); Industrial and Corporate Change (ICC); International Journal of Human Resource Management (IJHRM); International Journal of Research in Marketing (IJRM); Industrial Marketing Management (IMM); Journal of the Academy of Marketing Science (JAMS); Journal of Behavioral and Applied Management (JBAM); Journal of Business Research (JBR); Journal of Business Venturing (JBV); Journal of High Technology Management Research (JHTMR); Journal of International Business Studies (JIBS); Journal of Marketing (JM); Journal of Management (JOM); Journal of Management Studies (JOMS); Journal of Operations Management (JOPM); Journal of Product Innovation Management (JPIM); Journal of Small Business Management (JSBM); Journal of Strategic Marketing (JSM); Long Range Planning (LRP); Management Decision (MD); Management International Review (MIR); MIS Quarterly (MIS); Management Science (MS); Organization Science (OS); Research Policy (RP); Strategic Entrepreneurship Journal (SEJ); Strategic Management Journal (SMJ); Working Paper (WIP).

Meta-Analytic Procedures

We followed the Hunter and Schmidt (2004) random-effects model proce-dures used by Combs and Ketchen (2003) and Lux, Crook, and Woehr (2011). First, I calculated effect size estimates as the mean of the sample

Table 2.   Constructs and Sample Measures.

Construct	Sample Measures
Exploration	Annual interlocks established by a firm with another firm where no interlock existed previously (Beckman et al., 2004) Patent search scope (Katila & Ahuja, 2002) Extent of search in non-local domains external to the organization (Sidhu et al., 2007)
Exploitation	Modernization and automation of production processes, efforts to achieve economies of scale, capacity utilization (Menguc & Auh, 2008) Focus on product and process improvements (Bierly et al., 2001) Persistence of strategies utilizing existing knowledge (Katila & Ahuja, 2002)
Ambidexterity	Objectives for undertaking exploration and exploitation projects in the last three years (He & Wong, 2004) Extent of explorative/exploitative orientation (e.g., look for novel technologies, aggressively venture into new markets, commitment to improve quality/cost, increase customer satisfaction, improve reliability of products) (Lubatkin et al., 2006) Extent of organizational alignment (coherence among employees that they are working toward the same goals) and adaptability (the capacity to reconfigure activities to quickly meet changing demands) (Gibson & Birkinshaw, 2004)
Firm performance	Executives' satisfaction with 1) return on investment 2) return on assets, and 3) revenue growth (Zhan & Chen, 2010) ROA (Beckman et al., 2004) Three-year average of return on equity and revenue growth (Zahra & Hayton, 2008)

size weighted correlations ($\bar{r}$) from the primary studies. This corrects for sampling error because positive and negative sampling errors average out. Then, because reliability coefficients are not available for all studies, I corrected each correlation for measurement error using the mean of the available reliabilities reported in the primary studies (i.e., $\bar{r}_c = \frac{\bar{r}}{\sqrt{\bar{r}_{xx}}\sqrt{\bar{r}_{yy}}}$). This procedure yields the best estimate that accounts for measurement error when reliabilities are not reported for all studies (Hunter & Schmidt, 2004).

In meta-analysis, main effect relationships are positive or negative when confidence intervals do not overlap with zero. Thus, for Hypotheses 1 through 3a, I constructed confidence intervals around each effect size ($\bar{r}$) and tested whether the confidence interval around $\bar{r}$ included zero. For moderating effects, results are significant when confidence intervals do not overlap with one another. Thus, for Hypothesis 3b, I calculated $\bar{r}$ for the ambidexterity to performance relationship, and tested whether the effect was larger than the effect for either exploration or for exploitation (Hunter & Schmidt, 2004). For Hypotheses 4 and 5, I created groups according to whether performance was measured as a growth or operational measure (Combs et al., 2005). Firm growth includes sales, employee, or market share growth measures; operational performance includes process gains, operational effectiveness relative to competitors, and manufacturing efficiency metrics. Finally, for Hypotheses 6 and 7, I created groups according to whether performance was operationalized as "long-term" (if performance was measured for 3 years or longer) or "short-term" (if performance was measured as one year or less).

RESULTS

Table 3 reports the results of the hypotheses tests. Hypothesis 1, which predicted a positive relationship between exploration and performance, was supported with $\bar{r} = 0.18$ ($p < 0.01$). When corrected for measurement error, the estimate of the overall effect for the relationship between exploration and performance is $\bar{r}_c = 0.22$. Hypothesis 2, which predicted a positive relationship between exploitation and performance, was also supported ($\bar{r} = 0.16$, $\bar{r}_c = 0.20$, $p < 0.01$). Likewise, the results provide support for Hypothesis 3a, which posited a positive relationship between ambidexterity and performance ($\bar{r} = 0.13$, $\bar{r}_c = 0.15$, $p < 0.01$). However, Hypothesis 3b, which predicted a stronger relationship with performance for ambidexterity than for exploration or exploitation, was not supported with $\bar{r} = 0.13$ for ambidexterity, versus 0.18 for exploration and 0.16 for exploitation (*ns*). Although the magnitude of the relationship between exploration and firm growth ($\bar{r} = 0.16$) is greater than for exploitation ($\bar{r} = 0.10$), the difference is not significant; thus, Hypothesis 4 is not supported. Similarly, I failed to find support for Hypothesis 5, which suggested that the relationship between exploitation and operational performance would be greater than for exploration (with $\bar{r} = 0.24$ for both, *ns*). Hypotheses 6 and 7 suggested that exploration would exhibit a stronger relationship with long-term performance, while exploitation would demonstrate a stronger relationship with short-term performance; Hypotheses 7 and 8 were not supported (with $\bar{r} = 0.14$ vs. 0.09, *ns*, for long-term performance; $\bar{r} = 0.19$ versus 0.20, *ns*, for short-term performance). Taken together, I found support for Hypotheses 1−3a, and no support for Hypotheses 3b-7.

Table 3. Hypothesis Test Results.

	N	K	$\bar{r}$	$\bar{r}_c$	σ_e^2	$\sigma_{\bar{r}}^2$	Residual Variance	Percent Artifactual Variance	99% Confidence Interval	95% Confidence Interval	90% Confidence Interval	p value
H1: Exploration–performance	18,718	95	0.18	0.22	0.01	0.00	0.01	7.40%	0.15:0.21	0.16:0.20	0.16:0.19	<0.01
H2: Exploitation–performance	18,142	87	0.16	0.20	0.04	0.00	0.03	12.55%	0.12:0.21	0.13:0.20	0.14:0.19	<0.01
H3a/b: Ambidexterity–performance	4,144	17	0.13	0.15	0.02	0.00	0.02	16.58%	0.04:0.21	0.06:0.19	0.08:0.18	<0.01
H4: Exploration–firm growth	4,647	18	0.16	0.20	0.04	0.00	0.04	7.84%	0.05:0.27	0.08:0.24	0.10:0.22	ns
H4: Exploitation–firm growth	4,391	16	0.10	0.12	0.02	0.00	0.02	18.39%	0.02:0.18	0.04:0.16	0.05:0.14	
H5: Exploration–operational performance	5,958	35	0.24	0.30	0.05	0.01	0.05	11.12%	0.15:0.33	0.18:0.31	0.19:0.29	ns
H5: Exploitation–operational performance	5,560	29	0.24	0.30	0.03	0.00	0.03	14.97%	0.17:0.32	0.19:0.30	0.20:0.29	
H6: Exploration–long-term performance	6,544	30	0.14	0.17	0.02	0.00	0.02	19.54%	0.07:0.20	0.09:0.18	0.10:0.17	ns
H6: Exploitation–long-term performance	5,906	27	0.09	0.11	0.03	0.00	0.03	15.33%	0.01:0.17	0.04:0.15	0.05:0.13	
H7: Exploration–short-term performance	1,310	7	0.19	0.23	0.01	0.00	0.00	85.52%	0.12:0.26	0.14:0.24	0.15:0.23	ns
H7: Exploitation–short-term performance	2,108	10	0.20	0.25	0.04	0.00	0.03	12.26%	0.06:0.34	0.10:0.30	0.13:0.28	

Post Hoc Tests

Following the recommendations of Lavie et al., 2010, I identified several potential moderators, such as studies' specific operationalizations and contextual features, that may have driven past results, and I investigated their influence on the organizational learning activities—performance relationships. Although several moderators seemed potentially important, they also seemed to either lack the strong theoretical foundation necessary to develop hypotheses or fell slightly outside the primary focus – i.e., organizational learning activities and performance relationships. Because of this, I conducted post hoc tests. I conducted these tests by grouping effects according to the moderator of interest (e.g., operationalization of performance), calculating $\bar{r}$ for each group, and testing for differences (Hunter & Schmidt, 2004). I performed these tests to investigate moderating effects for the performance implications of exploration, exploitation, and ambidexterity.

Operationalizations
For the first set of tests, I focused on operationalizations. I first examined the operationalization of learning. The means by which firms explore and exploit, and thus, the way in which scholars measure explorative and exploitative learning may have a significant impact on performance. Clearly, organizations can learn through several means; however, as I coded for the meta-analysis, I noticed the studies' operationalizations coalesced around three general categories – executing innovative actions (Ahuja & Lampert, 2001; Gedajlovic et al., 2012; Piao, 2010), developing inter-organizational relationships (Lin et al., 2007; Zahra & Hayton, 2008), and engaging in strategic efforts that embrace learning activities (Bontis et al., 2002; Lubatkin et al., 2006). As such, I grouped studies into one of these three learning categories and tested for differences across groups.

Next, I also investigated the operationalization of performance. In addition to firm growth and operational performance, which were included in the hypotheses tests, I also created groups for technological, accounting, and stock market performance measures (Combs et al., 2005), and compared across all five groups. Additionally, I also compared lagged (i.e., performance assessed at least one year after learning was measured) versus non-lagged performance (i.e., performance measured at the same time as learning). The results of these operationalization tests are reported in Table 4. I found that Hypotheses 1–3a hold across each of these operationalizations (i.e., statistically different from zero at the $p < 0.01$ level), except when performance is computed with stock market measures. I also found that both exploration and exploitation exhibit a weaker relationship ($p < 0.05$) with accounting returns (e.g., net income) than technological or operational performance measures (where the difference is $p < 0.10$). Due to the lack of available studies, I was unable to conduct all post-hoc tests for ambidexterity. I did find that ambidexterity was not significantly related to performance when learning was measured via inter-organizational relationships; however, this finding was based on only two primary studies, and thus, not robust enough to derive strong evidence.

Contextual Factors

For the second set of tests, I focused on contextual factors, including geographical region, industry type, firm age, and firm size. Following Rosenbusch, Brinckmann, and Bausch (2011), I first coded geographical region as US/Canada, Asia, or Europe based on the country in which firms in the sample were headquartered — unspecified or multi-regional samples were excluded from this test. Second, I investigated whether the average age of firms in a sample shaped results. Accordingly, firm age was bifurcated into two groups — firms greater than and less than ten years old. Ten years provided a natural breaking point in the data and is also in line with other meta-analyses examining firm age as a moderator (e.g., Song, Podoynitsyna, Van Der Bij, & Halman, 2008). Third, in accordance with Dalton, Daily, Ellstrand, and Johnson (1998), firm size was coded as large for samples that were described as COMPUSTAT data, *Fortune* 1000 or large multinational firms, or had measures of average employee size exceeding 500 (e.g., Lechner & Floyd, 2012; Lin et al., 2009). Samples that were described as small- to medium-size businesses, new ventures, or had measures of employee size with average means of 500 or less were coded as small (e.g., Bierly & Daly, 2007; Martins & Kambil, 1999). Mixed samples were coded as large or small firms when more than 50 percent of the sample comprised the respective category. Finally, I grouped studies by industry type following Chandler and McEvoy (2000); I differentiated between high-tech firms, such as those in the biotechnology or pharmaceutical industries (e.g., Coombs et al., 2009; Hess & Rothaermel, 2011), and low-tech firms, such as those in the textile manufacturing or railroad transport industries (e.g., Baum & Dahlin, 2007; Wang & Li, 2008). I also report the results of these contextual factor tests in Table 4. Similar to the first set of tests, I found that Hypotheses 1−3a hold across each of these contextual factors results, except for ambidexterity among large firms, which is not significantly related to firm performance. After more careful examination of this finding, I determined this was primarily driven by the measurement of

Table 4. Post Hoc Tests.

	N	K	$\bar{r}$	$\bar{r}_c$	σ_e^2	$\sigma_{\bar{r}}^2$	Residual Variance	Percent Artifactual Variance	99% Confidence Interval	95% Confidence Interval	90% Confidence Interval
Learning measurement											
Innovation:exploration	8,018	33	0.18	0.21	0.02	0.00	0.02	15.92%	0.11:0.24	0.13:0.22	0.14:0.21
Innovation:exploitation	7,208	29	0.18	0.22	0.02	0.00	0.02	16.23%	0.11:0.24	0.13:0.23	0.14:0.22
Innovation:ambidexterity	2,426	6	0.12	0.15	0.02	0.00	0.02	13.54%	0.00:0.25	0.03:0.21	0.05:0.19
Relationships:exploration	3,595	17	0.13	0.16	0.02	0.00	0.02	22.65%	0.05:0.21	0.07:0.19	0.08:0.17
Relationships:exploitation	3,759	16	0.16	0.20	0.03	0.00	0.03	12.43%	0.06:0.27	0.09:0.24	0.10:0.22
Relationships:ambidexterity	269	2	−0.07	−0.09	0.03	0.01	0.02	23.32%	−0.36:0.22	−0.28:−0.13	−0.23:−0.09
Strategy:exploration	4,673	31	0.23	0.29	0.04	0.01	0.04	14.24%	0.15:0.32	0.17:0.30	0.19:0.28
Strategy:exploitation	3,997	28	0.17	0.21	0.06	0.01	0.05	11.06%	0.06:0.28	0.10:0.25	0.11:0.23
Strategy:ambidexterity	983	7	0.23	0.28	0.02	0.01	0.01	31.13%	0.11:0.35	0.14:0.31	0.16:0.29
Performance measurement[a]											
Technological:exploration	6,572	34	0.23	0.28	0.04	0.00	0.04	11.73%	0.15:0.31	0.17:0.29	0.18:0.27
Technological:exploitation	5,639	28	0.25	0.30	0.05	0.00	0.04	9.87%	0.15:0.34	0.18:0.31	0.19:0.30
Growth:exploration	4,647	18	0.16	0.20	0.04	0.00	0.04	7.84%	0.05:0.27	0.08:0.24	0.10:0.22
Growth:exploitation	4,391	16	0.10	0.12	0.02	0.00	0.02	18.39%	0.02:0.18	0.04:0.16	0.05:0.14
Accounting returns:exploration	4,004	29	0.13	0.16	0.03	0.01	0.02	25.01%	0.06:0.20	0.08:0.18	0.09:0.17
Accounting returns:exploitation	4,107	28	0.08	0.10	0.04	0.01	0.03	18.61%	0.00:0.17	0.02:0.14	0.04:0.13
Stock market:exploration	1,717	6	0.11	0.14	0.03	0.00	0.03	10.50%	−0.06:0.29	−0.01:0.24	0.02:0.21
Stock market:exploitation	1,712	6	0.11	0.13	0.04	0.00	0.03	9.53%	−0.08:0.29	−0.02:0.24	0.01:0.21
Operational:exploration	5,958	35	0.24	0.30	0.05	0.01	0.05	11.12%	0.15:0.33	0.18:0.31	0.19:0.29
Operational:exploitation	5,560	29	0.24	0.30	0.03	0.00	0.03	14.97%	0.17:0.32	0.19:0.30	0.20:0.29
Lagged performance											
Lagged:exploration	4,646	18	0.08	0.10	0.01	0.00	0.00	51.17%	0.03:0.13	0.05:0.12	0.06:0.11
Lagged:exploitation	4,826	19	0.10	0.12	0.03	0.00	0.03	12.29%	0.00:0.19	0.03:0.17	0.04:0.15
Non-lagged:exploration	2,567	18	0.18	0.22	0.04	0.01	0.03	18.76%	0.07:0.28	0.10:0.25	0.12:0.24
Non-lagged:exploitation	2,622	16	0.12	0.15	0.04	0.01	0.03	16.95%	0.01:0.23	0.04:0.20	0.06:0.18

Table 4. (Continued)

	N	K	$\bar{r}$	$\bar{r}_c$	σ_e^2	$\sigma_{\bar{r}}^2$	Residual Variance	Percent Artifactual Variance	99% Confidence Interval	95% Confidence Interval	90% Confidence Interval
Geographical region											
US/Canada:exploration	8,022	45	0.14	0.17	0.02	0.01	0.02	23.42%	0.08:0.19	0.10:0.18	0.11:0.17
US/Canada:exploitation	7,194	37	0.14	0.17	0.03	0.00	0.02	17.41%	0.07:0.20	0.09:0.18	0.10:0.17
Asia:exploration	3,220	13	0.22	0.27	0.02	0.00	0.02	15.27%	0.12:0.32	0.15:0.29	0.16:0.28
Asia:exploitation	3,063	12	0.23	0.28	0.03	0.00	0.03	11.08%	0.11:0.35	0.14:0.32	0.16:0.30
Europe:exploration	4,356	21	0.24	0.29	0.04	0.00	0.03	11.33%	0.14:0.34	0.17:0.31	0.19:0.30
Europe:exploitation	4,423	22	0.16	0.20	0.05	0.00	0.04	10.35%	0.05:0.27	0.08:0.24	0.10:0.22
Firm age											
Young:exploration	5,961	18	0.16	0.19	0.02	0.00	0.01	17.35%	0.09:0.23	0.11:0.21	0.12:0.19
Young:exploitation	5,870	19	0.15	0.18	0.04	0.00	0.04	7.13%	0.04:0.26	0.07:0.23	0.09:0.21
Young:ambidexterity	2,368	5	0.08	0.10	0.00	0.00	0.00	49.32%	0.01:0.15	0.03:0.13	0.05:0.12
Old:exploration	3,241	19	0.15	0.18	0.03	0.01	0.03	17.19%	0.05:0.25	0.08:0.22	0.10:0.20
Old:exploitation	2,939	16	0.10	0.12	0.03	0.01	0.02	19.43%	0.01:0.20	0.03:0.17	0.05:0.16
Old:ambidexterity	628	4	0.35	0.43	0.02	0.00	0.02	23.64%	0.18:0.52	0.23:0.47	0.26:0.44
Firm size											
Small:exploration	7,279	30	0.18	0.22	0.03	0.00	0.03	11.45%	0.10:0.25	0.13:0.23	0.14:0.22
Small:exploitation	7,159	30	0.14	0.17	0.03	0.00	0.03	13.18%	0.07:0.21	0.09:0.19	0.10:0.18
Small:ambidexterity	2,758	7	0.13	0.15	0.01	0.00	0.01	24.87%	0.04:0.21	0.06:0.19	0.08:0.17
Large:exploration	6,619	40	0.19	0.24	0.01	0.00	0.01	24.87%	0.16:0.23	0.17:0.22	0.17:0.21
Large:exploitation	6,396	33	0.21	0.26	0.05	0.00	0.04	9.16%	0.12:0.30	0.15:0.28	0.16:0.26
Large:ambidexterity	965	7	0.13	0.16	0.09	0.01	0.08	6.94%	−0.13:0.39	−0.06:0.31	−0.02:0.27
Industry											
Hi-tech industry:exploration	7,293	35	0.17	0.21	0.02	0.00	0.02	20.85%	0.11:0.23	0.13:0.21	0.14:0.20
Hi-tech industry:exploitation	6,864	31	0.16	0.20	0.03	0.00	0.03	12.70%	0.08:0.24	0.11:0.22	0.12:0.20
Low-tech industry:exploration	3,485	23	0.13	0.16	0.03	0.01	0.02	20.92%	0.05:0.22	0.07:0.19	0.08:0.18
Low-tech industry:exploitation	3,877	19	0.13	0.15	0.00	0.00	0.03	14.83%	0.03:0.22	0.06:0.19	0.07:0.18

[a]Growth and operational performance are also found in H4 and H5 in Table 3.

ambidexterity rather than fundamental differences between large and small firms. Four of the seven studies in this test used "balancing" measures, and the confidence interval widely varied (−0.02:0.27). I also found that ambidexterity among older firms generates much greater performance returns than ambidexterity among younger firms ($p < 0.01$). In the next section, I discuss these findings in further detail.

DISCUSSION

Based on data from over 21,000 organizational learning–performance relationships reported within 117 studies, the study offers evidence about the relationships among organizational learning activities and performance. Consistent with received theory, the results show that exploration, exploitation, and ambidexterity are related to performance at ($\bar{r}_c = 0.22, 0.20, 0.15$). Taken together, these findings offer strong evidence supporting March's (1991) assertions that exploration, exploitation, and ambidexterity are vital to the performance of an organization. Yet, the findings also challenge many other long-held views – that the returns from exploration are more distant than exploitation, that exploration is more strongly associated with growth, that exploitation is more strongly related to operational performance, and perhaps most importantly, that ambidexterity yields stronger performance effects than focusing solely on exploration or exploitation. I discuss each of these findings and their implications in the following paragraphs.

Exploration and Exploitation

First, the results indicate that both exploration and exploitation contribute roughly equally to performance with $\bar{r}_c = 0.22$ and 0.20, respectively. I find that the performance effects hold across numerous operationalizations and a diverse range of contexts. The relatively large effects suggest that exploration and exploitation are important determinants of performance; however, I see a need to build on these results to identify other contingencies. One avenue is to investigate more fine-grained learning strategies, such as product cannibalization, and how it shapes firm performance. Recently, Danneels and Sethi (2011) proposed that a willingness to cannibalize products promoted explorative new products. On the other hand, Voss and Voss (2013) posited that by replacing the old with the new, product cannibalization can create tensions among products, processes, and employees that could undermine organizational efficiency. Although these studies highlight the importance of product cannibalization as an exploratory activity, the answer as to whether cannibalization is an effective and profitable explorative learning strategy remains open.

Research could also examine organizations that rely heavily on exploitative activity, such as franchises (Combs, Ketchen, Shook, & Short, 2011). In essence, a franchise involves distribution of a proven and recognized product or service (i.e., exploitation). However, the recent recession presented franchisors, especially those in discretionary or higher end industries, with difficult decisions and explorative opportunities (Entrepreneur, 2010). To appeal to the cost-conscious consumer, franchisors were forced to decide whether to explore new alternatives, such as lower cost products and services, or stay the course. Although exploring new low-cost alternatives might appear alluring in the short-term, it could compromise the brand image associated with the organization in the longer-term. The recent economic climate might provide an interesting context for understanding the extent to which traditionally exploitative organizations pursue exploration in austere environments, and if so, whether such a move is beneficial or detrimental.

Ambidexterity

Most notably, the results run contrary to conventional wisdom with regard to ambidexterity. Despite many researchers' claims (e.g., Andriopoulos & Lewis, 2009; He & Wong, 2004; Raisch et al., 2009; Simsek, 2009) that a balance between exploration and exploitation enhances performance, I find no evidence that ambidexterity provides stronger performance effects than pursuit of either exploration or exploitation. I consider several potential explanations for this discovery.

First, this finding could reflect the different ways (or modes) in which organizations pursue ambidexterity. Although many scholars have emphasized the importance of various modes of balancing (cf. Lavie et al., 2010; Simsek, 2009), such as pursuing ambidexterity sequentially or simultaneously, few studies have examined whether these have differing performance implications. Traditional views of ambidexterity have called for the simultaneous pursuit of exploration and exploitation throughout the organization (e.g., March, 1991). However, several alternative ways of balancing these objectives have been advanced, such as cycling between these activities over time. Nevertheless, the literature is silent regarding which mode of balancing ambidexterity leads to the best firm performance. Perhaps, some modes of ambidexterity, such as cycling back-and-forth between exploration and exploitation, might have greater performance implications than organizations who pursue ambidexterity by simultaneously pursuing moderate levels of exploration and exploitation.

Recently, Fernhaber and Patel (2012) incorporated multiple ambidexterity measures into their study of absorptive capacity and ambidexterity. They calculated the extent to which firms engage in exploration and exploitation as well as the extent to which exploration and exploitation were congruent, and examined their varying impact on performance. Similarly, Venkatraman and colleagues (2007) used multiple measures by differentiating between simultaneous ambidexterity (contemporaneous balancing of exploration and exploitation) and sequential ambidexterity (dynamic, temporal sequencing of routines for exploration and exploitation). In line with this study's results, they found that sequential ambidexterity significantly predicted sales growth, whereas simultaneous ambidexterity did not. These varied methodological approaches provide important steps toward advancing ambidexterity research and building our contextual understanding for when ambidexterity may confer performance advantages. However, "Despite the rapidly expanding number of studies referring to organizational ambidexterity, empirical tests of the ambidexterity–performance relationship remain scarce" (Raisch & Birkinshaw, 2008, p. 393). This suggests that more empirical work regarding ambidexterity is needed.

Additionally, the results show that the ambidexterity–performance relationship is significantly stronger for older firms ($\bar{r}_c = 0.45$, $p < 0.01$) than for younger firms ($\bar{r}_c = 0.10$). This suggests that for more mature organizations, such as General Electric or IBM, ambidexterity is a large determinant of performance. Thus, ambidextrous learning should be a key focus. For nascent firms, rather than aiming for balance, they should likely focus on either exploration or exploitation efforts. Emerging firms should attempt to become known for exploration or exploitation, but as they grow and mature into more complex organizations, the need to not only balance but also integrate both exploration and exploitation activities may become increasingly important.

Similarly, the results of this research shed light on the long- and short-term performance implications for exploration and exploitation, and indirectly, ambidexterity. Although the learning literature points to the benefits of exploration for long-term performance and exploitation for short-term performance (March, 1991), extant empirical research does not support this assertion. Instead, the evidence indicates that the performance effects for both exploration and exploitation are greater in the short-term than the long-term. This infers that focusing on one learning activity vis-à-vis the other may be advantageous in the short-term, but is likely not optimal in the long-term. In the longer-term, engaging in ambidexterity might be a more profitable strategy; this could help explain why ambidexterity is most important to mature rather than nascent firms. Taken together, these ambidexterity findings have a number of critical implications.

The results regarding ambidexterity and older firms, and exploration and exploitation and long- and short-term performance broadly suggest that life-cycle theory may have an important place in the organizational learning literature. The potential application of life-cycle theory is two-fold. First, when considering balancing exploration and exploitation, much of the extant research has focused on *how much* the firm should explore versus exploit rather than *when* it should engage in each activity. However, explorative products and services have shelf-lives which may range from a few months to several years (Lichtenthaler, 2009). It seems likely that firms would want to exploit their initially "explorative technologies" for as long as possible, but not so long they become inflexible and outdated in their products and processes (Leonard-Barton, 1992). Firms that appropriately time their exploration and/or exploitation activities may incur greater performance returns than their competitors. A greater attention to time, and in particular, temporal sequencing (knowing when exploration and exploitation activities should follow one another) could benefit future learning research (e.g., Venkatraman et al., 2007). Thus, integration of product life-cycle theory with organizational learning could offer new insights into the benefits of ambidexterity. Secondly, given that older firms reap greater benefits from ambidexterity, future efforts could examine the role of the organizational life cycle on the success of learning activities. Perhaps, firms in the entrepreneurial stage of the life cycle possess the need for creative and explorative activity, but eventually, growth may guide organizations to a realization of their core proficiencies (Daft, 1983). From there, organizations may need to build upon and refine their core competencies (exploit), while continuing to innovate and explore new ideas (explore). Further integration of product and organizational life-cycle theories and organizational learning appears warranted.

In sum, the findings offer a number of ideas for future learning research. I challenge many long-held theoretical learning assumptions, and in doing so, I call attention to (1) the different ways (or modes) in which organizations can pursue ambidexterity, (2) the importance of firm age, timing, and life-cycle effects in the relationships among learning activities and performance, and (3) how organizations might align and adapt organizational strategy with organizational learning activities. Although this study has hopefully provided new avenues for future learning efforts, I also call for research of how additional, and currently unexplored, contextual features might impact learning and performance.

Limitations and Future Research

This study should be viewed in light of its limitations. A first limitation arises from issues inherent in the method. As with any meta-analysis, it is subject to capturing only those studies that report the necessary statistics for inclusion. Some published studies investigate learning activities but do not report the needed information (i.e., correlations) for inclusion in the analysis. Other studies, perhaps due to the "file drawer problem" (publication bias for studies reporting significant results), are simply never published (see Dalton & Dalton, 2005). To address this potential limitation, I looked for differences between what are perceived as top-tier publications and lower-tier articles/unpublished works. I did not find differences. I also conducted Rosenthal's (1979) *fail-safe N* test to determine the number of additional studies with null results that would be needed to alter the results. I determined that approximately 50 additional studies that report null findings would be needed to invalidate the exploration and exploitation results. This suggests that the results are robust.

A second limitation pertains to levels of analysis. In this study, I elected to focus on the firm level of analysis for learning and performance because most often exploration and exploitation discussions are described as organizational phenomenon. In some organizations, certain business units may focus exclusively on exploration, while other units exclusively on exploitation. As such, looking holistically at the activities of the firm rather than assessing the performance of a single business unit may help us better understand the implications of learning. Still, individual-, business unit-, or firm-level learning may have a distinct impact on organizations. I encourage future research to compare and contrast organizational learning at each of these levels.

A third limitation also seems a potentially fruitful line of future inquiry; it concerns evaluating overarching strategies and learning activities, particularly ambidexterity. For example, consider Porter's (1980) three "generic strategies" − overall low-cost, differentiation, and focus − and how learning activities can align with these strategies. Firms with a low-cost strategy may be less concerned with being innovative and exploring new alternatives; in order to deliver low-cost products and services, they may benefit from becoming increasingly efficient in exploiting existing processes and operations. Conversely, firms with a differentiation strategy may strive for consistently delivering new and innovative products and services through continuously exploring new avenues; exploitative efforts could actually tarnish a pioneering firm's reputation. Although firms with a single strategy may benefit from pursuit of either exploration or exploitation, firms with multiple strategies, such as low-cost and focused, may benefit from both exploration and exploitation (i.e., ambidexterity). In other words, ambidexterity may be optimal for firms with manifold strategies, but less desirable for those with a single strategic focus. Future research should investigate relationships involving overarching strategic types and organizational learning to further our understanding of the performance implications from learning, and especially, ambidexterity.

CONCLUSION

Organizational learning, and the activities of exploration, exploitation, and ambidexterity, have become guiding forces in strategic management inquiry. Although I lack support for the long-held assertion that ambidexterity leads to better performance than focusing mainly on exploration or exploitation, the findings indicate that explorative, exploitative, and ambidextrous activities "matter," and that they are important determinants of performance. I also investigate some key contingencies of these relationships, and discuss their implications. Overall, this examination of the last twenty years of organizational learning research provides increased clarity for March's (1991) influential work. It is my hope that the next twenty years of organizational learning research continue to usher in additional clarification and insights.

REFERENCES

Ahuja, G., & Lampert, M. C. (2001). Entrepreneurship in the large corporation: A longitudinal study of how established firms create breakthrough inventions. *Strategic Management Journal*, 22, 521–543.

Andriopoulos, C., & Lewis, M. W. (2009). Exploitation−exploration tensions and organizational ambidexterity: Managing paradoxes of innovation. *Organization Science*, *20*, 696−717.

Argyris, C., & Schön, D. A. (1978). *Organizational Learning*. Reading, MA: Addison-Wesley.

Baum, J. A. C., & Dahlin, K. (2007). Aspiration performance and railroads' patterns of experiential learning from train wrecks and crashes. *Organization Science*, *18*, 368−385.

Baum, J. A. C., Li, S. X., & Usher, J. M. (2000). Making the next move: How experiential and vicarious learning shape the locations of chains' acquisitions. *Administrative Science Quarterly*, *45*, 766−801.

Benner, M. J., & Tushman, M. L. (2003). Exploitation, exploration, and process management: The productivity dilemma revisited. *Academy of Management Review*, *28*, 238−256.

Bierly III, P. E., & Daly, P. S. (2007). Alternative knowledge strategies, competitive environment, and organizational performance in small manufacturing firms. *Entrepreneurship Theory and Practice*, *31*, 493−516.

Bontis, N., Crossan, M. M., & Hulland, J. (2002). Managing an organizational learning system by aligning stocks and flows. *Journal of Management Studies*, *39*, 437−469.

Cao, Q., Gedajlovic, E., & Zhang, H. (2009). Unpacking organizational ambidexterity: Dimensions, contingencies, and synergistic effects. *Organization Science*, *20*, 781−796.

Chandler, G. N., & McEvoy, G. M. (2000). Human resource management, TQM, and firm performance in small and medium-size enterprises. *Entrepreneurship Theory and Practice*, *25*, 43−58.

Cho, H. J., & Pucik, V. (2005). Relationship between innovativeness, quality, growth, profitability, and market value. *Strategic Management Journal*, *26*, 555−575.

Choi, Y. R., & Shepherd, D. A. (2004). Entrepreneurs' decisions to exploit opportunities. *Journal of Management*, *30*, 377−395.

Clarysse, B., Wright, M., & Van de Velde, E. (2011). Entrepreneurial origin, technological knowledge, and the growth of spin-off companies. *Journal of Management Studies*, *48*, 1420−1442.

Combs, J. G., Crook, T. R., & Shook, C. L. (2005). The dimensionality of organizational performance and its implications for strategic management research. In D. Ketchen & D. Bergh (Eds.), *Research methodology in strategy and management* (pp. 259−286). San Diego, CA: Elsevier.

Combs, J. G., & Ketchen, D. J. (2003). Why do firms use franchising as an entrepreneurial strategy?: A meta-analysis. *Journal of Management*, *29*, 443−465.

Combs, J. G., Ketchen, D. J., Shook, C. L., & Short, J. C. (2011). Antecedents and consequences of franchising: Past accomplishments and future challenges. *Journal of Management*, *37*, 99−126.

Coombs, J. E., Deeds, D. L., & Ireland, D. R. (2009). Placing the choice between exploration and exploitation in context: A study of geography and new product development. *Strategic Entrepreneurship Journal*, *3*, 261−279.

Cyert, R. M., & March, J. G. (1963). *A behavioral theory of the firm*. Oxford: Wiley-Blackwell.

Daft, R. L. (1983). *Organization theory and design*. New York, NY: West.

Daley, J. (2010). Out of the bunker for 2010. *Entrepreneur*.

Dalton, D. R., Daily, C. M., Ellstrand, A. E., & Johnson, J. L. (1998). Meta-analytic reviews of board composition, leadership structure, and financial performance. *Strategic Management Journal*, *19*, 269−290.

Dalton, D. R., & Dalton, C. M. (2005). Strategic management studies are a special case for meta-analysis. In D. Ketchen & D. Bergh (Eds.), *Research methodology in strategy and management* (Vol. 2, pp. 31−63). San Diego, CA: Elsevier.

Danneels, E., & Sethi, R. (2011). New product exploration under environmental turbulence. *Organization Science, 22*, 1026−1039.

D'Aveni, R. A. (1994). *Hypercompetition.* New York, NY: Free Press.

Delacroix, J., Swaminathan, A., & Solt, M. E. (1989). Density dependence versus population dynamics: An ecological study of failings in the California wine industry. *American Sociological Review, 54*, 245−262.

Duncan, R. (1976). The ambidextrous organizations: Designing dual structures for innovation. In R. H. Kilmann, L. R. Pondy & D. Slevin (Eds.), *The management of organizational design* (Vol. 1, pp. 167−188). New York, NY: North Holland.

Fernhaber, S. A., & Patel, P. C. (2012). How do young firms manage product portfolio complexity? The role of absorptive capacity and ambidexterity. *Strategic Management Journal, 33*, 1516−1539.

Gedajlovic, E., Cao, Q., & Zhang, H. (2012). Corporate shareholdings and organizational ambidexterity in high-tech SMEs: Evidence from a transitional economy. *Journal of Business Venturing, 27*, 652−665.

Gibson, C. B., & Birkinshaw, J. (2004). The antecedents, consequences, and mediating role of organizational ambidexterity. *Academy of Management Journal, 47*, 209−226.

Gupta, A. K., Smith, K. G., & Shalley, C. E. (2006). The interplay between exploration and exploitation. *Academy of Management Journal, 49*, 693−706.

Hannan, M. T., & Freeman, J. (1984). Structural inertia and organizational change. *American Sociological Review, 49*, 149−164.

He, Z. L., & Wong, P. K. (2004). Exploration vs. exploitation: An empirical test of the ambidexterity hypothesis. *Organization Science, 15*, 481−494.

Hedlund, G. (1994). A model of knowledge management and the N-form corporation. *Strategic Management Journal, 15*, 73−90.

Hess, A. M., & Rothaermel, F. T. (2011). When are assets complementary? Star scientists, strategic alliances, and innovation in the pharmaceutical industry. *Strategic Management Journal, 32*, 896−909.

Hill, S. A., & Birkinshaw, J. (2008). Strategy-organization configurations in corporate venture units: Impact on performance and survival. *Journal of Business Venturing, 23*, 423−444.

Hmieleski, K. M., & Baron, R. A. (2008). Regulatory focus and new venture performance: A study of entrepreneurial opportunity exploitation under conditions of risk versus uncertainty. *Strategic Entrepreneurship Journal, 2*, 285−299.

Hult, G. T., & Ketchen, D. J. (2001). Does market orientation matter?: A test of the relationship between positional advantage and performance. *Strategic Management Journal, 22*, 899−906.

Hunter, J. E., & Schmidt, F. L. (2004). *Methods of meta-analysis: Correcting error and bias in research findings.* Newbury Park, CA: Sage.

Ireland, R. D., Hitt, M. A., Camp, S. M., & Sexton, D. L. (2001). Integrating entrepreneurship and strategic management actions to create firm wealth. *Academy of Management Executive, 15*, 49−63.

Jansen, J. J. P., Van Den Bosch, F. A. J., & Volberda, H. W. (2005). Managing potential and realized absorptive capacity: How do organizational antecedents matter? *Academy of Management Journal, 48*, 999−1015.

Kang, S. C., & Snell, S. A. (2009). Intellectual capital architectures and ambidextrous learning: A framework for human resource management. *Journal of Management Studies, 46*, 65−92.

Lavie, D., & Rosenkopf, L. (2006). Balancing exploration and exploitation in alliance formation. *Academy of Management Journal, 49*, 797−818.

Lavie, D., Stettner, U., & Tushman, M. L. (2010). Exploration and exploitation within and across organizations. *Academy of Management Annals, 4*, 109−155.

Lechner, C., & Floyd, S. W. (2012). Group influence activities and the performance of strategic initiatives. *Strategic Management Journal, 33*, 478−495.

Leonard-Barton, D. (1992). Core capabilities and core rigidities: A paradox in managing new product development. *Strategic Management Journal, 13*, 111−117.

Leonard-Barton, D. (1995). *Wellsprings of knowledge*. Boston, MA: Harvard Business School Press.

Levitt, B., & March, J. G. (1988). Organizational learning. *Annual Review of Sociology, 14*, 319−340.

Lewin, A. Y., Long, C. P., & Carroll, T. N. (1999). The coevolution of new organizational forms. *Organization Science, 10*, 535−550.

Li, Y., Wei, Z., & Liu, Y. (2010). Strategic orientations, knowledge acquisition, and firm performance: The perspective of the vendor in cross-border outsourcing. *Journal of Management Studies, 47*, 1457−1482.

Lichtenthaler, U. (2009). Absorptive capacity, environmental turbulence, and the complementarity of organizational learning processes. *Academy of Management Journal, 52*, 822−846.

Lin, Z. J., Peng, M. W., Yang, H., & Sun, S. L. (2009). How do networks and learning drive MandAs? An institutional comparison between China and the United States. *Strategic Management Journal, 30*, 1113−1132.

Lin, Z., Yang, H., & Demirkan, I. (2007). The performance consequences of ambidexterity in strategic alliance formations: Empirical investigation and computational theorizing. *Management Science, 53*, 1645-1658.

Lubatkin, M. H., Simsek, Z., Ling, Y., & Veiga, J. F. (2006). Ambidexterity and performance in small- to medium-sized firms: The pivotal role of top management team behavioral integration. *Journal of Management, 32*, 646−672.

Lux, S., Crook, T. R. & Woehr, D. (2011). Mixing business with politics: A meta-analysis of the antecedents and outcomes of corporate political activity. *Journal of Management, 37*, 223−247.

March, J. G. (1991). Exploration and exploitation in organizational learning. *Organization Science, 2*, 71−87.

Markowitz, H. M. (1952). Portfolio selection. *Journal of Finance, 7*, 77−91.

Markowitz, H. M., Todd, G. P., & Sharpe, W. F. (2000). *Mean-variance analysis in portfolio choice and capital markets*. New York, NY: Wiley.

Martins, L. L., & Kambil, A. (1999). Looking back and thinking ahead: Effects of prior success on managers' interpretations of new information technologies. *Academy of Management Journal, 42*, 652−661.

Menguc, B., & Auh, S. (2008). The asymmetric moderating role of market orientation on the ambidexterity-firm performance relationship for prospectors and defenders. *Industrial Marketing Management, 37*, 455−470.

Meyer, A. D. (1991). What is strategy's distinctive competence? *Journal of Management, 17*, 821−833.

O'Reilly, C. A., & Tushman, M. L. (2004). The ambidextrous organization. *Harvard Business Review, 82*, 74–83.

O'Reilly, C. A., & Tushman, M. L. (2007). *Ambidexterity as a dynamic capability: Resolving the innovator's dilemma.* Cambridge, MA: Harvard Business School.

Peteraf, M. (1993). The cornerstones of competitive advantage: A resource-based view. *Strategic Management Journal, 14*, 179–191.

Piao, M. (2010). Thriving in the new: Implication of exploration on organizational longevity. *Journal of Management, 36*, 1529–1554.

Porter, M. E. (1980). *Competitive Strategy.* New York, NY: Free Press.

Prahalad, C. K., & Hamel, G. (1990). The core competence of the corporation. *Harvard Business Review, 68*, 71–91.

Raisch, S., & Birkinshaw, J. (2008). Organizational ambidexterity: Antecedents, outcomes, and moderators. *Journal of Management, 34*, 375–409.

Raisch, S., Birkinshaw, J., Probst, G., & Tushman, M. L. (2009). Organizational ambidexterity: Balancing exploitation and exploration for sustained performance. *Organization Science, 20*, 685–695.

Richard, P., Devinney, T., Yip. G. & Johnson. G. (2009). Measuring organizational performance: Towards methodological best practice. *Journal of Management, 35*, 718–804.

Rosenbusch, N., Brinckmann, J. & Bausch, A. (2011). Is innovation always beneficial? A meta-analysis of the relationship between innovation and performance in SMEs. *Journal of Business Venturing, 26*, 441–457.

Rosenkopf, L., & Nerkar, A. (2001). Beyond local search: Boundary-spanning, exploration, and impact in the optical disk industry. *Strategic Management Journal, 22*, 287–306.

Rosenthal, R. (1979). The file drawer problem and tolerance for null results. *Psychological Bulletin, 86*, 638–641.

Rothaermel, F. T. (2001). Incumbent's advantage through exploiting complementary assets via interfirm cooperation. *Strategic Management Journal, 22*, 687–699.

Rothaermel, F. T., & Deeds, D. L. (2004). Exploration and exploitation alliances in biotechnology: A system of new product development. *Strategic Management Journal, 25*, 201–221.

Schumpeter, J. (1934). *The theory of economic development.* Cambridge: Harvard University Press.

Simsek, Z. (2009). Organizational ambidexterity: Towards a multilevel understanding. *Journal of Management Studies, 46*, 597–624.

Song, M., Podoynitsyna, K., Van Der Bij, H. & Halman, J. I. M. (2008). Success factors in new ventures: A meta-analysis. *Journal of Product Innovation Management, 25*, 7–27.

Taylor, K. (2012). Entrepreneurs who turned service into a career. *Forbes.*

Teece, D. J., Pisano, G., & Shuen, A. (1997). Dynamic capabilities and strategic management. *Strategic Management Journal, 18*, 509–533.

Uotila, J., Maula, M., Keil, T., & Zahra, S. A. (2009). Exploration, exploitation, and financial performance: Analysis of S&P 500 corporations. *Strategic Management Journal, 30*, 221–231.

Venkatraman, N., Lee, C. H., & Iyer, B. (2007). *Strategic ambidexterity and sales growth: A longitudinal test in the software sector.* Unpublished Work (earlier version presented at the Academy of Management Meetings, 2005).

Voss, G. B., & Voss, Z. G. (2012). Strategic ambidexterity in small and medium-sized enterprises: Implementing exploration and exploitation in product and market domains. *Organization Science* (In press).

Voss, G. B., & Voss, Z. G. (2013). Strategic ambidexterity in small and medium-sized enterprises: Implementing exploration and exploitation in product and market domains. *Organization Science, 24*, 1459–1477.

Wang, H., & Li, J. (2008). Untangling the effects of overexploration and overexploitation on organizational performance: The moderating role of environmental dynamism. *Journal of Management, 34*, 925–951.

Zahra, S. A., & Hayton, J. C. (2008). The effect of international venturing on firm performance: The moderating influence of absorptive capacity. *Journal of Business Venturing, 23*, 195–220.

Zollo, M., & Winter, S. G. (2002). Deliberate learning and the evolution of dynamic capabilities. *Organization Science, 13*, 339–351.

CHAPTER 13

JUGGLING EXPLORATORY AND EXPLOITATIVE LEARNING WITH DYNAMIC NETWORKS IN THE EARLY DAYS OF SMALL COMPANIES

Jordi Comas

ABSTRACT

Networks and learning matter to small- and medium-sized enterprises (SMEs). Networks and learning are also further elaborations on the exploration−exploitation (EE) dilemma. Ambidexterity, that is, managing this apparent dilemma, can be difficult as a result of many constraints. One of these constraints is that of mutually exclusive network structures. Consequently, ambidexterity is the ability to change networks, depending on need using mixed data on four small companies formed as part of an undergraduate management class, I hypothesize how specific network properties of the advice-seeking relationship, including density, cohesion, centralization, and embeddedness, affect two outcomes. Specifically, early exploratory learning is proposed to be positively affected by less-dense networks that maintain cohesion without

Exploration and Exploitation in Early Stage Ventures and SMEs
Technology, Innovation, Entrepreneurship and Competitive Strategy, Volume 14, 319−357
Copyright © 2014 by Emerald Group Publishing Limited
All rights of reproduction in any form reserved
ISSN: 1479-067X/doi:10.1108/S1479-067X20140000014011

centralization and do not have relations embedded in other relations. In contrast, later exploitative learning should be associated with denser networks that also have higher cohesion, higher centralization, and greater embeddedness. The results provide some support for these hypotheses and suggest further research in two areas that will benefit SMEs. One, how do early networks affect learning mode? Two, how does the ability to rewire networks provide the relational infrastructure to shift from exploration to exploitation — that is, to be ambidextrous in the face of the exploration—exploitation tradeoff?

Keywords: Social networks; exploration; exploitation; learning; ideas

INTRODUCTION

This chapter analyzes how learning and networks within an organization can constitute a form of the exploration—exploitation tension. For this analysis, two key theoretical steps are required. First, exploration and exploitation are defined as types of learning. Second, social networks, especially those that involve advice-seeking, affect organizational learning because learning depends on knowledge flows, skills, and common understanding to solve problems.

Instead of within-firm learning, research on organizational learning and networks in SMEs has primarily examined the regional, innovation, and performance implications of interorganizational networks (Gronum, Verreynne, & Kastelle, 2012; Human & Provans, 1997; Powell, Kenneth, & Smith-Doerr, 1996). One reason for the lack of attention to intrafirm learning may be data scarcity; measuring learning requires not simply a sampling of success but also of unused knowledge, failures, and forgetting. Although some researchers focus on interfirm networks as one strategy for balancing exploration and exploitation (Lavie, 2007; Wadhwa & Kotha, 2006), my focus is on within-organization networks. However, this focus draws on the research on interfirm networks. Research on how interfirm networks affect small firms establishes a key concept: knowledge diversity as a function of network diversity. A pivotal study on regions and firm clusters is that of Saxenian (1990) who finds that the diversity of ties in Silicon Valley leads to diversity of knowledge. Extending this finding to intrafirm networks is the basis of the theory in this chapter. This builds on the ideas of social capital and value creation as elaborated by Tsai and

Ghoshal (1998); however, their work and the empirical research spawned by it tend to focus on intrafirm value creation in large firms. SMEs, by the nature of their size and tendency to be start-ups, are even more reliant on less-formal knowledge structures, such as interpersonal networks, as opposed to large firms, which are likely to have formalized knowledge management, learning units, tools, artifacts, and dedicated personnel (Jetter, 2006). Recent meta-analysis by Rosenbusch, Brinckmann, and Bausch (2011) challenges much of the literature on entrepreneurs and social capital that finds external networks are critical to performance; on the contrary, Rosenbusch et al. find that internal innovation has more of an impact, whereas those entrepreneurs with external partners "have no significant impact" (p. 442).

March's (1991) insight about the trade-offs of exploration and exploitation [EE] actually contains two key assumptions. First, an organization is a set of individual decision makers who collectively seek to adapt by problem-solving with respect to the environment. Second, this collectivity can exhibit different modes of learning, and a given mode is more adaptive to the environment. Thus, adaptation is learning about a changing environment. These modes are exploration and exploitation. For these reasons, I begin my analysis of the EE dilemma as one of organizational learning. March's (1991) article concludes with the formulation of the classic and apparent dilemma of organizational learning: organizations can either explore or exploit, but they cannot maximize both simultaneously. The trade-offs and the dilemma crystallize – for scholars and practitioners alike – key issues about the tricky dynamics of learning, organization, and performance. The heart of the issue, as March and others observe (Tushman & O'Reilly III, 1996), is that adaptation and performance may depend on the ability to balance the tradeoff, the zero-sum game. For example, Levinthal and March (1993) argue that "The basic problem confronting an organization is to engage in sufficient exploitation to ensure its current viability and, at the same time, to devote enough energy to exploration to ensure future viability" (p. 105). In reviewing the impact of knowledge on SMEs in 173 studies, Macpherson and Holt (2007) arrive at a similar conclusion:

> To further complicate matters, the formalization of such systems may create rigidities that, while they can improve knowledge transfer and exploitation, can stifle small firm flexibility and responsiveness. Moreover, the research on organizational systems and their usefulness as knowledge management tools is inconclusive. It does little to explore which specific systems can support exploitation and exploration and how the tensions between them can be addressed (p. 181).

Returning to the EE dilemma, I note that it is "apparent" because not long after its articulation, the corollary of ambidexterity was developed and researched (Lavie, Stettner, & Tushman, 2010). March's original insight is a good simulation; subsequent research examines those insights in empirical settings and finds that some organizations find ways to balance, negotiate, or manage the dilemma. The extent to which explore—exploit is a dilemma depends on the extent to which resources are themselves binary substitutions. Some of these resources are time, attention, material assets, skills embedded in people, and forms of collective learning (Lavie et al., 2010). Lavie et al. (2010) critique some studies of EE for not using a single measure of the two activities (p. 117). In this chapter, the two are measured as the mode of learning. Moreover, Lavie et al. (2010) also note the importance of not simply assuming that antecedents or constraints on exploitation and exploration are necessarily direct trade-offs. The network properties discussed here are all direct trade-offs.

In this chapter, I suggest and explore a new way of exploring/exploiting: social networks. Networks are relationships that are the conduits or links traversed by interaction and information (Cross & Borgatti, 2004). Thus, as I will argue, managing the explore—exploit tension is in part a problem of managing networks. Social networks and knowledge are both theoretically and empirically linked (Borgatti & Cross, 2003). Granovetter's "strength of weak ties" thesis can be understood as a function of networks and knowledge: knowledge diversity is greater among network ties beyond one's strongest (and thus, reciprocated) ties (Granovetter, 1973). In fact, network ties are implicit in any extension of the original EE thesis: the individual agents in March's simulation somehow aggregate knowledge of their environment; agents, if they are like humans, must communicate through connections. Furthermore, specific network properties are by definition binary substitutions. We can imagine that a very cohesive network reinforces norms; this is the basis of the voluminous literature on positive benefits to social capital (Coleman, 1988). Conversely, a network that is connected, but with lower overall cohesion — that is, a network rich in "structural holes" — may maximize knowledge variety (Burt, 2005). Like the trade-offs of exploring and exploiting, a network cannot be simultaneously cohesive and rich in structural holes. For SMEs, the network face of the EE dilemma is likely to be more acute. By the nature of their size, responsiveness to their environment, and greater focus on a narrower set of strategic and operational problems, SMEs are more like the agent-based model at the heart of March's initial study than are large firms (Rosenbusch et al., 2011).

In this chapter, I develop the idea of the network-learning constraint in the EE dilemma into two research questions. First, are particular network properties associated with exploring or exploiting? In general, I assume that exploring and exploiting are organizational learning activities; I focus on how knowledge is acquired and shared and how acquisition and sharing are the basis of finding solutions to an organization's perceived problems (Argote, McEvily, & Reagans, 2003). This approach is pragmatic in the sense that it focuses both on what members see as problems and on the subsequent deployment of solutions (Schulz, 2002). Second, given a dynamic environment, ambidexterity – that is, the capacity to manage, balance, or juggle the demands of the EE dilemma – is associated with changing the networks. In other words, network rewiring can enable shifts in learning.

Although simulation studies still seem to be popular for investigating networks and the EE thesis (Fang, Lee, & Schilling, 2010), in this chapter, I take advantage of an unusual setting to capture data of simultaneous processes of learning and network formation. These processes are similar in the founding of any small organization. Management 101 is an undergraduate course at a private, liberal-arts university in which four quasi-random sets of 30 students create organizations that traverse typical stages of creation and formalization. The four companies of this study are quasi-random because their membership is based on the students' independent course registration. Reading early papers from all of the participants reinforced that they overwhelmingly experienced being in a roomful of strangers. These organizations are not simulations. They are real because they create and sell a product that funds a service project. Although from any objective viewpoint, the stakes involved are not high (the companies usually borrow and pay back a few thousand dollars), the experience for those in the companies is both intense and consequential. The data relate to SMEs because the studied companies exhibit some similarities. They are populated with new members who face what they perceive as a series of linked and unstructured problems. They rely on past experience, knowledge, and contacts to address these problems. Formal roles are in flux. Networks of advice, communication, and friendship are also in flux. Using qualitative data, I assess whether the students, who over the course of the company adopt many roles, see their work and learning as exploration or exploitation.

The research follows a mixed-method design, a rarity in studies of SMEs: only 5% of the studies that are the subject of Macpherson and Holt (2007) meta-analysis use this method (p. 176). The choice of design is largely driven by the complexities of studying learning over time and across levels; to study the coevolution of networks and learning requires longitudinal network data and the ability to "zoom in on and zoom out from" how networks and individuals are related (Ibarra, Kilduff, & Tsai, 2005). To zoom in and out, this study includes two data sets. One contains quantitative measures of three networks (advice, communication, and friendship) at the beginning and end of the companies. The second contains qualitative data from several sources about the activities and experiences of the company members, both individually and collectively. The qualitative data includes student-written papers (resulting from an assignment requesting that they tell their stories in explicit behavioral terms), company-produced documents, my own observations, and interviews with students, TAs, and professors. (I am not a member of the teaching faculty.) I combined the two data sets into cases that integrated time-specific network observations and qualitative data. By looking within and across the four companies as cases in reasonably similar environments, I analyzed the two research questions.

In the remainder of this chapter, I develop hypotheses emerging from the two research questions. Then, I discuss the methods and research setting in more detail. I present the results and finally discuss some implications for organizational learning and networks, both in general and in the case of SMEs.

THEORY DEVELOPMENT

Networks for Exploration or Exploitation

The initial article that spawned this research stream is worth revisiting for the originality of its insights (March, 1991). From a simulation of interacting individuals and an organizational code of routines and collective knowledge, March concludes that knowledge transfer is quicker among people who interact more; however, an organization learns more about its environment when people learn more slowly than the organization does. Overall, March's results from the simulation establish the core idea that a greater equilibrium of accurate knowledge about an external environment is observed when *some* learners are stubborn (heterogeneity of learning speed) and when the organization is pliable (learns quickly from members). However, March's article does not specify any entity between individuals and organizations. In other words, to generalize, there are no groups, networks or other internal organizing elements. Nor does it address each individual's variable social position. These gaps are precisely where we can insert the concept of the network. The network links learners to each other within an organization so that the organization is not simply an aggregate of individuals. Moreover, network position determines access to relevant flows for learning, whether those flows involve information, influence, or affinity.

In general, many forms of knowledge creation or use are associated with better SME performance. Penrose's premise that firm growth depends on knowledge creation and usage sets the stage for exploring this relationship (Penrose, 1959). Researchers have found evidence of this relationship. For example, Mansury and Love (2008) find a positive relationship between innovation and growth for service-oriented SMEs. In a study of British manufacturing firms, Spicer and Sadler-Smith (2006) find that organizational learning has a positive impact on both financial and nonfinancial performance. A review of the literature by Macpherson and Holt (2007) finds 113 articles addressing the link between knowledge and small-firm performance. One conclusion they draw is that knowledge is too often treated as a static asset. They make a suggestion, which I follow, that researchers conceptualize knowledge as a relational construct (p. 185). More generally, they document that evidence of support for growth depends on other factors such as external and internal social capital (networks) and knowledge systems. This supports this study's approach of looking at the interaction between networks and learning. Rosenbusch et al.'s (2011) meta-analysis of innovation, similar to knowledge and learning activities, finds strong support for the notion that innovation benefits outweigh costs for SMEs. Those authors caution, however, that the manner in which SMEs pursue innovation matters. For example, innovation process and orientation matter more than direct spending on products (p. 452).

However, given the lack of a general theory of networks and learning for SMEs, I use the more general case of learning and networks in organizations to develop hypotheses and to discuss where SME research links to the general case. Regardless of an organization's size or age, scholars have demonstrated that organizations engage in exploratory or exploitative learning (Benner & Tushman, 2003; Gavetti & Levinthal, 2000; He & Wong, 2004; Levinthal & March, 1993; March, 1991). Exploration is "… experimentation with new alternatives. Its returns are uncertain, distant, and often negative" (March, 1991, p. 85). Moreover, the essence of exploitation is "the refinement and extension of existing competences, technologies, and paradigms. Its returns are positive, proximate, and predictable" (March, 1991, p. 85). Recent work has continued to use this definition. "In general, exploration is associated with organic structures, loosely coupled systems, path breaking, improvisation, autonomy and chaos, and emerging technologies and markets. Exploitation is associated with mechanistic structures, tightly coupled systems, path dependence, routinization, control and bureaucracy, and stable markets and technologies" (He & Wong, 2004, p. 481). These findings are paralleled in research on SMEs. For example, several studies focus on enhancing efficiency, including hard and soft technology deployment (such as ISO 9000) (Davig & Brown, 1992; Ghobadian, Mole, & O'Regan, 2003; Mole, Ghobadian, O'Regan, & Liu, 2004). In terms of exploration, SME researchers have found communication practices that support information exchange (Terziovski, 2002). Additionally, Young, Sapienza, and Baumer (2003) describe how flexibility in interfirm relationships allows access to new knowledge, encourages knowledge exploration, and contributes to increased productivity.

This chapter relies on a synthesis of organizational learning and understanding networks as relational structures. Important statements of the relational perspective include Wellman's (1988) argument that behavior be should interpreted "… in terms of structural constraints on activity rather than in terms of inner forces within units" (Wellman, 1988, p. 20). Structural analysis as a type of third way through the thicket of person−structure dualism is echoed in Burt's (1992) opening salvo: "People and organizations are not the source of action so much as they are vehicles for structurally induced action" (p. 5). Relationalism is a theoretical orientation that threads the needle between over- and under-socialized views of people and actions. To assemble a definition of networks as relational structures with organizational learning, I propose that we imagine learning as a knowledge flow through a network of conduits. This is the same as the "network flow" model that Borgatti and Halgin (2011) have advocated as the central model in network research.

This definition of learning as flows through networks enables a theory of networks and learning based on the research literature. In general, this theory relies on the amount of variation in knowledge resulting from network properties. A perfectly connected network will tend towards knowledge homogeneity. A disconnected network, really, atomized individuals, has the largest possible variety of knowledge (however, whether such a formation would even qualify as an organization is unresolved). Because exploration includes search, variation, experimentation, play, and so on, knowledge should be distributed unevenly, otherwise there will not be enough requisite variation to sustain the exploration. Since Granovetter's finding about the strength of weak ties, scholars have found that knowledge variation is a function of network heterogeneity (Reagans & McEvily, 2003).

As multiple actors combine and create knowledge, the overall knowledge variation of an entire company is maintained to the extent that those actors and subgroups are neither closely nor redundantly linked. This idea is echoed in research on organizational learning. Argote et al. (2003) write: "When properties of units, properties of relationships and properties of knowledge fit or are congruent with each other, knowledge retention, and transfer increase. Knowledge creation, by contrast, may be stimulated by a lack of congruence or parts that do not fit together" (p. 580). Conversely, because exploitation includes efficiency, selection, implementation and refinement, knowledge flows, and stocks that are too diverse or disparate will impede the efficient application of new knowledge. For example, Collins (1988) states: "The more tightly that individuals are tied into a network, the more they are affected by group standards." This general insight extends to other aspects of groups such as the amount of common knowledge or common understanding of problems the group faces. Collins and other early social capital researchers tend to use simple density as a sufficient measure of networks. Some empirical evidence for this tradeoff can be found in work by Yli-Renko, Autio, and Sapienza (2001). Those authors conclude that tie strength is inversely correlated to knowledge acquisition in UK technology firms; strong ties are correlated with less knowledge acquisition even though knowledge acquisition itself affects performance. Moreover, weaker ties lead to more firm-enhancing knowledge acquisition. Their explanation is the same: strong ties lead to knowledge redundancy.

Therefore, we can imagine a series of properties whose differences diminish or amplify exploration and exploitation because they affect the creation, retention, or transfer of knowledge. Kilduff and Tsai (2003, p. 30) describe four key network-level properties that are important to this discussion: density, reachability, centralization, and balance. In addition to Kilduff and Tsai's four properties, I consider two other properties to be relevant to organizational learning: clustering (Watts, 1999) and embedding (Granovetter, 1985; Uzzi, 1997). Thus, for SMEs, these six properties are key network properties. By definition, they are also mutually exclusive. Each of these six properties can be found in the literature affecting learning in some manner, either singly or in conjunction with other network properties. But, consistent with the complexity of organizational learning, we should look holistically at networks and not just focus on one property, such as density. Accordingly, I do not break down each property as it relates to exploration or exploitation, but rather, look at them as a particular configuration (Meyer, 1993).

Next, I review how these properties have been discussed in the literature as affecting organizational learning.

Density and reachability, for example, appear in Mizruchi and Brewster-Stearns' (2001) work examining two networks (approval and information-seeking) to predict bankers' ability to close deals. Although the predictive ability of information networks is unclear, this is not the case for approval networks: "sparsely connected groups are likely to contain a wider range of views and expertise than are more densely connected groups. This means that ideas supported by members of low-density groups will tend to have received more criticism and questioning and will benefit from a greater range of insights" (p. 653).

Centralization appears in Perry-Smith and Shalley's (2003) discussion of how creativity is most helped by having weak ties as opposed to strong ties — but only to a point. Too many ties can distract a creative person. Furthermore, being creative tends to make a person central, which sets up a type of tension reminiscent of exploration–exploitation tension.

Balance and clustering are both forms of cohesion. Balance can be observed over a network in terms of clique overlap or separation. Cliques overlap due to more closure in triads — the definition of balance. The value of cliques of overlapping, strong ties is demonstrated in Provan and Sebastian (1998). They find that effectiveness in organizational networks of mental health agencies decreases with overall integration but increases where cliques have high rates of multiplex overlaps. In short, a very cohesive network does not do as well as one that has less cohesion but a greater variety of types of clique members. I rely on clustering to capture the same idea of balance. Similar to balance, clustering is a measure of the amount of local closure that a network has (Watts, 1999). In other words, when looking at each person, the clustering coefficient measures the number of alters of that ego that are themselves tied or linked. This is conceptually similar to structural holes and their measurement (Latora, Nicosia, & Panzarasa, 2013).

Embeddedness is a familiar concept due to the impact of Granovetter (1985) and Uzzi (1997) in advancing our appreciation of nonmarket forces on firms that cause unexpected results. Uzzi's (1997) study of fashion firms, themselves SMEs, finds that even though such firms seek out strong, trust-based relationships to be competitive, those same close ties could paradoxically be a liability, leading him to describe the problem of "over-embeddedness." The problem is most evident for firms that rely too exclusively on purely economic ties embedded in other relationships. He proposes, in the language of institutional economics, that the best option for such firms is a variety of arm's length and embedded relationships (see p. 59). Again, we see that relational diversity affects performance.

Beyond looking at each property in isolation, we can also find evidence that specific configurations of multiple properties shape learning. Oh, Chung, and Labianca (2004), in their study of Korean work teams, find that: "The optimal configuration of informal socializing ties within a group is a moderate level of internal closure, whereas the optimal configuration of these groups across groups is a large number of bridging relationships to other group's leaders" (p. 869). Here, we see the benefits of balancing network configurations. A second confirmation comes from Reagans and Zuckerman's (2001) study of 224 corporate research and development teams. They find that "... A team that does not develop the connections among their members that enable it to coordinate effectively faces an uphill battle. However, when such networks remain concentrated among homogeneous sets of individuals, the team fails to generate the learning that can only come from interaction among different individuals" (p. 513). We can see that their results contribute to the idea that knowledge variation is a function of human networks in which greater cohesion and redundancy of links reduces variation, and the converse holds as well. From the research, then, I propose that particular network properties are associated with exploratory learning and their converse, with exploitative learning.

H1a. Network properties of lower density, lower cohesion, lower centralization, and less embedding will lead to exploring (exploratory organizational learning).

H1b. Network properties of higher density, higher cohesion, higher centralization, and more embedding will lead to exploiting (exploitative organizational learning).

A persistent challenge for organizations is how to balance competing needs for exploratory and exploitative learning with their own conscious and serendipitous engagement with each. There are some ways to escape the EE dilemma (Lavie et al., 2010). For example, Gupta, Smith, and Shalley (2006) rely on their conceptualization of continuity or orthogonality and number of domains to resolve this question (p. 698). They argue that when there is a continuous relationship in a single domain, logic dictates a punctuated equilibrium. When there is an orthogonal relationship across multiple domains, then ambidexterity is logical. Finally, using the semiconductor business as an example of an industry in which there is total specialization into fabrication firms (exploitation) and research and development firms (exploration), they argue that there are times and places (again, a contingency argument) in which specialization makes more sense than doomed attempts at ambidexterity (p. 699). Logically, a second solution to the EE dilemma is the combination of size and division of labor. A larger organization with specialized units can assign some to explore and others to exploit. However, to the extent that an entire organization needs to capture the knowledge of its environment and the learning that is inherent in adaptation, this strategy may have limits. Greater size or differentiation will cause new needs for communication and coordination whose costs may overwhelm any gains from the initial growth or specialization. A second solution is for managers to switch resources or capacities over time – to explore today and exploit tomorrow, as needed. However, this solution also has limits. Resources and capacities may be "sticky" and difficult to redeploy directly. This limitation is magnified for those resources and capacities that are behavioral, tacit, or otherwise embedded in an organization's social structures.

Networks are a new means of resolving the EE dilemma hinted at in the research. Levitt and March (1988) suggest researching networks and learning in their now-seminal article: "This diffusion of experience and routines from other organizations within a community of organizations complicates theories of routine-based learning. It suggests that understanding the relationship between experiential learning and routines, strategies, or technologies in organizations will require attention to organizational networks …" (p. 327). Although Levitt and March focus on interorganizational networks, diffusion and experience are also important within organizations. In March's (1991) modeling, the way to achieve ambidexterity – a "sweet spot" of balancing exploration and exploitation – is through simply having a heterogeneous mix of learners. Recently, interest in network analysis and organizational learning has been growing. Oh et al. (2004), in a study of group social capital and group effectiveness, write: "Thus, an increasingly complex and uncertain business environment has made understanding how individual group members manage this delicate balance of social relationships within their group, across organizational units, and across hierarchical levels increasingly important" (p. 860). Thus, with this constraint, there is now a third avenue for pursuing ambidexterity in exploration and exploitation: dynamic networks.

Substantial research has shown that various outcomes are improved or optimized when organizations balance the types of compromises implicit in the exploration–exploitation tradeoff (Brown & Eisenhardt, 1998; Ghemawat & Costa I Ricart, 1993; Tushman & O'Reilly III, 1996). A study of Korean work teams explicitly sets out to empirically test the "ambidex-trous" organization (He & Wong, 2004). The idea of the ambidextrous organization is that it can switch from exploration to exploitation as needed. However, it is not always easy to do this. Mizruchi and Stearns (2001) find a strategic paradox because bankers turn to strong ties for information gathering even though weaker ties lead to a higher probability of approval. The higher probability of bank deal approval is attributed to exposure to the inherently more diverse perspectives of the sparser network. The exploratory nature of sparser networks yields higher benefits even as bankers tend to exploit close ties for information gathering. This finding is replicated for SMEs by researchers attempting to identify optimal network structures in a dynamic environment (Fukugawa, 2006; Kleinbaum & Tushman, 2007; Pirolo & Presutti, 2010). Rather than a universal solution, the researchers find that there is a shift: weaker ties should be emphasized during the exploration or idea generation phase, whereas engaging strong ties is most appropriate for implementing or exploiting innovation.

There is a double contingency at work in the network-learning nexus. First, an organization's learning is contingent on its external environment; second, an organization's learning is contingent on its network of social relations, the enacted environment. For this reason, learning means that adaptation is in some sense not only adapting to an external environment but also adapting to an environment that is enacted by the very actions of the organization and its members. Negotiating the double contingency of learning-environment and learning-networks is neither straightforward nor simple. Ahuja (2000) suggests that due to variations in contingency needs, there is no universal optimal network structure. Although being explora-tory may be more adaptive or optimal long term, exploration is often crowded out by the short-term pursuit of exploitation (March, 1991). March describes how short-term adaptive pressures for survival, such as revenue growth, make taking on the less-defined process of exploratory learning difficult. For example, Weick and Westley (1996) discuss organiza-tional learning as an oxymoron. They assert that learning is about creating variation and organizing is about limiting variation for action. A parallel depiction is found in Cook and Brown's (1999) discussion of the "genera-tive dance" between knowledge and knowing, between epistemologies of possession and practice. Another example of this process is found in Hargadon and Fanelli's (2002) model of cycling between latent and explicit knowledge: "The generation of new knowledge or the successful replication of old knowledge depends not on the latent knowledge held by individuals nor the empirical knowledge of their surrounds, but rather on the cyclic

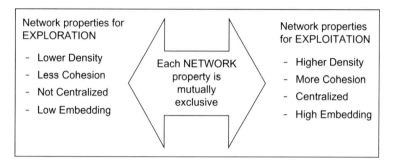

Fig. 1.   Network Properties as Exploration–Exploitation Trade-Offs.

interaction between the two, between the 'energy' that resides in latent knowledge and the 'matter' of empirical knowledge."

In Fig. 1 we can see the exploration–exploitation trade-offs in terms of binary choices in network properties. Ultimately, the question of adaption of a given organization is in part contingent on its environment, and this holds equally for intraorganizational networks.

H2. Dynamic networks will be associated with ambidexterity contingent on environmental pressure for exploration or exploitation.

RESEARCH SETTING

Management 101 companies are double-bottom-line organizations by design; they seek to maximize profit and community impact as they encounter three management themes: efficiency, effectiveness, and community (Comas, Hiller, & Miller, 2005). The companies they form are naturally deeply enmeshed in the culture and reality of life at a private, residential, liberal-arts college. The organizations are short-lived. Their success requires that a host of ideas arise and decisions occur within their evolving networks. The perception of many observers and participants over the last 25 years has been that the Management 101 companies are very dynamic organizations with both a wide variety of measurable outcomes and intersubjective perspectives and narratives. The 120 students in Management 101 are assigned to one of the four companies based on each student's selection of a course time. The student companies are largely left to evolve and develop on their own. A non-exhaustive list of major activities includes the following: managing stakeholders, developing products, marketing, requesting a loan, designing an organization, evaluating co-workers and subordinates, paying taxes, and coping with a variety of unforeseen challenges. While pursuing all of these tasks, relations (and thus, networks) are forming through instrumental and serendipitous processes (Kilduff & Tsai, 2003). Simultaneously, these tasks are responsive to their immediate environment and require the development, deployment, and refinement of knowledge; they are a means of adaptation.

From reading papers written during the first week of the class, it is clear that with a few exceptions, the students consider themselves to be in a group of relative strangers. They may know a few people or have a roommate in the class, but for the most part they are acutely aware that "everyone" in their class is a relative unknown. This is the source of my argument that the companies are emerging networks. The data bear out this presumption. The networks demonstrate a marked increase in connectivity, variation in overall shape, and low correlations of networks from initial measurement to final measurement.

Several scholars, especially in the fields of psychology and organizational behavior, have conducted experiments and simulations involving students. Argote and Ophir (2002) list five such studies out of thirteen seminal empirical studies in the field of organizational learning. For knowledge retention, Cohen and Bacdayan (1994), in a test of routines using a card-playing game, find that novel routines as new game rules slow down performance and experimentally confirm that routines are more behavioral than cognitive. For knowledge transfer, in a study quite similar in research design to this chapter, Gruenfeld, Martorana, and Fan look at a semester-long simulation of complex tasks and find that members who move between groups carry ideas with them, resulting in a greater variety of ideas, but that their ideas are less likely to be adopted (2000).

METHODS

Mixed Methods to Build Cases

This study used a mixed-method research design combining a quantitative analysis of networks and a qualitative analysis of archival, interview, and observational data (Ragin, 1987; Tasakkori & Teddle, 2003). Both analyses were fed into a cross-case analysis of the four companies (Eisenhardt, 1989;

Yin, 1994). The original research was not per se formulated to examine exploration and exploitation but more generally was formulated to study the coevolution of networks and learning. I developed cases of learning that unfolded in each company using standard qualitative techniques. Network analyses were conducted independently. These analyses of whether and to what degree a company's learning is exploratory or exploitative were then used to compare each company's learning to that of the other companies.

The categories of exploratory and exploitative learning emerged out of this analysis. I focused on the number of ideas, the longevity of ideas, uniqueness of ideas to the company, and the specific quality of radical or incremental knowledge involved. The last measure was context-dependent. To cope with the context-dependency, I relied on consultations with knowledgeable insiders (professors and TAs) and had them code ideas to check for consistency. They categorized the ideas as radical or incremental with 90% consistency.

Network Methods

The advice-seeking relationship in the Management 101 companies was the primary network under study because this relationship is critical for the creation and diffusion of organizational knowledge in the service of learning (Cross & Borgatti, 2004; Levinthal & March, 1993). Organizational learning is driven by the necessities confronted by members facing a range of both foreseen and emergent problems. These relationships are more important than simple communication flows because communication flows can be motivated by reporting requirements, problem-seeking, political maneuvering, and so on. A person may communicate with another frequently or intensely for reasons other than seeking key information to solve salient problems. Therefore, I primarily analyzed the observed problem-solving (advice) relationship. Communication captured, in part, the design of an organization and its subgroups because the question specifically addressed instrumental communication. Friendship relations capture the potential for affect to either mediate or constrain advice-seeking. Communication and friendship relationships were analyzed for embedding with advice-seeking. The survey was a full roster of the endogenous network. The network surveys used a 5-point Likert scale for questions regarding three relationships – communication, advice-seeking, and friendship. Where needed for certain analysis routines (i.e., where a dichotomous value was required), strong relationships were dichotomized at four or more.

- Communication relationship: With whom do you *directly* communicate (face-to-face, phone, email) as part of working at the company? (1 = Never, 3 = Occasionally [2–3 times a week], 5 = Frequent [multiple times/day].)
- Advice-seeking relationship: When you face a new problem or challenge related to any aspect of the company, who would you seek out for their input or advice (skipping yourself)? (1 = Never, 3 = Possible, 5 = Definite [first person I seek].)
- Friendship: How friendly have you become with each of the following people? (1 = Not very much, 3 = Somewhat (an acquaintance), 5 = Definite [a friend].)

Data were collected at two points. First, data were collected in the second week of the Management 101 class as small groups started to explore business and service projects. Second, data were collected at the end of the class after companies wrapped up their operations. Response rates for the network surveys varied and are presented in Table 1.

Missing data are a serious challenge to network research. It is a current area of interest among leading scholars (Stork & Richards, 1992). There are several possibilities for handling this problem. First, the researcher can delete the missing nodes thus lowering the total number of dyadic observations. I decided not to use this approach because I had small networks with a clear network-exogenous boundary: membership. It would have been quite cumbersome to possess qualitative data on particular ideas, events and individuals without corresponding network data. A second option for missing data is to estimate missing values using some reasonable rule

Table 1. Response Rates.

Company Identifier	Round 1	Round 2	Mean
OnTrack	58%	100%	79%
Inertia	68%	88%	78%
Backtrack	73%	90%	82%
Explorer	65%	97%	81%
Mean	66%	94%	
Mean for all companies, both rounds			80%

(Butts, 2003). I elected to estimate based on two rules derived from the underlying properties of the observed networks. Because of the partial nominations that resulted from using full roster surveys, the missing data were half of the total observations recorded. In other words, for a square network of N respondents, every actor had an $N-1$ length row of every possible nomination as well as an $N-1$ long column for every nomination received. A nonrespondent had an empty row of out-nominations but a partially filled column of in-nominations. To handle the missing data, I used a different technique for each type of data. First, there were respondent to nonrespondent links in which $x_i \rightarrow x_j$ was known, but $x_j \rightarrow x_i$ was not. For these, I assumed likely reciprocity and simulated missing data based on the observed reciprocity rate of the observed network. In the case of two nonrespondents (at most, 20% of a network) where $x_i \rightarrow x_j$ and $x_j \rightarrow x_i$ were unobserved, I used the density rate as the basis for a simulated network value. Thus, for example, in Company A, to impute missing values, the reciprocity rate was 35%, and the density was 7%. If George was a nonrespondent and Sue was a respondent who nominated George with a 4, a simulation would give George a reciprocal tie of the same strength with 35% probability. Meanwhile, for a tie between George and Andy, also a nonrespondent, the simulation of a strong tie used the underlying density rate of 7%.

Depending on the measure needed to examine a particular network property, particular iterations of the data are needed. In general, I tried to use measures that left the underlying data as unmodified as possible. When a binary, symmetric network was required, I symmetrized and dichotomized the relationships so that any combination that summed to eight (8) became a one (1) and all others were zero (0). These were strong ties. When a digraph was needed, that is, a network of asymmetric, binary relations, I simply dichotomized the network so that any value of four or greater was considered a strong relation. When valued graphs were required, I used the underlying full network of observed and imputed values (Table 2).

In sum, I pursued an open-ended, theory-building method in which qualitative and quantitative data were used recursively to develop ideas and concepts and then test the ideas against the four companies as cases.

Learning Measures

Recalling the definition of learning as creating and sharing solutions to problems, I needed a way to collect data that was likely to be ephemeral.

Table 2. Summary of Network Measures.

Network Property	Data Type and Description	Relationship to Learning
Density	Binary (strong advice) Number of links per node. A former student described how high density overwhelmed viable alternatives: "normally cliques kind of overwhelm it, especially when I took the class …"	Low density will reduce knowledge flows. High density will replicate or reinforce knowledge. Depending on the relationship, higher density may be the basis of greater identity or trust.
Cohesion as reachability	How reachable actors are to each other. Uses idea of shortest path (geodesic). Cohesion I – Binary (strong advice) Average number of links in strongest path (in this case, using strongest path as best to follow). Cohesion II – Valued digraph (advice) How close a network is to having *exactly* one link in all geodesic paths or to a network that is not cohesive (all isolates).	A more cohesive network allows for the spread and reinforcement of influence or ideas, so it will aid exploitation, whereas a less cohesive network promotes the incubation of ideas.
Cohesion as clustering coefficient	Binary (strong advice) The ratio of local (neighborhood) density of each actor relative to overall density. Higher ratios mean more clustering.	Few or no subgroups will limit exploratory learning and boost exploitative learning. Many subgroups will limit exploitative learning and boost exploratory learning.
Centralization	Binary (strong advice) The degree to which a network is centered on one individual (Freeman, 1979).	A centralized network will enjoy easier coordination and transfer of knowledge than will a more decentralized network.
Embeddedness	Valued, asymmetrical (for advice embedded in communication and advice embedded in friendship). The correlation of a tie, A→B in relation 1, when there is already a tie in relation 2.	High correlation between friendship and advice-seeking networks can reinforce idea flows while also suppressing variation. High correlation between communication and advice-seeking can reinforce idea flow while also suppressing variation.

To do this, I collected several types of data: student papers written at four points in the class, interviews with students and instructors, and archival material produced by the companies (such as company reports and plans). In addition students responded to an idea census at the same time network surveys were completed. The idea census was an open-ended grid asking a respondent to think of tasks, problems, or challenges (even if unsolved), possible solutions discussed (even if unused), and if possible, the source of the solution (i.e., the person or persons most associated). This form was modeled to encourage students to think broadly and not to hesitate to share hunches or impressions.

These results were used to validate archival and interview research, and vice versa. In addition, I made several observations of Management 101 classes, both in this semester and in others. Constant direct observation would have been preferable, but because the instructors were concerned about disruption of the class, approximately eight (8) hours of direct observations, evenly spaced across the semester, were recorded. The limited observations helped to ground my analysis of the other qualitative data. For this study, approximately 12 hours of interviews were conducted in addition to some follow-up interviews with instructors. For knowledge creation and transfer, I looked for specific ideas for projects, formal roles developed by the companies, procedures, and other concrete responses and actions.

For each company, I tracked the quality and number of ideas that had developed sufficiently to be included in the knowledge stocks available to members of the companies. I refer to these ideas as having been "in play" to capture the liminal state between being created and being retained (or adopted). For each company, I recorded the number of ideas, the number unique to that company, and the degree to which an idea was exploitative or exploratory in this context. An idea might have been unique to a company – for example, shot glasses – but not exploratory because it was repeated frequently by Management 101 companies over the class's 20-plus years of operation. Table 3 is an example of the type of data display I used to assemble insights and conclusions about each company's learning in accordance with widely used qualitative techniques (Miles & Huberman, 1994).

For these student-created companies, exploratory learning, dependent on new knowledge, was partially defined by the students' subjective perception and partially defined by how novel knowledge was (or was not, in the case of exploitation) in the Management 101 context. The service projects undertaken by the companies provided some of the clearest evidence of exploration. The companies were dependent on a community contact to develop

Table 3.   Sample Data Display of Early Learning.

Factor	Description
Number of ideas in play	Number of ideas viable enough to be observed or commented on by idea advocates or by other members of a company. A greater number indicates a more exploratory company.
Number unique to the company	Number of the above ideas that were in play for that company only. A greater number indicates a more exploratory company.
Number of unique ideas with longevity	Many ideas are dropped before decision day arrives. A unique idea that lasts until decision day has longevity. This ratio captures how many of the unique ideas (a sign of exploration) persisted.
Service project: final decision	Degree of unanimity plus assessment of decision as radical or incremental.
Business project: final decision	Degree of unanimity plus assessment of decision as radical or incremental.

and execute their service projects. More exploratory companies used this contact to develop more new knowledge and thus afford the possibility of more exploratory learning. At the same time, the potential downside of an exploratory network is evident in the service projects. If the project relied on one member's relation with the community contact, then learning was more likely to be confined to the local part of the company's network around that member. The learning may not flow well into the rest of the company. Further evidence of exploratory learning included the development of more novel business products, the design of the company, the application of new technologies (especially, in recent years, information technologies), the design of employee evaluation and incentive systems, the creation of internal routines, and the development of financial or business control systems. As appropriate, I discuss the evidence of exploratory or exploitative learning for each of these areas later.

Adaptation and Performance Measures

To capture adaptation, two measures were used. First, an adaptation score was calculated that was the average gap between stated objectives and accomplishments. As students shifted from forming a company to performing, they submitted elaborate operational plans to a supervisory board. These plans necessarily culminated in an intensive process of information gathering and knowledge creation captured in roles, new organizational units, plans, and routines. At the end of the class, the companies submitted a final report, which included reporting on the various objectives covered in the operational plans. These objectives were as follows: financial performance (revenue, break-even point), labor by company members, service hours by company members, time to sell out inventory, donations to service project, and costs. The average of each gap between the stated objective and the final realized outcome is the adaptation score. Looking at these variances, some of the measured objectives seem more likely to vary than others. For example, the revenue for most companies was straightforward because there was a fixed inventory and simple pricing scheme. Based on discussions with the course instructors, the following estimates were weighted to reflect their greater stochasticity and thus importance in capturing adaptation to environment: service hours, donations, time to sell out, and department costs. Therefore, a high score (close to 100%) reflected closeness between a given company's projections and its prior estimates. To be very effective in realizing one's plans is a measure of adaptation because it reflects that a company has been able to collect information about itself and its environment and successfully turn that information into working knowledge.

A second measure of adaptation was the score assigned by the instructors. This final grade for the company was also a multidimensional assessment. For example, students were evaluated in terms of effectiveness, efficiency, and community. Based on instructors' comments, I decomposed the company grade into the components so I could discuss which companies were seen as better at effectiveness and efficiency because those elements generally correspond to exploration and exploitation.

RESULTS

Initially, I present an overview of the findings. These summarize the results from the underlying cases with a high level of granularity. The results are based on more detailed analysis of both the networks and the performance of the four companies. After this overview, I present more detail on each of the four companies as a case; this reflects the iterative process of cross-case comparison. To provide a more general orientation, in Table 4, I summarize each of the four Management 101 companies' projects.

In Table 5 (a and b), we see that one of the four companies best fit the expectations of both network-learning hypotheses. The summaries in

Table 4. Overview of Each Company's Projects.

	Business Project	Service Project	Key Statement
A OnTrack	Exploratory: "Tooters" T-shirts	Exploratory: Two-part project for SAUL House (residence for the mentally challenged): Building library and renovating house	"Another company also decided to sell T-shirts, which put a lot of competitive pressure on us. In retaliation, we opted to move up our Business and Finance Operating Plans by one lab session, which would hopefully allow us to place our order first. Although that was a great idea in theory, it imposed very demanding time constraints on many members of the company." *We see an awareness of shifting from idea exploration to idea exploitation.*
B Late Exploit	Exploitative/mixed: T-shirts (very incremental) to be designed after the decision to proceed (riskier)	Exploratory: Renovating an after school program's facilities (YMCA)	"The departments and divisions made the company feel smaller. Company members were not working directly with 29 other people; instead, there were three to eight other people who shared a workload. These divisions became like a home within the company for everyone." *Here we see the tight cohesion within departments that cemented the more consistently exploitative learning.*
C Backtrack	Exploitative: Pint glasses	Exploitative: Habitat for Humanity	"… [A]t first everyone was very timid and shy. Nobody wanted to ruffle anybody's feathers. However, this only lasted a short time. The next phase was the appropriately named 'storming phase.' This was definitely a very stormy time within the company. As coalition groups began to develop, true personalities began to poke through some of the protective shells that had been built earlier in the semester." *The student is describing how a group tended to engage in productive tension and idea generation later in the company's life cycle.*
D Explorer	Exploitative/mixed: Baseball caps	Exploratory: Provide meals and support for families at Ronald McDonald house	"All companies will face many problems and have to find ways to get around them. A company's strength can be seen by how well they can attack a problem because no matter how good a company is doing financially, it is the crises that can tear a company apart." *The student is discussing that there is a new problem-solving sequence every time a problem comes up. The sense of novel solutions persisted throughout this company's life cycle.*

Table 5 draw on the raw data in Table 6. The network measures in Table 6 are analyzed two ways. First, for each company, I determine whether its network properties are more conducive to exploration or exploitation by comparing them with each other and with the core logic of the measure. In that case, cells are shaded when a measure is more conducive to exploration. Second, I examine the direction of the measure. If it moves from exploration to exploitation, I call it adaptive. So, for example, Company D was exploratory early in clustering (10.7%) and still is fairly exploratory at Time 2 (24.2%). Even though this fits H1 at T1, low clustering is conducive to knowledge variation; the trajectory is not adaptive.

Overall, Company A supports H1 because it is a dynamic network aligned to exploration initially that changes to aligned to exploitation later. Moreover, it supports H2 because it is the best in understanding its environment; it also performs the best on the global measure of effectiveness and efficiency. The other three companies provide partial support of the hypotheses. Let's begin with the company that started with the most promise. Company D began with network measures that were aligned towards exploration. We see that it is the second-best company in terms of anticipating its environment. However, it lacks the shift to a network better suited to exploit its knowledge. Company D and Company C, which also lack this shift, are essentially tied as the third and fourth worst-performing companies. Meanwhile, Company B, which performs the least well in predicting its environment, has the network that at the outset was least suited for exploration. This supports the hypothesis that initial exploratory networks do better at learning about their environments. However, B prevails over this difficulty when it comes to performing. Having exploitative network capabilities when shifting from planning to performance may explain its superior performance (clearly second) to the two companies that ended up with exploratory instead of exploitative network capabilities.

In general, there is moderate support for the proposition that the companies with changes in learning modes have more dynamic networks. As discussed below, there is also some evidence of a friction between learning intention and network structure. This friction is best explained by the congruence model that is employed where causality is not a deterministic trajectory from networks to learning or the other way around, but rather, networks and learning processes are a double contingency. For example, Late Exploit (B) and Backtrack (C) have fairly clear intentions to pursue more radical projects that would qualify as exploratory learning. In both cases, the will to explore clashes with the structure to exploit.

Table 5. Overview of Results.

	A OnTrack	B Late Exploit	C Backtrack	D Explorer
(a): H1: Networks shape learning				
Network properties (exploratory shaded) → type of learning (exploratory bolded)				
H1a: Exploratory networks at T1 lead to more exploratory learning	**5/7 network measures are exploratory**	2/7 network measures are exploratory	2/7 network measures are exploratory	**5/7 network measures are exploratory**
H1b: Exploitative networks at T2 lead to more exploitative learning	7/7 network measures are exploitative	6/7 network measures are exploitative	2/7 network measures are exploitative	3/7 network measures are exploitative
Learning summary	**Exploring** to Exploiting	Exploiting to Exploiting	Moderate Exploiting to Moderate **Exploring**	Moderate **Exploring** to **Exploring**
Number of ideas in play	10	13	**14**	**15**
Number unique to the company (proportion of total which more are radical)	**5 (50%)**	6 (46%)	5 (35%)	**5 (33%)**
Number of unique ideas with longevity	**4 (80%)**	**4 (50%)**	2 (40%)	**3 (60%)**
Confirms H1?	Strongly	Strongly	Moderately	Moderately

Table 5. (*Continued*)

(b): H2: Ambidextrous network→Adaptation (exploring bolded for clarity)

	A OnTrack	B Late Exploit	C Backtrack	D Explorer
H2: Companies with networks better matched to contingency of environment will perform better. Here, the environment expects a shift from exploration to exploitation	**Exploring** to Exploiting	Exploiting to Exploiting	Moderate Exploiting to Moderate **Exploring**	Moderate **Exploring** to **Exploring**
H2 Measure 1 – anticipating the environment	1st	4th	3rd	2nd
Adaptation by planning (100%= perfect prediction)	88%	66%	77%	83%
H2 Measure 2 – performance comments	Best on both measures	Second-best	Lacked exploitative capability because networks evolved incorrectly	Lacked exploitative capability. Network never developed exploitative capability
Effectiveness rank	1	2	3	4
Efficiency rank	1	2	4	3
Confirmation of H2	Strong	Moderate	Moderate	Moderate

A (OnTrack) and B (Late Exploit) Show Stronger Support

What is the evidence that particular network properties capable of exploiting or exploring? First, Company A, with the most exploratory network properties, was also the company doing the most exploring in the data on learning. Both of its final projects are innovative or unusual for Management 101 companies. Company A has the most persistent ideas in the initial stages, both overall and as a proportion of initial ideas. This by itself is evidence of heterogeneous knowledge and as the network measures indicate, of lower density, lower cohesion, low centralization, and low embedding. Here is one vignette from Company A:

"It's going to be a war," Leigh said to Sari as she listened to Wayne, another company member, finish a presentation about the soon-to-be controversial idea of the "Tooter's" T-shirt. Wayne, with substantial support, was pushing for a T-shirt that would use the notorious "Hooter's" restaurant logo on a T-shirt for an on-campus academic support office. Wayne thought his idea was a sure winner. Clearly, as the quotation shows, unanimity was not soon in coming. A further indication of A's more exploratory learning is the number of project ideas that survived to decision day. These multiple projects resided in the more fragmented subgroups, and their existence increased the amount of variation in internal knowledge in the company. One of the more striking facets of their exploratory learning was that in Company A, a larger number of viable ideas persisted until the fateful decision day. Many companies that semester saw coalitions collapse in the face of influence pressures in favor of what were seen as more popular ideas (and their coalitions). The sense of difference among the groups tugging and pulling to get their ideas adopted by the entire company is strongly evident in members' comments about the need to pull together and find common ground. One participant wrote:

> I was sitting in my room the next day … chronicling the events that led up to our eventual decision of shirts. My roommate was blown away by the amount of discussion and conflict that had taken place because the decisions for her company were rather easy. I told her I was scared, not about the actual product, but how this company was going to work together to not only recognize that there will be opposition but also actually deal with the opposition.

At that point in the company's history, Company A seemed to be a late bloomer because these internal conflicts led to the need to extend the decision-making process for two days. The students saw this as a problem unto itself, but the instructors and TAs were much less concerned.

Company A's networks became more exploitative compared to its starting point and to those of the other companies. This translated into good performance in terms of Company A's best adaptation score as well as performance.

Company B (Late Exploit) intended to be more unique. In some sense, its intentions were perhaps swamped by a network whose connectivity and relative centralization swamped the knowledge variation needed to see more exploratory ideas borne out. Company B's networks had some of the strongest indicators of exploitive capability at the beginning of the company and at the end (Table 6). The following vignette illustrates this trend.

At the early stages of the company, B had the individuals and ideas to pursue more exploratory possibilities. The raw number of possible ideas in play was higher. In addition, early contenders for service projects would have been relative newcomers to the Management 101 universe. However, these ideas were quickly abandoned, and idea coalitions were quickly swamped by a rising tide of connectivity. Many coalitions formed and folded quickly, exchanging members in the process. The exchange led to more connectivity, which in turn led to 18 people joining the shot glass coalition. In the early days of the company, this was a large and dominant coalition, compared with other companies. Only intervention by the instructor broke up the group. A further example of how similar ideas moved quickly throughout the company and reinforced themselves is the fact that many participants commented on how they quickly decided that working with children would be the goal of the service project. Subsequently, all three of the service projects in play focused on children, consistent with the definition of exploiting existing knowledge and focusing on incremental learning. In the face of outside pressure from university administration about a particular project promoting drinking (and perhaps promiscuous behavior), the company responded by deciding to produce a T-shirt, but without specifying the type or design. To a student TA, this was a very "easy" decision because T-shirts are by far the most common business projects and can always be sold. Another observer described how Company B "Wanted to go down in the history of Management 101 as a unique [company] and they sold out uniqueness to T-shirts; instead [of being unique] they wanted something that would sell." These learning moments appear consistent with a learning trajectory that starts with a network conducive to exploitative learning, especially considering the extent to which they relied on the recorded experiences of previous companies.

As Late Exploit shifted from brainstorming to executing its projects, they were very focused on efficiency. Their job descriptions were cut whole cloth from previous companies' archives; many companies match jobs to project-specific goals. One story that reveals some of the opportunities that Company B lost due to a lack of exploratory learning is that it greatly underestimated the demand for their T-shirts. Expecting to sell out in six days, they instead sold out in a few hours. However, part of the reason that the company under-ordered was because of poor market research early on, which did not generate enough working knowledge about the environment. Of course, we cannot say that more exploratory learning would have definitely prevented this problem, but the tendency towards exploitative learning contributes to a lack of awareness about the need for better market research; for Company B, it was easier to simply affirm what it assumed it knew about the demand.

By the end of the semester, Company B was notable for having the worst adaptation score and the second-best performance. Looking at Companies A and B together echoes March's findings – early exploitation can lead to good results, but sometimes results are less good than when earlier exploration is followed by later exploitation.

C (Backtracker) and D (Explorer) Are Suggestive

Company C started as a network more conducive to exploitation. Many coalitions folded quickly, limiting the amount of ideas and knowledge variation. This was especially true for some potentially more radical business ideas. One participant said she felt that the company merely took the path of least resistance at this stage. A TA commented on this weak group pattern: "Up until decision-day every coalition tried to disband and Tammy [the professor] had to make two of them stay around, just to have an option." A different participant described how, while advocating for projects, many individuals tried to get her and others to support a particular project out of a sense of loyalty or friendship. This is precisely the effect of embedding of friendship and advice ties. Finally, a third participant reflected that "Also, during the storming phase, I felt the entire company avoided groupthink very well, a problem that has plagued other companies. In fact, on decision day, the ability for company members to abandon their product ideas for a better product not only was effective but also helped to establish a strong community that would prevail for the rest of the semester."

I have a different reaction to this reflection by the eventual CEO. Although he is proud of a lack of groupthink, a different perspective is that the lack of strong groups to incubate multiple options – his idea of group-think – made it easier for the entire company to quickly agree, which is a form of groupthink that simply has more members. He attributes the company's quick decisions to an interest in promoting community. The network patterns suggest that the community, in the form of a relatively denser and more cohesive network, was already there and led to greater efficiency in decision-making at the potential risk of more exploratory decision-making.

However, as Backtracker shifted to a more performing mode, a wider range of exploratory learning appeared. Although not as exploratory as OnTrack, the record does support the view that Backtracker engaged in more exploratory learning over the company's lifetime than either Inertia or OnTrack, the two most exploitative companies. Let us examine the evidence. Due to the presence of several athletes in the company, scheduling became an ongoing problem because each company member was supposed to participate in the service project (building a house with Habitat for Humanity). Several solutions were attempted, some of which did not work (through no fault of the company members). However, the search for more novel solutions persisted. More novel practical knowledge grew out of a variety of marketing endeavors, including a video commercial. One of these marketing projects backfired because it provoked the university administration's concerns that Backtracker's pint glass product overtly encouraged dangerous drinking. This response from the environment forced Company C to respond by withdrawing the advertisement (a poster). Moreover, a new emphasis on incorporating alcohol awareness into that company's project developed, further evidence of novel knowledge creation. Meanwhile, the service project had been criticized for not being thorough. Thus, Company C added an entirely new project involving visiting an area homeless shelter. This had been an earlier coalition idea, but it stands in contrast to OnTrack, which began to exploit existing knowledge to expand its service project. In reality, Backtracker had two service projects united by its common concern with housing. They also had some members starting a program to collect donated food. Partly as an adaptation to the lack of depth originally planned for its service project, Backtracker added service journals. All of these additions to the service project enhanced the company's impact. At the shift to performing, Backtracker developed its own internal procedures for tracking cash flows and producing company reports and archives. The Vice President of Reports tried a newer system that delegated more content control to company members. Overall, their earlier exploitative learning left key aspects of their environment unknown. Later, when the company needed to exploit solutions, it was compelled to become exploratory to find solutions.

Company D (Explorer), in terms of network capabilities, started with exploratory capabilities and mostly strengthened them. For example, at Time 1, it had the second lowest density (4.1%) and clustering coefficient (10.7%). By Time 2, it had decreased the embedding of advice in communication networks and still had relatively low clustering (24%), little centralization, and relatively less cohesion (any two nodes are still nearly three links away, whereas in Companies A and B, it is much closer to only two links). Does this early, mild exploring, which develops into later exploring, appear in the learning data?

Early on, Company D demonstrated more exploratory learning. It had a greater number of ideas in play as it searched for projects. Certain groups, with higher density, stayed together and eventually carried their ideas to fruition. This persistence of the group and the novelty of the service project show the greater degree of exploratory learning undertaken by Company D.

As Company D shifted to performing, adaptive pressures encouraged it to develop novel knowledge to solve problems. The most persistent of these problems concerned the company's product supplier. The initial delivery date was delayed two weeks, a lifetime for short-lived companies. To handle this, the company increased marketing efforts and attempts at presales. Likewise, in their service project – providing meals to a Ronald McDonald House – it repeatedly found numbers of families that varied, compared with the number expected at the House. This led the company to begin delivering meals to family members visiting loved ones in the hospital during meals, an adaptation that led to new scheduling procedures. There was also a problem with buy-in to the service project. One participant attributed this to the lack of any of the original advocates remaining in the service division once jobs had been assigned. This improved, she said. The improvement likely involved the creation of new organizational knowledge about the goals of both the company and the charity – knowledge lost in the absence of more density and cohesion in the company.

Explorer has some similarities to OnTrack in terms of a large gain in density (from 0.04 to 0.09). The low initial density, along with low centralization in geodesic and eigenvalue terms, suggests a more exploratory-friendly network. Unlike OnTrack, Explorer is less dynamic in terms of how changes in connectivity (density) translate into movement towards a more exploitation-conducive network. Increasing density does not produce changes in cohesion or centralization. Explorer remains fairly low in both dimensions. This unlocks a particular puzzle. We see increasing density and

Table 6. Summary of Network Measures.

Measure	Density (Standard Deviation)	Cohesion I (Links in Geodesic)	Cohesion II (Close to Having One Link in each Geodesic)	Centralization	Weighted Clustering Coefficient	Embedding Advice and Communication	Embedding Advice and Friendship
Relationship to exploration (converse is exploitation)	Low	High	Low	High	Low	Low	Low
A OnTrack							
Time 1	**0.03 (0.18)**	2.08	56%	**11%**	**0%**	**0.46**	0.23
Time 2	0.13 (0.39)	2.3	50%	50%	28.9%	0.62	0.68
Adaptive	Y	N	N	Y	Y	Y	Y
B Late Exploit							
Time 1	0.081 (0.27)	**2.84**	**43%**	20%	23.3%	0.5	0.47
Time 2	0.10 (0.30)	2.3	52%	46%	**23.5%**	0.62	0.59
Adaptive	N	Y	Y	Y	N	Y	Y
C Backtrack							
Time 1	0.06 (0.24)	2.5	48%	12%	37.5%	0.56	**0.19**
Time 2	**0.07 (0.26)**	**3**	**43%**	24%	39.3%	0.62	**0.41**
Adaptive	N	N	N	N	N	N	Y
D Explorer							
Time 1	**0.04 (0.20)**	2.75	50%	13%	10.7%	0.48	0.49
Time 2	0.09 (0.29)	2.74	48%	**19%**	24.2%	**0.46**	0.59
Adaptive	N	N	N	N	N	N	Y

1. For all four companies, at each T1 or T2, most exploratory is in **bold**, most exploitative is underlined.
2. Shaded cells indicate exploratory network properties.
3. Adaptation is determined by direction (from exploratory to exploitative).

its standard deviation, but not an increase in actors' cohesion or centrality. However, this increasing number of ties must go somewhere. The answer is found in increasing transitivity and clustering: new ties tend to close off triads and to increase local density, even as overall network cohesion does not increase. This is underscored by the falling variation in centralization scores across all actors (heterogeneity falls to 4.5%). This is not a measure reported for other companies because it is unchanged for the other three. I include it here because it is interesting that the variation in centralization is falling – a sign of a flattening network, one with more consistent centralization scores for each actor. This is a move away from hierarchy or centrality for a few actors. Lessening embeddedness in communication and advice reinforces the persistent exploration trajectory. Explorer is the only company with embedding measures that have stubbornly resisted the strong trend towards embedding seen in every other company. In sum, Company D presents a picture of a network that is most conducive to exploratory learning from the outset.

DISCUSSION

SMEs are essential to economic growth because they account for the largest proportion of the world's enterprises and make a substantial contribution to economic development and growth (OECD, 2009). Simultaneously, there is broad evidence that not only knowledge and learning but also networks are key drivers of SME formation and growth. However, their specific interactions are still an area to theorize and research. This chapter contributes to the field because its hypotheses develop the reasons that learning and networks matter. Although suggestive, there is evidence to support the two hypotheses proposed. First, network configurations are capabilities for exploratory or exploitative learning. Second, dynamic networks are associated with ambidexterity in pursuing exploration and exploitation – ambidexterity is like rewiring a network and can affect adaptation. Company A offers the strongest support for both hypotheses. It began as a more fragmented network with clusters of connected people and low embedding. This enabled more exploratory learning. Then, as the company switched to operating, its network changed dramatically. This change matches the best performance of the four. The other three companies offered other support for the hypotheses. For example, Company B, despite having weak early exploration, performs second-best while also having a network that is very conducive to exploiting knowledge. Companies C and D, in different ways, became more exploratory in the midst of the operating stage; their networks match their own efforts at exploratory learning. At most, the limits of the data mean we can use the results to continue to develop a theory about how a network theory of flows can affect EE tension and might be dexterously avoided, or if networks impose true trade-offs, juggled at best.

These results can form the basis of further empirical work with SMEs to uncover how networks affect learning and also how they can be structured or managed depending on the needs of a firm or organization. In reviewing system adoption in general to acquire growth from knowledge for SMEs, McPherson and Holt argue that managing growth requires "… Knowing when, how and what systems are appropriate" (p. 181). This can be extended to knowing when, how, and what networks are appropriate.

Further research into SMEs could test the suggested findings here. For example, do particular network properties correlate to exploratory or exploitative learning? Companies B and C are interesting in that they sought to be more novel or unique in their actions, indicators of an intent to explore, but perhaps their early higher density, greater cohesion, greater centralization, and greater embedding worked against that intent. Furthermore, given other scholarship that suggests that the EE tensions may not be narrowly restricted to pure trade-offs, network properties are by definition such trade-offs. In this case, ambidexterity is achieved over time because networks must change. For larger organizations, ambidexterity in networks can also be seen in how networks cross-cut their domains of activity. However, for smaller organizations with fewer domains of activity, the overall network, as was measured in the Management 101 companies, may be the relevant unit of measure.

There are limits to the data. Although the companies' experiences have some facial similarity to what SMEs confront, they are also limited in generalizability due to their short life spans and their officer-selection process (i.e., their process of selecting their own officers). These results are the most generalizable to smaller start-ups or even proto-organizations: networks of entrepreneurs or others who are collecting ideas and knowledge as part of starting up firms. For example, incubators or other entrepreneurship-rich milieus may be similar to the Management 101 companies. In addition, the relationships suggested here between networks, learning and EE tensions may extend to organizations that are similar to SMEs but are not officially labeled as such, including organizations that engage in open-source innovation or production (Raymond, 2001) or even more radical forms of organization such as co-operatives (Young, Dworkin, Moving Images Video Project, & Bullfrog Films, 2013), social movements (Davis, 2005), or Argentina-style "horizontalism" (Sitrin, 2012).

This suggests a final critical point. A long-standing question is how amenable networks are to direct change efforts. Embeddedness research in economic sociology and management suggests that the noneconomic or rational processes that create networks are not part of a conscious strategy (Granovetter, 1985; Uzzi, 1997). If this is the case, it may be worth exploring how initial conditions and choices of networks shape network and learning trajectories over time. None of the Management 101 companies clearly chose to have greater exploring or exploiting network capabilities when they started. Their early networks resulted from random factors such as prior acquaintance, where people sat, and ineffable processes of attraction or repulsion among people. For SME founders, executives, and managers, these are important points. Networks are the result of a mix of strategic choices and serendipitous processes. Knowing whether it is strategy or chance that creates and alters networks and how over time those networks shape knowledge flows can help to unlock the promise of exploring and exploiting at the most opportune times.

ACKNOWLEDGEMENT

I acknowledge the helpful comments of Mihai Banciu, Tammy Hiller, John Miller, Mark Ciaverelli, and Carl Milofsky as well as the editorial assistance of Michael Zimmerman and Tooba Ali

REFERENCES

Ahuja, G. (2000). The duality of collaboration: Inducements and opportunities in the formation of interfirm linkages. *Strategic Management Journal, 21*(3), 317−343.

Argote, L., McEvily, B., & Reagans, R. (2003). Introduction to the special issue on managing knowledge in organizations: Creating, retaining, and transferring knowledge. *Management Science, 49*(4), 5−8.

Argote, L., & Ophir, R. (2002). Intraorganizational learning. In J. A. C. Baum (Ed.), *Blackwell companion to organizations* (pp. 181−207). Oxford, UK: Blackwell.

Benner, M. J., & Tushman, M. (2003). Exploitation, exploration, and process management: The productivity dilemma revisited. *Academy of Management Review, 28*(2), 238−256.

Borgatti, S. P., & Cross, R. (2003). A relational view of information seeking and learning in social networks. *Management Science, 49*(4), 432–445.

Borgatti, S. P., & Halgin, D. S. (2011). On network theory. *Organization Science, 22*(5), 1168–1181. doi:10.1287/orsc.1100.0641

Brown, S. L., & Eisenhardt, K. M. (1998). *Competing on the edge: Strategy as structured chaos.* Boston, MA: Harvard Business School.

Burt, R. (1992). *Structural holes: The social structure of competition.* Cambridge, MA: Harvard University Press.

Burt, R. S. (2005). *Brokerage and closure: An introduction to social capital.* Oxford; NY: Oxford University Press.

Butts, C. (2003). Network inference, error, and informant (in)accuracy: A Bayesian approach. *Social Networks, 25*(2), 103–140.

Cohen, M. D., & Bacdayan, P. (1994). Organizational routines are stored as procedural memory: Evidence from a laboratory study. *Organization Science, 5*(4), 554–568.

Coleman, J. S. (1988). Social capital in the creation of human capital. *American Journal of Sociology, 94*, 95–120.

Collins, R. (1988). *Theoretical sociology.* San Diego, CA: Harcourt Brace Jovanovich.

Comas, J., Hiller, T., & Miller, J. (2005). Management 101 as a community of practice. In D. W. Butin (Ed.), *Service learning in higher education: Critical issues and trends* (pp. 107–125). New York, NY: Palgrave Press.

Cook, S. D., & Brown, J. S. (1999). Bridging epistemologies: The generative dance between organizational knowledge and organizational knowing. *Organization Science, 10*(4), 381–400.

Cross, R., & Borgatti, S. (2004). Ties that share: Relational characteristics that facilitate information sharing. In M. Huysman & V. Wulf (Eds.), *Social capital and information technology* (pp. 137–162). MIT Press.

Davig, W., & Brown, S. (1992). Incremental decision making in small manufacturing firms. *Journal of Small Business Management, 30*(2), 53–60.

Davis, G. F. (2005). *Social movements and organization theory.* New York, NY: Cambridge University Press.

Eisenhardt, K. (1989). Building theories from case study research. *Academy of Management Review, 14*(4), 532–550.

Fang, C., Lee, J., & Schilling, M. A. (2010). Balancing exploration and exploitation through structural design: The isolation of subgroups and organizational learning. *Organization Science, 21*(3), 625–642. doi:10.1287/orsc.1090.0468

Freeman, L. C. (1979). Centrality in social networks conceptual clarification. *Social networks, 1*(3), 215–239.

Fukugawa, N. (2006). Determining factors in innovation of small firm networks: A case of cross industry groups in Japan. *Small Business Economics, 27*(2–3), 181–193.

Gavetti, G., & Levinthal, D. (2000). Looking forward and looking backward: Cognitive and experiential search. *Administrative Science Quarterly, 45*(2), 113–137.

Ghemawat, P., & Costa I Ricart, J. E. (1993). The organizational tension between static and dynamic efficiency. *Strategic Management Journal, 14*(Winter), 59–73.

Ghobadian, A., Mole, K., & O'Regan, N. (2003). New process technologies: Barriers to adoption in small firms. *International Journal of Manufacturing Technology and Management, 5*(5), 549–562.

Granovetter, M. (1973). The strength of weak ties. *American Journal of Sociology, 78*(6), 1360–1380.

Granovetter, M. (1985). Economic action and social structure: The problem of embeddedness. *American Journal of Sociology, 91,* 481−510.

Gronum, S., Verreynne, M.-L., & Kastelle, T. (2012). The role of networks in small and medium-sized enterprise innovation and firm performance. *Journal of Small Business Management, 50*(2), 257−282.

Gruenfeld, D., Martorana, P., & Fan, E. (2000). What do groups learn from their worldliest members? direct and indirect influence in dynamic teams. *Organizational Behavior and Human Decision Processes, 82*(1), 45−59.

Gupta, A. K., Smith, K. G., & Shalley, C. E. (2006). The interplay between exploration and exploitation. *Academy of Management Journal, 49*(4), 693−706.

Hargadon, A., & Fanelli, A. (2002). Action and possibility: Reconciling dual perspectives of knowledge in organizations. *Organization Science, 13*(3), 290−302.

He, Z., & Wong, P. (2004). Exploration vs. exploitation: An empirical test of the ambidextrity hypothesis. *Organization Science, 15*(4), 481−494.

Human, S. E., & Provan, K. G. (1997). An emergent theory of structure and outcomes in small-firm strategic manufacturing networks. *Academy of Management Journal Academy of Management Journal, 40*(2), 368−403.

Ibarra, H., Kilduff, M., & Tsai, W. (2005). Zooming in and out: Connecting individuals and collectivities at the frontiers of organizational network research. *Organization Science, 16*(4), 359−371.

Jetter, A. (2006). *Knowledge integration the practice of knowledge management in small and medium enterprises.* Heidelberg: Physica-Verlag. Retrieved from http://public.eblib.com/ EBLPublic/PublicView.do?ptiID=304792

Kilduff, M., & Tsai, W. (2003). *Social networks and organizations.* Thousand Oaks, CA: Sage.

Kleinbaum, A. M., & Tushman, M. L. (2007). Building bridges: The social structure of interdependent innovation. *Strategic Entrepreneurship Journal, 1*(1−2), 103−122. doi:10.1002/sej.14

Latora, V., Nicosia, V., & Panzarasa, P. (2013). Social cohesion, structural holes, and a tale of two measures. *Journal of Statistical Physics, 151*(3−4), 745−764.

Lavie, D. (2007). Alliance portfolios and firm performance: A study of value creation and appropriation in the US software industry. *Strategic Management Journal, 28*(12), 1187−1212.

Lavie, D., Stettner, U., & Tushman, M. L. (2010). Exploration and exploitation within and across organizations. *The Academy of Management Annals, 4*(1), 109−155. doi:10.1080/ 19416521003691287

Levinthal, D. A., & March, J. G. (1993). The myopia of learning. *Strategic Management Journal, 14*(S2), 95−112.

Levitt, B., & March, J. G. (1988). Organizational learning. *Annual Review of Sociology, 14*(1), 319−340.

Macpherson, A., & Holt, R. (2007). Knowledge, learning and small firm growth: A systematic review of the evidence. *Research Policy, 36*(2), 172−192.

Mansury, M. A., & Love, J. H. (2008). Innovation, productivity and growth in US business services: A firm-level analysis. *Technovation, 28*(1−2), 52−62. doi:10.1016/ j.technovation.2007.06.002

March, J. G. (1991). Exploration and exploitation in organizational learning. *Organization Science, 2*(1), 71−87.

Meyer, A. D. (1993). Configurational approaches to organizational analysis. *Academy of Management Journal, 36*(6), 1175−1196.

Miles, M. B., & Huberman, A. M. (1994). *Qualitative data analysis: An expanded sourcebook* (2nd ed.). Thousand Oaks, CA: Sage.

Mizruchi, M. S., & Stearns, L. B. (2001). Getting deals done: The use of social networks in bank decision-making. *American Sociological Review, 66,* 647–671.

Mole, K. F., Ghobadian, A., O'Regan, N., & Liu, J. (2004). The use and deployment of soft process technologies within UK manufacturing SMEs: An empirical assessment using logit models. *Journal of Small Business Management, 42*(3), 303–324. doi:10.1111/j.1540-627X.2004.00113.x

OECD. (2009). *The impact of the global crisis on SME and entrepreneurship financing and policy responses.* Retrieved from http://www.oecd.org/document/6/0,3746,en_2649_34197_43182598_1_1_1_1,00.html. Accessed on January 2, 2014.

Oh, K., Chung, M.-H., & Labianca, G. (2004). Group social capital and group effectiveness: The role of informal socializing ties. *Academy of Management Journal, 47*(6), 860–875.

Penrose, E. T. (1959). *The theory of the growth in the firm.* Oxford, England: Blackwell.

Perry-Smith, J. E., & Shalley, C. E. (2003). The social side of creativity: A static and dynamic social network perspective. *Academy of Management Journal, 28*(1), 89–107.

Pirolo, L., & Presutti, M. (2010). The impact of social capital on the start-ups' performance growth. *Journal of Small Business Management, 48*(2), 197–227. doi:10.1111/j.1540-627X.2010.00292.x

Powell, W., Kenneth, K., & Smith-Doerr, L. (1996). Interorganizational collaboration and the locus of innovation: Networks of learning in biotechnology. *Administrative Science Quarterly, 41*(1), 116–145.

Provan, K. G., & Sebastian, J. G. (1998). Networks within networks: Service link overlap, organizational cliques, and network effectiveness. *Academy of Management Journal, 41*(4), 453–463.

Ragin, C. C. (1987). *The comparative method: Moving beyond qualitative and quantitative strategies.* Berkley, CA: University of California Press.

Raymond, E. S. (2001). *The Cathedral and the Bazaar: Musings on Linux and open source by an accidental revolutionary.* Cambridge, MA: O'Reilly.

Reagans, R., & McEvily, B. (2003). Network structure and knowledge transfer: The effects of cohesion and range. *Administrative Science Quarterly, 48*(2), 240.

Reagans, R., & Zuckerman, E. (2001). Networks, diversity, and productivity: The social capital of corporate R&D teams. *Organization Science, 12*(4), 502–517.

Rosenbusch, N., Brinckmann, J., & Bausch, A. (2011). Is innovation always beneficial? A meta-analysis of the relationship between innovation and performance in SMEs. *Journal of Business Venturing, 26,* 441–457.

Saxenian, A. (1990). Regional networks and the resurgence of silicon valley. *California, CA Management Review, 33*(1), 89.

Schulz, M. (2002). Organizational learning. In J. A. C. Baum (Ed.), *The Blackwell companion to organizations* (pp. 415–451). Oxford, UK: Blackwell Publishing.

Sitrin, M. (2012). *Everyday revolutions: Horizontalism and autonomy in Argentina.* London: Zed Books.

Spicer, D. P., & Sadler-Smith, E. (2006). Organizational learning in smaller manufacturing firms. *International Small Business Journal, 24*(2), 133–158. doi:10.1177/0266242606061836

Stork, D., & Richards, W. D. (1992). Nonrespondents in communication network studies problems and possibilities. *Group and Organization Management*, *17*(2), 193–209. doi:10.1177/1059601192172006

Tasakkori, A., & Teddle, C. (2003). *Handbook of mixed methods in social and behavioral research*. Thousand Oaks, CA: Sage.

Terziovski, M. (2002). Achieving performance excellence through an integrated strategy of radical innovation and continuous improvement. *Measuring Business Excellence*, *6*(2), 5–14. doi:10.1108/13683040210431419

Tsai, W., & Ghoshal, S. (1998). Social capital and value creation: The role of intrafirm networks. *Academy of Management Journal*, *41*(4), 464–476.

Tushman, M., & O'Reilly III, C. (1996). The ambidextrous organization: Managing evolutionary and revolutionary change. *California Management Review*, *38*(4), 8–31.

Uzzi, B. (1997). Social structure and competition in interfirm networks: The paradox of embeddedness. *Administrative Science Quarterly*, *42*, 35–67.

Wadhwa, A., & Kotha, S. (2006). Knowledge creation through external venturing: Evidence from the telecommunications equipment manufacturing industry. *Academy of Management Journal*, *49*(4), 819–835.

Watts, D. J. (1999). *Small worlds: The dynamics of networks between order and randomness*. Princeton, NJ: Princeton University Press.

Weick, K. E., & Westley, F. (1996). Organizational learning: Affirming an oxymoron. In S. Clegg, C. Hardy, & W. Nord (Eds.), *Handbook of organization studies* (pp. 440–458). London: Sage.

Wellman, B. (1988). Structural analysis: From method and metaphor to theory and substance. In B. Wellman & S. D. Berkowitz (Eds.), *Social structures: A network approach* (pp. 19–62). Cambridge, MA: Cambridge University Press.

Yin, R. (1994). *Case study research: Design and methods*. Thousand Oaks, CA: Sage.

Yli-Renko, H., Autio, E., & Sapienza, H. J. (2001). Social capital, knowledge acquisition, and knowledge exploitation in young technology-based firms. *Strategic Management Journal*, *22*(6–7), 587–613. doi:10.1002/smj.183

Young, G., Sapienza, H., & Baumer, D. (2003). The influence of flexibility in buyer–seller relationships on the productivity of knowledge. *Journal of Business Research*, *56*(6), 443–451. doi:10.1016/S0148-2963(01)00243-0

Young, M., Dworkin, M., & Moving Images Video Project. (2013). *Shift change*. USA. Bullfrog Films. Retrieved from http://bucknell.worldcat.org/title/shift-change/oclc/8300 05018&referer = brief_results

ABOUT THE EDITORS

Uriel Stettner is an Assistant Professor of Strategy, Innovation, and Entrepreneurship at Tel Aviv University. Dr. Stettner obtained his Ph.D. from Tel Aviv University and completed his post-doctoral research at the Technion – Israel Institute of Technology. He was a Visiting Assistant Professor at Georgia Institute of Technology in 2013. His research interests include the performance implications of organizational boundary choices, strategic innovation, technological innovation and management as well as organizational knowledge creation and appropriation. He has published his research in high-quality outlets such as the *Strategic Management Journal* and the *Academy of Management Annals*. He has had extensive experience in several start-up firms operating in the software and semiconductor industries and held a variety of managerial and technology focused positions in both Israel and the United States.

Barak S. Aharonson is an Assistant Professor of Strategy, Innovation, and Entrepreneurship at Tel Aviv University. Before joining Tel-Aviv University, Aharonson served on the Management faculty at Stern School of Business at NYU and at Olin Business School at Washington University in St. Louis. He received his Ph.D. from Rotman School of Management at the University of Toronto. The main focus of his research is on patterns of competition and cooperation among firms, and their influence on a firm's behavior. He has published his research in high-quality outlets such as *Research Policy*, *Strategic Organization*, *Industrial and Corporate Change*, and *Advances in Strategic Management*. His projects examine a firm's competitive versus co-operative behavior and knowledge diffusion in networks, geographic agglomerations and technological space. Barak is co-convenor of the Standing Working Group on Organizational Network Research in The European Group for Organizational Studies.

Terry L. Amburgey is a Professor of Strategic Management at the Rotman School of Management. His research is focused on the dynamics of inter-organizational networks and organizational evolution with a particular focus on biotechnology. Terry is co-convenor of the Standing Working

Group on Organizational Network Research in The European Group for Organizational Studies. His research has been published in a variety of outlets including *Administrative Science Quarterly*, *Academy of Management Journal*, *Strategic Management Journal*, *Strategic Organization, and Advances in Strategic Management*.

ABOUT THE AUTHORS

Meriam Bezemer holds a Masters Degree in History and a Bachelors Degree in German Language and Culture and has been involved throughout this Spatial Information Industry project as a QUT research assistant.

Peter T. Bryant is an Assistant Professor of Entrepreneurship at IE Business School in Madrid. He began his academic career in Sydney 2007, after earning his Ph.D. in Management from Macquarie University in Sydney, Australia. During the preceding 15 years, Peter worked as a manager in the airline, banking, consulting and venture capital industries in Sydney, Australia. He subsequently managed the commercialization of new technologies through the creation of spinoff companies at The University of Sydney. In this role, he accomplished successful IPOs and VC deals. In Peter's academic career, he researches in the fields of entrepreneurial management and strategy, and their relationship to the dynamics of industrial change and the evolution of organizational capabilities. His research is published in the *Journal of Business Venturing*, *Entrepreneurship Theory and Practice*, *Management Decision*, *Applied Psychology: An International review*, *Neuroscience* and *Neuroeconomics*, as well as professional outlets including *The Economist and Harvard Business Review*. Peter is currently co-editing the volume on organizations and management for Elsevier's new encyclopaedia of the Social and Behavioral Sciences.

Graziano Coller is an Assistant Professor in Management Accounting and Control at the Department of Economics and Management of the University of Trento, Italy. He holds a M.A. in Economics and Business from the University of Trento and a Ph.D. in Economics and Management from Scuola Superiore Sant'Anna in Pisa. His research is focused on cost-based decision making, accuracy of cost information, and costing systems design. Currently, through analytical models and numerical experiments (computer simulations), he is investigating cost-based pricing heuristics and the role of accuracy of cost information in decision making. Through in-depth case studies, he is also investigating the relationship between management control systems and strategy.

Paolo Collini is a Professor in Management accounting and control at the University of Trento in Italy. He holds a Master in business administration from Boston University and a Ph.D. from the Ca' Foscari University in Venice. His research interests can be summarized into three main areas: (i) the analysis of the relation between cost information and decision making, with a strong focus on pricing decisions: using a simulation/numerical experiment approach, market mechanism are taken into the analysis to relate both accounting accuracy and decision making heuristics to profit maximization; (ii) the interaction between strategic decision making and management control systems through case studies; (iii) the performance management systems exploring its effectiveness and its fairness mainly by using real life data and laboratory experiments. In the past, his work focused on the relation between manufacturing and management accounting and Strategic Cost Management. He has been member of editorial boards of *European Accounting Review*, *International Journal of Contemporary Hospitality Management*. He is actively involved as reviewer for a number of international and national journals. He has been national representative in the Board of European Accounting Association from 2006 to 2012, and Dean of the Faculty of Economics since 2012. He is currently Deputy Rector at the University of Trento.

Jordi Comas is an Assistant Professor in the School of Management of Bucknell University in Lewisburg, PA, USA. Dr. Comas researches social networks as well as organization and social theory. His work brings these perspectives to differing contexts including virtual worlds, organizational learning, international development, and terrorism. Most recently, his work has appeared in the journal *First Monday*. He earned an M.A. in sociology from the University of Virginia followed by a Ph.D. in Management from IESE/Universidad de Navarra.

Janke Dittmer is a Partner with Gilde Healthcare, a transatlantic venture and growth capital firm investing in innovative, private Healthcare companies. Prior to joining Gilde, he was a Venture General Manager and Head of Business Development & Strategy within Philips' Corporate Venturing unit in Healthcare. Before his time at Philips, Janke was an Engagement Manager at McKinsey & Company advising clients in the High Tech sector on growth strategies and strategic marketing. Janke cofounded a Nanotech company in the Silicon Valley after serving as a Fellow at the Lawrence Berkeley National Lab. Mr Dittmer earned a Ph.D. in Physics from the University of Cambridge in the United Kingdom and did a Post-Doc in

Nanotechnology at the University of California, Berkeley. Janke is one of the founders of the International Venture Club.

Linda F. Edelman is an Associate Professor of Strategic Management at Bentley University. Before coming to Bentley, she studied at London Business School and was a research fellow at the Warwick Business School for two years. Professor Edelman is the author of over 15 book chapters and 30 peer reviewed journal articles. In addition, she has made over 50 scholarly and professional international presentations. Her work has appeared in many of the top management and entrepreneurship journals such as *Journal of Business Venturing, Entrepreneurship Theory and Practice, Industrial and Corporate Change,* and *Organization Studies.* She serves on three editorial boards, is an ad hoc reviewer for the NSF and other scholarly organizations. Currently, Dr. Edelman teaches strategic management to undergraduates, graduates, doctoral students, and executives. Her recent research examines strategic industry dynamics, women and nascent entrepreneurs, SME internationalization and entrepreneurial finance.

M. Laura Frigotto is an Assistant Professor in Organization management and theory at the Department of Economics and Management of the University of Trento, Italy. Her research addresses the emergence of novelty in organizations within theories of organizational learning, strategic change, and innovation. She mainly builds on empirical evidence referring to key or outlier empirical cases. She has investigated small-medium enterprises, high-reliability organizations, scientific communities as well as simulated contexts, with methods including in-depth case studies, participant observation, archival and textual analysis, interviews, questionnaires, bibliometric and network analysis, computer modeling. In particular, in small-medium enterprises (SMEs), she investigated the role of management control systems for the exploration of new directories of strategic and organizational evolution. Laura holds a M.A. in Economics and Business from the University of Trento (2001), a (postgraduate) Master in Innovation Management from Scuola Superiore Sant'Anna in Pisa (2002) and a Ph.D. in Management and Business from the Ca' Foscari University in Venice (2007). Before starting her Ph.D., she worked in the business development division of both a multinational company and an SME in the information technology sector. She was Visiting Scholar at Stanford University in 2007 and in 2012 for a research project that was awarded with ex-alumni grant by the Scandinavian Consortium for Organizational Research at Stanford (SCANCOR).

Robert Galliers is Bentley University's inaugural University Distinguished Professor, having previously served as Provost. Prior to joining Bentley, he was Professor of Information Systems and Research Director at the London School of Economics (LSE), Lucas Professor of Business Management Systems and Dean of Warwick Business School, and Foundation Professor and Head of the School of Information Systems at Curtin University, Australia. He has held visiting professorships at various leading institutions internationally. He has served as President of the Association for Information Systems (AIS) and received its LEO Award for exceptional lifetime achievement in 2102. He is also a Fellow of the AIS, the British Computer Society, and the Royal Society of Arts. He is editor-in-chief of the *Journal of Strategic Information Systems*, has published more than 80 articles in many leading IS and Management journals, and has three journal best paper awards to his name. He has also authored or co-authored 11 books, the most recent being: *The Oxford Handbook of Management Information Systems* (Oxford University Press, 2011), *Exploring Information Systems Research* (Routledge, 2007), and four editions of the best seller, *Strategic Information Management* (Butterworth-Heinemann, 1994, 1999, 2003; Routledge, 2009). His work has been cited approximately 7,000 according to *Google Scholar*. He has given over 40 keynote addresses at major international conferences. His research focuses in the main on information systems strategizing practice, and the innovation and management of change associated with the application of IT systems within and between organizations.

Moon-Goo Huh is a professor of Strategy and Organization at the School of Business Administration, Kyungpook National University, Korea. He received his Ph.D. and MBA in management from the Korea University Business School, Korea. Prior to joining Kyungpook National University, he worked as a Senior Research Fellow and Director at POSCO Research Institute and also an Advisor to POSCO. He has authored four books, and his scholarly work has appeared in *Korean Management Review*, *Korean Journal of Management*, *Journal of Strategic Management*, and *Academy of Management Best Paper Proceedings*, among others. Moon-Goo has won five best paper awards, and has also consistently received teaching excellence awards. During the past 10 years, his research has been granted by National Research Foundation of Korea, Korean Ministry of Education. He served as President of the Korean Society of Strategic Management in 2013. His current research interests include firm innovation, exploration and exploitation, modes of ambidexterity, knowledge creation, and social capital.

Guktae Kim is a Ph.D. (doctoral) student at the School of Business Administration, Kyungpook National University, Korea. He received the bachelor's and master's degrees of science in business administration from the Kyungpook National University, Daegu, Korea, in 2011 and 2013, respectively. He won the Best Paper Award in the 2012 Korean Academic Society of Business Administration Annual Meeting from the *Maeil Business Newspaper* and the Best Paper Award in the *2013 Korean Society of Strategic Management Spring Conference*. He presented a paper in the 2013 Annual Meeting of the Academy Management and the paper was published in the Best Paper Proceedings. His current research interests include exploration, exploitation, organizational ambidexterity, innovation, dynamic capabilities and organizational culture.

Blake D. Mathias is a Ph.D. Candidate in the Organizations and Strategy doctoral program at the University of Tennessee, Knoxville. His research interests are at the intersection of psychology and entrepreneurship, focusing on the topics of entrepreneurial decision-making, identity, and cognition. His work has been published in the *Journal of Business Ethics* and the *Frontiers of Entrepreneurship Research*. His research has also been presented at a number of conferences, including the *Academy of Management Conference, Southern Management Association Conference, Babson College Entrepreneurship Research Conference,* and the *United States Association for Small Business Conference*. At the 2012 Babson Conference, his paper entitled "Role With It: The Impact of Role Identities on Entrepreneurs' Evaluation and Selection of Opportunities" received the *National Federation of Independent Business* award for the best conference paper.

Judy Matthews, Ph.D., is a Senior Lecturer in the School of Management in the QUT Business School, Queensland University of Technology, actively engaged in research in design led innovation. Until January 2007, she was a Senior Lecturer in the School of Management, Marketing and International Business in the College of Business and Economics at the Australian National University and from 2002 to 2005 was the Director of Master of Management Programs at the National Graduate School of Management at the Australian National University. In 2005–2006, she taught units in Organisational Behaviour and Knowledge Management to senior managers in China (through interpreters) in a Master of Management (Technology and Innovation) program at Tsinghua University, Beijing. Judy works with individuals, groups and organisations to improve their understanding and practice of the leadership and management of people and organisations, and the issues, themes and processes that make a difference in managing the innovation and effective knowledge generation and implementation. Judy has worked with government agencies to identify barriers to innovation and developed some practical customised solutions to improve innovation. In 2004, Dr. Matthews was a Visiting Scholar at the ESRC Centre for Research on Innovation and Competition at the University of Manchester, United Kingdom and the Innovation Policy Centre at Simon Fraser University in Vancouver, Canada.

Joseph A. McCahery is Professor of International Economic Law at Tilburg University School of Law and Tilburg Law and Economics Center (TILEC). He is also Program Director of Finance and Law at the Duisenberg School of Finance in Amsterdam. Before coming to Tilburg, he taught at the University of Amsterdam and Warwick University. He has held visiting appointments at the University of Pennsylvania Law School and the Solvay School of Business (ULB). He has been an advisor to several governments, international institutions, and corporations. McCahery works in the area of banking, corporate law, corporate finance, and securities market regulation. He has many publications in top law and finance journals and has written or co-edited 10 books, including *Institutional Investor Activism: Hedge Funds, Private Equity, and Regulation and Governance* (Oxford University Press, 2014). He obtained his Ph.D. from Warwick University in 1998.

Gaëtan Mourmant is an Associate Professor at École de Management Strasbourg – HuManiS (EA 1347). He holds a Ph.D. from Paris Dauphine University and Georgia State University. For several years, he worked as a Marketing Database Analyst in a global, financial institution. As a consultant, he managed more than 50 IT projects. His research interests focus on Grounded Theory Methodology, entrepreneurship, and IT personnel turnover. He has published papers in the *European Journal of Information Systems*, as well as the *International Conference of Information Systems*.

Fred Niederman serves as the Shaughnessy Endowed Professor of MIS at Saint Louis University. His Ph.D. and MBA are from the University of Minnesota in 1990. His research interests include global information management, MIS personnel, and using MIS to support teams and groups. Recently, he has been investigating the integration of MIS functions after corporate mergers and acquisitions. He is a proponent of grounded theory and theory building as a way to enrich the MIS discipline and build intellectual content customized specifically to our field of practice. He serves on editorial boards for *JAIS, CAIS, Human Resource Management, Journal of International Management*, and the *Journal of Global Information Management*. He recently served as co-program chair for the 2010 ICIS conference in St. Louis, Missouri, and is an active member in the MIS "senior scholars."

Craig Randall is an Assistant Professor of Business at FGCU where he focuses on strategy, entrepreneurship, and innovation. He has a B.S. in Electrical Engineering from Carnegie Mellon University, an MBA from Harvard Business School, and a Ph.D. from Bentley University. Craig began his professional career programming and designing control systems. After receiving his MBA, he worked in technology; first in Product Management, then as VP of Marketing/Sales, and finally as a company founder. His first of four software startups went public in 1998. His last was purchased by a public company after four years of always profitable 30% quarterly growth.

Shengce Ren is an Associate Professor and Business Administration Department Head in Shanghai Maritime University. He was a Visiting Scholar at Imperial College, London. Prior to joining Shanghai Maritime University, Dr. Ren held positions as a financial analyst position at a PC firm and as a manager and partner at a Consulting firm. Dr. Ren has consulted in strategy and organization for more than 30 corporations across various sectors and governments in China. Dr. Ren's research focuses on strategic management of innovation, intellectual property (IP) rights and organizational learning for Chinese firms. He authored more than 30 peer-reviewed articles in the *Frontier of Business Research in China*, *Nankai Business Review*, *Chinese Journal of Management Science*, *EURAM*, among others, and five books. His research has been granted by National Science Foundation of China (NSFC), Chinese Ministry of Education and Chinese Post-doctor Foundation, among others.

Anna Sabidussi is an Associate Professor of Innovation and Entrepreneurship at TiasNimbas, Business School, Tilburg University. Dr. Sabidussi's research focus is at the cross-road of innovation management and entrepreneurship. The precedent professional experience in banking and investments supports a portfolio approach to strategic business decisions. Her research mainly concerns corporate entrepreneurship, exploration and exploitation balance and external technology sourcing strategies (strategic alliances, mergers and acquisitions). Before joining TiasNimbas, she worked as Assistant Professor at Eindhoven University of Technology and Wageningen University & Research Centrum.

Sukanlaya Sawang, Ph.D. is an active researcher with professional experience from Australia, Japan, Thailand and USA. Sukanlaya worked at Chulalongkorn University, Thailand, as a full time Psychology Lecturer, consultant and trainer, before she moved to Australia. Currently, Sukanlaya is Senior Lecturer (tenured) and higher degree research student coordinator in the QUT Business School. She is also an active research member of Australian Centre for Entrepreneurship Research and a board member of Asian Cognitive Behavioural Therapy Association. Sukanlaya's research to date has primarily focussed on two main areas within the field of organisational effectiveness: cross-cultural studies, psychological well-being; and innovation adoption. Sukanlaya has developed considerable research and impact within these spheres. For example, her work related stress and employee engagement research identifies a specific work-related stress pattern across ethnicity and develops culturally based stress measures to minimize the negative work performance. Another example of Sukanlaya's research is in SMEs innovation which identifies critical success factors which enhance SMEs innovation performance. Her research within this sector addresses critical issues at individual, organisational and governmental levels and significantly contributes to the sector, which is widely recognised as the backbone of the Australian economy. Sukanlaya received a number of awards — including the 'Emerald Management Reviews Citation of Excellence'; the 'Best Paper Awards' from the Academy of Management (AOM); and the 'AGSE International Entrepreneurship Research Exchange' award. The AOM award winning paper has been published in *Technovation* journal. She has successfully applied for two competitive grants from the CRC Rail Innovation and the CRC Spatial Information.

Peiran Su is Lecturer in Strategic Management/Operations Management at the University of the West of Scotland, United Kingdom. His research areas are strategic management and innovation management. He studies strategic and organizational implications of failure events within high technology firms. His research appears in *Technology Analysis & Strategic Management*, the Academy of Management annual meetings, etc. Peiran received PhD Strategic Management from University College Dublin, Ireland. He was Assistant Professor of Technology and Innovation Management at Technical University of Denmark.

Noriko Taji is Professor of MBA School & Department of Business Administration, Director of The Research Institute for Innovation Management of HOSEI University. She received her Master from Hitotsubashi University and Ph.D. from Kobe University in Japan. She had worked in industries for nine years including an IT startup. She teaches innovation management, qualitative research method etc. in the undergraduate, MBA, doctoral program at Tohoku University and Chuo University. Main topics of her research are innovation management, high-tech startups strategy and entrepreneurship.

Erik P. M. Vermeulen is Professor of Business and Financial Law at Tilburg University and Tilburg Law and Economics Center (TILEC). He is also Senior Counsel Corporate of Philips (a technology company) in the Netherlands. Much of his current research focuses on the life cycle of a company – from idea to fully mature company, the sources of capital available at each stage of a company's development, and the importance of collaborations and partnerships with other firms to ensure innovation, growth, and value creation. In the context of the corporate life cycle, he also examines international trends in corporate governance and the development of company law and securities regulations. Furthermore, his research focuses on financial markets and innovation policies and ecosystems. His work has been widely published in top journals and books. In 2006, he became the Director of the International Business Law LLM Program at Tilburg University. He teaches courses on corporate governance, venture capital, entrepreneurship, joint ventures, and company law. He has also been a Visiting Professor at Ghent University in Belgium, Pontificia Universidad Javeriana, Universidad Icesi and Universidad Externado in Colombia, Interdisciplinary Center (IDC) Herzliya in Israel, Kyushu University and Kobe University in Japan, and the University of Liechtenstein. In addition, he has worked on national and international projects with organizations, such as the European Commission, the OECD, the Dutch Development Finance Institution, UNCITRAL and local governments in the Netherlands, concerning financial and venture capital markets, corporate law, and corporate governance of listed and non-listed companies. Erik is one of the founders of the International Venture Club.

Katerina Voutsina is a Lecturer at the American College of Greece. She holds a Ph.D. degree in Management from the London School of Economics and Political Science (LSE). After completing her doctoral studies, she worked as a Research Fellow/Lecturer in the Department of Management at LSE and as a Visiting Lecturer in the Warwick Business

School. Her research interests focus on the organizational and socio-economic aspects of nascent entrepreneurship and technological innovation. Outputs of her work have been published in international referred journals and presented in international conferences. She was involved in the England's National Programme for Information Technology by evaluating the implementation and adoption of nationwide electronic health records in secondary care in England. For several years, she has served as a reviewer for scholarly journals and academic conferences.

Roxanne Zolin, Ph.D., is an Associate Professor in the School of Management, Queensland University of Technology. Roxanne did her Ph.D. at Stanford University, where she also holds a Masters in Sociology. In addition Roxanne has a Master of Business (Marketing) from Monash University, Melbourne, and a Bachelor of Business (Management) from Queensland Institute of Technology. Her research overturns stereotypes finding that women entrepreneurs perform equal to men and immigrant entrepreneurs are more likely to start international new businesses. Roxanne has won numerous grants, attends prestigious conferences, such as the Babson College Entrepreneurship Research Conference, and has published over 30 papers and chapters in high ranking journals such as *Entrepreneurship & Regional Development, Journal of Business Research* and *Thunderbird International Review*. Roxanne started a software development company, which built organizational simulations for business training. Her marketing consultancy helped start over 500 new businesses with 80% self-supporting in their first year. Roxanne was National Marketing Manager for Myers, the world's 15th largest department store chain. Her sales promotions won three national awards from the Sales Promotion Association of Australia. Roxanne helped start the AusCongo Network, Inc. to fight poverty in Australia and the Democratic Republic of the Congo. They have a business centre in Mbuji-Maya, the poorest city in the poorest large country of the world. Since starting the community has self-organized into nine industry groups. The Centre runs a "Nano-Finance" program, which trains businesses by providing small loans prior to lending larger amounts.